ACCA

STUDY TEXT

PAPER F6

TAXATION (UK)
FA 2007

In this new syllabus second edition approved by ACCA

- We **discuss** the **best strategies** for studying for ACCA exams
- We **highlight** the **most important elements** in the syllabus and the **key skills** you will need
- We **signpost** how each chapter links to the syllabus and the study guide
- We **provide** lots of **exam focus points** demonstrating what the examiner will want you to do
- We **emphasise key points** in regular **fast forward summaries**
- We **test your knowledge** of what you've studied in **quick quizzes**
- We **examine your understanding** in our **exam question bank**
- We **reference all the important topics** in our **full index**

BPP's **i-Learn** and **i-Pass** products also support this paper.

FOR EXAMS IN JUNE AND DECEMBER 2008

First edition March 2007
Second edition August 2007

ISBN 9780 7517 4574 0
(previous edition 9780 7517 3292 4)

British Library Cataloguing-in-Publication Data
A catalogue record for this book is available from the British Library

Published by

BPP Learning Media Ltd
BPP House, Aldine Place
London W12 8AA

www.bpp.com/learningmedia

Printed in Great Britain by
WM Print Ltd
Frederick Street
Walsall
WS2 9NE

Your learning materials, published by BPP Learning Media Ltd, are printed on paper sourced from sustainable, managed forests.

We are grateful to the Association of Chartered Certified Accountants for permission to reproduce past examination questions. The suggested solutions in the exam answer bank have been prepared by BPP Learning Media Ltd.

Contents

Page

How the BPP ACCA-approved Study Text can help you pass
How the BPP ACCA-approved Study Text can help you pass 7
Example chapter 9
Learning styles 13

Studying efficiently and effectively
What you need to study efficiently and effectively 17
Timetabling your studies 18
Short of time: Skim study technique 19
Revision 20

Studying F6
Approaching F6 23
Syllabus 25
Study Guide 29
The exam paper 37

Pilot paper questions 39

Part A Taxation of individuals
1 Introduction to the UK tax system 49
2 The computation of taxable income and the income tax liability 57
3 Employment income 71
4 Taxable and exempt benefits. The PAYE system 81
5 Pensions 103
6 Property income 111
7 Computing trading income 119
8 Capital allowances 131
9 Assessable trading income 151
10 Trading losses 165
11 Partnerships and limited liability partnerships 179
12 National insurance contributions 189

Part B Taxation of chargeable gains
13 Computing chargeable gains 199
14 Computing chargeable gains – further aspects 209
15 Chattels and the principal private residence exemption 219
16 Business reliefs 229
17 Shares and securities 239
18 Self assessment and payment of tax by individuals 251

Part C Taxation of companies
19 Computing profits chargeable to corporation tax 267
20 Computing the corporation tax liability 281
21 Losses 291
22 Groups 303
23 Overseas matters for companies 313
24 Self assessment and payment of tax by companies 323

Part D Value added tax

25 An introduction to VAT 333
26 Further aspects of VAT 351

Exam question bank 361
Exam answer bank 389

Pilot Paper questions and answers 431

Tax Tables 455

Index 459

Review form and free prize draw

The BPP Learning Media Effective Study Package

Distance Learning from BPP Professional Education

You can access our exam-focused interactive e-learning materials over the **Internet**, via BPP Learn Online, hosted by BPP Professional Education.

BPP Learn Online offers **comprehensive tutor support**, **revision guidance** and **exam tips**.

Visit www.bpp.com/acca/learnonline for further details.

Learning to Learn Accountancy

BPP's ground-breaking **Learning to Learn Accountancy** book is designed to be used both at the outset of your ACCA studies and throughout the process of learning accountancy. It challenges you to consider how you study and gives you helpful hints about how to approach the various types of paper which you will encounter. It can help you **focus your studies on the subject and exam**, enabling you to **acquire knowledge, practise and revise efficiently and effectively**.

How the BPP ACCA-approved Study Text can help you pass

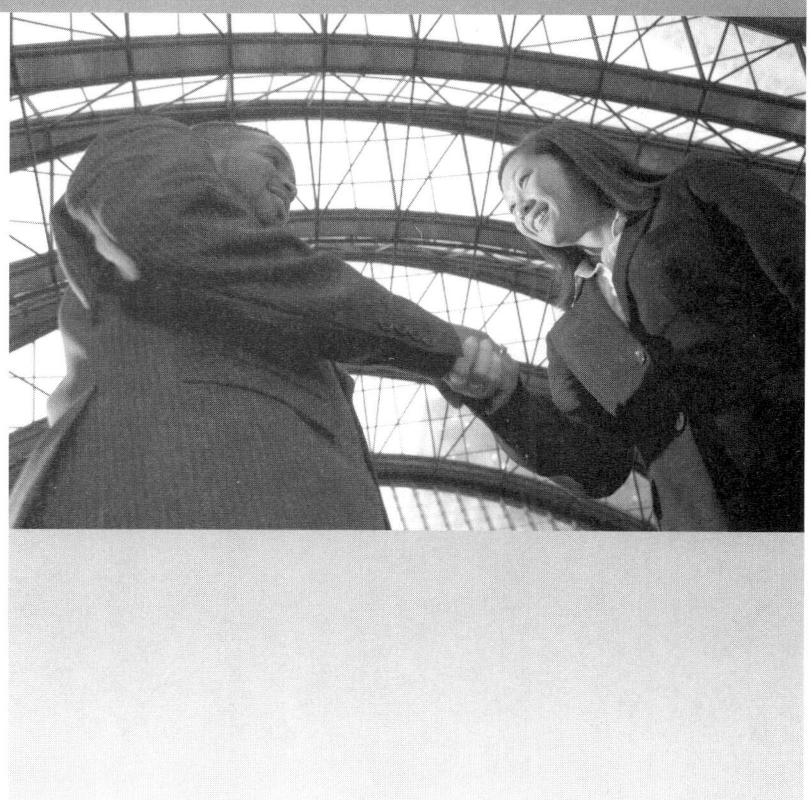

How the BPP ACCA-approved Study Text can help you pass

Tackling studying

We know that studying for a number of exams can seem daunting, particularly when you have other commitments as well.

- We therefore provide guidance on **what you need to study efficiently and effectively** – to use the limited time you have in the best way possible
- We explain the **purposes** of the **different features** in the BPP Study Text, demonstrating how they help you and improve your chances of passing

Developing exam awareness

We never forget that you're aiming to pass your exams, and our Texts are completely focused on helping you do this.

- In the section **Studying F6** we introduce the key themes of the syllabus, describe the skills you need and summarise how to succeed
- The **Introduction** to each chapter of this Study Text sets the chapter in the context of the syllabus and exam
- We provide specific tips, **Exam focus points**, on what you can expect in the exam and what to do (and not to do!) when answering questions

And our Study Text is **comprehensive**. It covers the syllabus content. No more, no less.

Using the Syllabus and Study Guide

We set out the Syllabus and Study Guide in full.

- Reading the **introduction to the Syllabus** will show you what **capabilities** (skills) you'll have to demonstrate, and how this exam links with other papers.
- The topics listed in the **Syllabus** are the **key topics** in this exam. By quickly looking through the Syllabus, you can see the breadth of the paper. Reading the Syllabus will also highlight topics to look out for when you're reading newspapers or *student accountant* magazine.
- The **Study Guide** provides the **detail**, showing you precisely what you'll be studying. Don't worry if it seems a lot when you look through it; BPP's Study Text will carefully guide you through it all.
- Remember the Study Text shows, at the start of every chapter, which areas of the Syllabus and Study Guide are covered in the chapter.

Testing what you can do

Testing yourself helps you develop the skills you need to pass the exam and also confirms that you can recall what you have learnt.

- We include **Questions** within chapters, and the **Exam Question Bank** provides lots more practice.
- Our **Quick Quizzes** test whether you have enough knowledge of the contents of each chapter.
- Question practice is particularly important if English is not your first written language. ACCA offers an **International Certificate in Financial English** promoting language skills within the international business community.

Example chapter

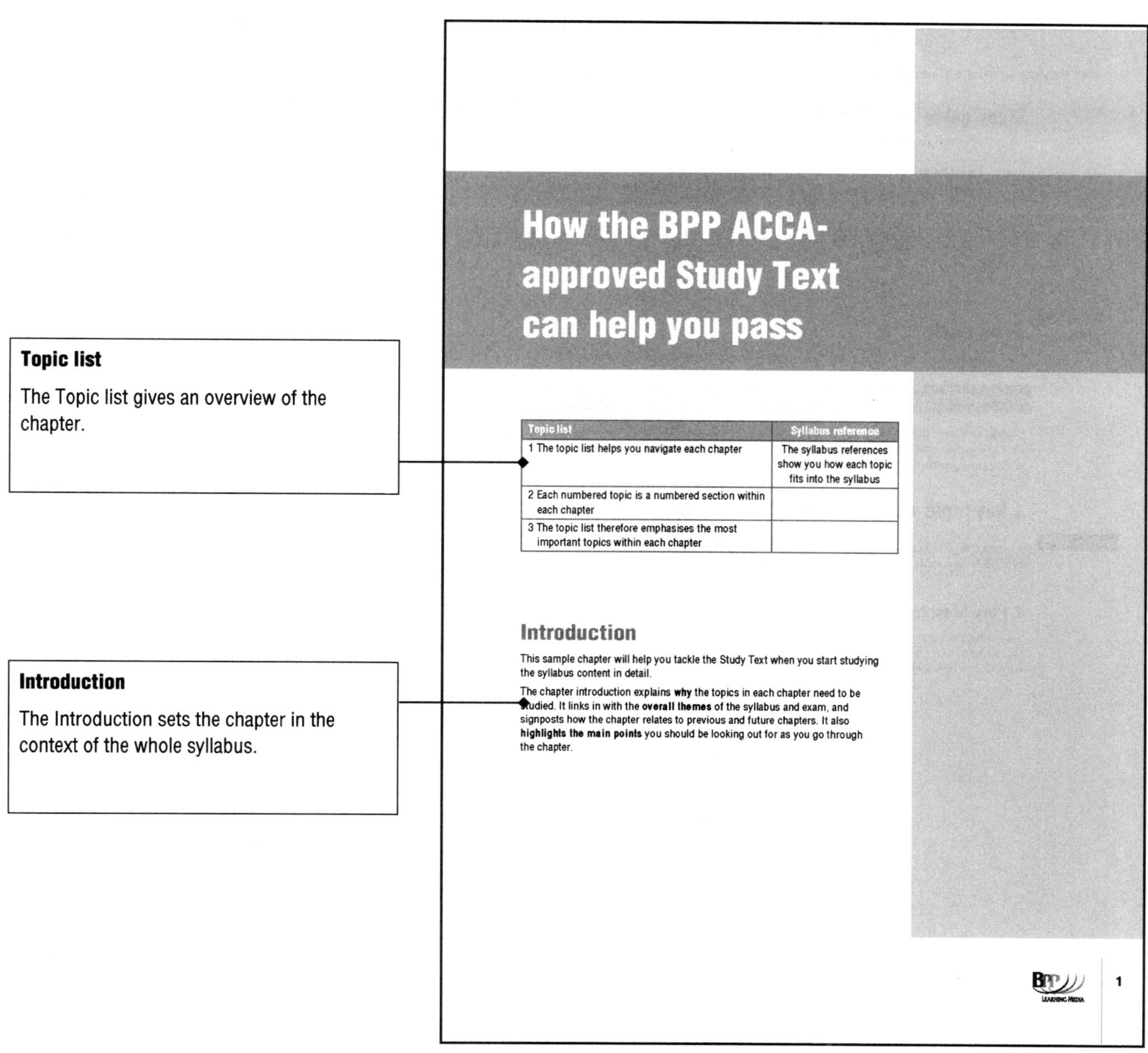

Topic list

The Topic list gives an overview of the chapter.

Introduction

The Introduction sets the chapter in the context of the whole syllabus.

How the BPP ACCA-approved Study Text can help you pass

Topic list	Syllabus reference
1 The topic list helps you navigate each chapter	The syllabus references show you how each topic fits into the syllabus
2 Each numbered topic is a numbered section within each chapter	
3 The topic list therefore emphasises the most important topics within each chapter	

Introduction

This sample chapter will help you tackle the Study Text when you start studying the syllabus content in detail.

The chapter introduction explains **why** the topics in each chapter need to be studied. It links in with the **overall themes** of the syllabus and exam, and signposts how the chapter relates to previous and future chapters. It also **highlights the main points** you should be looking out for as you go through the chapter.

1

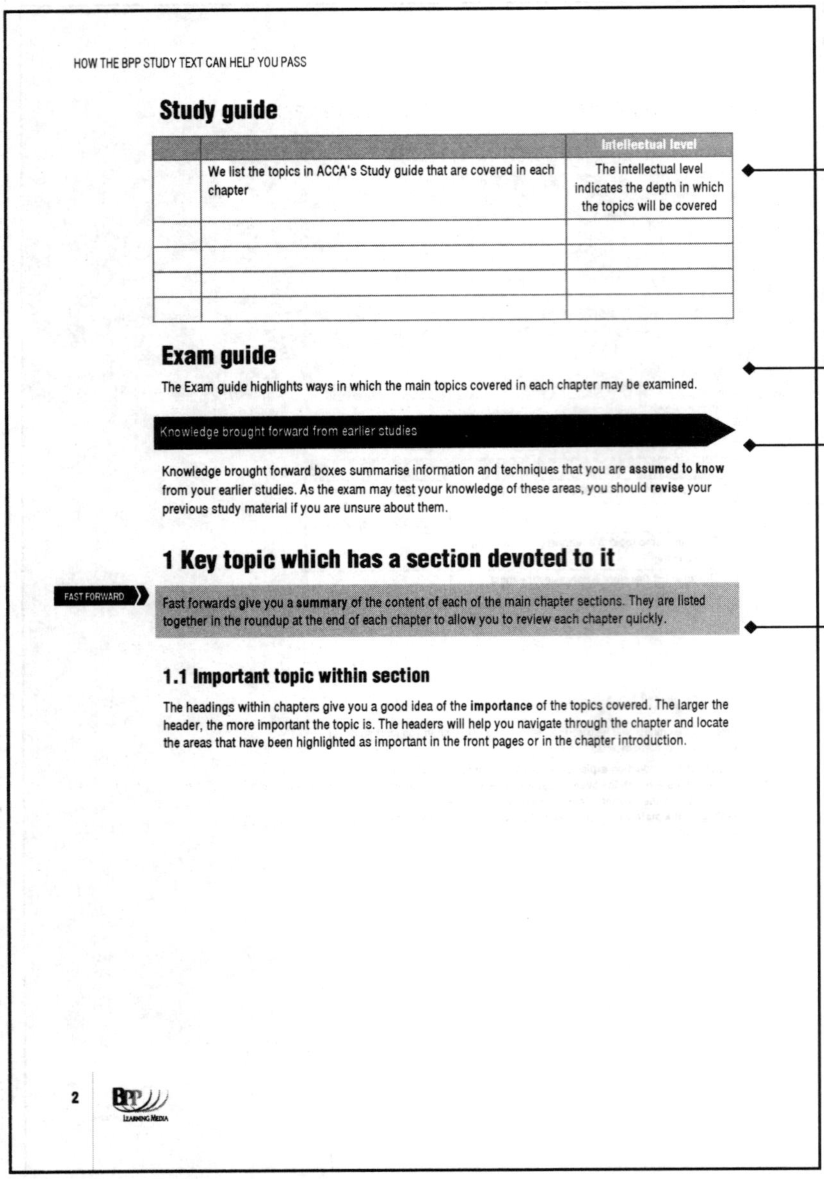

HOW THE BPP STUDY TEXT CAN HELP YOU PASS

Study guide

		Intellectual level
	We list the topics in ACCA's Study guide that are covered in each chapter	The intellectual level indicates the depth in which the topics will be covered

Exam guide

The Exam guide highlights ways in which the main topics covered in each chapter may be examined.

Knowledge brought forward from earlier studies

Knowledge brought forward boxes summarise information and techniques that you are **assumed to know** from your earlier studies. As the exam may test your knowledge of these areas, you should **revise** your previous study material if you are unsure about them.

1 Key topic which has a section devoted to it

FAST FORWARD

Fast forwards give you a **summary** of the content of each of the main chapter sections. They are listed together in the roundup at the end of each chapter to allow you to review each chapter quickly.

1.1 Important topic within section

The headings within chapters give you a good idea of the **importance** of the topics covered. The larger the header, the more important the topic is. The headers will help you navigate through the chapter and locate the areas that have been highlighted as important in the front pages or in the chapter introduction.

2 BPP LEARNING MEDIA

Study guide

The Study guide links with ACCA's own guidance.

Exam guide

The Exam guide describes the examinability of the chapter.

Knowledge brought forward

Knowledge brought forward shows you what you need to remember from previous exams.

Fast forward

Fast forwards allow you to preview and review each section easily.

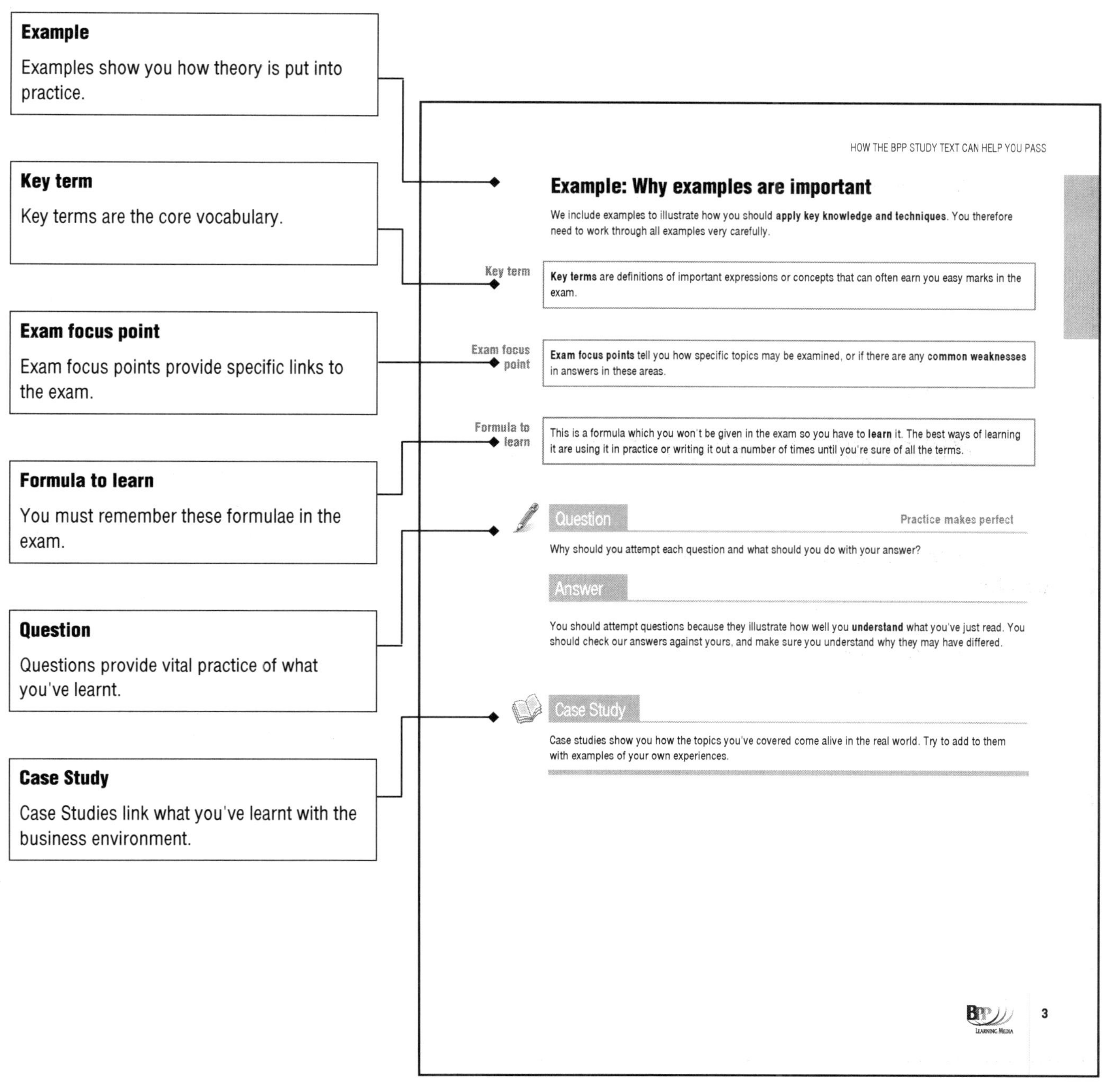
Example
Examples show you how theory is put into practice.
Key term
Key terms are the core vocabulary.
Exam focus point
Exam focus points provide specific links to the exam.
Formula to learn
You must remember these formulae in the exam.
Question
Questions provide vital practice of what you've learnt.
Case Study
Case Studies link what you've learnt with the business environment.
HOW THE BPP STUDY TEXT CAN HELP YOU PASS
Example: Why examples are important
We include examples to illustrate how you should apply key knowledge and techniques. You therefore need to work through all examples very carefully.
Key term
Key terms are definitions of important expressions or concepts that can often earn you easy marks in the exam.
Exam focus point
Exam focus points tell you how specific topics may be examined, or if there are any common weaknesses in answers in these areas.
Formula to learn
This is a formula which you won't be given in the exam so you have to learn it. The best ways of learning it are using it in practice or writing it out a number of times until you're sure of all the terms.
Question
Practice makes perfect
Why should you attempt each question and what should you do with your answer?
Answer
You should attempt questions because they illustrate how well you understand what you've just read. You should check our answers against yours, and make sure you understand why they may have differed.
Case Study
Case studies show you how the topics you've covered come alive in the real world. Try to add to them with examples of your own experiences.
3

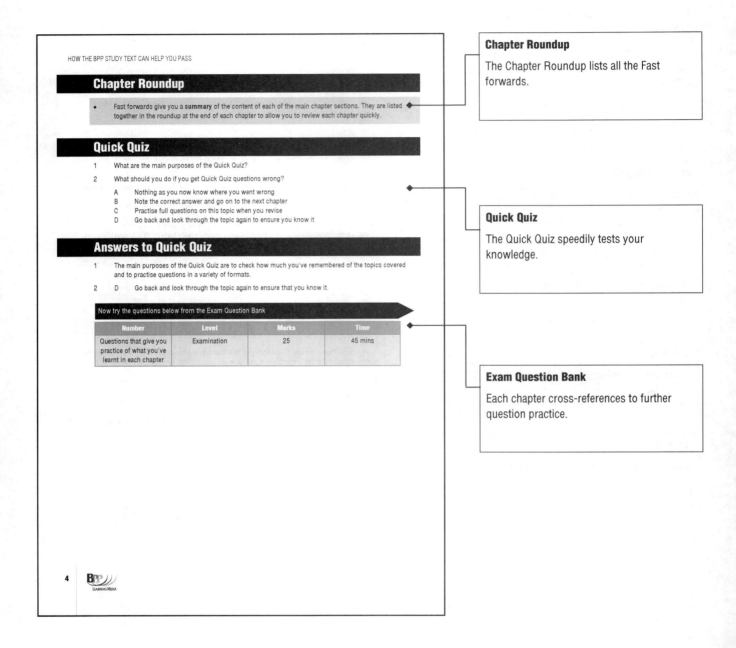

Chapter Roundup

- Fast forwards give you a **summary** of the content of each of the main chapter sections. They are listed together in the roundup at the end of each chapter to allow you to review each chapter quickly.

Quick Quiz

1 What are the main purposes of the Quick Quiz?

2 What should you do if you get Quick Quiz questions wrong?

A Nothing as you now know where you went wrong
B Note the correct answer and go on to the next chapter
C Practise full questions on this topic when you revise
D Go back and look through the topic again to ensure you know it

Answers to Quick Quiz

1 The main purposes of the Quick Quiz are to check how much you've remembered of the topics covered and to practise questions in a variety of formats.

2 D Go back and look through the topic again to ensure that you know it.

Now try the questions below from the Exam Question Bank

Number	Level	Marks	Time
Questions that give you practice of what you've learnt in each chapter	Examination	25	45 mins

Chapter Roundup

The Chapter Roundup lists all the Fast forwards.

Quick Quiz

The Quick Quiz speedily tests your knowledge.

Exam Question Bank

Each chapter cross-references to further question practice.

Learning styles

BPP's guide to studying, *Learning to Learn Accountancy*, provides guidance on identifying how you learn and the variety of intelligences that you have. We shall summarise some of the material in *Learning to Learn Accountancy*, as it will help you understand how to you are likely to approach the Study Text:

If you like	Then you might focus on	How the Study Text helps you
Word games, crosswords, poetry	Going through the detail in the Text	Chapter introductions, Fast forwards and Key terms help you determine the detail that's most significant
Number puzzles, Sudoku, Cluedo	Understanding the Text as a logical sequence of knowledge and ideas	Chapter introductions and headers help you follow the flow of material
Drawing, cartoons, films	Seeing how the ways material is presented show what it means and how important it is	The different features and the emphasis given by headers and emboldening help you see quickly what you have to know
Attending concerts, playing a musical instrument, dancing	Identifying patterns in the Text	The sequence of features within each chapter helps you understand what material is really crucial
Sport, craftwork, hands on experience	Learning practical skills such as preparing a set of accounts	Examples and question practice help you develop the practical skills you need

If you want to learn more about developing some or all of your intelligences, *Learning to Learn Accountancy* shows you plenty of ways in which you can do so.

Studying efficiently and effectively

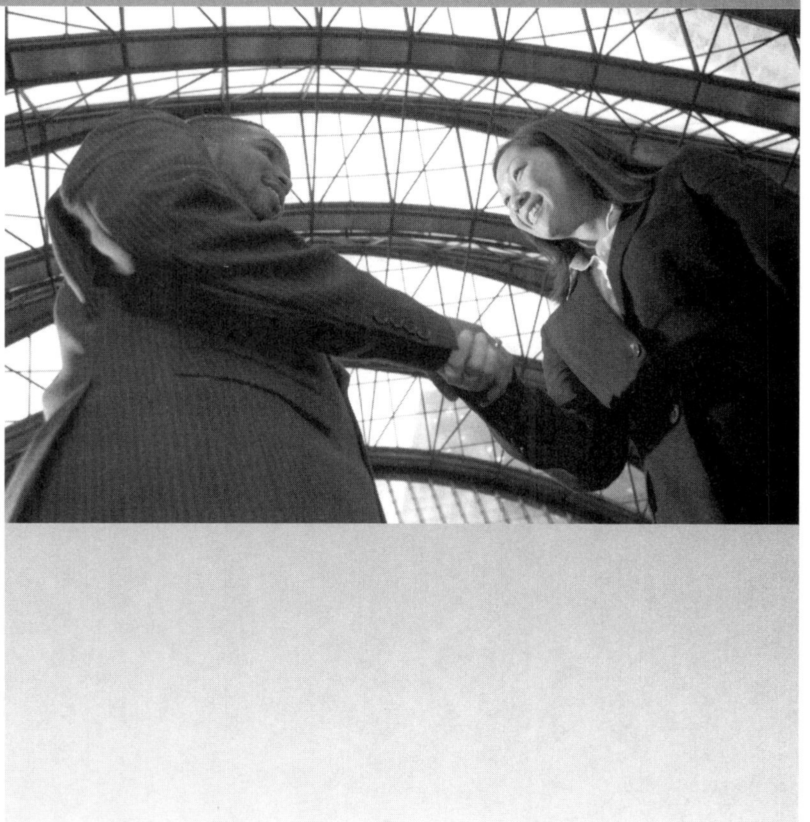

What you need to study efficiently and effectively

Positive attitude

Yes there is a lot to learn. But look at the most recent ACCA pass list. See how many people have passed. They've made it; you can too. Focus on all the **benefits** that passing the exam will bring you.

Exam focus

Keep the exam firmly in your sights throughout your studies.

- Remember there's lots of **helpful guidance** about F6 in the first part of the Study Text including BPP's guide to Passing F6, the syllabus, study guide and pilot paper.
- Look out for all the **references to the exam** in chapter introductions, exam focus points and other places in the Study Text.

Organisation

Before you start studying you must organise yourself properly

- We show you how to **timetable** your study so that you can ensure you have enough time to cover all of the syllabus – and revise it.
- Think carefully about the way you take **notes**. You needn't copy out too much, but if you can summarise key areas, that shows you understand them.
- Choose the notes **format** that's most helpful to you: lists, diagrams, mindmaps.
- Consider the **order** in which you tackle each chapter. If you prefer to get to grips with a theory before seeing how it's applied, you should read the explanations first. If you prefer to see how things work in practice, read the examples and questions first.

Active brain

There are various ways in which you can keep your brain active when studying and hence improve your **understanding** and **recall** of material.

- Keep asking yourself how does what I'm studying fit into the **whole picture** of this exam. If you're not sure, look back at the chapter introductions and Study Text front pages.
- Go carefully through every **example** and try every **question** in the Study Text and in the Exam Question Bank. You will be thinking deeply about the syllabus and increasing your understanding.

Review, review, review

Regularly reviewing the topics you're studying will help fix them in your memory. Your BPP Texts help you review in many ways.

- Important points are emphasised **in bold**
- **Chapter roundups** summarise the **Fast forward** key points in each chapter
- **Quick quizzes** test your grasp of the essentials

BPP Passcards present summaries of topics in different visual formats to enhance your chances of remembering them.

Timetabling your studies

As your time is limited, it's vital that you calculate how much time you can allocate to each chapter. Following the approach below will help you do this.

Step 1 Calculate how much time you have

Work out the time you have available per week, given the following.

- The standard you have set yourself
- The time you need to set aside later to work on the Practice & Revision Kit, Passcards, i-Learn and i-Pass
- The other exam(s) you are sitting
- Practical matters such as work, travel, exercise, sleep and social life

		Hours
Note your time available in box A.	A	

Step 2 Allocate your time

• Take the time you have available per week for this Study Text shown in box A, multiply it by the number of weeks available and insert the result in box B.	B	
• Divide the figure in box B by the number of chapters in this Study Text and insert the result in box C.	C	

Remember that this is only a rough guide. Some of the chapters in this Study Text are longer and more complicated than others, and you will find some subjects easier to understand than others.

Step 3 Implement your plan

Set about studying each chapter in the time shown in box C. You'll find that once you've established a timetable, you're much more likely to study systematically.

Short of time: Skim study technique?

You may find you simply do not have the time available to follow all the key study steps for each chapter, however you adapt them for your particular learning style. If this is the case, follow the **skim study** technique below.

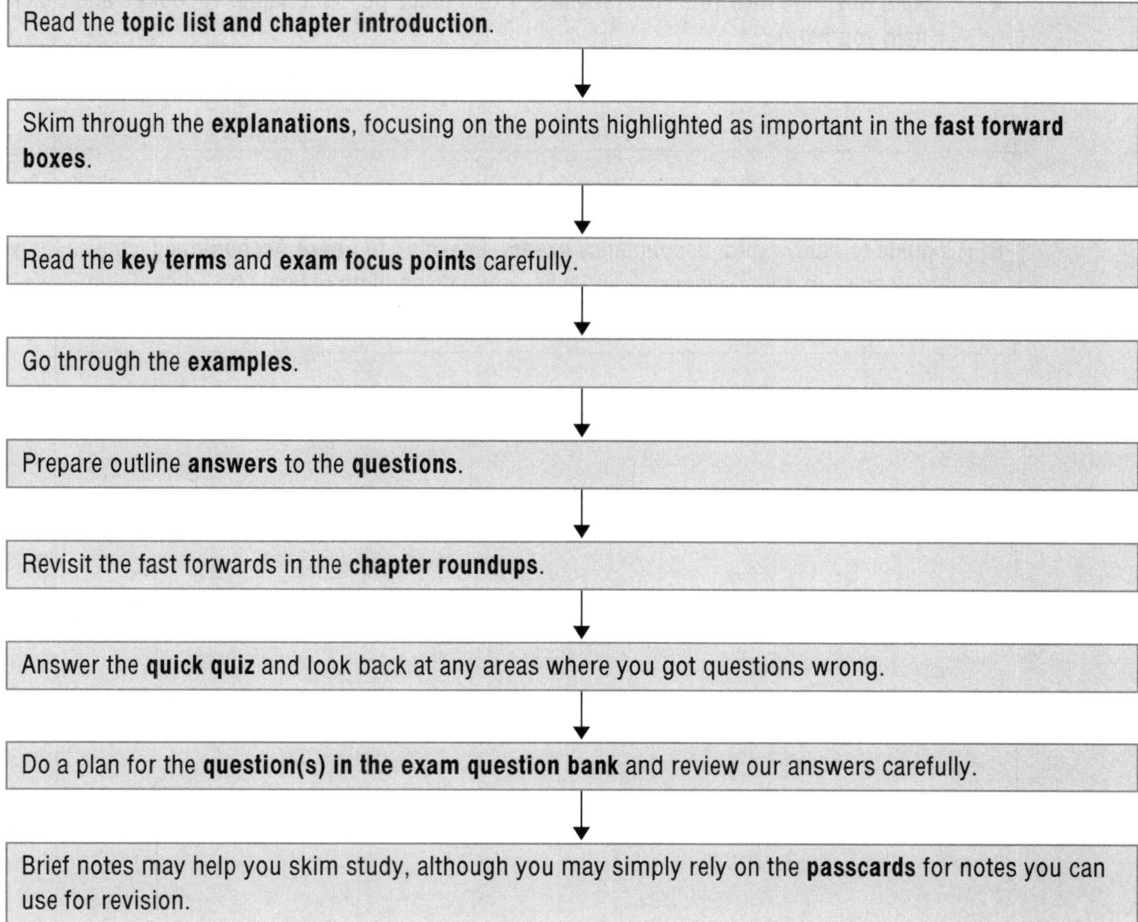

Read the **topic list and chapter introduction**.
Skim through the **explanations**, focusing on the points highlighted as important in the **fast forward boxes**.
Read the **key terms** and **exam focus points** carefully.
Go through the **examples**.
Prepare outline **answers** to the **questions**.
Revisit the fast forwards in the **chapter roundups**.
Answer the **quick quiz** and look back at any areas where you got questions wrong.
Do a plan for the **question(s) in the exam question bank** and review our answers carefully.
Brief notes may help you skim study, although you may simply rely on the **passcards** for notes you can use for revision.

Revision

When you are ready to start revising, you should still refer back to this Study Text.

- As a source of **reference** (you should find the index particularly helpful for this)
- As a way to **review** (the Fast forwards, Exam focus points, Chapter roundups and Quick quizzes help you here)

Remember to keep careful hold of this Study Text – you will find it invaluable in your work.

Learning to Learn Accountancy

BPP's guide to studying for accountancy exams, **Learning to Learn Accountancy**, challenges you to think about how you can study effectively and gives you lots and lots of vital tips on studying, revising and taking the exams.

Studying F6

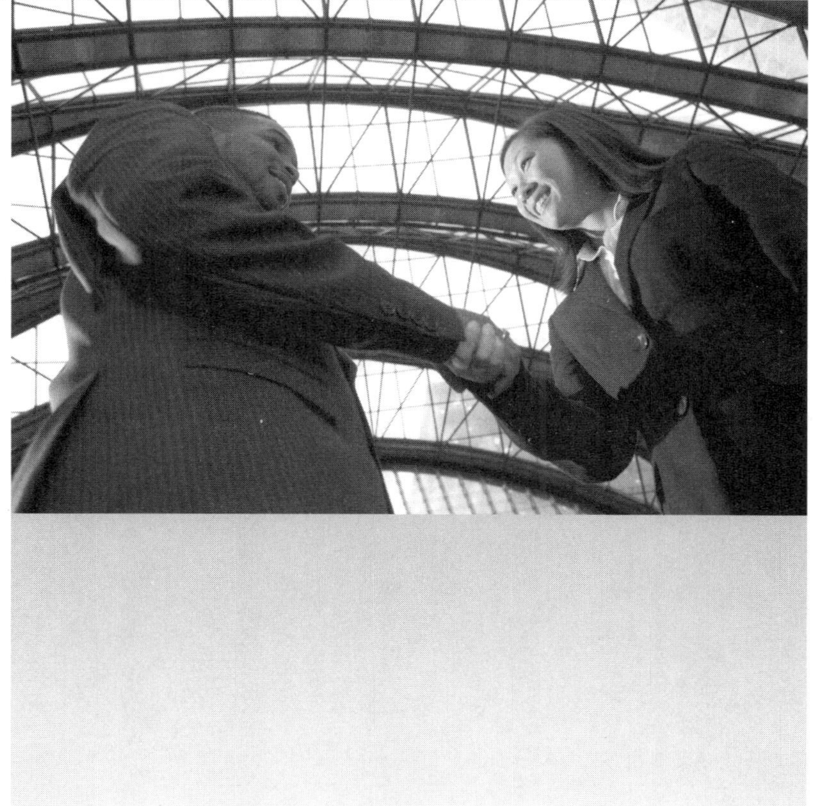

Approaching F6

1 What F6 Taxation is about

The UK tax system

The syllabus introduces the rationale behind – and the functions of – the tax system.

The taxes

It then covers the **main UK taxes** which apply to individuals and businesses.

Income tax and corporation tax cover the widest areas of the syllabus, forming the basis for questions 1 and 2 totalling 55% of the marks. Value added tax is likely to be covered in one of these questions, in which case at least 10 of the 55 marks will be awarded for VAT, although it is possible that a separate question on VAT will be included instead. Capital gains will be covered in Question 3, for which 20 marks will be available. National insurance may be examined in any question on income tax or corporation tax.

You will be expected to have a detailed knowledge of these taxes, but **no previous knowledge is assumed**. You should study the basics carefully and **learn the proforma computations**. It then becomes straightforward to complete these by slotting in figures from your detailed workings.

As well as being able to calculate tax liabilities you will be expected to explain the basis of the calculations and how a taxpayer can minimise or defer tax liabilities

Compliance

The final part of the syllabus covers the **compliance obligations** of the taxpayer. Although not a major part of the syllabus it is likely to form an element in one or more questions in the exam. A knowledge of tax is incomplete without an understanding of how the tax is collected.

2 What's required

Knowledge

You will require a **core knowledge of the basic principles** of each of the taxes applying to individuals and businesses. You must be able to draw together the strands of your knowledge to complete detailed computations of tax liabilities.

Calculations

Calculation questions will be of two types:

- Short calculations illustrating a single aspect of a tax, not forming part of a complete overview
- Longer calculations for which you will have to prepare proformas. The majority of marks in questions 1 and 2 are likely to be available for these. The proformas you will need to prepare are for the computation of an income tax or corporation tax liability

Explanation

As well as testing your knowledge you will be asked to demonstrate the skill of **explaining the underlying principles**. Explaining means providing a simple summary of the rules and how they apply to the particular situation. You will only gain marks if your explanations are clearly focused on the question, superfluous explanations will not achieve extra marks.

Application

You will be required to apply tax planning techniques. At this level this involves identifying available options and testing them to see which has the greater effect on tax liabilities. If you reject an option, say so and explain why.

3 How to pass

Cover the whole syllabus

All of the questions in the exam are **compulsory**. This gives the examiner plenty of opportunity to test all major areas of the syllabus on every paper, but sadly doesn't give you much opportunity to avoid questions you don't like. **Do not study the syllabus selectively** as the format of the paper enables all topics to be tested in some way in most exams.

Practise

Our text gives you ample opportunity to **practise** by providing questions within chapters, quick quiz questions and questions in the exam question bank at the end. In addition the BPP Practice and Revision Kit provides lots more question practice.

Examiners routinely identify **time management** as being a problem. It is particularly important, therefore, that towards the end of your course when you practise questions you only allow yourself the time you will be given in the exam.

Answer selectively

The examiner will expect you to consider carefully what is **relevant** and significant enough to include in your answers. Exam answers are likely to show various signs that students are not taking the necessary care:

- Include all the information in the answer that you are asked for; if you are dealing with a loss relief question and are asked to state the loss carried forward don't waste marks by omitting to do so
- Do not include unnecessary information, if you are asked a specific question on one topic do not write all you know if it is outside the specific area
- Indicate where you have deliberately excluded an item from a computation, if something is exempt from tax say so to show you have not just ignored it.

Employ good exam technique

The following aspects of exam technique are particularly relevant in this exam:

- **Subheadings and leaving spaces between paragraphs** help to demonstrate that your answer is clearly structured and emphasise the points you're making
- **Short paragraphs** (2-3 sentences) help you keep to the point; however avoid 2-3 word bullet points
- **Clear numerical workings** can gain you many marks even if you make a mistake in your calculations
- **Time management** is likely to be less of a problem if you do the longer questions (Questions 1 and 2) first.

Syllabus

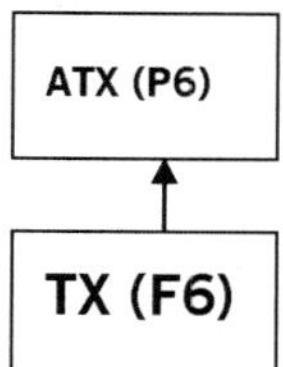

AIM

To develop knowledge and skills relating to the tax system as applicable to individuals, single companies, and groups of companies.

MAIN CAPABILITIES

On successful completion of this paper candidates should be able to:

A Explain the operation and scope of the tax system

B Explain and compute the income tax liabilities of individuals

C Explain and compute the corporation tax liabilities of individual companies and groups of companies

D Explain and compute the chargeable gains arising on companies and individuals

E Explain and compute the effect of national insurance contributions on employees, employers and the self employed

F Explain and compute the effects of value added tax on incorporated and unincorporated businesses

G Identify and explain the obligations of tax payers and/or their agents and the implications of non-compliance

RELATIONAL DIAGRAM OF MAIN CAPABILITIES

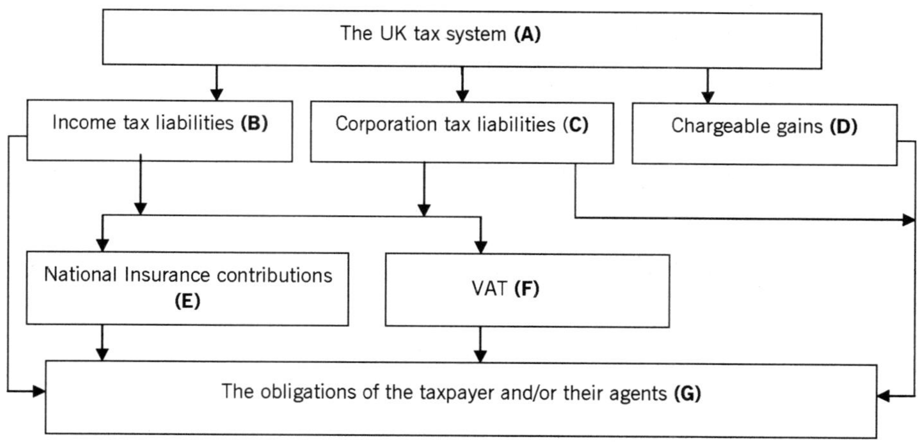

INTELLECTUAL LEVELS

The syllabus is designed to progressively broaden and deepen the knowledge, skills and professional values demonstrated by the student on their way through the qualification.

The specific capabilities within the detailed syllabuses and study guides are assessed at one of three intellectual or cognitive levels:

Level 1: Knowledge and comprehension
Level 2: Application and analysis
Level 3: Synthesis and evaluation

Very broadly, these intellectual levels relate to the three cognitive levels at which the Knowledge module, the Skills module and the Professional level are assessed.

Each subject area in the detailed study guide included in this document is given a 1, 2, or 3 superscript, denoting intellectual level, marked at the end of each relevant line. This gives an indication of the intellectual depth at which an area could be assessed within the examination. However, while level 1 broadly equates with the Knowledge module, level 2 equates to the Skills module and level 3 to the Professional level, some lower level skills can continue to be assessed as the student progresses through each module and level. This reflects that at each stage of study there will be a requirement to broaden, as well as deepen capabilities. It is also possible that occasionally some higher level capabilities may be assessed at lower levels.

RATIONALE

The syllabus for Paper F6, *Taxation,* introduces candidates to the subject of taxation and provides the core knowledge of the underlying principles and major technical areas of taxation as they affect the activities of individuals and businesses.

Candidates are introduced to the rationale behind – and the functions of – the tax system. The syllabus then considers the separate taxes that an accountant would need to have a detailed knowledge of, such as income tax from self-employment, employment and investments, the corporation tax liability of individual companies and groups of companies, the national insurance contribution liabilities of both employed and self employed persons, the value added tax liability of businesses, and the chargeable gains arising on disposals of investments by both individuals and companies.

Having covered the core areas of the basic taxes, candidates should be able to compute tax liabilities, explain the basis of their calculations, apply tax planning techniques for individuals and companies and identify the compliance issues for each major tax through a variety of business and personal scenarios and situations.

DETAILED SYLLABUS

A. The UK tax system

1. The overall function and purpose of taxation in a modern economy
2. Different types of taxes
3. Principal sources of revenue law and practice
4. Tax avoidance and tax evasion

B. Income tax liabilities

1. The scope of income tax
2. Income from employment
3. Income from self-employment
4. Property and investment income
5. The comprehensive computation of taxable income and income tax liability
6. The use of exemptions and reliefs in deferring and minimising income tax liabilities

C. Corporation tax liabilities

1. The scope of corporation tax
2. Profits chargeable to corporation tax
3. The comprehensive computation of corporation tax liability
4. The effect of a group corporate structure for corporation tax purposes
5. The use of exemptions and reliefs in deferring and minimising corporation tax liabilities

D. Chargeable gains

1. The scope of the taxation of capital gains
2. The basic principles of computing gains and losses.
3. Gains and losses on the disposal of movable and immovable property
4. Gains and losses on the disposal of shares and securities
5. The computation of capital gains tax payable by individuals
6. The use of exemptions and reliefs in deferring and minimising tax liabilities arising on the disposal of capital assets

E. National insurance contributions

1. The scope of national insurance
2. Class 1 and Class 1A contributions for employed persons
3. Class 2 and Class 4 contributions for self-employed persons

F. Value added tax

1. The scope of value added tax (VAT)
2. The VAT registration requirements
3. The computation of VAT liabilities
4. The effect of special schemes

G. The obligations of taxpayers and/or their agents

1. The systems for self-assessment and the making of returns
2. The time limits for the submission of information, claims and payment of tax, including payments on account
3. The procedures relating to enquiries, appeals and disputes
4. Penalties for non-compliance

Study Guide

A THE UK TAX SYSTEM

1. The overall function and purpose of taxation in a modern economy

a) Describe the purpose (economic, social etc) of taxation in a modern economy.[2]

2. Different types of taxes

a) Identify the different types of capital and revenue tax.[1]

b) Explain the difference between direct and indirect taxation.[2]

3. Principal sources of revenue law and practice

a) Describe the overall structure of the UK tax system.[1]

b) State the different sources of revenue law.[1]

c) Appreciate the interaction of the UK tax system with that of other tax jurisdictions.[2]

4. Tax avoidance and tax evasion

a) Explain the difference between tax avoidance and tax evasion.[1]

b) Explain the need for an ethical and professional approach.[2]

Excluded topics

- *Anti-avoidance legislation.*

B INCOME TAX LIABILITIES

1. The scope of income tax

a) Explain how the residence of an individual is determined.[1]

Excluded topics

- *The treatment of a person who comes to the UK to work or a person who leaves the UK to take up employment overseas.*
- *Foreign income, non-residents and double taxation relief.*
- *Income from trusts and settlements.*

2. Income from employment

a) Recognise the factors that determine whether an engagement is treated as employment or self-employment.[2]

b) Recognise the basis of assessment for employment income.[2]

c) Compute the income assessable.[2]

d) Recognise the allowable deductions, including travelling expenses.[2]

e) Discuss the use of the statutory approved mileage allowances.[2]

f) Explain the PAYE system.[1]

g) Identify P11D employees.[1]

h) Compute the amount of benefits assessable.[2]

i) Explain the purpose of a dispensation from HM Revenue & Customs.[2]

k) Explain how charitable giving can be made through a payroll deduction scheme.[1]

Excluded topics

- *The calculation of a car benefit where emission figures are not available.*
- *Share and share option incentive schemes for employees.*
- *Payments on the termination of employment, and other lump sums received by employees.*

3 Income from self-employment

a) Recognise the basis of assessment for self-employment income.[2]

b) Describe and apply the badges of trade.[2]

c) Recognise the expenditure that is allowable in calculating the tax-adjusted trading profit.[2]

d) Recognise the relief that can be obtained for pre-trading expenditure.[2]

e) Compute the assessable profits on commencement and on cessation.[2]

f) Change of accounting date
   i) Recognise the factors that will influence the choice of accounting date.[2]
   ii) State the conditions that must be met for a change of accounting date to be valid.[1]
   iii) Compute the assessable profits on a change of accounting date.[2]

g) Capital allowances
   i) Define plant and machinery for capital allowances purposes.[1]
   ii) Compute writing down allowances and first year allowances.[2]
   iii) Compute capital allowances for motor cars.[2]
   iv) Compute balancing allowances and balancing charges.[2]
   v) Recognise the treatment of short life assets.[2]
   vi) Explain the treatment of long life assets.[2]
   vii) Define an industrial building for industrial buildings allowance purposes.[1]
   viii) Compute industrial buildings allowance for new and second-hand buildings.[2]
   ix) Compute the balancing adjustment on the disposal of an industrial building.[2]

h) Relief for trading losses
   i) Understand how trading losses can be carried forward.[2]
   ii) Explain how trading losses can be carried forward following the incorporation of a business.[2]
   iii) Understand how trading losses can be claimed against total income and chargeable gains.[2]
   iv) Explain and compute the relief for trading losses in the early years of a trade.[1]
   v) Explain and compute terminal loss relief.[1]

i) Partnerships and limited liability partnerships
   i) Explain how a partnership is assessed to tax.[2]
   ii) Compute the assessable profits for each partner following a change in the profit sharing ratio.[2]
   iii) Compute the assessable profits for each partner following a change in the membership of the partnership.[2]
   iv) Describe the alternative loss relief claims that are available to partners.[1]
   v) Explain the loss relief restriction that applies to the partners of a limited liability partnership.[1]

Excluded topics

- *The 100% first-year allowance for information and communication technology equipment.*
- *The 50% first-year allowance for small businesses that applied for the period 1 April 2004 to 31 March 2005.*
- *The 100% first-year allowance for expenditure on renovating business premises in disadvantaged areas.*
- *The 100% first-year allowance for flats above shops.*
- *The 100% first-year allowance for water technologies.*
- *Capital allowances for agricultural buildings, patents, scientific research and know how.*
- *Enterprise zones.*
- *The disposal of an industrial building at less than original cost following a period of non-industrial use (sales for more than original cost are examinable).*
- *Investment income and charges of a partnership.*
- *The allocation of notional profits and losses for a partnership.*
- *Farmers averaging of profits.*
- *The averaging of profits for authors and creative artists.*

- *Loss relief for shares in unquoted trading companies.*

4. Property and investment income

a) Compute property business profits.[2]

b) Explain the treatment of furnished holiday lettings.[1]

c) Describe rent-a-room relief.[1]

d) Compute the amount assessable when a premium is received for the grant of a short lease.[2]

e) Understand how relief for a property business loss is given.[2]

f) Compute the tax payable on savings income.[2]

g) Compute the tax payable on dividend income.[2]

h) Explain the treatment of individual savings accounts (ISAs) and other tax exempt investments.[1]

5 The comprehensive computation of taxable income and income tax liability

a) Prepare a basic income tax computation involving different types of income.[2]

b) Calculate the amount of personal allowance available to people aged 65 and above.[2]

c) Compute the amount of income tax payable.[2]

d) Explain the treatment of charges on income.[2]

e) Explain the treatment of gift aid donations.[1]

f) Explain the treatment of property owned jointly by a married couple, or by a couple in a civil partnership.[1]

Excluded topics

- *The blind person's allowance and the married couple's allowance.*
- *Tax credits.*
- *Maintenance payments.*
- *The income of minor children.*

6. The use of exemptions and reliefs in deferring and minimising income tax liabilities

a) Explain and compute the relief given for contributions to personal pension schemes, using the rules applicable from 6 April 2006.[2]

b) Describe the relief given for contributions to occupational pension schemes, using the rules applicable from 6 April 2006.[1]

c) Explain how a married couple or couple in a civil partnership can minimise their tax liabilities.[2]

Excluded topics

- *The conditions that must be met in order for a pension scheme to obtain approval from HM Revenue & Customs.*
- *The enterprise investment scheme.*
- *Venture capital trusts.*

C CORPORATION TAX LIABILITIES

1. The scope of corporation tax

a) Define the terms 'period of account', 'accounting period', and 'financial year'.[1]

b) Recognise when an accounting period starts and when an accounting period finishes.[1]

c) Explain how the residence of a company is determined.[2]

Excluded topics

- *Investment companies.*
- *Close companies.*
- *Companies in receivership or liquidation.*
- *Reorganisations.*

- *The purchase by a company of its own shares.*
- *Personal service companies.*

2. Profits chargeable to corporation tax

a) Recognise the expenditure that is allowable in calculating the tax-adjusted trading profit.[2]

b) Explain how relief can be obtained for pre-trading expenditure.[1]

c) Compute capital allowances (as for income tax).[2]

d) Compute property business profits.[2]

e) Explain the treatment of interest paid and received under the loan relationship rules.[1]

f) Explain the treatment of gift aid donations.[2]

g) Understand how trading losses can be carried forward.[2]

h) Understand how trading losses can be claimed against income of the current or previous accounting periods.[2]

i) Recognise the factors that will influence the choice of loss relief claim.[2]

j) Explain how relief for a property business loss is given.[1]

k) Compute profits chargeable to corporation tax.[2]

Excluded topics

- *Research and development expenditure.*
- *Non-trading deficits on loan relationships.*
- *Relief for intangible assets.*

3. The comprehensive computation of corporation tax liability

a) Compute the corporation tax liability and apply marginal relief.[2]

b) Explain the implications of receiving franked investment income.[2]

c) Explain how exemptions and reliefs can defer or minimise corporation tax liabilities.[2]

Excluded topics

- *The minimum rate of corporation tax of 19%.*
- *The corporate venturing scheme.*

4. The effect of a group corporate structure for corporation tax purposes

a) Define an associated company and recognise the effect of being an associated company for corporation tax purposes.[2]

b) Define a 75% group, and recognise the reliefs that are available to members of such a group.[2]

c) Define a 75% capital gains group, and recognise the reliefs that are available to members of such a group.[2]

d) Calculate double taxation relief for withholding tax and underlying tax.[2]

e) Explain the basic principles of the transfer pricing rules.[2]

Excluded topics

- *Relief for trading losses incurred by an overseas subsidiary.*
- *Consortia.*
- *Pre-entry gains and losses.*
- *The anti-avoidance provisions where arrangements exist for a company to leave a group.*
- *The tax charge that applies where a company leaves a group within six years of receiving an asset by way of a no gain/no loss transfer.*
- *Controlled foreign companies.*

- *Foreign companies trading in the UK.*
- *Expense relief in respect of overseas tax.*
- *The restriction of double taxation relief for underlying tax to the full rate of corporation tax.*
- *The carry back and carry forward of unrelieved foreign tax, or any aspect of the on-shore pooling rules.*
- *Transfer pricing transactions not involving an overseas company.*

5. The use of exemptions and reliefs in deferring and minimising corporation tax liabilities:

The use of such exemptions and reliefs is implicit within all of the above sections 1 to 4 of part C of the syllabus, concerning corporation tax.

D CHARGEABLE GAINS

1. The scope of the taxation of capital gains

a) Describe the scope of capital gains tax.[2]

b) Explain how the residence and ordinary residence of an individual is determined.[2]

c) List those assets which are exempt.[1]

Excluded topics

- *Assets situated overseas and double taxation relief.*
- *Partnership capital gains.*

2. The basic principles of computing gains and losses.

a) Compute capital gains for both individuals and companies.[2]

b) Calculate the indexation allowance available to companies, and identify the indexation allowance available to individuals.[2]

c) Explain the treatment of capital losses for both individuals and companies.[1]

d) Explain the treatment of transfers between a husband and wife or between a couple in a civil partnership.[2]

e) Compute the amount of allowable expenditure for a part disposal.[2]

f) Explain the treatment where an asset is damaged, lost or destroyed, and the implications of receiving insurance proceeds and reinvesting such proceeds.[2]

Excluded topics

- *Assets held at 31 March 1982.*
- *Small part disposals of land.*
- *Losses in the year of death.*
- *Relief for losses incurred on loans made to traders.*
- *Negligible value claims.*

3. Gains and losses on the disposal of movable and immovable property

a) Identify when chattels and wasting assets are exempt.[1]

b) Compute the chargeable gain when a chattel is disposed of.[2]

c) Calculate the chargeable gain when a wasting asset is disposed of.[2]

d) Compute the exemption when a principal private residence is disposed of.[2]

e) Calculate the chargeable gain when a principal private residence has been used for business purposes.[2]

f) Identify the amount of letting relief available when a principal private residence has been let out.[2]

Excluded topics

- *The disposal of leases and the creation of sub-leases.*

4. Gains and losses on the disposal of shares and securities

a) Calculate the value of quoted shares where they are disposed of by way of a gift.[2]

b) Explain and apply the identification rules as they apply to individuals and to companies, including the same day, nine day, and thirty day matching rules.[2]

c) Explain the pooling provisions.[2]

d) Explain the treatment of bonus issues, rights issues, takeovers and reorganisations.[2]

e) Explain the exemption available for gilt-edged securities and qualifying corporate bonds.[1]

Excluded topics

- *A detailed question on the pooling provisions for shares.*
- *Calculation of the indexation allowance for individual taxpayers (where shares and securities are concerned, a figure will be given for the value of the 1985 pool as at 5 April 1998).*
- *The small part disposal rules applicable to rights issues.*
- *Substantial shareholdings.*
- *Gilt-edged securities and qualifying corporate bonds other than the fact that they are exempt.*

5. The computation of capital gains tax payable by individuals

a) Recognise a business asset for the purposes of taper relief.[2]

b) Compute taper relief for business and non-business assets.[2]

c) Compute the amount of capital gains tax payable.[2]

6. The use of exemptions and reliefs in deferring and minimising tax liabilities arising on the disposal of capital assets

a) Explain and apply rollover relief as it applies to individuals and companies.[2]

b) Explain and apply holdover relief for the gift of business assets.[2]

c) Explain and apply the incorporation relief that is available upon the transfer of a business to a company.[2]

Excluded topics

- *Reinvestment relief.*

E NATIONAL INSURANCE CONTRIBUTIONS

1. The scope of national insurance

a) Describe the scope of national insurance.[1]

2. Class 1 and Class 1A contributions for employed persons

a) Compute Class 1 NIC.[2]

b) Compute Class 1A NIC.[2]

Excluded topics

- *The calculation of directors' national insurance on a month by month basis.*
- *Contracted out contributions.*

3. Class 2 and Class 4 contributions for self-employed persons

a) Compute Class 2 NIC.[2]

b) Compute Class 4 NIC.[2]

Excluded topics

- *The offset of trading losses against non-trading income.*

F VALUE ADDED TAX

1. The scope of value added tax (VAT)

a) Describe the scope of VAT.[2]

b) List the principal zero-rated and exempt supplies.[1]

2. The VAT registration requirements

a) Recognise the circumstances in which a person must register for VAT.[2]

b) Explain the advantages of voluntary VAT registration.[2]

c) Explain the circumstances in which pre-registration input VAT can be recovered.[2]

d) Explain how and when a person can deregister for VAT.[1]

Excluded topics

- *Group registration.*

3. The computation of VAT liabilities

a) Explain how VAT is accounted for and administered.[2]

b) Recognise the tax point when goods or services are supplied.[2]

c) List the information that must be given on a VAT invoice.[1]

d) Explain and apply the principles regarding the valuation of supplies.[2]

e) Recognise the circumstances in which input VAT is non-deductible.[2]

f) Compute the relief that is available for impairment losses on trade debts.[2]

g) Explain the circumstances in which the default surcharge, a serious misdeclaration penalty, and default interest will be applied.[1]

Excluded topics

- *Imports, exports and trading within the European Community*
- *Partial exemption*
- *In respect of property and land: leases, do-it-yourself builders, and a landlord's option to tax.*
- *Penalties apart from those listed in the study guide (repeated misdeclarations are excluded).*

4. The effect of special schemes

a) Describe the cash accounting scheme, and recognise when it will be advantageous to use the scheme.[2]

b) Describe the annual accounting scheme, and recognise when it will be advantageous to use the scheme.[2]

c) Describe the flat rate scheme, and recognise when it will be advantageous to use the scheme.[2]

Excluded topics

- *The second-hand goods scheme.*
- *The capital goods scheme.*
- *The special schemes for retailers.*

G THE OBLIGATIONS OF TAX PAYERS AND/OR THEIR AGENTS

1. The systems for self-assessment and the making of returns

a) Explain and apply the features of the self-assessment system as it applies to individuals.[2]

b) Explain and apply the features of the self-assessment system as it applies to companies.[2]

2. The time limits for the submission of information, claims and payment of tax, including payments on account

a) Recognise the time limits that apply to the filing of returns and the making of claims.[2]

b) Recognise the due dates for the payment of tax under the self-assessment system.[2]

c) Compute payments on account and balancing payments/repayments for individuals.[2]

d) Explain how large companies are required to account for corporation tax on a quarterly basis.[2]

e) List the information and records that taxpayers need to retain for tax purposes.[1]

Excluded topics

- *The payment of CGT by annual instalments.*

3. The procedures relating to enquiries, appeals and disputes

a) Explain the circumstances in which HM Revenue & Customs can enquire into a self-assessment tax return.[2]

b) Explain the procedures for dealing with appeals and disputes.[1]

4. Penalties for non-compliance

a) Calculate interest on overdue tax.[2]

b) State the penalties that can be charged.[2]

The exam paper

The syllabus is assessed by a three-hour paper-based examination.

The paper will be predominantly computational and will have five questions, all of which will be compulsory.

- Question one will focus on income tax and question two will focus on corporation tax. The two questions will be for a total of 55 marks, with one of the questions being for 30 marks and the other being for 25 marks.
- Question three will focus on chargeable gains (either personal or corporate) and will be for 20 marks.
- Questions four and five will be on any area of the syllabus and will respectively be for 15 marks and 10 marks.

There will always be at a minimum of 10 marks on value added tax. These marks will normally be included within question one or question two, although there might be a separate question on value added tax.

National insurance contributions will not be examined as a separate question, but may be examined in any question involving income tax or corporation tax.

Groups and overseas aspects of corporation tax will only be examined in question two, and will account for no more than one third of the marks available for that question.

Questions one or two might include a small element of chargeable gains.

Any of the five questions might include the consideration of issues relating to the minimisation or deferral of tax liabilities.

Analysis of pilot paper

1. Computation of income tax payable. Record keeping requirement.
2. Computation of adjusted trading profit and corporation tax liability. VAT.
3. Computation of capital gains tax liability.
4. Computing basis periods in opening years and on a change in accounting date.
5. Corporation tax losses.

The pilot paper is reproduced in full on the following pages. You will also find the pilot paper with BPP's answers at the back of this text.

Pilot paper

Paper F6

Time allowed

Reading and planning: 15 minutes
Writing: 3 hours

ALL FIVE questions are compulsory and MUST be attempted.

Do NOT open this paper until instructed by the supervisor.

During reading and planning time only the question paper may be annotated. You must NOT write in your answer booklet until instructed by the supervisor.

This question paper must not be removed from the examination hall.

Warning

The pilot paper cannot cover all of the syllabus nor can it include examples of every type of question that will be included in the actual exam. You may see questions in the exam that you think are more difficult than any you see in the pilot paper.

Question 1

On 31 December 2007 Mark Kett ceased trading as a marketing consultant. He had been self-employed since 6 April 2002, and had always made his accounts up to 5 April. On 1 January 2008 Mark commenced employment as the marketing manager of Sleep-Easy plc. The company runs a hotel. The following information is available for the tax year 2007/08:

Self-employment

(1) Mark's tax adjusted trading profit for the nine-month period ended 31 December 2007 is £20,700. This figure is before taking account of capital allowances.

(2) The tax written down values for capital allowances purposes at 6 April 2007 were as follows:

	£
General pool	13,800
Expensive motor car	14,600

The expensive motor car was used by Mark, and 40% of the mileage was for private purposes.

(3) On 15 June 2007 Mark had purchased office furniture for £1,900. All of the items included in the general pool were sold for £18,800 on 31 December 2007. On the cessation of trading Mark personally retained the expensive motor car. Its value on 31 December 2007 was £11,800.

Employment

(1) Mark is paid a salary of £3,250 (gross) per month by Sleep-Easy plc, from which income tax of £620 per month has been deducted under PAYE.

(2) During the period from 1 January 2008 to 5 April 2008 Mark used his private motor car for business purposes. He drove 2,500 miles in the performance of his duties for Sleep-Easy plc, for which the company paid an allowance of 16 pence per mile. The relevant HM Revenue & Customs authorised mileage rate to be used as the basis of an expense claim is 40 pence per mile.

(3) On 1 January 2008 Sleep-Easy plc provided Mark with an interest free loan of £64,000 so that he could purchase a new main residence.

(4) During the period from 1 January 2008 to 5 April 2008 Mark was provided with free meals in Sleep-Easy plc's staff canteen. The total cost of these meals to the company was £400.

Property income

(1) Mark let out a furnished property throughout the tax year 2007/08. He received gross rents of £8,600, 5% of which was paid to a letting agency. During December 2007 Mark spent £540 on replacing dilapidated furniture and furnishings.

(2) From 6 April 2007 to 31 December 2007 Mark let out a spare room in his main residence, receiving rent of £350 per month.

Investment income

(1) During the tax year 2007/08 Mark received dividends of £2,880, interest from government stocks (gilts) of £1,900, and interest of £430 from an individual savings account (ISA). These were the actual cash amounts received.

(2) On 3 May 2007 Mark received a premium bond prize of £100.

Other information

(1) On 15 December 2007 Mark made a gift aid donation of £780 (net) to a national charity.

(2) Mark's payments on account of income tax in respect of the tax year 2007/08 totalled £11,381.

Required

(a) Compute the income tax payable by Mark for the tax year 2007/08, and the balancing payment or repayment that will be due for the year. **(22 marks)**

(b) Advise Mark as to how long he must retain the records used in preparing his tax return for the tax year 2007/08, and the potential consequences of not retaining the records for the required period. **(3 marks)**

(Total = 25 marks)

> **Question 1**
>
> There is likely to be a comprehensive question covering a wide range of income. You will be expected to complete detailed workings and you must always state why you have excluded any item from your computation rather than ignoring it. You do not have to use the three column approach to calculating taxable income, but it does make the income tax computation much simpler and less prone to error if you do. In a computational question you are likely also to see a written part where you are required to discuss some aspect of income tax, such as administrative requirements.

Question 2

(a) Scuba Ltd is a manufacturer of diving equipment. The following information is relevant for the year ended 31 December 2007:

Operating profit

The operating profit is £170,400. The expenses that have been deducted in calculating this figure include the following:

	£
Depreciation and amortisation of lease	45,200
Entertaining customers	7,050
Entertaining employees	2,470
Gifts to customers (diaries costing £25 each displaying Scuba Ltd's name)	1,350
Gifts to customers (food hampers costing £80 each)	1,600

Leasehold property

On 1 April 2007 Scuba Ltd acquired a leasehold office building that is used for business purposes. The company paid a premium of £80,000 for the grant of a twenty-year lease.

Purchase of industrial building

Scuba Ltd purchased a new factory from a builder on 1 July 2007 for £240,000, and this was immediately brought into use. The cost was made up as follows:

	£
Drawing office serving the factory	34,000
General offices	40,000
Factory	98,000
Land	68,000
	240,000

Plant and machinery

On 1 January 2007 the tax written down values of plant and machinery were as follows:

	£
General pool	47,200
Expensive motor car	22,400

The following transactions took place during the year ended 31 December 2007:

		Cost (Proceeds)
		£
3 January 2007	Purchased machinery	18,020
29 February 2007	Purchased a computer	1,100
4 May 2007	Purchased a motor car	10,400
18 August 2007	Purchased machinery	7,300
15 November 2007	Sold a lorry	(12,400)

The motor car purchased on 4 May 2007 for £10,400 is used by the factory manager, and 40% of the mileage is for private journeys. The lorry sold on 15 November 2007 for £12,400 originally cost £19,800.

Scuba Ltd is a small company as defined by the Companies Acts.

Property income

Scuba Ltd lets a retail shop that is surplus to requirements. The shop was let until 31 December 2006 but was then empty from 1 January 2007 to 30 April 2007. During this period Scuba Ltd spent £6,200 on decorating the shop, and £1,430 on advertising for new tenants. The shop was let from 1 May 2007 to 31 December 2007 at a quarterly rent of £7,200, payable in advance.

Interest received

Interest of £430 was received from HM Revenue & Customs on 31 October 2007 in respect of the overpayment of corporation tax for the year ended 31 December 2006.

Other information

Scuba Ltd has no associated companies, and the company has always had an accounting date of 31 December.

Required

(i) Compute Scuba Ltd's tax adjusted trading profit for the year ended 31 December 2007. You should ignore value added tax (VAT); **(15 marks)**

(ii) Compute Scuba Ltd's corporation tax liability for the year ended 31 December 2007. **(4 marks)**

(b) Scuba Ltd registered for value added tax (VAT) on 1 April 2005. The company's VAT returns have been submitted as follows:

Quarter ended	*VAT paid (refunded)*	*Submitted*
	£	
30 June 2005	18,600	One month late
30 September 2005	32,200	One month late
31 December 2005	8,800	On time
31 March 2006	3,400	Two months late
30 June 2006	(6,500)	One month late
30 September 2006	42,100	On time
31 December 2006	(2,900)	On time
31 March 2007	3,900	On time
30 June 2007	18,800	On time
30 September 2007	57,300	Two months late
31 December 2007	9,600	On time

Scuba Ltd always pays any VAT that is due at the same time that the related return is submitted.

During February 2008 Scuba Ltd discovered that a number of errors had been made when completing its VAT return for the quarter ended 31 December 2007. As a result of these errors the company will have to make an additional payment of VAT to HM Revenue & Customs.

Required

(i) State, giving appropriate reasons, the default surcharge consequences arising from Scuba Ltd's submission of its VAT returns for the quarter ended 30 June 2005 to the quarter ended 30 September 2007 inclusive. **(8 marks)**

(ii) Explain how Scuba Ltd can voluntarily disclose the errors relating to the VAT return for the quarter ended 31 December 2007, and state whether default interest will be due, if (1) the net errors in total are less than £2,000, and (2) the net errors in total are more than £2,000. **(3 marks)**

(Total = 30 marks)

Question 2

You are likely to get a detailed corporation tax question, requiring workings supporting each of the figures in the final computations of corporation tax payable. Part (b) of the question deals with VAT. Taking a methodical approach to part (b) is crucial. Ensure that adequate reasoning is given in your answer to obtain the maximum marks. In part (b)(ii) you are asked to give an explanation in two scenarios – be sure that you cover both.

Question 3

Paul Opus disposed of the following assets during the tax year 2007/08:

(1) On 10 April 2007 Paul sold 5,000 £1 ordinary shares in Symphony Ltd, an unquoted trading company, for £23,600. He had originally purchased 40,000 shares in the company on 23 June 2005 for £110,400.

(2) On 15 June 2007 Paul made a gift of his entire shareholding of 10,000 £1 ordinary shares in Concerto plc to his daughter. On that date the shares were quoted on the Stock Exchange at £5.10–£5.18, with recorded bargains of £5.00, £5.15 and £5.22. Paul's shareholding had been purchased on 29 April 1992 for £14,000. The shareholding is less than 1% of Concerto plc's issued share capital, and Paul has never been employed by Concerto plc. The indexation factor from April 1992 to April 1998 is 0.170, and from April 1992 to June 2007 it is 0.483.

(3) On 9 August 2007 Paul sold a motor car for £16,400. The motor car had been purchased on 21 January 2004 for £12,800.

(4) On 4 October 2007 Paul sold an antique vase for £8,400. The antique vase had been purchased on 19 January 2007 for £4,150.

(5) On 31 December 2007 Paul sold a house for £220,000. The house had been purchased on 1 April 2001 for £114,700. Paul occupied the house as his main residence from the date of purchase until 30 June 2004. The house was then unoccupied until it was sold on 31 December 2007.

(6) On 16 February 2008 Paul sold three acres of land for £285,000. He had originally purchased four acres of land on 17 July 2006 for £220,000. The market value of the unsold acre of land as at 16 February 2008 was £90,000. The land has never been used for business purposes.

(7) On 5 March 2008 Paul sold a freehold holiday cottage for £125,000. The cottage had originally been purchased on 28 July 2006 for £101,600 by Paul's wife. She transferred the cottage to Paul on 16 November 2007 when it was valued at £114,800. The cottage is not a business asset for taper relief purposes.

Paul's taxable income for the tax year 2007/08 is £15,800.

Required

Compute Paul's capital gains tax liability for the tax year 2007/08, and advise him by when this should be paid. **(20 marks)**

> **Question 3**
>
> This question included seven disposals of assets on which you had to calculate the gain. Although each computation was straight forward it tested a different aspect of CGT. Remember always to include your workings, and state why you exclude any disposal ('motor cars are exempt assets') to obtain maximum marks. Part (2) required you to calculate the indexation allowance on a disposal of shares from the FA 1985 pool. The study guide states that '*where shares and securities are concerned, a figure will be given for the value of the 1985 pool as at 5 April 1998*' so this was strictly outside the scope of your studies.

Question 4

Li Fung commenced in self-employment on 1 October 2003. She initially prepared accounts to 30 June, but changed her accounting date to 31 March by preparing accounts for the nine-month period to 31 March 2007. Li's trading profits since she commenced self-employment have been as follows:

	£
Nine-month period ended 30 June 2004	18,600
Year ended 30 June 2005	24,900
Year ended 30 June 2006	22,200
Nine-month period ended 31 March 2007	16,800
Year ended 31 March 2008	26,400

Required

(a) State the qualifying conditions that must be met for a change of accounting date to be valid. **(3 marks)**

(b) Compute Li's trading income assessments for each of the five tax years 2003/04, 2004/05, 2005/06, 2006/07 and 2007/08. **(9 marks)**

(c) Advise Li of the advantages and disadvantages for tax purposes of changing her accounting date from 30 June to 31 March. **(3 marks)**

(Total = 15 marks)

> **Question 4**
>
> This was a question on basis periods in opening years and on a change of accounting date. As well as calculating assessable profits you were required to state conditions (facts) and also advantages and disadvantages (conclusions). This combination of facts, calculations and conclusions is likely to be typical of the sort of question that you will meet.

Question 5

Loser Ltd's results for the year ended 30 June 2005, the nine month period ended 31 March 2006, the year ended 31 March 2007 and the year ended 31 March 2008 are as follows:

	Year ended 30 June 2005	*Period ended 31 March 2006*	*Year ended 31 March 2007*	*Year ended 31 March 2008*
	£	£	£	£
Trading profit/(loss)	86,600	(25,700)	27,300	(78,300)
Property business profit	–	4,500	8,100	5,600
Gift aid donations	(1,400)	(800)	(1,200)	(1,100)

Loser Ltd does not have any associated companies.

Required

(a) State the factors that will influence a company's choice of loss relief claims. You are not expected to consider group relief. **(3 marks)**

(b) Assuming that Loser Ltd claims relief for its losses as early as possible, compute the company's profits chargeable to corporation tax for the year ended 30 June 2005, the nine month period ended 31 March 2006, the year ended 31 March 2007 and the year ended 31 March 2008. Your answer should clearly identify the amount of any losses that are unrelieved. **(5 marks)**

(c) Explain how your answer to (b) above would have differed if Loser Ltd had ceased trading on 31 March 2008. **(2 marks)**

(Total = 10 marks)

Question 5

This was a question on corporation tax losses. First it required a written explanation, then a calculation and it ended with a comment on the effect of slightly changing the scenario, thereby encompassing a range of issues. Always read the question carefully, part (b) told you to assume that loss relief was claimed as early as possible, and to state clearly any unrelieved losses. If you did not, you would lose easy marks.

Part A
Taxation of individuals

1

Introduction to the UK tax system

Topic list	Syllabus reference
1 The overall function and purpose of taxation in a modern economy	A1(a)
2 Different types of taxes	A2(a), (b)
3 Principal sources of revenue law and practice	A3(a)-(c)
4 Tax avoidance and tax evasion	A4(a), (b)

Introduction

We start our study of tax with an introduction to the UK tax system.

First we consider briefly the purpose of raising taxes, both economic and social. We next consider the specific UK taxes, both revenue and capital, and also direct and indirect.

We see how the collection of tax is administered in the UK, and where the UK tax system interacts with overseas tax jurisdictions.

Finally we highlight the difference between tax avoidance and tax evasion.

When you have finished this chapter you should be able to discuss the broad features of the tax system. In the following chapters we will consider specific UK taxes, starting with income tax.

Study guide

		Intellectual level
A1	**The overall function and purpose of taxation in a modern economy**	
(a)	Describe the purpose (economic, social etc) of taxation in a modern economy.	2
A2	**Different types of taxes**	
(a)	Identify the different types of capital and revenue tax.	1
(b)	Explain the difference between direct and indirect taxation.	2
A3	**Principal sources of revenue law and practice**	
(a)	Describe the overall structure of the UK tax system.	1
(b)	State the different sources of revenue law.	1
(c)	Appreciate the interaction of the UK tax system with that of other tax jurisdictions.	2
A4	**Tax avoidance and tax evasion**	
(a)	Explain the difference between tax avoidance and tax evasion.	1
(b)	Explain the need for an ethical and professional approach.	2

Exam guide

You are unlikely to be asked a whole question on this part of the syllabus. You may, however, be asked to comment on one aspect, such as the difference between tax avoidance and tax evasion, as part of a question.

1 The overall function and purpose of taxation in a modern economy

FAST FORWARD

Economic, social and environmental factors may affect the government's tax policies.

1.1 Economic factors

In terms of economic analysis, government **taxation represents a withdrawal from the UK economy** while its expenditure acts as an injection into it. So the government's net position in terms of taxation and expenditure, together with its public sector borrowing policies, has an effect on the level of economic activity within the UK.

The government favours longer-term planning, currently publishing and then sticking to three year plans for expenditure. These show the proportion of the economy's overall resources which will be allocated by the government and how much will be left for the private sector.

This can have an effect on demand for particular types of goods, eg health and education on the one hand, which are predominately the result of public spending, and consumer goods on the other, which results from private spending. Changing demand levels will have an impact on employment levels within the different sectors, as well as on the profitability of different private sector suppliers.

Within that overall proportion left in the private sector, **the government uses tax policies to encourage and discourage certain types of activity**.

It **encourages**:

(a) **saving** on the part of the individual, by offering tax incentives such as tax-free Individual Savings Accounts and tax relief on pension contributions

(b) **donations to charities**, through the Gift Aid scheme

(c) **entrepreneurs** who build their own business, through reliefs from capital gains tax

(d) **investment in industrial buildings and plant and machinery** through capital allowances;

while it **discourages**:

(a) **smoking** and **alcoholic drinks**, through the duties placed on each type of product;

(b) **motoring**, through fuel duties.

Governments can and do argue that these latter taxes and duties to some extent mirror the extra costs to the country as a whole of such behaviours, such as the cost of coping with smoking related illnesses. However, the Government needs to raise money for spending in areas where there are no consumers on whom the necessary taxes can be levied, such as defence, law and order, overseas aid and the cost of running the government and Parliament.

1.2 Social factors

Social justice lies at the heart of politics, since what some think of as just is regarded by others as completely unjust. Attitudes to the redistribution of wealth are a clear example.

In a free market some individuals generate greater amounts of income and capital than others and once wealth has been acquired, it tends to grow through the reinvestment of investment income received. This can lead to the rich getting richer and the poor poorer, with economic power becoming concentrated in relatively few hands.

Some electors make the value judgement that these trends should be countered by **taxation policies which redistribute income and wealth** away from the rich towards the poor. This is one of the key arguments in favour of some sort of capital gains tax and inheritance tax, taxes which, relative to the revenue raised, cost a very great deal to collect.

Different taxes have different social effects:

(a) **Direct taxes** based on income and profits (income tax), gains (capital gains tax) or wealth (inheritance tax) **tax only those who have these resources**.

(b) **Indirect taxes** paid by the consumer (VAT) **discourage spending** and encourage saving. Lower or nil rates of tax can be levied on essentials, such as food.

(c) **Progressive taxes** such as income tax, where the proportion of the income or gains paid over in tax increases as income/gains rise, **target those who can afford to pay**. Personal allowances and the rates of taxation can be adjusted so as to ensure that those on very low incomes pay little or no tax.

(d) Taxes on capital or wealth ensure that that people cannot avoid taxation by having an income of zero and just living off the sale of capital assets.

Almost everyone would argue that taxation should be **equitable** or 'fair', but there are many different views as to what is equitable.

An **efficient tax** is one where the costs of collection are low relative to the tax paid over to the government. The government publishes figures for the administrative costs incurred by government departments in operating the taxation systems, but there are also compliance costs to be taken into account. Compliance costs are those incurred by the taxpayer, whether they be the individual preparing tax returns under the self assessment system or the employer operating the PAYE system to collect income tax or the business collecting value added tax. Some of the more equitable taxes may be less efficient to collect.

1.3 Environmental factors

The taxation system is moving slowly to accommodate the environmental concerns which have come to the fore over the last twenty years or so, especially the concerns about renewable and non-renewable sources of energy and global warming.

Examples of taxes which have been introduced for environmental reasons are:

(a) the **climate change levy**, raised on businesses in proportion to their consumption of energy. Its claimed purpose is to encourage reduced consumption;

(b) the **landfill tax** levied on the operators of landfill sites on each tonne of rubbish/waste processed at the site. Its claimed purpose is to encourage recycling by taxing waste which has to be stored;

(c) the changes to **taxation of company cars and the provision of private fuel** to be dependent on CO_2 emissions. Its claimed purpose is to encourage the manufacture and purchase of low CO_2 emission cars to reduce emissions into the atmosphere caused by driving.

Only the last of these will be directly felt by individuals, even if the other taxes are passed on by being factored into a business's overheads.

2 Different types of taxes

FAST FORWARD

Central government raises revenue through a wide range of taxes. Tax law is made by **statute.**

2.1 Taxes in the UK

Central government raises revenue through a wide range of taxes. Tax law is made by **statute.**

The main taxes, their incidence and their sources, are set out in the table below.

Tax	Suffered by	Source
Income tax	**Individuals** **Partnerships**	Capital Allowances Act 2001 (CAA 2001); Income Tax (Earnings and Pensions) Act 2003 (ITEPA 2003); Income Tax (Trading and Other Income) Act 2005 (ITTOIA 2005); Income Tax Act 2007 (ITA 2007)
Corporation tax	**Companies**	Income and Corporation Taxes Act 1988 (ICTA 1988) and subsequent Finance Acts, CAA 2001 as above
Capital gains tax	**Individuals** **Partnerships** **Companies** (which pay tax on capital gains in the form of corporation tax)	Taxation of Chargeable Gains Act 1992 (TCGA 1992) and subsequent Finance Acts
Value added tax	**Businesses**, both incorporated and unincorporated	Value Added Tax Act 1994 (VATA 1994) and subsequent Finance Acts

You will also meet National Insurance. **National insurance is payable by employers, employees and the self employed.** Further details of all these taxes are found later in this Text.

The other taxes referred to in the previous section, such as inheritance tax and landfill tax, are not examinable at F6.

Finance Acts are passed each year, incorporating proposals set out in the **Budget**. They make changes which apply mainly to the tax year ahead. **This Study Text includes the provisions of the Finance Act 2007**. This is examinable in June and December 2008.

2.2 Revenue and capital taxes

Revenue taxes are those charged on income. In this Text this covers:

(a) **income tax**,
(b) **corporation tax**, and
(c) **national insurance**.

Capital taxes are those charged on capital gains or on wealth. In this Text this covers **CGT**.

2.3 Direct and indirect taxes

Direct taxes are those charged on **income, gains and wealth**, whilst **indirect taxes** are **those paid by the consumer to the supplier**, and thence to the Government. **VAT** is an indirect tax, whilst income tax, national insurance, corporation tax and CGT are direct taxes.

3 Principal sources of revenue law and practice

FAST FORWARD

Tax is administered by HM Revenue and Customs (HMRC).

3.1 The overall structure of the UK tax system

The **Treasury** formally imposes and collects taxation. The management of the Treasury is the responsibility of the Chancellor of the Exchequer. **The administrative function for the collection of tax is undertaken by Her Majesty's Revenue and Customs (HMRC).**

The HMRC staff are referred to in the tax legislation as **'Officers of the Revenue and Customs'**. They are responsible for supervising the self-assessment system and agreeing tax liabilities. Officers who collect tax may be referred to as **receivable management officers**. These officers are local officers who are responsible for following up amounts of unpaid tax referred to them by the **HMRC Accounts Office.**

The **Revenue and Customs Prosecutions Office (R&CPO)** has been established to provide legal advice and institute and conduct criminal prosecutions in England and Wales where there has been an investigation by HMRC.

The **General Commissioners** (not to be confused with the Commissioners for HMRC) are appointed (at the moment) by the Lord Chancellor to hear **appeals** against HMRC decisions. They are part-time and unpaid. They are appointed for a local area (a **division**). They appoint a clerk who is often a lawyer or accountant and who is paid for his services.

The **Special Commissioners** are also appointed by the Lord Chancellor. They are full-time paid professionals. They generally hear the more complex appeals.

Many taxpayers arrange for their accountants to prepare and submit their tax returns. The taxpayer is still the person responsible for submitting the return and for paying whatever tax becomes due: the accountant is only acting as the taxpayer's agent.

3.2 Different sources of revenue law

As stated above, taxes are imposed by statute. This comprises not only **Acts of Parliament** but also regulations laid down by **Statutory Instruments**. Statute is interpreted and amplified by **case law**.

HM Revenue and Customs also issue:

(a) **Statements of practice**, setting out how they intend to apply the law

(b) **Extra-statutory concessions**, setting out circumstances in which they will not apply the strict letter of the law where it would be unfair

(c) A wide range of **explanatory leaflets**

(d) **Business economic notes**. These are notes on particular types of business, which are used as background information by HMRC and are also published

(e) The **Tax Bulletin**. This is a newsletter giving HMRC's view on specific points

(f) The **Internal Guidance**, a series of manuals used by HMRC staff

A great deal of information and HMRC publications can be found on the HM Revenue and Customs' Internet site (www.hmrc.gov.uk).

Although the HMRC publications do not generally have the force of law some of the VAT notices do where power has been delegated under regulations. This applies, for example, to certain administrative aspects of the cash accounting scheme.

3.3 The interaction of the UK tax system with that of other tax jurisdictions

3.3.1 The European Union

Membership of the European Union can be expected to have a significant effect on UK taxes although **there is not yet a general requirement imposed on the EU member states to move to a common system of taxation or to harmonise their individual tax systems**. The states may, however, agree jointly to enact specific laws, known as '**Directives**', which provide for a common code of taxation within particular areas of their taxation systems.

The most important example to date is VAT, where the UK is obliged to pass its laws in conformity with the rules laid down in the European legislation. The VAT Directives still allow for a certain amount of flexibility between member states, eg in setting rates of taxation. There are only limited examples of Directives in the area of Direct Taxes, generally concerned with cross-border dividend and interest payments and corporate reorganisations.

However, under the EU treaties, member states are also obliged to permit freedom of movement of workers, freedom of movement of capital and freedom to establish business operations within the EU. These treaty provisions have 'direct effect', ie **a taxpayer is entitled to claim that a UK tax provision is ineffective because it breaches one or more of the freedoms guaranteed under European Law**.

The European Court of Justice has repeatedly held that taxation provisions which discriminate against non-residents (ie treat a non-resident less favourably than a resident in a similar situation) are contrary to European Law, unless there is a very strong public interest justification.

There are provisions regarding the **exchange of information** between European Union Revenue authorities.

3.3.2 Other countries

The UK has entered into **double tax treaties** with various countries, such as the USA. These contain rules which prevent income and gains being taxed twice, but often contain non-discrimination provisions, preventing a foreign national from being treated more harshly than a national. There are also usually rules for the **exchange of information** between the different Revenue authorities.

Even where there is no double tax relief, the UK tax system gives relief for foreign taxes paid.

4 Tax avoidance and tax evasion

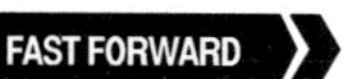

Tax avoidance is the legal minimisation of tax liabilities, tax evasion is illegal.

4.1 Tax evasion

Tax evasion consists of seeking to mislead HMRC by either:

(a) **suppressing information to which they are entitled** (eg failing to notify HMRC that you are liable to tax, understating income or gains or omitting to disclose a relevant fact, eg that business expenditure had a dual motive), or

(b) **providing them with deliberately false information** (eg deducting expenses which have not been incurred or claiming capital allowances on plant that has not been purchased).

Minor cases of tax evasion have generally been settled out of court on the payment of penalties. However, there is now a **statutory offence of evading income tax**, which enables such matters as deliberate failure to operate PAYE to be dealt with in magistrates' courts.

Serious cases of tax evasion, particularly those involving fraud, will continue to be the subject of criminal prosecutions which may lead to fines and/or imprisonment on conviction.

4.2 Tax avoidance

Tax avoidance is more difficult to define.

In a very broad sense, it could include **any legal method of reducing your tax burden**, eg taking advantage of tax shelter opportunities explicitly offered by tax legislation such as ISAs. However, the term is more commonly used in a more narrow sense, to denote ingenious arrangements designed to produce unintended tax advantages for the taxpayer.

The effectiveness of tax avoidance schemes has often been examined in the courts. Traditionally the tax rules were applied to the legal form of transactions, although this principle was qualified in later cases. It was held that the Courts could disregard transactions which were preordained and solely designed to avoid tax.

Traditionally, the response of HMRC has been to seek to mend the loopholes in the law as they come to their attention. In general, there is a presumption that the effect of such changes should not be backdated.

The Finance Act 2004 introduced new **disclosure obligations** on promoters of certain tax avoidance schemes, and on taxpayers, to provide details to HMRC of any such schemes used by the taxpayer. This enables HMRC to introduce counter avoidance measures at the earliest opportunity.

4.3 The distinction between avoidance and evasion

The distinction between tax evasion and tax avoidance is generally clear cut, since tax avoidance is an entirely legal activity and does not entail misleading HMRC.

However, care should be taken in giving advice in some circumstances. For example, a taxpayer who does not return income or gains because he wrongly believes that he has successfully avoided having to pay tax on them may, as a result, be guilty of tax evasion.

4.4 The need for an ethical and professional approach

Under self assessment, all taxpayers (whether individuals or companies) are responsible for disclosing their taxable income and gains and the deductions and reliefs they are claiming against them.

The practising accountant often acts for taxpayers in their dealings with HMRC and situations can arise where the accountant has concerns as to whether the taxpayer is being honest in providing information to the accountant for onward transmission.

How the accountant deals with such situations is a matter of professional judgement, but in deciding what to do, the accountant will be expected to uphold the standards of the Association of Chartered Certified Accountants. He must act honestly and objectively, with due care and diligence, and showing the highest standards of integrity.

Chapter Roundup

- Economic, social and environmental factors may affect the government's tax policies.
- Central government raises revenue through a wide range of taxes. Tax law is made by **statute.**
- Tax is administered by HM Revenue and Customs (HMRC).
- Tax avoidance is the legal minimisation of tax liabilities, tax evasion is illegal.

Quick Quiz

1. What is the difference between a direct and an indirect tax?
2. What is an Extra Statutory Concession?
3. Is tax avoidance legal?

Answers to Quick Quiz

1. A direct tax is one charged on income or gains, an indirect tax is paid by a consumer to the supplier, who then passes it to HMRC.
2. In Extra Statutory Concession is a relaxation by HMRC of the strict rules where their imposition would be unfair.
3. Yes tax avoidance is legal; tax evasion is illegal.

The computation of taxable income and the income tax liability

2

Topic list	Syllabus reference
1 The scope of income tax	B1(a)
2 Computing taxable income	B5(a)
3 Various types of income	B4(f), (g), B5(a)
4 Tax exempt income	B4(h)
5 Deductible interest	B5(d)
6 Personal allowance	B5(b)
7 Computing tax payable	B5(c)
8 Gift Aid	B5(e)
9 Jointly held property	B5(f) B6(c)

Introduction

In the previous chapter we considered the UK tax system generally. Now we look at income tax, which is a tax on what individuals make from their jobs, their businesses and their savings and investments. We consider the scope of income tax and see how to collect together all of an individual's income in a personal tax computation, and we also see which income can be excluded as being exempt from tax.

Next we look at the circumstances in which interest paid can be deducted in the income tax computation.

Each individual is entitled to a personal allowance, and only if that is exceeded will any tax be due. Older taxpayers are entitled to a higher allowance, the age allowance, although this is restricted if the taxpayer's income is too high.

We then learn how to work out the tax on the individual's taxable income, and we see how donations to charity under the gift aid scheme can save tax.

Finally we consider how income from property held jointly by married couples or civil partners is allocated for tax purposes.

In later chapters, we look at particular types of income in more detail.

Study guide

		Intellectual level
B1	**The scope of income tax**	
(a)	Explain how the residence of an individual is determined.	1
B4	**Property and investment income**	
(f)	Compute the tax payable on savings income.	2
(g)	Compute the tax payable on dividend income.	2
(h)	Explain the treatment of individual savings accounts (ISAs) and other tax exempt investments.	1
B5	**The comprehensive computation of taxable income and income tax liability**	
(a)	Prepare a basic income tax computation involving different types of income.	2
(b)	Calculate the amount of personal allowance available to people aged 65 and above.	2
(c)	Compute the amount of income tax payable.	2
(d)	Explain the treatment of interest paid.	2
(e)	Explain the treatment of gift aid donations.	1
(f)	Explain the treatment of property owned jointly by a married couple, or by a couple in a civil partnership.	1
B6	**The use of exemptions and reliefs in deferring and minimising income tax liabilities**	
(c)	Explain how a married couple or couple in a civil partnership can minimise their tax liabilities.	2

Exam guide

It is very likely that you will have to prepare an income tax computation in your exam. You should familiarise yourself with the layout of the computation, and the three types of income: non-savings, savings and dividends. It is then a simple matter of slotting the final figures into the computation from supporting workings for the different types of income.

Gift aid donations are likely to feature regularly, and you will come across the technique of extending the basic rate band again when you deal with pensions later in this Text.

1 The scope of income tax

An individual may be resident and/or ordinarily in the UK, and his liability to UK income tax will be determined accordingly.

1.1 Introduction

A taxpayer's **residence and ordinary residence** have important consequences in establishing the tax treatment of his UK and overseas income and capital gains.

1.2 Residence

An individual is resident in the UK for a given tax year if, in that tax year, he satisfies either of the following criteria.

(a) **He is present in the UK for 183 days or more** (days of arrival and departure are excluded).

(b) **He makes substantial annual visits to the UK**. Visits averaging 91 days or more a year for each of four or more consecutive years will make the person resident for each of these tax years (for someone emigrating from the UK, the four years are reduced to three).

If days are spent in the UK because of exceptional circumstances beyond the individual's control (such as illness), those days are ignored for the purposes of the 91 day rule (but not for the 183 day rule above).

1.3 Tax consequences

Generally, a UK resident is liable to UK income tax on his UK and overseas income whereas a non-resident is liable to UK income tax only on income arising in the UK.

Exam focus point

The taxation of the overseas income of a UK resident and the taxation of non-residents is outside the scope of your syllabus.

2 Computing taxable income

FAST FORWARD

In a personal income tax computation, we bring together income from all sources, splitting the sources into non-savings, savings and dividend income.

An individual's income from all sources is brought together in a personal tax computation. Three columns are needed to distinguish between non-savings income, savings income and dividend income. Here is an example. All items are explained later in this Text.

RICHARD: INCOME TAX COMPUTATION 2007/08

	Non-savings income £	*Savings income* £	*Dividend income* £	*Total* £
Income from employment	43,000			
Building society interest		1,000		
National Savings & Investments a/c interest		360		
UK dividends			1,000	
Total income	43,000	1,360	1,000	
Less interest paid	(2,000)			
Net income	41,000	1,360	1,000	43,360
Less personal allowance	(5,225)			
Taxable income	35,775	1,360	1,000	38,135

	£	£
Income tax		
Non savings income		
£2,230 × 10%		223
£32,370 × 22%		7,121
£1,175 × 40%		470
		7,814
Savings income		
£1,360 × 40%		544
Dividend income		
£1,000 × 32.5%		325
Tax liability		8,683
Less tax suffered		
Tax credit on dividend income	100	
PAYE tax on salary (say)	7,800	
Tax on building society interest	200	
		(8,100)
Tax payable		583

Key term

Total income is all income subject to income tax. Each of the amounts which make up total income is called a **component**. **Net income** is total income after deductible interest and trade losses. **Taxable income** is net income less the personal allowance. The **tax liability** is the amount of tax charged on the individual's income. **Tax payable** is the balance of the liability still to be settled in cash.

Income tax is charged on **'taxable income'**. Non-savings income is dealt with first, then savings income and then dividend income.

For non-savings income, the first £2,230 (the starting rate band) is taxed at the starting rate (10%), the next £32,370 (the basic rate band) is taxed at the basic rate (22%) and the rest at the higher rate (40%). We will look at the taxation of the other types of income later in this chapter.

The remainder of this chapter gives more details of the income tax computation.

3 Various types of income

3.1 Classification of income

All income received must be classified according to the nature of the income. This is because different computational rules apply to different types of income. The main types of income are:

(a) **Income from employment and pensions**
(b) **Profits of trades, professions and vocations**
(c) **Income from property letting**
(d) **Savings and investment income, including interest and dividends.**

The rules for computing employment income, profits from trades, professions and vocations and property letting income will be covered in later chapters. These types of income are non-savings income.

FAST FORWARD

An individual may receive interest net of 20% tax suffered at source. The amount received must be grossed up by multiplying by 100/80 and must be included gross in the income tax computation. Similarly dividends are received net of a 10% tax credit and must be grossed up for inclusion in the tax computation.

3.2 Savings income

3.2.1 What is savings income?

Savings income is interest. Interest is paid on bank and building society accounts, on Government securities, such as Treasury Stock, and on company debentures and loan stock.

Interest may be paid net of 20% tax or it may be paid gross.

3.2.2 Savings income received net of 20% tax

The following savings income is received net of 20% tax. **This is called income taxed at source.**

(a) Bank and building society interest paid to individuals (but not National Savings & Investments bank account interest)

(b) Interest paid to individuals by unlisted UK companies on debentures and loan stocks

The amount received is grossed up by multiplying by 100/80 and is included gross in the income tax computation. The tax deducted at source is deducted in computing tax payable and may be repaid.

Exam focus point

In examinations you may be given either the net or the gross amount of such income: read the question carefully. If you are given the net amount (the amount received or credited), you should gross up the figure at the rate of 20%. For example, net building society interest of £160 is equivalent to gross income of £160 × 100/80 = £200 on which tax of £40 (20% of £200) has been suffered.

3.2.3 Savings income received gross

Some savings income is received gross, ie without tax having been deducted. Examples are:

(a) National Savings & Investments bank account Interest
(b) Interest on government securities (these are also called 'gilts')
(c) Interest from quoted company debentures and loan stock.

3.3 Dividend income

Dividends on UK shares are received net of a 10% tax credit. This means a dividend of £90 has a £10 tax credit, giving gross income of £100 to include in the income tax computation. The tax credit can be deducted in computing tax payable but it cannot be repaid.

This treatment applies to dividends received from open ended investment companies (OEICs) and to dividend distributions from unit trusts.

4 Tax exempt income

4.1 Types of tax exempt investments

Income from certain investments is exempt from income tax.

Exam focus point

In examinations you may be given details of exempt income. You should state in your answer that the income is exempt to show that you have considered it and have not just overlooked it.

4.2 Individual savings accounts

An individual savings account (ISA) is a special tax exempt way of saving. Each year an individual can invest either

(a) up to £7,000 in a maxi ISA, or
(b) up to £3,000 in a mini cash ISA and/or up to £4,000 in a stocks and shares ISA.

Funds invested in a maxi ISA are used to buy stock market investments, such as shares in quoted companies or OEICs, units in unit trusts, fixed interest investments, or insurance policies.

Dividend income and interest received from ISAs is exempt from income tax, whether it is paid out to the investor or retained and reinvested within the ISA.

4.3 Savings certificates

Savings certificates are issued by National Savings and Investments (NS&I). They may be fixed rate certificates or index linked, and are for fixed terms of between two and five years. On maturity the profit is tax exempt. This profit is often called interest.

4.4 Premium bonds

Prizes received from premium bonds are exempt from tax.

5 Deductible interest

FAST FORWARD

Deductible interest is deducted from total income to compute net income.

5.1 Interest payments

An individual who pays interest in a tax year is entitled to relief in that tax year if the loan is for one of the following purposes:

(a) **Loan to buy plant or machinery for partnership use**. Interest is allowed for three years from the end of the tax year in which the loan was taken out. If the plant is used partly for private use, the allowable interest is apportioned.

(b) **Loan to buy plant or machinery for employment use.** Interest is allowed for three years from the end of the tax year in which the loan was taken out. If the plant is used partly for private use, the allowable interest is apportioned.

(c) **Loan to buy interest in employee-controlled company.** The company must be an unquoted trading company resident in the UK with at least 50% of the voting shares held by employees.

(d) **Loan to invest in partnership.** The investment may be a share in the partnership or a contribution to the partnership of capital or a loan to the partnership. The individual must be a partner (other than a limited partner) and relief ceases when he ceases to be a partner.

(e) **Loan to invest in a co-operative.** The investment may be shares or a loan. The individual must spend the greater part of his time working for the co-operative.

Tax relief is given by deducting the interest from total income to calculate net income for the tax year in which the interest is paid. It is deducted from **non-savings income first, then from savings income and lastly from dividend income**.

5.2 Example

Frederick has taxable trading income for 2007/08 of £42,000, savings income of £1,320 (gross) and dividend income of £1,000 (gross).

Frederick pays interest of £1,370 in 2007/08 on a loan to invest in a partnership.

Frederick's taxable income is:

	Non-savings income	*Savings income*	*Dividend income*	*Total*
	£	£	£	£
Total income	42,000	1,320	1,000	44,320
Less: interest paid	(1,370)			(1,370)
Net income	40,630	1,320	1,000	42,950
Less: personal allowance	(5,225)			(5,225)
Taxable income	35,405	1,320	1,000	37,725

6 Personal allowance

FAST FORWARD

All persons are entitled to a personal allowance. It is deducted from net income, first against non savings income, then against savings income and lastly against dividend income. Taxpayers aged 65-74 are entitled to an age allowance, and taxpayers aged 75 and over to a higher age allowance.

6.1 Basic personal allowance

Once taxable income from all sources has been aggregated and any deductible interest deducted, the remainder is the taxpayer's net income. An allowance, the personal allowance, is deducted from net income. Like deductible interest, it reduces non savings income first, then savings income and lastly dividend income.

All persons under the age of 65 (including children) are entitled to the personal allowance of £5,225.

6.2 Age allowance

An individual aged 65-74 receives an age allowance of £7,550 instead of the personal allowance of £5,225.

An individual aged 75 or over receives a higher age allowance of £7,690 instead of the personal allowance of £5,225.

If the individual's net income exceeds £20,900 the age allowance is reduced by £1 for each £2 by which net income exceeds £20,900. The age allowance cannot be reduced below £5,225.

An individual is entitled to the age allowance, or higher age allowance, provided he attains the age of 65 or 75 respectively before the end of the tax year, or would have had he not died before his birthday.

6.3 Example: personal allowance

Three taxpayers have the following net income for 2007/08.

A £21,800
B £26,800
C £25,300

Calculate their taxable income assuming taxpayers A and B are aged 68 and taxpayer C is aged 78.

Taxable income is:	*A*	*B*	*C*
	£	£	£
Net income	21,800	26,800	25,300
Less age allowance (Working)	(7,100)	(5,225)	(5,490)
Taxable income	14,700	21,575	19,810

Working

Net income	21,800	26,800	25,300
Less income limit	(20,900)	(20,900)	(20,900)
Excess	900	5,900	4,400
Age allowance	7,550	7,550	7,690
Less half the excess £900/5,900/4,400 × 1/2	(450)	(2,950)	(2,200)
	7,100	4,600	5,490
Minimum		5,225	

Question

Calculation of taxable income

Susan (aged 41) has taxable partnership income of £37,000 for 2007/08. She has a loan of £7,000 at 10% interest used to buy into her partnership, and another loan of £5,000 at 6% interest to buy double glazing for her house. She receives gross interest from Gilts of £2,500 a year. What is her taxable income for 2007/08?

Answer

	Non-savings income	*Savings income*	*Total*
	£	£	£
Partnership income	37,000		
Gilts interest		2,500	
Total income	37,000	2,500	
Less deductible interest £7,000 × 10% (note)	(700)		
Net income	36,300	2,500	38,800
Less personal allowance	(5,225)		
Taxable income	31,075	2,500	33,575

Note. The loan to purchase double glazing for her house is not for a purpose which would qualify for tax relief.

7 Computing tax payable

FAST FORWARD

Work out income tax on the taxable income. Deduct the tax credit on dividend income and any income tax suffered at source to arrive at tax payable. The tax credit on dividend income cannot be repaid if it exceeds the tax liability calculated so far. Other tax suffered at source can be repaid.

7.1 Taxable income

Income tax payable is computed on an individual's taxable income, which comprises the net income less the personal or age allowance. The rate of income tax payable depends on the nature of the income: non-savings, savings income, or dividend income.

7.2 Steps in the income tax computation

Step 1 **The first step in preparing a personal tax computation is to set up three columns**
One column for non-savings income, one for savings income and one for dividend income. Add up income from different sources. The sum of these is known as 'total income'.

Step 2 **Deal with non-savings income first**
Income of up to £2,230 is taxed at 10%. Next any income in the basic rate band is taxed at 22%, and finally income above the basic rate threshold is taxed at 40%.

Step 3 **Now deal with savings income**
If any of the starting or basic rate bands remain **after taxing non savings income**, they can be used here. Savings income is taxed at 10% in the starting rate band. If savings income falls within the basic rate band it is taxed at 20% (not 22%). Once income is above the higher rate threshold, it is taxed at 40%.

Step 4 **Lastly, tax dividend income**
If dividend income falls within the starting or basic rate bands, it is taxed at 10% (never 20% or 22%). If, however, the dividend income exceeds the basic rate threshold of £34,600, it is taxable at 32.5%.

Step 5 Add the amounts of tax together. The resulting figure is the income tax liability.

Step 6 Next, deduct the tax credit on dividends. Although deductible this tax credit cannot be repaid if it exceeds the tax liability calculated so far.

Step 7 Finally deduct the tax deducted at source from savings income and any PAYE. These amounts can be repaid to the extent that they exceed the income tax liability.

7.3 Examples: personal tax computations

(a) Kathe has a salary of £10,000 and receives dividends of £4,500.

	Non-savings income	*Dividend income*	*Total*
	£	£	£
Earnings	10,000		
Dividends £4,500 × 100/90		5,000	
Net income	10,000	5,000	15,000
Less personal allowance	(5,225)		
Taxable income	4,775	5,000	9,775

	£
Income tax	
Non savings income	
£2,230 × 10%	223
£2,545 × 22%	560
Dividend income	
£5,000 × 10%	500
Tax liability	1,283
Less tax credit on dividend	(500)
Tax payable	783

Some of the tax payable has probably already been paid on the salary under PAYE.

The dividend income falls within the basic rate band so it is taxed at 10% (*not* 22%).

(b) Jules has a salary of £20,000, business profits of £30,000, net dividends of £6,750 and building society interest of £3,000 net. He is entitled to relief on interest paid of £2,000.

	Non-savings income	*Savings income*	*Dividend income*	*Total*
	£	£	£	£
Business profits	30,000			
Employment income	20,000			
Dividends £6,750 × 100/90			7,500	
Building society interest £3,000 × 100/80	–	3,750	–	
Total income	50,000	3,750	7,500	
Less interest paid	(2,000)			
Net income	48,000	3,750	7,500	59,250
Less personal allowance	(5,225)			
Taxable income	42,775	3,750	7,500	54,025

	£
Income tax	
Non savings income	
£2,230 × 10%	223
£32,370 × 22%	7,121
£8,175 × 40%	3,270
Savings income	
£3,750 × 40%	1,500
Dividend income	
£7,500 × 32.5%	2,437
Tax liability	14,551
Less tax credit on dividend income	(750)
Less tax suffered on building society interest	(750)
Tax payable	13,051

Savings income and dividend income fall above the basic rate threshold so they are taxed at 40% and 32.5% respectively.

(c) Jim does not work. He receives net bank interest of £38,000. He is entitled to relief on interest paid of £2,000.

	Savings income	*Total*
	£	£
Bank interest × 100/80/Total income	47,500	
Less interest paid	(2,000)	
Net income	45,500	45,500
Less personal allowance	(5,225)	
Taxable income	40,275	40,275

	£
Savings income	
£2,230 × 10%	223
£32,370 × 20%	6,474
£5,675 × 40%	2,270
Tax liability	8,967
Less tax suffered	(9,500)
Tax repayable	(533)

Savings income within the basic rate band is taxed at 20% (*not* 22%).

7.4 The complete proforma

Here is a complete proforma computation of taxable income. It is probably too much for you to absorb at this stage, but refer back to it as you come to the chapters dealing with the types of income shown. You will also see how trading losses fit into the proforma later in this study text.

	Non-savings income	*Savings income*	*Dividend income*	*Total*
	£	£	£	£
Trading income	X			
Employment income	X			
Property business income	X			
Building society interest (gross)		X		
Other interest (gross)		X		
(as many lines as necessary)				
Dividends (gross)			X	
Total income	X	X	X	
Less interest paid	(X)	(X)	(X)	
Net income	X	X	X	X
Less personal allowance	(X)	(X)	(X)	
Taxable income	X	X	X	X

8 Gift Aid

Extend the basic rate band by the gross amount of any gift aid payment.

8.1 Gift aid donations

Key term

One-off and regular charitable gifts of money qualify for tax relief under the **gift aid scheme** provided the donor gives the charity a gift aid declaration.

Gift aid declarations can be made in writing, electronically through the internet or orally over the phone. A declaration can cover a one-off gift or any number of gifts made after a specified date (which may be in the past).

The gift must not be repayable, and must not confer any more than a minimal benefit on the donor. Gift aid may be used for entrance fees (for example to National Trust properties or historic houses) provided the right of admission applies for at least one year or the visitor pays at least 10% more than the normal admission charge.

8.2 Tax relief for gift aid donations

A gift aid donation is treated as though it is paid net of basic rate tax (22%). Additional tax relief for higher rate taxpayers is given in the personal tax computation by increasing the donor's basic rate band by the gross amount of the gift. To arrive at the gross amount of the gift you must multiply the amount paid by 100/78.

No additional relief is due for basic rate taxpayers. Extending the basic rate band is then irrelevant as taxable income is below the basic rate threshold.

Question

Gift Aid

James earns a salary of £60,530 but has no other income. In 2007/08 he paid £7,800 (net) under the gift aid scheme.

Compute James' income tax liability for 2007/08.

Answer

		Non-savings income
		£
Salary/Net income		60,530
Less: personal allowance		(5,225)
Taxable income		55,305
Income tax	£	£
Starting rate band	2,230 × 10%	223
Basic rate band	32,370 × 22%	7,121
Basic rate band (extended)	10,000 × 22%	2,200
Higher rate band	10,705 × 40%	4,282
	55,305	13,826

The basic rate band is extended by the gross amount of the gift (£7,800 × 100/78).

9 Jointly held property

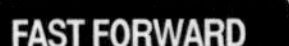

FAST FORWARD

Income on property held jointly by married couples and members of a civil partnership is treated as if it were shared equally unless the couple make a joint declaration of the actual shares of ownership.

9.1 Allocation of joint income

If property is held jointly by a married couple or civil partners the income arising from that property is taxed as if it was shared equally between the members of the couple.

This 50:50 split applies even if the property is not owned in equal shares, **unless the members of the couple make a joint declaration to HMRC specifying the actual proportion to which each is entitled.**

Civil partners are members of a same sex couple which has registered as a civil partnership under the Civil Partnerships Act 2004.

9.2 Example: joint income

Janet owns 40% of a holiday cottage and John, her husband, owns the other 60%.

If no declaration is made each will be taxed on one half of the income arising when he property is let out.

If a declaration is made, Janet will be taxed on her 40% of the income and John will be taxed on his 60%.

9.3 Tax planning for married couples/civil partners

Where one member of a married couple/civil partnership is a basic rate taxpayer and the other a higher rate taxpayer, income tax liabilities can be minimised by transferring income producing assets from the higher rate taxpayer to the other spouse or civil partner.

If assets are owned jointly but in unequal proportions, then:

(a) if the higher rate taxpayer owns more than 50% of the asset, no declaration of beneficial interest should be made so that the income is shared equally, or

(b) if the higher rate taxpayer owns less than 50% of the asset, a declaration of beneficial interest should be made so that the other spouse or civil partner is taxed on their full amount of income.

Thus in the above example a declaration is beneficial if Janet is a higher rate taxpayer whilst John is a basic rate taxpayer,

Chapter Roundup

- An individual may be resident and/or ordinarily in the UK, and his liability to UK income tax will be determined accordingly.
- In a personal income tax computation, we bring together income from all sources, splitting the sources into non-savings, savings and dividend income.
- An individual may receive interest net of 20% tax suffered at source. The amount received must be grossed up by multiplying by 100/80 and must be included gross in the income tax computation. Similarly dividends are received net of a 10% tax credit and must be grossed up for inclusion in the tax computation.
- Deductible interest is deducted from total income to compute net income.
- All persons are entitled to a personal allowance. It is deducted from statutory total income, first against non savings income, then against savings income and lastly against dividend income. Taxpayers aged 65-74 are entitled to an age allowance, and taxpayers aged 75 and over to a higher personal allowance.
- Work out income tax on the taxable income. Deduct the tax credit on dividend income and any income tax suffered at source to arrive at tax payable. The tax credit on dividend income cannot be repaid if it exceeds the tax liability calculated so far. Other tax suffered at source can be repaid.
- Extend the basic rate band by the gross amount of any gift aid payment.
- Income on property held jointly by married couples and members of a civil partnership is treated as if it were shared equally unless the couple make a joint declaration of the actual shares of ownership.

Quick Quiz

1. When will an individual be resident in the UK?
2. At what rates is income tax charged on non-savings income?
3. List one type of savings income that is received by individuals net of 20% tax.
4. How is dividend income taxed?
5. If Dennis has taxable income of £35,300 and makes gift aid payments of £390, on how much of his income will he pay higher rate tax?
6. Mike and Matt have registered a civil partnership. Mike owns 25% of an investment property and Matt owns 75%. How will the income be taxed?

Answers to Quick Quiz

1. An individual is resident in the UK if he is here for 183 days or more, or he makes visits to the UK averaging 91 days or more a year for each of four consecutive years.
2. Income tax on non-savings income is charged at 10% in the starting rate band, at 22% in the basic rate band and at 40% in the higher rate band.
3. Bank (or building society) interest.
4. Dividend income in the starting and basic rate band is taxed at 10%. Dividend income in excess of the higher rate threshold is taxed at 32.5%
5. The basic rate band is extended by £390 × 100/78 = £500 to £35,100. Dennis will be liable to higher rate tax on £35,300 – £35,100 = £200.
6. Mike and Matt will each be taxed on 50% of the income from the investment property unless they make a joint declaration in which case Mike will be taxed on 25% of the income and Matt on 75%.

Now try the questions below from the Exam Question Bank

Number	Level	Marks	Time
Q1	Introductory	7	13 mins
Q2	Introductory	7	13 mins
Q3	Examination	15	27 mins

3 Employment income

Topic list	Syllabus reference
1 Employment and self employment	B2(a)
2 Basis of assessment for employment income	B2(c) B2(b)
3 Allowable deductions	B2(c) B2(d)
4 Statutory mileage allowances	B2(c) B2(e)
5 Charitable donations under the payroll deduction scheme	B2(c) B2(k)

Introduction

In the previous chapter we saw how to construct the income tax computation. Now we start to look in greater detail at the different types of income that people may receive so that the income can be slotted into the computation.

Many people earn money by working. We look at the important distinction between employment and self employment, so that we can consider the way in which people are taxed on the wages or salaries from their jobs.

Sometimes the employee may incur expenses when carrying out his job. We look at the rules determining when these can be deducted from employment income for tax purposes. We also look at the rules covering mileage payments made by employers to employees who use their own cars for business journeys. Finally employees can make tax efficient contributions to charity under the payroll giving scheme.

In the next chapter we look at how benefits received as a result of employment are taxed and at how tax is deducted from employment income under the PAYE system.

Study guide

		Intellectual level
B2	**Income from employment**	
(a)	Recognise the factors that determine whether an engagement is treated as employment or self-employment.	2
(b)	Recognise the basis of assessment for employment income.	2
(c)	Compute the income assessable.	2
(d)	Recognise the allowable deductions, including travelling expenses.	2
(e)	Discuss the use of the statutory approved mileage allowances.	2
(k)	Explain how charitable giving can be made through a payroll deduction scheme.	1

Exam guide

You are very likely to be asked a question concerning at least one aspect of employment taxation in your exam. This could range from a discussion of the distinction between employment and self employment to a full computation of employment income, including benefits.

1 Employment and self employment

FAST FORWARD

Employment involves a contract **of** service whereas self employment involves a contract **for** services. The distinction between employment and self employment is decided by looking at all the facts of the engagement.

1.1 Employment income

Employment income includes income arising from an employment under a contract of service.

Some people, however, set themselves up in business and carry out work for customers under a contract for services.

Before we can calculate employment income, we must be sure that the individual is employed rather than self employed. This can only be decided by looking at all the facts of the engagement.

1.2 Employment and self employment

Exam focus point

Many of the tax rules have come about as a result of legal cases. In the exam you are not required to know the relevant cases. However we have included the case names in the Text for your information.

The distinction between employment (receipts taxable as earnings) and self employment (receipts taxable as trading income) is a fine one. Employment involves a contract of service, whereas self employment involves a contract for services. Taxpayers tend to prefer self employment, because the rules on deductions for expenses are more generous.

Factors which may be of importance include:

- The degree of control exercised over the person doing the work
- Whether he must accept further work
- Whether the other party must provide further work

- Whether he provides his own equipment
- Whether he hires his own helpers
- What degree of financial risk he takes
- What degree of responsibility for investment and management he has
- Whether he can profit from sound management
- Whether he can work when he chooses
- The wording used in any agreement between the parties.

Relevant cases include:

(a) *Edwards v Clinch 1981*

A civil engineer acted occasionally as an inspector on temporary ad hoc appointments.

Held: there was no ongoing office which could be vacated by one person and held by another so the fees received were from self employment not employment.

(b) *Hall v Lorimer 1994*

A vision mixer was engaged under a series of short-term contracts.

Held: the vision mixer was self employed, not because of any one detail of the case but because the overall picture was one of self-employment.

(c) *Carmichael and Anor v National Power plc 1999*

Individuals engaged as visitor guides on a casual 'as required' basis were not employees. An exchange of correspondence between the company and the individuals was not a contract of employment as there was no provision as to the frequency of work and there was flexibility to accept work or turn it down as it arose. Sickness, holiday and pension arrangements did not apply and neither did grievance and disciplinary procedures.

A worker's status also affects national insurance contributions (NIC). The self-employed generally pay less than employees. NIC is covered later in this Text.

2 Basis of assessment for employment income

FAST FORWARD

General earnings are taxed in the year of receipt. Money earnings are generally received on the earlier of the time payment is made and the time entitlement to payment arises.

2.1 Outline of the charge

Employment income includes income arising from an employment under a contract of service and the income of office holders, such as directors. The term 'employee' is used in this Text to mean anyone who receives employment income (ie both employees and directors).

General earnings are an employee's earnings (see key term below) plus the 'cash equivalent' of any taxable non-monetary benefits.

Key term

'Earnings' means any salary, wage or fee, any gratuity or other profit or incidental benefit obtained by the employee if it is money or money's worth (something of direct monetary value or convertible into direct monetary value) or anything else which constitutes a reward of the employment.

Taxable earnings from an employment in a tax year are the general earnings received in that tax year.

2.2 When are earnings received?

General earnings consisting of money are treated as received at the earlier of:

- **The time when payment is made**
- **The time when a person becomes entitled to payment of the earnings.**

If the employee is a director of a company, earnings from the company are received on the earliest of:

- The earlier of the two alternatives given in the general rule (above)
- The time when the amount is credited in the company's accounting records
- The end of the company's period of account (if the amount was determined by then)
- The time the amount is determined (if after the end of the company's period of account).

Taxable benefits (see next chapter) **are generally treated as received when they are provided to the employee.**

The receipts basis does not apply to pension income. Pensions are taxed on the amount accruing in the tax year, whether or not it has actually been received in that year.

2.3 Net taxable earnings

Total taxable earnings less total allowable deductions (see below) **are net taxable earnings of a tax year**. Deductions cannot usually create a loss: they can only reduce the net taxable earnings to nil. If there is more than one employment in the tax year, separate calculations are required for each employment.

3 Allowable deductions

FAST FORWARD

Deductions for expenses are extremely limited. Relief is available for the costs that an employee is obliged to incur in travelling in the performance of his duties or in travelling to the place he has to attend in performance of his duties. Relief is **not** available for normal commuting costs.

3.1 The general rules

Deductions for expenses are extremely limited and are notoriously hard to obtain. Although there are some specific deductions, which are covered below, the general rule is that relief is limited to:

- **Qualifying travel expenses**
- **Other expenses the employee is obliged to incur and pay as holder of the employment which are incurred wholly, exclusively and necessarily in the performance of the duties of the employment.**

3.2 Travel expenses

3.2.1 Qualifying travel expenses

Tax relief is not available for an employee's normal commuting costs. This means relief is not available for any costs an employee incurs in getting from home to his normal place of work. However **employees are entitled to relief for travel expenses that they are obliged to incur and pay in travelling in the performance of their duties or travelling to or from a place which they have to attend in the performance of their duties (other than a permanent workplace).**

3.2.2 Example: travel in the performance of duties

Judi is an accountant. She often travels to meetings at the firm's offices in the North of England returning to her office in Leeds after the meetings. Relief is available for the full cost of these journeys as the travel is undertaken in the performance of her duties.

Question — Relief for travelling costs

Zoe lives in Wycombe and normally works in Chiswick. Occasionally she visits a client in Wimbledon and travels direct from home. Distances are shown in the diagram below:

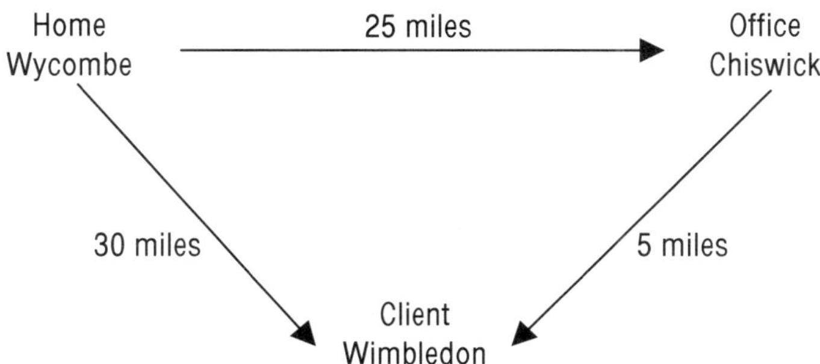

What tax relief is available for Zoe's travel costs?

Answer

Zoe is not entitled to tax relief for the costs incurred in travelling between Wycombe and Chiswick since these are normal commuting costs. However, relief is available for all costs that Zoe incurs when she travels from Wycombe to Wimbledon to visit her client.

To prevent manipulation of the basic rule normal commuting will not become a business journey just because the employee stops en-route to perform a business task (eg make a 'phone call). Nor will relief be available if the journey is essentially the same as the employee's normal journey to work.

3.2.3 Example: normal commuting

Judi is based at her office in Leeds City Centre. One day she is required to attend a 9.00 am meeting with a client whose premises are around the corner from her Leeds office. Judi travels from home directly to the meeting. As the journey is substantially the same as her ordinary journey to work relief is not available.

Site based employees (eg construction workers, management consultants etc) **who do not have a permanent workplace, are entitled to relief for the costs of all journeys made from home to wherever they are working**. This is because these employees do not have an ordinary commuting journey or any normal commuting costs.

3.2.4 Temporary workplace

If an employee is seconded to work at another location for some considerable time, then the question arises as to whether the journey from home to that workplace can become normal commuting. There is a 24 month rule.

Tax relief is available for travel, accommodation and subsistence expenses incurred by an employee who is working at a temporary workplace on a secondment expected to last up to 24 months. If a secondment is initially expected not to exceed 24 months, but it is extended, relief ceases to be due from the date the employee becomes aware of the change.

When looking at how long a secondment is expected to last, HMRC will consider not only the terms of the written contract but also any verbal agreement by the employer and other factors such as whether the employee buys a house etc.

Question **Temporary workplace**

Philip works for Vastbank at its Newcastle City Centre branch. Philip is sent to work full-time at another branch in Morpeth for 20 months at the end of which he will return to the Newcastle branch. Morpeth is about 20 miles north of Newcastle.

What travel costs is Philip entitled to claim as a deduction?

Answer

Although Philip is spending all of his time at the Morpeth branch it will not be treated as his normal work place because his period of attendance will be less than 24 months. Thus Philip can claim relief in full for the costs of travel from his home to the Morpeth branch.

3.3 Other expenses

Relief is given for other expenses incurred **wholly, exclusively and necessarily in the performance of the duties** of the employment. **The word 'exclusively' strictly implies that the expenditure must give no private benefit at all. If it does, none of it is deductible. In practice HMRC may ignore a small element of private benefit or make an apportionment between business and private use.**

Whether an expense is 'necessary' is not determined by what the employer requires. The test is whether the duties of the employment could not be performed without the outlay.

The following cases illustrate how the requirements are interpreted. Remember you are not expected to know the case names, they are given for information only.

- *Sanderson v Durbridge 1955*

  The cost of evening meals taken when attending late meetings was not deductible because it was not incurred in the performance of the duties.

- *Blackwell v Mills 1945*

  As a condition of his employment, an employee was required to attend evening classes. The cost of his text books and travel was not deductible because it was not incurred in the performance of the duties.

- *Lupton v Potts 1969*

  Examination fees incurred by a solicitor's articled clerk were not deductible because they were incurred neither wholly nor exclusively in the performance of the duties, but in furthering the clerk's ambition to become a solicitor.

- *Brown v Bullock 1961*

  The expense of joining a club that was virtually a requisite of an employment was not deductible because it would have been possible to carry on the employment without the club membership, so the expense was not necessary.

- *Elwood v Utitz 1965*

  A managing director's subscriptions to two residential London clubs were claimed by him as an expense on the grounds that they were cheaper than hotels.

  The expenditure was deductible as it was necessary in that it would be impossible for the employee to carry out his London duties without being provided with first class accommodation. The residential facilities (which were cheaper than hotel accommodation) were given to club members only.

- *Lucas v Cattell 1972*

  The cost of business telephone calls on a private telephone is deductible, but **no part of the line or** telephone **rental charges is deductible**.

- *Fitzpatrick v IRC 1994; Smith v Abbott 1994*

  Journalists cannot claim a deduction for the cost of buying newspapers which they read to keep themselves informed, since they are merely preparing themselves to perform their duties.

The cost of clothes for work is not deductible, except for certain trades requiring protective clothing where there are annual deductions on a set scale.

An employee required to work at home may be able to claim a deduction for the marginal costs of working from home, such as an appropriate proportion of his or her expenditure on lighting and heating. Employers can pay up to £2 per week without the need for supporting evidence of the costs incurred by the employee. Payments above the £2 limit require evidence of the employee's actual costs.

3.4 Other deductions

Certain expenditure is specifically deductible in computing net taxable earnings:

(a) **Contributions to registered occupational pension schemes**

(b) **Subscriptions to professional bodies** on the list of bodies issued by the HMRC (which includes most UK professional bodies), if relevant to the duties of the employment

(c) Payments for certain liabilities relating to the employment and for insurance against them (see below).

Employees may also claim capital allowances on plant and machinery (other than cars or other vehicles) necessarily provided for use in the performance of those duties. The computation of capital allowances is discussed later in this Text.

3.5 Liabilities and insurance

If a director or employee incurs a liability related to his employment or pays for insurance against such a liability, the cost is a deductible expense. If the employer pays such amounts, there is no taxable benefit.

A liability relating to employment is one which is imposed in respect of the employee's acts or omissions as employee. Thus, for example, liability for negligence would be covered. Related costs, for example the costs of legal proceedings, are included.

For insurance premiums to qualify, the insurance policy must:

(a) Cover only liabilities relating to employment, vicarious liability in respect of liabilities of another person's employment, related costs and payments to the employee's own employees in respect of their employment liabilities relating to employment and related costs, and

(b) It must not last for more than two years (although it may be renewed for up to two years at a time), and the insured person must not be not required to renew it.

4 Statutory mileage allowances

FAST FORWARD

Employers may pay a mileage allowance to employees who use their own car on business journeys. Payments up to the statutory limits are tax free, any excess is taxable, and a deduction can be claimed if the payment is lower.

A single authorised mileage allowance for business journeys in an employee's own vehicle applies to all cars and vans. There is no income tax on payments up to this allowance and employers do not have to report mileage allowances up to this amount. The allowance for 2007/08 is 40p per mile on the first 10,000 miles in the tax year with each additional mile over 10,000 miles at 25p per mile.

The authorised mileage allowance for employees using their own motor cycle is 24p per mile. For employees using their own pedal cycle it is 20p per mile.

If employers pay less than the statutory mileage allowance, employees can claim tax relief up to that level.

The statutory mileage allowance does not prevent employers from paying higher rates, but any excess will be subject to income tax. There is a similar (but slightly different) system for NICs, covered later in this Text.

Employers can make income tax and NIC free payments of up to 5p per mile for each fellow employee making the same business trip who is carried as a passenger. If the employer does not pay the employee for carrying business passengers, the employee cannot claim any tax relief.

Question

Mileage allowance

Sophie uses her own car for business travel. During 2007/08, Sophie drove 15,400 miles in the performance of her duties. Sophie's employer paid her a mileage allowance. How is the mileage allowance treated for tax purposes assuming that the rate paid is:

(a) 35p a mile, or
(b) 25p a mile?

Answer

(a)

	£
Mileage allowance received (15,400 × 35p)	5,390
Less: tax free [(10,000 × 40p) + (5,400 × 25p)]	(5,350)
Taxable benefit	40

£5,350 is tax free and the excess amount received of £40 is a taxable benefit.

(b)

	£
Tax free amount [(10,000 × 40p) + (5,400 × 25p)]	5,350
Less: mileage allowance received (15,400 × 25p)	(3,850)
Shortfall	1,500

There is no taxable benefit and Sophie can claim a deduction from her employment income for the shortfall of £1,500.

5 Charitable donations under the payroll deduction scheme

FAST FORWARD

Employees can make tax deductible donations to charity under the payroll deduction scheme. The amount paid is deducted from gross pay.

Employees can make charitable donations under the payroll deduction scheme by asking their employer to make deductions from their gross earnings. The deductions are then passed to a charitable agency which will either distribute the funds to the employees' chosen charities on receipt of their instructions, or provide the employee with vouchers that can be encashed by the recipient charities.

The donation is an allowable deduction from the employee's earnings for tax purposes. Tax relief is given at source as the employer must deduct the donation from gross pay before calculating PAYE due thereon.

Chapter Roundup

- Employment involves a contract **of** service whereas self employment involves a contract **for** services. The distinction between employment and self employment is decided by looking at all the facts of the engagement.
- General earnings are taxed in the year of receipt. Money earnings are generally received on the earlier of the time payment is made and the time entitlement to payment arises.
- Deductions for expenses are extremely limited. Relief is available for the costs that an employee is obliged to incur in travelling in the performance of his duties or in travelling to the place he has to attend in performance of his duties. Relief is **not** available for normal commuting costs.
- Employers may pay a mileage allowance to employees who use their own car on business journeys. Payments up to the statutory limits are tax free, any excess is taxable, and a deduction can be claimed if the payment is lower.
- Employees can make tax deductible donations to charity under the payroll deduction scheme. The amount paid is deducted from gross pay.

Quick Quiz

1. On what basis are earnings taxed?
2. What are the conditions for general expenses of employment to be deductible?
3. What relief can Karen claim if she is paid 35p for each mile that she drives her own car on company business and she drives 5,000 miles in 2007/08?
4. Could Karen claim any extra relief if she was accompanied by a work colleague for 1,000 of those miles?

Answers to Quick Quiz

1 Earnings are taxed on a receipts basis.

2 The expenses must be incurred wholly, exclusively and necessarily in the performance of the duties of the employment.

3 Karen could claim relief of 5,000 x (40 – 35)p = £250.

4 Karen could not claim any extra relief if she was accompanied by a work colleague for 1,000 of those miles. If her employer had made extra payments of up to 5p per mile for those journeys the extra payment would have been tax free.

Now try the question below from the Exam Question Bank

Number	Level	Marks	Time
Q4	Examination	15	27 mins

Taxable and exempt benefits. The PAYE system

4

Topic list	Syllabus reference
1 P11D employees	B2(g)
2 Benefits taxable on all employees	B2(h)
3 Benefits taxable on P11D employees	B2(h)
4 Exempt benefits	B2(h)
5 P11D dispensations	B2(i)
6 The PAYE system	B2(f)

Introduction

In the previous chapter we discussed when a worker was an employee and when he was self employed. We then considered the taxation of salaries and wages and the deduction of expenses and charitable donations.

In this chapter we look at benefits provided to employees. Benefits are an integral part of many remuneration packages, but the tax cost of receiving a benefit must not be overlooked. Special rules apply to fix the taxable value of certain benefits.

Finally we look at how tax is deducted from employment income under the PAYE system. Tax is deducted from cash payments, and benefits are dealt with through the PAYE code.

In the next chapter we look at how employees can save for their retirement through pension provision and the tax reliefs available.

Study guide

		Intellectual level
B2	**Income from employment**	
(f)	Explain the PAYE system.	1
(g)	Identify P11D employees.	1
(h)	Compute the amount of benefits assessable.	2
(i)	Explain the purpose of a dispensation from HM Revenue & Customs.	2

Exam guide

Benefits are a very important part of employment income and you are likely to come across them in your exam. Most employees these days are P11D employees, but you may need to know which benefits apply to excluded employees. If you come across exempt benefits in a question, note this in your answer to show that you have considered each item.

The PAYE system is a very sophisticated system of deduction of tax at source and you should be able to explain how it can cope with collecting the correct amount of tax. The construction of the PAYE code is important.

1 P11D employees

FAST FORWARD

Most employees are taxed on benefits under the benefits code. 'Excluded employees' (lower paid/non-directors) are only subject to part of the provisions of the code.

1.1 Excluded employees

There is comprehensive legislation which covers the taxation of benefits.

The legislation generally applies to all employees. However, only certain parts of it apply to 'excluded employees'.

An excluded employee is an employee in lower paid employment who is either not a director of a company or is a director but has no material interest in the company ('material' means control of more than 5% of the ordinary share capital) and either:

(a) He is full time working director, or
(b) The company is non-profit-making or is established for charitable purposes only.

The term 'director' refers to any person who acts as a director or any person in accordance with whose instructions the directors are accustomed to act (other than a professional adviser).

1.2 Lower paid employment

Lower paid employment is one where earnings for the tax year are less than £8,500. To decide whether this applies, add together the total earnings and benefits that would be taxable if the employee were **not** an excluded employee.

A number of specific deductions must be taken into account to determine lower paid employment. These include contributions to registered pension schemes and payroll charitable deductions. However, general deductions from employment income (see earlier in this Text) are not taken into account.

1.3 P11D employees

Employees, including directors, who are not excluded employees may be referred to as '**P11D employees**'; the P11D is the form that the employer completes for each such employee with details of expenses and benefits.

Question — **Excluded employee**

Tim earns £6,500 per annum working full time as a sales representative at Chap Co Ltd. The company provides the following staff benefits to Tim:

Private health insurance	£300
Company car	£1,500
Expense allowance	£2,000

Tim used £1,900 of the expense allowance on business mileage petrol and on entertaining clients.

Is Tim an excluded employee?

Answer

No. Although Tim's taxable income is less than £8,500 this is only after his expense claim. The figure to consider and compare to £8,500 is the £10,300 as shown below.

		£
Salary		6,500
Benefits:	health insurance	300
	car	1,500
	expense allowance	2,000
Earnings to consider if Tim is an 'excluded employee'		10,300
Less claim for expenses paid out		(1,900)
Taxable income		8,400

2 Benefits taxable on all employees

2.1 Introduction

All employees, including excluded employees, are taxable on the provision of:

- vouchers
- living accommodation.

For excluded employees, other benefits are taxed on their "second-hand value", which is usually nil. The special rules for P11D employees are covered in the next Section.

2.2 Vouchers

If any employee (including an excluded employee):

(a) receives cash vouchers (vouchers exchangeable for cash)
(b) uses a credit token (such as a credit card) to obtain money, goods or services, or
(c) receives exchangeable vouchers (such as book tokens), also called non-cash vouchers

he is taxed on the cost for the employer of providing the benefit, less any amount made good.

The first 15p per working day of meal vouchers (eg luncheon vouchers) is not taxed.

2.3 Accommodation

FAST FORWARD

The benefit in respect of accommodation is its annual value. There is an additional benefit if the property cost over £75,000.

2.3.1 Annual value charge

The taxable value of accommodation provided to an employee (including an excluded employee) is the rent that would have been payable if the premises had been let at their annual value (sometimes called 'rateable value'). **If the premises are rented** rather than owned by the employer, then **the taxable benefit is the higher of the rent actually paid and the annual value**. If property does not have a rateable value HMRC estimate a value.

2.3.2 Additional benefit charge

If a property was bought by the employer for a cost of more than £75,000, an additional amount is chargeable as follows:

> (Cost of providing the living accommodation – £75,000) × the official rate of interest at the start of the tax year.

Thus with an official rate of 6.25%, the total benefit for accommodation costing £90,000 and with an annual value of £2,000 would be £2,000 + £(90,000 – 75,000) × 6.25% = £2,937.

The 'cost of providing' the living accommodation is the aggregate of the cost of purchase and the cost of any improvements made before the start of the tax year for which the benefit is being computed. It is therefore not possible to avoid the charge by buying an inexpensive property requiring substantial repairs and improving it.

Where the property was acquired more than six years before first being provided to the employee, the market value when first so provided plus the cost of subsequent improvements is used as the cost of providing the living accommodation. However, unless the actual cost plus improvements up to the start of the tax year in question exceeds £75,000, the additional charge cannot be imposed, however high the market value.

Exam focus point

The 'official rate' of interest will be given to you in the exam.

2.3.3 Job related accommodation

There is no taxable benefit in respect of job related accommodation. Accommodation is job related if:

(a) Residence in the accommodation **is necessary for the proper performance of the employee's duties** (as with a caretaker), or

(b) The accommodation is provided **for the better performance of the employee's duties** and the employment is of a kind in which it is **customary for accommodation to be provided** (as with a policeman), or

(c) The **accommodation is provided as part of arrangements in force because of a special threat to the employee's security**.

Directors can only claim exemptions (a) or (b) if:

(i) They have no **material interest** ('material' means over 5%) in the company, and

(ii) Either they are **full time working directors** or the company is **non-profit making or is a charity**.

2.3.4 Other points

Any contribution paid by the employee is deducted from the annual value of the property and then from the additional benefit.

If the employee is given a cash alternative to living accommodation, the benefits code still applies in priority to treating the cash alternative as earnings. If the cash alternative is greater than the taxable benefit, the excess is treated as earnings.

Question — **Accommodation**

Mr Quinton was provided with a company flat in Birmingham in January 2007. The rateable value of the house is £1,200. The property cost his employer £125,000, but was valued at £150,000 in January 2007. Mr Quinton paid rent of £500 pa.

What is the taxable benefit for 2007/08 assuming:

(a) His employer purchased the property in 2005, or

(b) His employer purchased the property in 1999, or

(c) Mr Quinton was required to live in the flat as he was employed as the caretaker for the company premises (of which the flat was part).

Answer

(a)

	£
Annual value	1,200
Less: rent paid	(500)
	700
Additional amount £(125,000 – 75,000) × 6.25%	3,125
Taxable benefit	3,825

(b)

	£
Annual value	1,200
Less: rent paid	(500)
	700
Additional amount £(150,000 – 75,000) × 6.25%	4,687
Taxable benefit	5,387

As Mr Quinton first moved in more than six years after the company bought the flat, the value at the date he moved in is used.

(c) Job related accommodation: taxable benefit £ nil

3 Benefits taxable on P11D employees

3.1 Introduction

Special rules apply to determine the taxable value of expenses and benefits paid to or provided for P11D employees.

3.2 Expenses

3.2.1 General business expenses

If business expenses on such items as travel or hotel stays, are reimbursed by an employer, the reimbursed amount is a taxable benefit for P11D employees. To avoid being taxed on this amount, **an employee must then make a claim to deduct it as an expense** under the rules set out below.

A P11D dispensation may be obtained from HMRC to avoid the need to report expenses and claim a deduction (see earlier in this Text).

3.2.2 Private incidental expenses

When an individual has to spend one or more nights away from home, his employer may reimburse expenses on items incidental to his absence (for example laundry and private telephone calls). **Such incidental expenses are exempt** if:

(a) The expenses of travelling to each place where the individual stays overnight, throughout the trip, are incurred necessarily in the performance of the duties of the employment (or would have been, if there had been any expenses).

(b) The total (for the whole trip) of incidental expenses not deductible under the usual rules is no more than £5 for each night spent wholly in the UK and £10 for each other night. If this limit is exceeded, all of the expenses are taxable, not just the excess. The expenses include any VAT.

This incidental expenses exemption applies to expenses reimbursed, and to benefits obtained using credit tokens and non-cash vouchers.

3.2.3 Expenses related to living accommodation

In addition to the benefit of living accommodation itself, P11D **employees are taxed on related expenses paid by the employer**, such as:

(a) **Heating, lighting or cleaning the premises**
(b) **Repairing, maintaining or decorating the premises**
(c) **The provision of furniture (the annual value is 20% of the cost).**

If the accommodation is 'job related', however, the **taxable amount is restricted to a maximum of 10% of the employee's 'net earnings'**. For this purpose, net earnings comprises the total employment income, net of expenses and pension contributions, but excluding these related expenses.

Council tax and water or sewage charges paid by the employer are taxable in full as a benefit unless the accommodation is 'job-related'.

3.3 Cars

FAST FORWARD

Employees who have a company car are taxed on a % of the car's list price which depends on the level of the car's CO_2 emissions. The same % multiplied by £14,400 determines the benefit where private fuel is also provided.

3.3.1 Cars provided for private use

A car provided by reason of the employment to a P11D employee or member of his family or household for private use gives rise to a taxable benefit. 'Private use' includes home to work travel.

A tax charge arises whether the car is provided by the employer or by some other person. The benefit is computed as shown below, even if the car is taken as an alternative to another benefit of a different value.

The starting point for calculating a car benefit is the list price of the car (plus accessories). **The percentage of the list price that is taxable depends on the car's CO_2 emissions.**

3.3.2 Taxable benefit

For cars that emit CO_2 of 140g/km (2007/08) or less, the taxable benefit is 15% of the car's list price. This percentage increases by 1% for every 5g/km (rounded down to the nearest multiple of 5) by which CO_2 emissions exceed 140g/km up to a maximum of 35%.

Exam focus point

> The CO_2 baseline figure will be given to you in the tax rates and allowances section of the exam paper.

Diesel cars have a supplement of 3% of the car's list price added to the taxable benefit. The maximum percentage, however, remains 35% of the list price.

3.3.3 List price

The price of the car is the sum of the following items.

(a) **The list price of the car** for a single retail sale at the time of first registration, including charges for delivery and standard accessories. The manufacturer's, importer's or distributor's list price must be used, even if the retailer offered a discount. A notional list price is estimated if no list price was published.

(b) **The price (including fitting) of all optional accessories provided when the car was first provided** to the employee, excluding mobile telephones and equipment needed by a disabled employee. The extra cost of adapting or manufacturing a car to run on road fuel gases is not included.

(c) **The price (including fitting) of all optional accessories fitted later** and costing at least £100 each, excluding mobile telephones and equipment needed by a disabled employee. Such accessories affect the taxable benefit from and including the tax year in which they are fitted. However, accessories which are merely replacing existing accessories and are not superior to the ones replaced are ignored. Replacement accessories which *are* superior are taken into account, but the cost of the old accessory is then ignored.

There is a special rule for **classic cars**. If the car is at least 15 years old (from the time of first registration) at the end of the tax year, and its market value at the end of the year (or, if earlier, when it ceased to be available to the employee) is over £15,000 and greater than the price found under the above rules, that market value is used instead of the price. The market value takes account of all accessories (except mobile telephones and equipment needed by a disabled employee).

Capital contributions made by the employee in that and previous tax years up to a maximum of £5,000 are deducted from the list price. Capital contributions are payments by the employee in respect of the price of the car or accessories for the same car. Contributions beyond the maximum are ignored.

If the price or value exceeds £80,000, then £80,000 is used instead. This £80,000 is after capital contributions have been taken into account.

Question — Car benefit

Nigel Issan is provided with a diesel car which had a list price of £22,000 when it was first registered. The car has CO_2 emissions of 203g/km.

You are required to calculate Nigel's car benefit for 2007/08.

Answer

Car benefit £22,000 × 30% (15% + (200 – 140) × 1/5 + 3%) = £6,600

Note that 203 is rounded down to 200 to be exactly divisible by 5.

3.3.4 Reductions in the benefit

The benefit is reduced on a time basis where a car is first made available or ceases to be made available during the tax year or is incapable of being used for a continuous period of not less than 30 days (for example because it is being repaired).

The benefit is reduced by any payment the user must make for the private use of the car (as distinct from a capital contribution to the cost of the car). The benefit cannot become negative to create a deduction from the employee's income.

Question — Time apportioning benefits

Vicky Olvo starts her employment on 6 January 2008 and is immediately provided with a new petrol car with a list price of £25,000. The car was more expensive than her employer would have provided and she therefore made a capital contribution of £6,200. The employer was able to buy the car at a discount and paid only £23,000. Vicky contributed £100 a month for being able to use the car privately. CO_2 emissions are 267g/km.

You are required to calculate her car benefit for 2007/08.

Answer

	£
List price *	25,000
Less capital contribution (maximum)	(5,000)
	20,000

	£
£20,000 × 35%** × 3/12 ***	1,750
Less contribution to running costs (£100 × 3)	(300)
Car benefit	1,450

* The discounted price is not relevant

** 15% + (265 – 140) × 1/5 = 40% restricted to 35% max

*** Only available for 3 months in 2007/08.

3.3.5 Pool cars

Pool cars are exempt. A car is a pool car if **all** the following conditions are satisfied:

(a) It is used by more than one employee and is not ordinarily used by any one of them to the exclusion of the others

(b) Any private use is merely incidental to business use

(c) It is not normally kept overnight at or near the residence of an employee.

3.3.6 Ancillary benefits

There are many ancillary benefits associated with the provision of cars, such as insurance, repairs, vehicle licences and a parking space at or near work. No extra taxable benefit arises as a result of these, with the exception of the cost of providing a driver.

3.4 Fuel for cars

3.4.1 Introduction

Where fuel is provided there is a further benefit in addition to the car benefit.

No taxable benefit arises where either

(a) **All the fuel provided was made available only for business travel**, or

(b) **The employee is required to make good, and has made good, the whole of the cost of any fuel provided for his private use**.

Unlike most benefits, a reimbursement of only part of the cost of the fuel available for private use does not reduce the benefit.

3.4.2 Taxable benefit

The taxable benefit is a percentage of a base figure. The base figure for 2007/08 is £14,400. The percentage is the same percentage as is used to calculate the car benefit (see above).

Exam focus point

> The fuel base figure will be given to you in the tax rates and allowances section of the exam paper.

3.4.3 Reductions in the benefit

The fuel benefit is reduced in the same way as the car benefit **if the car is not available for 30 days or more**.

The fuel benefit is also reduced if private fuel is not available for part of a tax year. However, if private fuel later becomes available in the same tax year, the reduction is not made. If, for example, fuel is provided from 6 April 2007 to 30 June 2007, then the fuel benefit for 2007/08 will be restricted to just three months. This is because the provision of fuel has permanently ceased. However, if fuel is provided from 6 April 2007 to 30 June 2007, and then again from 1 September 2007 to 5 April 2008, then the fuel benefit will not be reduced since the cessation was only temporary.

Question — **Car and fuel benefit**

An employee was provided with a new car (2,500 cc) costing £15,000. The car emits 191g/km of CO_2. During 2007/08 the employer spent £900 on insurance, repairs and a vehicle licence. The firm paid for all petrol, costing £1,500, without reimbursement. The employee paid the firm £270 for the private use of the car. Calculate the taxable benefit.

Answer

Round CO_2 emissions figure down to the nearest 5, ie 190 g/km.

Amount by which CO_2 emissions exceed the baseline:

(190 – 140) = 50 g/km

Divide by 5 = 10

Taxable percentage = 15% + 10% = 25%

	£
Car benefit £15,000 × 25%	3,750
Fuel benefit £14,400 × 25%	3,600
	7,350
Less contribution towards use of car	(270)
	7,080

If the contribution of £270 had been towards the petrol the benefit would have been £7,350.

3.5 Vans and heavier commercial vehicles

If a van (of normal maximum laden weight up to 3,500 kg) **is made available for an employee's private use, there is an annual scale charge of £3,000**. The scale charge covers ancillary benefits such as insurance and servicing. The benefit is scaled down if the van is not available for the full year (as for cars) and is reduced by any payment made by the employee for private use.

There is, however, **no taxable benefit where an employee takes a van home** (ie uses the van for home to work travel) but is not allowed any other private use.

Where private fuel is provided, there is an additional charge of £500. If the van is unavailable for part of the year or fuel for private use is only provided for part of the year, the benefit is scaled down.

If a commercial vehicle of normal maximum laden weight over 3,500 kg is made available for an employee's private use, but the employee's use of the vehicle is not wholly or mainly private, no taxable benefit arises except in respect of the provision of a driver.

3.6 Beneficial loans

FAST FORWARD

Cheap loans are charged to tax on the difference between the official rate of interest and any interest paid by the employee.

3.6.1 Taxable benefit

Employment related loans to P11D employees and their relatives give rise to a benefit equal to:

(a) **Any amounts written off** (unless the employee has died), and

(b) **The excess of the interest based on an official rate prescribed by the Treasury, over any interest actually charged ('taxable cheap loan')**. Interest payable during the tax year but paid after the end of the tax year is taken into account.

The following loans are normally not treated as taxable cheap loans for calculation of the interest benefits (but not for the purposes of the charge on loans written off).

(a) A loan on normal commercial terms made in the ordinary course of the employer's money-lending business.

(b) A loan made by an individual in the ordinary course of the lender's domestic, family or personal arrangements.

3.6.2 Calculating the interest benefit

There are two alternative methods of calculating the taxable benefit. The simpler **'average' method** automatically applies unless the taxpayer or HMRC elect for the alternative **'strict' method**. (HMRC normally only make the election where it appears that the 'average' method is being deliberately exploited.) In both methods, the benefit is the interest at the official rate minus the interest payable.

The 'average' method averages the balances at the beginning and end of the tax year (or the dates on which the loan was made and discharged if it was not in existence throughout the tax year) and applies the official rate of interest to this average. If the loan was not in existence throughout the tax year only the number of complete tax months (from the 6th of the month) for which it existed are taken into account.

The 'strict' method is to compute interest at the official rate on the actual amount outstanding on a daily basis.

Question — **Loan benefit**

At 6 April 2007 a taxable cheap loan of £30,000 was outstanding to an employee earning £12,000 a year, who repaid £20,000 on 7 December 2007. The remaining balance of £10,000 was outstanding at 5 April 2008. Interest paid during the year was £250. What was the benefit under both methods for 2007/08, assuming that the official rate of interest was 6.25%?

Answer

Average method

	£
$6.25\% \times \frac{30{,}000 + 10{,}000}{2}$	1,250
Less interest paid	(250)
Benefit	1,000

Alternative method (strict method)

	£
$£30{,}000 \times \frac{245}{365}$ (6 April – 6 December) $\times$ 6.25%	1,259
$£10{,}000 \times \frac{120}{365}$ (7 December – 5 April) $\times$ 6.25%	205
	1,464
Less interest paid	(250)
Benefit	1,214

HMRC might opt for the alternative method.

Note. You must always show the workings for the average method. If it appears likely that the taxpayer should or HMRC might opt for the alternative method you will need to show those workings as well.

3.6.3 The de minimis test

The interest benefit is not taxable if the total of all non-qualifying loans to the employee did not exceed £5,000 at any time in the tax year.

A qualifying loan is one on which all or part of any interest paid would qualify for tax relief (see further below).

When the £5,000 threshold is exceeded, a benefit arises on interest on the whole loan, not just on the excess of the loan over £5,000.

3.6.4 Qualifying loans

If the whole of the interest payable on a qualifying loan is eligible for tax relief as deductible interest, then no taxable benefit arises. If the interest is only partly eligible for tax relief, then the employee is treated as receiving earnings because the actual rate of interest is below the official rate. He is also treated as paying interest equal to those earnings. This **deemed interest paid may qualify as a business expense or as deductible interest in addition to any interest actually paid.**

Question — **Beneficial loans**

Anna, who is single, has an annual salary of £30,000, and two loans from her employer.

(a) A season ticket loan of £2,300 at no interest
(b) A loan, 90% of which was used to buy a partnership interest, of £54,000 at 3% interest

The official rate of interest is to be taken as 6.25%.

What is Anna's tax liability for 2007/08?

Answer

	£
Salary	30,000
Season ticket loan (non-qualifying): not over £5,000	0
Loan to buy shares (qualifying): £54,000 × (6.25 – 3 = 3.25%)	1,755
Earnings/Total income	31,755
Less deductible interest paid (£54,000 × 6.25%× 90%)	(3,038)
Net income	28,717
Less personal allowance	(5,225)
Taxable income	23,492
Income tax	
£2,230 × 10%	223
£21,262 × 22%	4,678
Tax liability	4,901

3.7 Private use of other assets

FAST FORWARD: 20% of the value of assets made available for private use is taxable.

When assets are made available to employees or members of their family or household, the taxable benefit is the higher of 20% of the market value when first provided as a benefit to any employee, or on the rent paid by the employer if higher. The 20% charge is time-apportioned when the asset is provided for only part of the year. The charge after any time apportionment is reduced by any contribution made by the employee.

Certain assets, such as bicycles provided for journeys to work, are exempt. These are described later in this chapter.

If an asset made available is subsequently acquired by the employee, **the taxable benefit on the acquisition is the *greater* of:**

- The **current market value minus the price paid by the employee.**
- The **market value when first provided minus any amounts already taxed (ignoring contributions by the employee) minus the price paid by the employee.**

This rule prevents tax free benefits arising on rapidly depreciating items through the employee purchasing them at their low secondhand value.

There is an exception to this rule for bicycles which have previously been provided as exempt benefits. The taxable benefit on acquisition is restricted to current market value, minus the price paid by the employee.

3.8 Example: assets made available for private use

A suit costing £400 is purchased by an employer for use by an employee on 6 April 2006. On 6 April 2007 the suit is purchased by the employee for £30, its market value then being £50.

The benefit in 2006/07 is £400 × 20% = £80

The benefit in 2007/08 is £290, being the *greater* of:

		£
(a)	Market value at acquisition by employee	50
	Less price paid	(30)
		20
(b)	Original market value	400
	Less taxed in respect of use	(80)
		320
	Less price paid	(30)
		290

Question — **Bicycles**

Rupert is provided with a new bicycle by his employer on 6 April 2007. The bicycle is available for private use as well as commuting to work. It cost the employer £1,500 when new. On 6 October 2007 the employer transfers ownership of the bicycle to Rupert when it is worth £800. Rupert does not pay anything for the bicycle.

What is the total taxable benefit on Rupert for 2007/08 in respect of the bicycle?

Answer

Use benefit	Exempt
Transfer benefit (use MV at acquisition by employee only)	
MV at transfer	£800

3.9 Scholarships

If scholarships are given to members an employee's family, the **employee is taxable on the cost** unless the scholarship fund's or scheme's payments by reason of people's employments are not more than 25% of its total payments.

3.10 Other benefits

FAST FORWARD

There is a residual charge for other benefits, usually equal to the cost to the employer of the benefits.

We have seen above how certain specific benefits are taxed. **There is a sweeping up charge for all other benefits. Under this rule the taxable value of a benefit is the cost of the benefit less any part of that cost made good by the employee to the persons providing the benefit.**

The residual charge applies to any benefit provided for a P11D employee or a member of his family or household, by reason of the employment. There is an exception where the employer is an individual and the provision of the benefit is made in the normal course of the employer's domestic, family or personal relationships.

3.11 Example: other benefits

A private school offers free places to the children of its staff. The marginal cost to the school of providing the place is £2,000 pa, although the fees charged to other pupils is £5,000 pa.

The taxable value of the benefit to the staff is the actual cost of £2,000 per pupil, not the full £5,000 charged to other pupils.

4 Exempt benefits

FAST FORWARD

There are a number of exempt benefits including removal expenses, childcare, meal vouchers and workplace parking.

Various benefits are exempt from tax. These include:

(a) **Entertainment provided to employees by genuine third parties** (eg seats at sporting/cultural events), even if it is provided by giving the employee a voucher.

(b) **Gifts of goods** (or vouchers exchangeable for goods) from third parties (ie not provided by the employer or a person connected to the employer) if the total cost (incl. VAT) of all gifts by the same donor to the same employee in the tax year is £250 or less. If the £250 limit is exceeded, the full amount is taxable, not just the excess.

(c) **Non-cash awards for long service** if the period of service was at least 20 years, no similar award was made to the employee in the past 10 years and the cost is not more than £50 per year of service.

(d) **Awards under staff suggestion schemes if**:

   (i) There is a formal scheme, open to all employees on equal terms.

   (ii) The suggestion is outside the scope of the employee's normal duties.

   (iii) Either the award is not more than £25, or the award is only made after a decision is taken to implement the suggestion.

   (iv) Awards over £25 reflect the financial importance of the suggestion to the business, and either do not exceed 50% of the expected net financial benefit during the first year of implementation or do not exceed 10% of the expected net financial benefit over a period of up to five years.

   (v) Awards of over £25 are shared on a reasonable basis between two or more employees putting forward the same suggestion.

   If an award exceeds £5,000, the excess is always taxable.

(e) **The first £8,000 of removal expenses if:**

(i) The employee does not already live within a reasonable daily travelling distance of his new place of employment, but will do so after moving.

(ii) The expenses are incurred or the benefits provided by the end of the tax year following the tax year of the start of employment at the new location.

(f) The cost of running a **workplace nursery or playscheme (without limit). Otherwise up to £55 a week of childcare is tax free** if the employer contracts with an approved childcarer or provides childcare vouchers to pay an approved childcarer. The childcare must be available to all employees and the childcare must either be registered or approved home-childcare.

(g) **Sporting or recreational facilities available to employees generally and not to the general public**, unless they are provided on domestic premises, or they consist of an interest in or the use of any mechanically propelled vehicle or any overnight accommodation. Vouchers only exchangeable for such facilities are also exempt, but membership fees for sports clubs are taxable.

(h) **Assets or services used in performing the duties of employment** provided any private use of the item concerned is insignificant. This exempts, for example, the benefit arising on the private use of employer-provided tools.

(i) **Welfare counselling** and similar minor benefits if the benefit concerned is available to employees generally.

(j) **Bicycles or cycling safety equipment provided to enable employees to get to and from work or to travel between one workplace and another**. The equipment must be available to the employer's employees generally. Also, it must be used mainly for the aforementioned journeys.

(k) **Workplace parking**

(l) **Up to £15,000 a year paid to an employee who is on a full-time course lasting at least a year**, with average full-time attendance of at least 20 weeks a year. If the £15,000 limit is exceeded, the whole amount is taxable.

(m) **Work related training and related costs. This includes the costs of** training material and assets either made during training or incorporated into something so made.

(n) **Air miles or car fuel coupons** obtained as a result of business expenditure but used for private purposes.

(o) **The cost of work buses and minibuses or subsidies to public bus services.**

A works bus must have a seating capacity of 12 or more and a works minibus a seating capacity of 9 or more but not more than 12 and be available generally to employees of the employer concerned. The bus or minibus must mainly be used by employees for journeys to and from work and for journeys between workplaces.

(p) **Transport/overnight costs where public transport is disrupted by industrial action,** late night taxis and travel costs incurred where car sharing arrangements unavoidably breakdown.

(q) The private use of one **mobile phone**. Top up vouchers for exempt mobile phones are also tax free. If more than one mobile phone is provided to an employee for private use only the second or subsequent phone is a taxable benefit valued using 'cost of provision to the employer'.

(r) **Employer provided uniforms** which employees must wear as part of their duties.

(s) The cost of **staff parties** which are open to staff generally provided that the **cost per head per year (including VAT) is £150 or less**. The £150 limit may be split between several parties. If exceeded, the full amount is taxable, not just the excess over £150.

(t) **Private medical insurance premiums paid to cover treatment when the employee is outside the UK in the performance of his duties**. Other medical insurance premiums are taxable as is the cost of medical diagnosis and treatment except for routine check ups. Eye tests and glasses for employees using VDUs are exempt.

(u) **The first 15p per day of meal vouchers (eg luncheon vouchers).**

(v) **Cheap loans that do not exceed £5,000** at any time in the tax year (see above).

(w) **Job related accommodation** (see above).

(x) **Employer contributions towards additional household costs incurred by an employee who works wholly or partly at home**. Payments up to £2 pw (£104 pa) may be made without supporting evidence (see earlier in this Text).

(y) **Meals or refreshments for cyclists** provided as part of official 'cycle to work' days.

(z) **Personal incidental expenses** (see earlier in this Text).

Where a voucher is provided for a benefit which is exempt from income tax the provision of the voucher itself is also exempt.

5 P11D dispensations

As we have seen expense payments to P11D employees should be reported to HMRC. They form part of the employee's employment income and a claim must be made to deduct the expenses in computing net employment income.

To avoid this cumbersome procedure **the employer and HMRC can agree for a dispensation to apply to avoid the need to report expenses covered by the dispensation, and the employee then need not make a formal claim for a deduction.**

Dispensations can only apply to genuine business expenses. Some employers only reimburse business expenses, so that a dispensation may be agreed to cover all payments. Other employers may agree to cover a particular category of expenses, such as travel expenses.

A dispensation cannot be given for mileage allowances paid to employees using their own cars for business journeys as these payments are governed by a statutory exemption (see earlier in this Text).

6 The PAYE system

Most tax in respect of employment income is deducted under the PAYE system. The objective of the PAYE system is to collect the correct amount of tax over the year. An employee's PAYE code is designed to ensure that allowances etc are given evenly over the year.

6.1 Introduction

6.1.1 Cash payments

The objective of the PAYE system is to deduct the correct amount of tax over the year. Its scope is very wide. It applies to most cash payments, other than reimbursed business expenses, and to certain non cash payments.

In addition to wages and salaries, PAYE applies to round sum expense allowances and payments instead of benefits. It also applies to any readily convertible asset.

A readily convertible asset is any asset which can effectively be exchanged for cash. The amount subject to PAYE is the amount that would be taxed as employment income. This is usually the cost to the employer of providing the asset.

Tips paid direct to an employee are normally outside the PAYE system (although still assessable as employment income). An exception may apply in the catering trades where tips are often pooled. Here the PAYE position depends on whether a 'tronc', administered other than by the employer, exists.

It is the employer's duty to deduct income tax from the pay of his employees, whether or not he has been directed to do so by HMRC. **If he fails to do this he** (or sometimes the employee) **must pay over the tax which he should have deducted and the employer may be subject to penalties**. Interest will also run from 14 days after the end of the tax year concerned on any underpaid PAYE. Officers of HMRC can inspect employer's records in order to satisfy themselves that the correct amounts of tax are being deducted and paid over to HMRC.

6.1.2 Benefits

PAYE is not normally operated on benefits; instead the employee's PAYE code is restricted (see below).

However, PAYE must be applied to remuneration in the form of a taxable non-cash voucher if at the time it is provided:

(a) the voucher is capable of being exchanged for readily convertible assets; or
(b) the voucher can itself be sold, realised or traded.

PAYE must normally be operated on cash vouchers and on each occasion when a director/employee uses a credit-token (eg a credit card) to obtain money or goods which are readily convertible assets. However, a cash voucher or credit token which is used to defray expenses is not subject to PAYE.

6.2 How PAYE works

6.2.1 Operation of PAYE

To operate PAYE the employer needs:

(a) deductions working sheets
(b) codes for employees that reflect the tax allowances to which the employees are entitled
(c) tax tables.

The employer works out the amount of PAYE tax to deduct on any particular pay day by using the employee's code number (see below) in conjunction with the PAYE tables. The tables are designed so that tax is normally worked out on a cumulative basis. This means that with each payment of earnings the running total of tax paid is compared with tax due on total earnings to that date. The difference between the tax due and the tax paid is the tax to be deducted on that particular payday.

National insurance tables are used to work out the national insurance due on any payday.

6.2.2 Records

The employer must keep records of each employee's pay and tax at each pay day. The records must also contain details of National Insurance. The employer has a choice of three ways of recording and returning these figures:

(a) he may use the official deductions working sheet (P11)
(b) he may incorporate the figures in his own pay records using a substitute document
(c) he may retain the figures on a computer.

These records will be used to make a return at the end of the tax year.

6.3 Payment under the PAYE system

Under PAYE income tax and national insurance is normally paid over to HMRC monthly, 14 days after the end of each tax month.

If an employer's average monthly payments under the PAYE system are less than £1,500, the employer may choose to pay quarterly, within 14 days of the end of each tax quarter. Tax quarters end on 5 July, 5 October, 5 January and 5 April. Payments can continue to be made quarterly during a tax year even if the monthly average reaches or exceeds £1,500, but a new estimate must be made and a new decision taken to pay quarterly at the start of each tax year. Average monthly payments are the average net monthly payments due to HMRC for income tax and NICs.

6.4 PAYE codes

An employee is normally entitled to various allowances. Under the PAYE system an amount reflecting the effect of a proportion of these allowances is set against his pay each pay day. To determine the amount to set against his pay the allowances are expressed in the form of a code which is used in conjunction with the Pay Adjustment Table (Table A).

An employee's code may be any one of the following:

L	tax code with basic personal allowance
P	tax code with age 65-74 age allowance
Y	tax code with age 75+ age allowance

The codes BR, DO and OT are generally used where there is a second source of income and all allowances have been used in a tax code which is applied to the main source of income.

Generally, a tax code number is arrived at by deleting the last digit in the sum representing the employee's tax free allowances. Every individual is entitled to a personal tax free allowance of £5,225. The code number for an individual who is entitled to this but no other allowance is 522L.

The code number may also reflect other items. For example, **it will be restricted to reflect benefits, small amounts of untaxed income** and **unpaid tax on income from earlier years**. If an amount of tax is in point, it is necessary to gross up the tax in the code using the taxpayer's estimated marginal rate of income tax.

Question

PAYE codes

Adrian is a 40 year old single man (suffix letter L) who earns £15,000 pa. He has benefits of £560 and his unpaid tax for 2005/06 was £57.50. Adrian is entitled to a tax free personal allowance of £5,225 in 2007/08.

Adrian pays income tax at the marginal rate of 22%.

What is Adrian's PAYE code for 2007/08?

Answer

	£
Personal allowance	5,225
Benefits	(560)
Unpaid tax £57.50 × 100/22	(261)
Available allowances	4,404

Adrian's PAYE code is 440L

Codes are determined and amended by HMRC. They are normally notified to the employer on a code list. The employer must act on the code notified to him until amended instructions are received from HMRC, even if the employee has appealed against the code.

By using the code number in conjunction with the tax tables, an employee is generally given 1/52nd or 1/12th of his tax free allowances against each week's/month's pay. However because of the cumulative nature of PAYE, if an employee is first paid in, say, September, that month he will receive six months' allowances against his gross pay. In cases where the employee's previous PAYE history is not known, this could lead to under-deduction of tax. To avoid this, codes for the employees concerned have to be operated on a 'week 1/month1' basis, so that only 1/52nd or 1/12th of the employee's allowances are available each week/month.

6.5 PAYE forms

FAST FORWARD

Employers must complete forms P60, P14, P35, P9D, P11D and P45 as appropriate. A P45 is needed when an employee leaves. Forms P9D and P11D record details of benefits. Forms P60, P14 and P35 are year end returns.

At the end of each tax year, the employer must provide each employee with a form P60. This shows total taxable earnings for the year, tax deducted, code number, NI number and the employer's name and address. **The P60 must be provided by 31 May following the year of assessment.**

Following the end of each tax year, the employer must send HMRC:

(a) **by 19 May**:

(i) **End of year Returns P14** (showing the same details as the P60)
(ii) **Form P35** (summary of total tax and NI deducted from all employees)

(b) **by 6 July**:

(i) **Forms P11D** (benefits etc for directors and employees paid £8,500+ pa)
(ii) **Forms P11D(b)** (return of Class 1A NICs (see later in this Text))
(iii) **Forms P9D** (benefits etc for other employees)

A copy of the form P11D (or P9D) must also be provided to the employee by 6 July. The details shown on the P11D include the full cash equivalent of all benefits, so that the employee may enter the details on his self-assessment tax return. Specific reference numbers for the entries on the P11D are given to assist with the preparation of the employee's self assessment tax return.

When an employee leaves, a form P45 (particulars of Employee Leaving) must be prepared. This form shows the employee's code and details of his income and tax paid to date and is a four part form. One part is sent to HMRC, and three parts handed to the employee. One of the parts (part 1A) is the employee's personal copy.

If the employee takes up a new employment, he must hand the other two parts of the form P45 to the new employer. The new employer will fill in details of the new employment and send one part to HMRC, retaining the other. The details on the form are used by the new employer to calculate the PAYE due on the next payday. If the employee dies a P45 should be completed, and the whole form sent to HMRC.

If an employee joins with a form P45, the new employer can operate PAYE. If there is no P45 the employer still needs to operate PAYE. **The employee is required to complete a form P46**.

If he declares that the employment is his first job since the start of the tax year and he has not received a taxable state benefit, or that it is now his only job but he previously had another job or received a taxable state benefit, the emergency code (522L for 2007/08) applies, on a cumulative basis or week 1/month 1 basis respectively. If the employee declares that he has another job or receives a pension the employer must use code BR.

The P46 is sent to HMRC, unless the pay is below the PAYE and NIC thresholds, and the emergency code applies. In this case no PAYE is deductible until the pay exceeds the threshold.

6.6 Penalties

A form P35 is due on 19 May after the end of the tax year. In practice, a 7 day extension to the due date of 19 May is allowed.

Where a form P35 is late, a penalty of £100 per month per 50 employees may be imposed. This penalty cannot be mitigated. **This penalty ceases 12 months after the due date and a further penalty of up to 100% of the tax (and NIC) for the year which remains unpaid** at 19 April may be imposed. This penalty can be mitigated. HMRC automatically reduce the penalty by concession to the greater of £100 and the total PAYE/NIC which should be reported on the return.

Where a person has fraudulently or negligently submitted an incorrect form P35 the penalty is 100% of the tax (and NIC) attributable to the error. This penalty can be mitigated.

6.7 PAYE settlement agreements

PAYE settlement agreements (PSAs) are arrangements under which employers can make single payments to settle their employees' income tax liabilities on expense payments and benefits which are minor, irregular or where it would be impractical to operate PAYE.

Chapter Roundup

- Most employees are taxed on benefits under the benefits code. 'Excluded employees' (lower paid/non-directors) are only subject to part of the provisions of the code.
- The benefit in respect of accommodation is its annual value. There is an additional benefit if the property cost over £75,000.
- Employees who have a company car are taxed on a % of the car's list price which depends on the level of the car's CO_2 emissions. The same % multiplied by £14,400 determines the benefit where private fuel is also provided.
- Cheap loans are charged to tax on the difference between the official rate of interest and any interest paid by the employee.
- 20% of the value of assets made available for private use is taxable.
- There is a residual charge for other benefits, usually equal to the cost to the employer of the benefits.
- There are a number of exempt benefits including removal expenses, childcare, meal vouchers and workplace parking.
- Most tax in respect of employment income is deducted under the PAYE system. The objective of the PAYE system is to collect the correct amount of tax over the year. An employee's PAYE code is designed to ensure that allowances etc are given evenly over the year.
- Employers must complete forms P60, P14, P35, P9D, P11D and P45 as appropriate. A P45 is needed when an employee leaves. Forms P9D and P11D record details of benefits. Forms P60, P14 and P35 are year end returns.

Quick Quiz

1 What accommodation does not give rise to a taxable benefit?

2 When may an employee who is provided with a fuel by his employer avoid a fuel scale charge?

3 To what extent are removal expenses paid for by an employer taxable?

4 Give an example of a PAYE code.

Answers to Quick Quiz

1 Job related accommodation

2 There is no fuel scale charge if:

(a) All the fuel provided was made available only for business travel, or
(b) The full cost of any fuel provided for private use was completely reimbursed by the employee.

3 The first £8,000 of removal expenses are exempt. Any excess is taxable.

4 522L.

Now try the question below from the Exam Question Bank

Number	Level	Marks	Time
Q5	Examination	15	27 mins

5

Pensions

Topic list	Syllabus reference
1 Types of pension scheme and membership	B6(a), (b)
2 Contributing to a pension scheme	B6(a), (b)
3 Receiving benefits from pension arrangements	B6(a), (b)

Introduction

In the previous two chapters we have discussed the taxation of employment income. Many employers offer their employees the option of joining an occupational pension scheme, and they may choose instead or in addition to take out a personal pension scheme run by a financial institution such as a bank or building society.

Self-employed or non-working individuals can only make provision for a pension using a personal pension scheme.

Whichever type of scheme is chosen the amount of tax relief available is calculated in the same way, and this is covered in this chapter. Note however that contributions to occupational schemes are usually deducted from gross pay before PAYE is calculated whilst contributions to personal pensions are paid net of basic rate tax.

Study guide

		Intellectual level
B6	**The use of exemptions and reliefs in deferring and minimising income tax liabilities**	
(a)	Explain and compute the relief given for contributions to personal pension schemes, using the rules applicable from 6 April 2006.	2
(b)	Describe the relief given for contributions to occupational pension schemes, using the rules applicable from 6 April 2006.	1

Exam guide

Pension contributions can be paid by all individuals and you may come across them as part of an income tax question. You may be required to discuss the types of pension schemes available and the limits on the tax relief due, or you may have to deal with them in an income tax computation. You must be sure that you know how to deal with the two ways of giving relief – contributions to occupational schemes are deducted from earnings whilst contributions to personal pensions are paid net of basic rate tax and higher rate tax relief is given by extending the basic rate band.

1 Types of pension scheme and membership

FAST FORWARD

An employee may be a member of his employer's occupational pension scheme. Any individual whether a member of an occupational pension scheme or not, can take out a 'personal pension' plan with a financial institution such as an insurance company, bank or building society.

1.1 Introduction

An individual is encouraged by the Government to make financial provision to cover his needs when he reaches a certain age. There are state pension arrangements which provide some financial support, but the Government would prefer an individual to make his own pension provision.

Therefore tax relief is given for private pension provision. This includes relief for contributions to pension schemes and an exemption from tax on income and gains arising in a pension fund.

1.2 Pension arrangements

An individual may make pension provision in a number of ways.

1.2.1 Occupational pension scheme

Key term

Employers may set up an **occupational pension scheme**. Such schemes may either require contributions from employees or be non-contributory. The employer may use the services of an insurance company (an insured scheme) or may set up a totally self administered pension fund.

There are two kinds of occupational pension scheme – earnings-related (**defined benefits arrangements**) and investment-related (**money purchase arrangements**). In a **defined benefits arrangements** – also known as a **final salary scheme** – the pension is generally based on employees' earnings at retirement and linked to the number of years they have worked for the firm.

A **money purchase pension** – also known as a **defined contribution scheme** – does not provide any guarantee regarding the level of pension which will be available. The individual invests in the pension scheme and the amount invested is used to build up a pension.

1.2.2 Personal pensions

Key term

Personal pensions are money purchase schemes, which are provided by banks, insurance companies and other financial institutions.

Stakeholder pensions are a particular type of personal pension scheme. They must satisfy certain rules, such as a maximum level of charges, ease of transfer etc.

Any individual (whether employed or not) may join a personal pension scheme.

1.2.3 More than one pension arrangement

An individual may make a number of different pension arrangements depending on his circumstances. For example, he may be a member of an occupational pension scheme and also make pension arrangements independently with a financial provider. If the individual has more than one pension arrangement, the rules we will be looking at in detail later apply to all the pension arrangements he makes. For example, **there is a limit on the amount of contributions that the individual can make in a tax year. This limit applies to all the pension arrangements that he makes, not *each* of them.**

The rules below apply to registered pension schemes, ie those registered with HMRC.

2 Contributing to a pension scheme

FAST FORWARD

Anyone can contribute to a personal pension scheme, even if they are not earning, subject to the contributions threshold of £3,600 (gross).

2.1 Contributions by a scheme member

Any individual **under the age of 75 can make tax relievable pension contributions** in a tax year.

The maximum amount of contributions attracting tax relief made by an individual in a tax year is the higher of:

(a) **the individual's relevant UK earnings chargeable to income tax in the year; and**
(b) **the basic amount (set at £3,600 for 2007/08).**

Relevant UK earnings are broadly employment income, trading income and income from furnished holiday lettings (see later in this Text).

If the individual does not have any UK earnings in a tax year, the maximum pension contribution he can obtain tax relief on is £3,600.

Where an individual contributes to more than one pension scheme, the aggregate of his contributions will be used to give the total amount of tax relief.

There is an interaction between this provision and the annual allowance, which will be discussed later.

2.2 Methods of giving tax relief

FAST FORWARD

Contributions to personal pension plans are paid net of basic rate tax. Higher rate relief is given through the personal tax computation. Contributions to occupational pension schemes are usually paid under the net pay scheme.

2.2.1 Pension tax relief given at source

This method will be used where an individual makes a contribution to a pension scheme run by a personal pension provider such as an insurance company.

Relief is given at source by the contributions being deemed to be made net of basic rate tax. This applies whether the individual is an employee, self-employed or not employed at all and whether or not he has taxable income. HMRC then pay an amount of basic rate tax to the pension provider.

Further tax relief is given if the individual is a higher rate taxpayer. The relief is given by increasing the basic rate band for the year by the gross amount of contributions for which he is entitled to relief. (You will recognise this as the same way in which relief is given for gift aid donations.)

Exam focus point

Make sure your workings show clearly how you have extended the basic rate tax band. Note the difference between this method and that used for net pay arrangements (see below).

Question — **Higher rate relief**

Joe has earnings of £50,000 in 2007/08. He pays a personal pension contribution of £7,020 (net). He has no other taxable income.

Show Joe's tax liability for 2007/08.

Answer

	Non savings income
	£
Earnings/Net income	50,000
Less PA	(5,225)
Taxable income	44,775

Tax

	£
£2,230 × 10%	223
£32,370 × 22%	7,121
£9,000 (7,020 × 100/78) × 22%	1,980
£1,175 × 40%	470
44,775	9,794

2.2.2 Net pay arrangements

An occupational scheme will normally operate net pay arrangements.

In this case, the employer will deduct gross pension contributions from the individual's earnings before operating PAYE. The individual therefore obtains tax relief at his marginal rate of tax automatically.

Question — **Net pay arrangements**

Maxine has taxable earnings of £50,000 in 2007/08. Her employer deducts a pension contribution of £9,000 from these earnings before operating PAYE. She has no other taxable income.

Show Maxine's tax liability for 2007/08.

Answer

	Non-savings income
	£
Earnings/Total income	50,000
Less pension contribution	(9,000)
Net income	41,000
Less PA	(5,225)
Taxable income	35,775

Tax

	£
£2,230 × 10%	223
£32,370 × 22%	7,121
£1,175 × 40%	470
35,775	7,814

This is the same result as Joe in the previous example. Joe had received basic rate tax relief of £(9,000 – 7,020) = £1,980 at source, so his overall tax position was £(9,794 – 1,980) = £7,814.

2.3 Contributions not attracting tax relief

An individual can also make contributions to his pension arrangements which do not attract tax relief, for example out of capital. The member must notify the scheme administrator if he makes contributions in excess of the higher of his UK relevant earnings and the basic amount.

Such contributions do not count towards the annual allowance limit (discussed below) but will affect the value of the pension fund for the lifetime allowance.

2.4 Employer pension contributions

Where the individual is an employee, his **employer may make contributions to his pension scheme** as part of his employment benefits package. Such contributions are **exempt benefits** for the employee.

There is **no limit** on the amount of the contributions that may be made by an employer but **they always count towards the annual allowance** and will also affect the value of the pension fund for the lifetime allowance (see further below).

All contributions made by an employer are made gross and the employer will usually obtain tax relief for the contribution by deducting it as an expense in calculating trading profits for the period of account in which the payment is made.

2.5 Annual allowance

FAST FORWARD

There is an overriding limit on the amount that can be paid into an individual's pension schemes for each tax year. This is called the **annual allowance**.

The annual allowance restricts the amount of tax relievable contributions that can be paid into an individual's pension scheme each year. The amount of the annual allowance for 2007/08 is **£225,000**.

If pension contributions exceed the annual allowance there is a charge to income tax on the individual on the excess at the rate of 40%.

Question

Charge on excess contributions

For 2007/08 Freda has trading profits of £400,000 and made gross personal pension contributions of £260,000.

Calculate Freda's income tax liability for the year and state how she will obtain relief for the pension contributions she makes.

Answer

Freda has earnings of £400,000 for the tax year 2007/08. The contributions of £260,000 qualify for tax relief, and she will have paid £202,800 (£260,000 less 22%) to the pension company. Higher rate tax relief will be given by extending Freda's basic rate tax band for 2007/08 by £260,000. However, there will be tax charge at the rate of 40% on the excess of contributions above the annual allowance of £225,000. Freda's income tax liability for the tax year 2007/08 is as follows:

		£
Trading profit		400,000
Personal allowance		(5,225)
Taxable income		394,775
		£
Income tax:	£2,230 at 10%	223
	£292,370 at 22%	64,321
	£100,175 at 40%	40,070
		104,614
Excess contribution charge £35,000 (260,000 – 225,000) at 40%		14,000
Tax liability		118,614

3 Receiving benefits from pension arrangements

3.1 Pension benefits

Normally an individual may take one quarter of his pension fund as a tax free lump sum, and the balance as a pension. The benefits need not all be taken at one time, but may be phased over several years, but not beyond age 75.

3.2 The lifetime allowance

FAST FORWARD

An individual is not allowed to build up an indefinitely large pension fund. There is a maximum value for a pension fund called the **lifetime allowance**.

The amount of the lifetime allowance for 2007/08 is **£1,600,000**.

If the pension fund exceeds the lifetime allowance at the time the benefit starts to be taken ('vested') this will give rise to an income tax charge on the excess value of the fund. The rate of the charge is 55% if the excess value is taken as a lump sum, or 25% if the funds are left in the scheme to provide a pension.

Chapter Roundup

- An employee may be a member of his employer's occupational pension scheme. Any individual whether a member of an occupational pension scheme or not, can take out a 'personal pension' plan with a financial institution such as an insurance company, bank or building society.
- Anyone can contribute to a personal pension scheme, even if they are not earning, subject to the contributions threshold of £3,600 (gross).
- Contributions to personal pension plans are paid net of basic rate tax. Higher rate relief is given through the personal tax computation. Contributions to occupational pension schemes are usually paid under the net pay scheme.
- There is an overriding limit on the amount that can be paid into an individual's pension schemes for each tax year. This is called the **annual allowance.**
- An individual is not allowed to build up an indefinitely large pension fund. There is a maximum value for a pension fund called the **lifetime allowance**.

Quick Quiz

1 What is the limit on tax relievable contributions to a registered pension scheme?

2 What are the consequences of the total of employee and employer pension contributions exceeding the annual allowance?

3 What are the consequences of exceeding the lifetime allowance?

Answers to Quick Quiz

1. Higher of relevant UK earnings and the basic amount (£3,600).
2. The excess is subject to the annual allowance charge on the employee at 40%.
3. If the lifetime allowance is exceeded the excess is charged at 55% (if taken as a lump sum) or 25% (if taken as a pension).

Now try the question below from the Exam Question Bank

Number	Level	Marks	Time
Q6	Introductory	7	13 mins
Q7	Examination	15	27 mins

Property income

Topic list	Syllabus reference
1 Property business income	B4(a)
2 Furnished holiday lettings	B4(b)
3 Rent a room relief	B4(c)
4 Premiums on leases	B4(d)
5 Property business losses	B4(e)

Introduction

We have finished looking at an individual's employment income and can turn our attention to other income to be slotted into the tax computation.

We are now going to look at the computation and taxation of the profits of a property letting business. First we see how to work out the profit (you may like to return to this section once you have studied chapters 7 and 8).

Next we look at the special conditions which must be satisfied if a letting is to be treated as a furnished holiday lettings and at the extra tax reliefs available if it is.

We then consider the special relief available to taxpayers who let out rooms in their own homes, rent a room relief.

Finally we see how part of a premium for granting a short lease is taxed as income.

In the following chapters we shall turn our attention to the profits of an actual trade, profession or vocation.

Study guide

		Intellectual level
B4	**The use of exemptions and reliefs in deferring and minimising income tax liabilities**	
(a)	Compute property business profits.	2
(b)	Explain the treatment of furnished holiday lettings.	1
(c)	Describe rent-a-room relief.	1
(d)	Compute the amount assessable when a premium is received for the grant of a short lease.	2
(e)	Understand how relief for a property business loss is given.	2

Exam guide

You are very likely to have to compute property income as part of question. You may find it in the context of income tax or corporation tax – the basic computational rules are the same (apart from interest paid which is not included as an expense for corporation tax purposes). Rent a room relief is an important relief for individuals (it does not apply to companies), and the special rules for furnished holiday lettings will only be examined in an income tax context. Remember that property income is non-savings income even though a property portfolio is usually regarded as an investment.

1 Property business income

FAST FORWARD: Property business profits are calculated on an accruals basis.

1.1 Profits of a property business

Income from land and buildings in the UK is taxed as non-savings income.

The profits of the UK property business are computed for tax years. Each tax year's profit is taxed in that year.

1.2 Computation of profits

A taxpayer with UK rental income is treated as running a business, his 'UK property business'. All the rents and expenses for all properties are pooled, to give a single profit or loss. Profits and losses are computed in the same way as trading profits are computed for tax purposes, on an **accruals basis**.

Expenses will often include rent payable where a landlord is himself renting the land which he in turn lets to others. For individuals, interest on loans to buy or improve properties is treated as an expense (on an accruals basis).

Relief is available for irrecoverable rent as an impaired debt.

1.3 Capital allowances

FAST FORWARD

If property is let furnished a wear and tear allowance may be claimed in respect of the furniture. Capital allowances are not available.

Capital allowances are given on plant and machinery used in the UK property business and on industrial buildings, in the same way as they are given for a trading business with an accounting date of 5 April. Capital allowances are not normally available on plant or machinery used in a dwelling but someone who lets property furnished can instead claim the 10% wear and tear allowance.

Under the *10%* **wear and tear** basis, the actual cost of furniture is ignored. Instead, an annual deduction is given of 10% of rents. The rents are first reduced by amounts which are paid by the landlord but are normally a tenant's burden. These amounts include any **water rates** and **council tax** paid by the landlord.

Exam focus point

In the exam look at the question carefully to see if the property is let furnished. If so it is eligible for the 10% wear and tear deduction.

Question — Property business income

Over the last few years Pete has purchased several properties in Manchester as 'buy to let' investments.

5 Whitby Ave is let out furnished at £500 per month. A tenant moved in on 1 March 2006 but left unexpectedly on 1 May 2008 having paid rent only up to 31 December 2007. The tenant left no forwarding address.

17 Bolton Rd has been let furnished to the same tenant for a number of years at £800 per month.

A recent purchase, 27 Turner Close has been let unfurnished since 1 August 2007 at £750 per month having been empty whilst Pete redecorated it after its purchase in March 2007.

Pete's expenses during 2007/08 are:

	No 5	*No 17*	*No 27*
	£	£	£
Insurance	250	250	200
Letting agency fees	–	–	100
Repairs	300	40	–
Redecoration	–	–	500

No 27 was in a fit state to let when Pete bought it but he wanted to redecorate the property as he felt this would allow him to achieve a better rental income.

Water rates and council tax are paid by the tenants.

What is Pete's property business income for 2007/08?

Answer

	No 5	*No 17*	*No 27*
	£	£	£
Accrued income			
12 × £500	6,000		
12 × £800		9,600	
8 × £750			6,000
Less:			
Insurance	(250)	(250)	(200)
Letting agency fees			(100)
Repairs	(300)	(40)	(500)
Impairment (irrecoverable rent)			
3 × 500	(1,500)		
Wear and Tear Allowance			
£(6,000 – 1,500) × 10%	(450)		
£9,600 × 10%		(960)	
Property business income	3,500	8,350	5,200
Taxable property income for 2007/08			£17,050

2 Furnished holiday lettings

FAST FORWARD

Special rules apply to income from furnished holiday lettings. Whilst the income is taxed as normal as property business income, relief for losses is available as if they were trading losses. Capital allowances are available on the furniture, and the income is relevant earnings for pension purposes.

2.1 Introduction

There are special rules for furnished holiday lettings (FHLs). The letting is treated as if it were a trade. This means that, although the income is taxed as income from a UK property business, the provisions which apply to actual trades also apply to furnished holiday lettings, as follows:

(a) Relief for losses is available as if they were trading losses, including the facility to set losses against other income. The usual UK property business loss reliefs do not apply (see below).

(b) Capital allowances are available on furniture.

(c) The income qualifies as relevant UK earnings for pension relief (see earlier in this Text).

(d) Capital gains tax rollover relief, business asset taper relief and relief for gifts of business assets are available (see later in this Text).

Note, however, that the basis period rules for trades do not apply, and the profits or losses must be computed for tax years.

2.2 Conditions

The letting must be of furnished accommodation made on a **commercial basis with a view to the realisation of profit**. The property must also satisfy the following three conditions.

(a) **The availability condition** – the accommodation is available for **commercial let** as **holiday accommodation** to the **public** generally, for **at least 140 days during the year**.

(b) **The letting condition** – the accommodation is **commercially let** as holiday accommodation to members of the public **for at least 70 days during the year**.

(c) **The pattern of occupation condition** – **not more than 155 days in the year fall during periods of longer term occupation**. Longer term occupation is defined as **a continuous period of more than 31 days during which the accommodation is in the same occupation** unless there are abnormal circumstances.

If someone has furnished holiday lettings and other lettings, **draw up two profit and loss accounts as if they had two separate UK property businesses**. This is so that the profits and losses treated as trade profits and losses can be identified.

3 Rent a room relief

FAST FORWARD

Rents received from letting a room in the taxpayer's home may be tax free under the rent-a-room scheme.

3.1 The exemption

If an individual lets a room or rooms, furnished, in his or her main residence as living accommodation, then a special exemption may apply.

The limit on the exemption is gross rents (before any expenses or capital allowances) of £4,250 a year. This limit is halved if any other person (eg spouse/civil partner) also received income from renting accommodation in the property.

If gross rents are not more than the limit, the rents are wholly exempt from income tax and expenses are ignored. However, the taxpayer may claim to ignore the exemption, for example to generate a loss by taking into account both rent and expenses.

Exam focus point

If you are asked to calculate property income in an exam don't overlook rent a room relief, but be sure to state whether the relief applies.

3.2 Alternative basis

If gross rents exceed the limit, the taxpayer will be taxed in the ordinary way, ignoring the rent a room scheme, unless he elects for the 'alternative basis'. If he so elects, he will be taxable on gross receipts less £4,250 (or £2,125 if the limit is halved), with no deductions for expenses.

An election to ignore the exemption or an election for the alternative basis must be made by the 31 January which is 22 months from the end of the tax year concerned. An election to ignore the exemption applies only for the tax year for which it is made, but an election for the alternative basis remains in force until it is withdrawn or until a year in which gross rents do not exceed the limit.

Question

Rent a room relief

Sylvia owns a house near the sea in Norfolk. She has a spare bedroom and during 2007/08 this was let to a chef working at a nearby restaurant for £85 per week which includes the cost of heating, lighting etc.

Sylvia estimates that her lodger costs her an extra:

£50 on gas
£25 on electricity
£50 on insurance

each year.

How much property income must Sylvia pay tax on?

Answer

Sylvia has a choice:

(1) Total rental income of £85 × 52 = £4,420 exceeds £4,250 limit so taxable income is £170 (ie 4,420 – 4,250) if rent a room relief claimed.

(2) Alternatively she can be taxed on her actual profit:

	£
Rental income	4,420
Less expenses (50 + 25 + 50)	(125)
	4,295

Sylvia would be advised to claim rent a room relief.

4 Premiums on leases

When a premium or similar consideration is received on the grant (that is, by a landlord to a tenant) **of a short lease (50 years or less), part of the premium is treated as rent received in the year of grant.**

The premium taxed as rent is the whole premium, less 2% of the premium for each complete year of the lease, except the first year.

This rule does not apply on the **assignment** of a lease (one tenant selling his entire interest in the property to another).

4.1 Example: income element of premium

Janet granted a lease to Jack on 1 March 2008 for a period of 40 years. Jack paid a premium of £16,000. How much of the premium received by Janet is taxed as rent received?

	£
Premium received	16,000
Less 2% × (40 –1) × £16,000	(12,480)
Taxable as rent received	3,520

Note that if Janet had **assigned** the lease, no part of the amount received would be taxed as rent received.

4.2 Premiums paid by traders

Where a trader pays a premium for a lease he may deduct an amount from his taxable trading profits in each year of the lease. The amount deductible is the figure treated as rent received by the landlord divided by the number of years of the lease. For example, suppose that B, a trader, pays A a premium of £30,000 for a ten year lease. A is treated as receiving £30,000 – (£30,000 × (10 – 1) × 2%) = £24,600. B can therefore deduct £24,600/10 = £2,460 in each of the ten years. He starts with the accounts year in which the lease starts and apportions the relief to the nearest month.

4.3 Premiums for granting subleases

A tenant may decide to sublet property and to charge a premium on the grant of a lease to the subtenant. This premium is treated as rent received in the normal way (because this is a grant and not an assignment, the original tenant retaining an interest in the property). **Where the tenant originally paid a premium for his own head lease, this deemed rent is reduced by:**

$$\text{Rent part of premium for head lease} \times \frac{\text{duration of sublease}}{\text{duration of head lease}}$$

If the relief exceeds the part of the premium for the sub-lease treated as rent (including cases where there is a sub-lease with no premium), the balance of the relief is treated as rent payable by the head tenant, spread evenly over the period of the sub-lease. This rent payable is an expense, reducing the overall property business profit.

Question — **Taxable premium received**

Charles granted a lease to David on 1 March 1997 for a period of 40 years. David paid a premium of £16,000. On 1 June 2007 David granted a sublease to Edward for a period of ten years. Edward paid a premium of £30,000. Calculate the amount treated as rent out of the premium received by David.

Answer

	£
Premium received by David	30,000
Less £30,000 × 2% × (10-1)	(5,400)
	24,600
Less allowance for premium paid	
(£16,000 – (£16,000 × 39 × 2%)) × 10/40	(880)
Premium treated as rent	23,720

You may wish to return to this section once you have covered trade profits in the next chapter.

5 Property business losses

FAST FORWARD A loss on a property letting business is carried forward to set against future property business profits.

A loss from a UK property business is carried forward to set against the first future profits from the UK property business. It may be carried forward until the UK property business ends, but it must be used as soon as possible.

As explained above, however, FHL losses are dealt with under the special rules that apply to trading losses (see later in this Text). Only if these are not claimed would a FHL loss be available to carry forward.

Chapter Roundup

- Property business profits are calculated on an accruals basis.
- If property is let furnished a wear and tear allowance may be claimed in respect of the furniture. Capital allowances are not available.
- Special rules apply to income from furnished holiday lettings. Whilst the income is taxed as normal as property business income, relief for losses is available as if they were trading losses. Capital allowances are available on the furniture, and the income is relevant earnings for pension purposes.
- Rents received from letting a room in the taxpayer's home may be tax free under the rent-a-room scheme.
- A loss on a property letting business is carried forward to set against future property business profits.

Quick Quiz

1 How is capital expenditure relieved for furnished lettings?

2 How much income per annum is tax free under the rent a room scheme?

Answers to Quick Quiz

1 Except for furnished holiday lettings where capital allowances are available for the cost of furniture, capital expenditure on furnishings is relieved through the 10% wear and tear allowance. The deduction is equal to 10% of rents less council tax and water rates.

2 £4,250

Now try the questions below from the Exam Question Bank

Number	Level	Marks	Time
Q8	Examination	15	27 mins

7

Computing trading income

Topic list	Syllabus reference
1 The badges of trade	B3(b)
2 The adjustment of profits	B3(c)
3 Pre-trading expenditure	B3(d)

Introduction

The final figure to slot into the income tax computation is income from self employment.

We are therefore going to look at the computation of profits of unincorporated businesses. We work out a business's profit as if it were a separate entity (the separate entity concept familiar to you from basic bookkeeping) but, as an unincorporated business has no legal existence apart from its proprietor, we cannot tax it separately. We have to feed its profit into the proprietor's personal tax computation.

Later chapters will consider capital allowances, which are allowed as an expense in the computation of profits, the taxation of business profit, and how trading losses can be relieved. We will then extend our study to partnerships, ie to groups of two or more individuals trading together.

Study guide

		Intellectual level
B3	**Income from self-employment**	
(b)	Describe and apply the badges of trade.	2
(c)	Recognise the expenditure that is allowable in calculating the tax-adjusted trading profit.	2
(d)	Recognise the relief that can be obtained for pre-trading expenditure.	2

Exam guide

You are likely to have to compute trading profits at some point in the exam. The computation may be for an individual, a partnership or a company. In each case the same principles are applied. You must however watch out for the adjustments which only apply to individuals, such as private use expenses.

1 The badges of trade

FAST FORWARD

The badges of trade are used to decide whether or not a trade exists. If one does exist, the accounts profits need to be adjusted in order to establish the taxable profits.

Key term

A trade is defined in the legislation only in an unhelpful manner as including every trade, manufacture, adventure or concern in the nature of a trade. It has therefore been left to the courts to provide guidance. This guidance is summarised in a collection of principles known as the **'badges of trade'**. These are set out below. They apply to both corporate and unincorporated businesses.

Exam focus point

You are not expected to know case names – we have included these below for your information only. The rules relating to trades apply equally to all professions and vocations.

1.1 The subject matter

Whether a person is trading or not may sometimes be decided by examining the subject matter of the transaction. Some assets are commonly held as investments for their intrinsic value: an individual buying some shares or a painting may do so in order to enjoy the income from the shares or to enjoy the work of art. A subsequent disposal may produce a gain of a capital nature rather than a trading profit. But **where the subject matter of a transaction is such as would not be held as an investment** (for example 34,000,000 yards of aircraft linen (*Martin v Lowry 1927*) or 1,000,000 rolls of toilet paper (*Rutledge v CIR 1929*)), **it is presumed that any profit on resale is a trading profit.**

1.2 The frequency of transactions

Transactions which may, in isolation, be of a capital nature will be interpreted as trading transactions where their **frequency indicates the carrying on of a trade**. It was decided that whereas normally the purchase of a mill-owning company and the subsequent stripping of its assets might be a capital transaction, where the taxpayer was embarking on the same exercise for the fourth time he must be carrying on a trade (*Pickford v Quirke 1927*).

1.3 The length of ownership

The courts may infer adventures in the nature of trade where **items purchased are sold soon afterwards**.

1.4 Supplementary work and marketing

When work is done to make an asset more marketable, or steps are taken to find purchasers, the courts will be more ready to ascribe a trading motive. When a group of accountants bought, blended and recasked a quantity of brandy they were held to be taxable on a trading profit when the brandy was later sold (*Cape Brandy Syndicate v CIR 1921*).

1.5 A profit motive

The absence of a profit motive will not necessarily preclude a tax charge as trading income, but its presence is a strong indication that a person is trading. The purchase and resale of £20,000 worth of silver bullion by the comedian Norman Wisdom, as a hedge against devaluation, was held to be a trading transaction (*Wisdom v Chamberlain 1969*).

1.6 The way in which the asset sold was acquired

If goods are acquired deliberately, trading may be indicated. If goods are acquired unintentionally, for example by gift or inheritance, their later sale is unlikely to be trading.

1.7 The taxpayer's intentions

Where a transaction is clearly trading on objective criteria, **the taxpayer's intentions are irrelevant**. If, however, a transaction has (objectively) a dual purpose, the taxpayer's intentions may be taken into account. An example of a transaction with a dual purpose is the acquisition of a site partly as premises from which to conduct another trade, and partly with a view to the possible development and resale of the site.

This test is not one of the traditional badges of trade, but it may be just as important.

2 The adjustment of profits

The net profit in the profit and loss account must be adjusted to find the taxable trading profit.

2.1 Illustrative adjustment

Although the **net profit before taxation** shown in the accounts is the starting point in computing the taxable trade profits, many adjustments may be required to calculate the taxable amount.

Exam focus point

You must start with the net profit before taxation and only adjust for items where there is a difference between the tax and accounting treatment of an item of income and expenditure. Do not try to rewrite the profit and loss account.

Here is an illustrative adjustment.

	£	£
Net profit per accounts		140,000
Add: expenditure charged in the accounts which is not deductible from trading profits	50,000	
income taxable as trading profits which has not been included in the accounts	30,000	
		80,000
		220,000
Less: profits included in the accounts but which are not taxable trading profits	40,000	
expenditure which is deductible from trading profits but has not been charged in the accounts	20,000	
		(60,000)
Profit adjusted for tax purposes		160,000

You may refer to deductible and non-deductible expenditure as allowable and disallowable expenditure respectively. The two sets of terms are interchangeable.

2.2 Accounting policies

The fundamental concept is that the profits of the business must be calculated in accordance with generally accepted accounting practice. These profits are subject to any adjustment specifically required for income tax purposes.

2.3 Deductible and non-deductible expenditure

FAST FORWARD

Disallowable (ie non-deductible) expenditure must be added back to the accounts profit in the computation of the taxable trading profit. Any item not deducted wholly and exclusively for trade purposes is disallowable expenditure. Certain other items, such as depreciation, are specifically disallowable.

2.3.1 Introduction

Certain expenses are specifically disallowed by the legislation. These are covered below. If however a deduction is specifically permitted this overrides the disallowance.

2.3.2 Payments contrary to public policy and illegal payments

Fines and penalties are not deductible. However, **HMRC usually allow employees' parking fines incurred in parking their employer's cars while on their employer's business. Fines relating to proprietors, however, are never allowed.**

A payment is not deductible if making it constitutes an offence by the payer. This covers protection money paid to terrorists, and also bribes. Statute also prevents any deduction for payments made in response to blackmail or extortion.

2.3.3 Capital expenditure

Capital expenditure is not deductible. This denies a deduction for depreciation or amortisation. The most contentious items of expenditure will often be repairs (revenue expenditure) **and improvements** (capital expenditure).

- The cost of restoration of an asset by, for instance, replacing a subsidiary part of the asset is revenue expenditure. Expenditure on a new factory chimney replacement was allowable since the chimney was a subsidiary part of the factory (*Samuel Jones & Co (Devondale) Ltd v CIR 1951*). However, in another case a football club demolished a spectators' stand and replaced it with a modern equivalent. This was held not to be repair, since repair is the restoration by renewal or replacement of subsidiary parts of a larger entity, and the stand formed a distinct and *separate* part of the club (*Brown v Burnley Football and Athletic Co Ltd 1980*).
- The cost of initial repairs to improve an asset recently acquired to make it fit to earn profits is disallowable capital expenditure. In *Law Shipping Co Ltd v CIR 1923* the taxpayer failed to obtain relief for expenditure on making a newly bought ship seaworthy prior to using it.
- The cost of initial repairs to remedy normal wear and tear of recently acquired assets is allowable. *Odeon Associated Theatres Ltd v Jones 1971* can be contrasted with the *Law Shipping* judgement. Odeon were allowed to charge expenditure incurred on improving the state of recently acquired cinemas.

Capital allowances may, however, be available as a deduction for capital expenditure from trading profits (see later in this Text).

Two exceptions to the 'capital' rule are worth noting.

(a) The costs of **registering patents and trade marks** are deductible.

(b) **Incidental costs of obtaining loan finance**, or of attempting to obtain or redeeming it, are deductible other than a discount on issue or a premium on redemption (which are really alternatives to paying interest).

2.3.4 Expenditure not wholly and exclusively for the purposes of the trade

Expenditure is not deductible if it is not for trade purposes (the remoteness test), or if it reflects more than one purpose (the duality test). The private proportion of payments for motoring expenses, rent, heat and light and telephone expenses of a proprietor is not deductible. If an exact apportionment is possible relief is given on the business element. Where the payments are to or on behalf of employees, the full amounts are deductible but the employees are taxed under the benefits code (see earlier in this Text).

The remoteness test is illustrated by the following cases.

- *Strong & Co of Romsey Ltd v Woodifield 1906*
  A customer injured by a falling chimney when sleeping in an inn owned by a brewery claimed compensation from the company. The compensation was not deductible: 'the loss sustained by the appellant was not really incidental to their trade as innkeepers and fell upon them in their character not of innkeepers but of householders'.
- *Bamford v ATA Advertising Ltd 1972*
  A director misappropriated £15,000. The loss was not allowable: 'the loss is not, as in the case of a dishonest shop assistant, an incident of the company's trading activities. It arises altogether outside such activities'.
- Expenditure which is wholly and exclusively to benefit the trades of several companies (for example in a group) but is not wholly and exclusively to benefit the trade of one specific company is not deductible *(Vodafone Cellular Ltd and others v Shaw 1995).*
- *McKnight (HMIT) v Sheppard (1999)* concerned expenses incurred by a stockbroker in defending allegations of infringements of Stock Exchange regulations. It was found that the expenditure was incurred to prevent the destruction of the taxpayer's business and that as the expenditure was incurred for business purposes it was deductible. It was also found that although the expenditure had the effect of preserving the taxpayer's reputation, that was not its purpose, so there was no duality of purpose.

The **duality test** is illustrated by the following cases.

- *Caillebotte v Quinn 1975*
  A self-employed carpenter spent an average of 40p per day when obliged to buy lunch away from home but just 10p when he lunched at home. He claimed the excess 30p. It was decided that the payment had a dual purpose and was not deductible: a taxpayer 'must eat to live not eat to work'.
- *Mallalieu v Drummond 1983*
  Expenditure by a lady barrister on black clothing to be worn in court (and on its cleaning and repair) was not deductible. The expenditure was for the dual purpose of enabling the barrister to be warmly and properly clad as well as meeting her professional requirements.
- *McLaren v Mumford 1996*
  A publican traded from a public house which had residential accommodation above it. He was obliged to live at the public house but he also had another house which he visited regularly. It was held that the private element of the expenditure incurred at the public house on electricity, rent, gas, etc was not incurred for the purpose of earning profits, but for serving the non-business purpose of satisfying the publican's ordinary human needs. The expenditure, therefore had a dual purpose and was disallowed.

However, the cost of overnight accommodation when on a business trip may be deductible and reasonable expenditure on an evening meal and breakfast in conjunction with such accommodation is then also deductible.

2.3.5 Impaired trade receivables (bad debts)

Only impairment debts incurred wholly and exclusively for the purposes of the trade are deductible for taxation purposes. Thus loans to employees written off are not deductible unless the business is that of making loans, or it can be shown that the writing-off of the loan was earnings paid out for the benefit of the trade. If a trade debt is released as part of a voluntary arrangement under the Insolvency Act 1986, or a compromise or arrangement under s 425 Companies Act 1985, the amount released is deductible as an impaired debt.

Under FRS 26 Financial Instruments: measurement, a review of all trade receivables should be carried out to assess their fair value at the balance sheet date, and any impairment debts written off. As a specific provision, no adjustment to the accounts profit is needed for impairment review.

2.3.6 Unpaid remuneration and employee benefit contributions

If earnings for employees are charged in the accounts but are not paid within nine months of the end of the period of account, the cost is only deductible for the period of account in which the earnings are paid. When a tax computation is made within the nine month period, it is initially assumed that unpaid earnings will not be paid within that period. The computation is adjusted if they are so paid.

Earnings are treated as paid at the same time as they are treated as received for employment income purposes.

Similar rules apply to employee benefit contributions.

2.3.7 Entertaining and gifts

The general rule is that expenditure on entertaining and gifts is non-deductible. This applies to amounts reimbursed to employees for specific entertaining expenses and gifts, and to round sum allowances which are exclusively for meeting such expenses.

There are specific exceptions to the general rule:

- **Entertaining for and gifts to employees are normally deductible** although where gifts are made, or the entertainment is excessive, a charge to tax may arise on the employee under the benefits legislation.
- **Gifts to customers not costing more than £50 per donee per year are allowed if they carry a conspicuous advertisement for the business and are not food, drink, tobacco or vouchers exchangeable for goods.**
- Gifts to charities may also be allowed although many will fall foul of the 'wholly and exclusively' rule above. If a gift aid declaration is made in respect of a gift, tax relief will be given under the gift aid scheme, not as a trading expense.

2.3.8 Lease charges for expensive cars

Although leasing costs will normally be an allowable expense, there is a restriction for costs relating to expensive cars. **If the retail price of the car when new exceeds £12,000 the deductible part of any leasing charge is reduced by multiplying it by the fraction (£12,000 + RP) / 2RP, where RP is the retail price of the car.**

Thus for a car with a retail price of £20,000 and an annual leasing charge of £5,000 the allowable deduction is £5,000 × [(12,000 + 20,000)/2 × 20,000] = £4,000, so £1,000 of the charge is added back.

This restriction does not apply to low emission cars, ie those with carbon dioxide emissions not exceeding 120 g/km and electrically propelled cars.

2.3.9 Patent royalties and copyright royalties

Patent royalties and copyright royalties paid in connection with an individual's trade are deductible as trading expenses.

2.3.10 National insurance contributions

No deduction is allowed for any national insurance contributions **except for employer's contributions**. For your exam, these are Class 1 secondary contributions and Class 1A contributions (see later in this Text).

2.3.11 Penalties and interest on tax

Penalties and interest on late paid tax are not allowed as a trading expense. For the purpose of your exam, tax includes income tax, capital gains tax and VAT.

2.3.12 Appropriations

Salary or interest on capital paid to a proprietor are not deductible. A salary paid to a member of the traders family is allowed as long as it is not excessive in respect of the work performed by that family member.

The private proportion of payments for motoring expenses, rent, heat and light and telephone expenses of a proprietor is not deductible. Where the payments are to or on behalf of employees, the full amounts are deductible but are taxed on the employees as benefits for income tax.

Payments of the proprietor's income tax and national insurance contributions are not deductible.

Question — Adjusted taxable trade profits

Here is the profit and loss account of John Dodd, a trader.

PROFIT AND LOSS FOR THE YEAR ENDED 31 MAY 2007

	£	£
GROSS OPERATING PROFIT		30,000
Less: wages and salaries	7,000	
rent and rates	2,000	
depreciation	1,500	
motor expenses	5,000	
entertainment expenses – customers	750	
office expenses	1,350	
		(17,600)
NET PROFIT		12,400

You ascertain the following:

(a) Salaries include £1,000 paid to John Dodd's wife who works part time in the business.

(b) Motor expenses are £3,000 for John Dodd's car used 20% privately and £2,000 for his part-time salesman's car used 40% privately.

(c) There are also capital allowances of £860.

What is the adjusted taxable trade profit for the year ended 31 May 2007?

Answer

ADJUSTED PROFIT COMPUTATION: John Dodd
YEAR TO 31 MAY 2007

	£	£
Profit per accounts		12,400
Add: depreciation	1,500	
proprietor private motor expenses (£3,000 × 20%)	600	
entertainment expenses	750	
		2,850
		15,250
Deduct:		
Capital allowances		(860)
Adjusted trading profit		14,390

Note. The employee's private motor expenses are allowable for the trader but the provision of the car will be taxed on the employee as an income tax benefit. The salary paid to John Dodd's wife is allowed as it is reasonable remuneration for the work actually done.

2.3.13 Subscriptions and donations

The general 'wholly and exclusively' rule determines the deductibility of expenses. Subscriptions and donations are not deductible unless the expenditure is for the benefit of the trade. The following are the main types of subscriptions and donations you may meet and their correct treatments.

- Trade subscriptions (such as to a professional or trade association) are generally deductible.
- Charitable donations are deductible only if they are small and to local charities.
- Political subscriptions and donations are generally not deductible.
- When a business makes a gift of equipment manufactured, sold or used in the course of its trade to an educational establishment or for a charitable purpose, nothing need be brought into account as a trading receipt.

2.3.14 Legal and professional charges

Legal and professional charges relating to capital or non-trading items are not deductible. These include charges incurred in acquiring new capital assets or legal rights, issuing shares, drawing up partnership agreements and litigating disputes over the terms of a partnership agreement.

Professional charges are deductible if they relate directly to trading. Deductible items include:

- Legal and professional charges incurred defending the taxpayer's title to fixed assets
- Charges connected with an action for breach of contract
- Expenses of the **renewal** (not the original grant) of a lease for less than 50 years
- Charges for trade debt collection
- Normal charges for preparing accounts/assisting with the self assessment of tax liabilities

Accountancy expenses arising out of an enquiry into the accounts information in a particular year's return are not allowed where the enquiry reveals discrepancies and additional liabilities for the year of enquiry, or any earlier year, which arise as a result of negligent or fraudulent conduct.

Where, however, the enquiry results in no addition to profits, or an adjustment to the profits for the year of enquiry only and that assessment does not arise as a result of negligent or fraudulent conduct, the additional accountancy expenses are allowable.

2.3.15 Interest

Interest paid by an individual on borrowings for trade purposes is deductible as a trading expense on an accruals basis, so no adjustment to the accounts figure is needed.

Individuals cannot deduct interest on overdue tax.

2.3.16 Miscellaneous deductions

Here is a list of various other items that you may meet.

Item	Treatment	Comment
Educational courses for staff	Allow	
Educational courses for proprietor	Allow	If to update existing knowledge or skills, not if to acquire new knowledge or skills
Removal expenses (to new business premises)	Allow	Only if not an expansionary move
Travelling expenses to the trader's place of business	Disallow	*Ricketts v Colquhoun 1925*: unless an itinerant trader (*Horton v Young 1971*)
Counselling services for employees leaving employment	Allow	If qualify for exemption from employment income charge on employees
Pension contributions (to schemes for employees and company directors)	Allow	If paid, not if only provided for; special contributions may be spread over the year of payment and future years
Premiums for insurance: • against an employee's death or illness • to cover locum costs or fixed overheads whilst the policyholder is ill	Allow	Receipts are taxable
Damages paid	Allow	If not too remote from trade: *Strong and Co v Woodifield 1906*
Improving an individual's personal security	Allow	Provision of a car, ship or dwelling is excluded

2.4 Income taxable as trading income but excluded from the accounts

The usual example is when a proprietor takes goods for his own use. In such circumstances the normal selling price of the goods is added to the accounting profit. In other words, the proprietor is treated for tax purposes as having made a sale to himself (*Sharkey v Wernher 1955*) (you do not need to know this case name). This rule does not apply to supplies of services, which are treated as sold for the amount (if any) actually paid (but the cost of services to the trader or his household is not deductible).

2.5 Accounting profits not taxable as trading income

FAST FORWARD

Receipts not taxable as trading profit must be deducted from the accounts profit. For example, rental income and interest received are not taxable as trading profit. The rental income is taxed instead as property business income, whilst the interest is taxed as savings income.

There are three types of receipts which may be found in the accounting profits but which must be excluded from the taxable trading profit computation. These are:

(a) **Capital receipts**
(b) **Income taxed in another way** (at source or as another type of income)
(c) **Income specifically exempt from tax**

However, compensation received in one lump sum for the loss of income is likely to be treated as income (*Donald Fisher (Ealing) Ltd v Spencer 1989*).

Income taxed as another type of income, for example rental income, is excluded from the computation of taxable trading profits but it is brought in again further down in the computation as property business income. Similarly capital receipts are excluded from the computation of taxable trading profits but they may be included in the computation of chargeable gains (see later in this Text).

2.6 Deductible expenditure not charged in the accounts

FAST FORWARD

Amounts not charged in the accounts that are deductible from trading profits must be deducted when computing the taxable trading income. An example is capital allowances.

Capital allowances (see the next chapter) **are** an example of **deductible expenditure not charged in the accounts.**

A second example is **an annual sum** which can be deducted by a trader that has paid **a lease premium to a landlord who is taxable on the premium as property business income** (see earlier in this Text). Normally, the amortisation of the lease will have been deducted in the accounts and must be added back as an appropriation of profit.

Question **Adjustment of profits**

Here is the profit and loss account of S Pring, a trader.

	£	£
Gross operating profit		30,000
Taxed interest received		860
		30,860
Wages and salaries	7,000	
Rent and rates	2,000	
Depreciation	1,500	
Impairment of trade receivables	150	
Entertainment expenses	750	
Patent royalties	1,200	
Bank interest	300	
Legal expenses on acquisition of new factory	250	
		(13,150)
Net profit		17,710

(a) Salaries include £500 paid to Mrs Pring who works full time in the business.
(b) No staff were entertained.
(c) Taxed interest and patent royalties were received and paid net but have been shown gross.

Compute the taxable trade profits.

Answer

	£	£
Profit per accounts		17,710
Add: depreciation	1,500	
entertainment expenses	750	
legal expenses (capital)	250	
		2,500
		20,210
Less interest received (to tax as taxed income)		(860)
Taxable trading profit		19,350

3 Pre-trading expenditure

Pre-trading expenditure incurred within the seven years prior to the commencement of trade is allowable if it would have been allowable had the trade already started.

Expenditure incurred before the commencement of trade is deductible, if it is incurred within seven years of the start of trade and it is of a type that would have been deductible had the trade already started. **It is treated as a trading expense incurred on the first day of trading**.

Chapter Roundup

- The badges of trade are used to decide whether or not a trade exists. If one does exist, the accounts profits need to be adjusted in order to establish the taxable profits.
- The net profit in the profit and loss account must be adjusted to find the taxable trading profit.
- Disallowable (ie non-deductible) expenditure must be added back to the accounts profit in the computation of the taxable trading profit. Any item not deducted wholly and exclusively for trade purposes is disallowable expenditure. Certain other items, such as depreciation, are specifically disallowable.
- Receipts not taxable as trading profit must be deducted from the accounts profit. For example, rental income and interest received are not taxable as trading profit. The rental income is taxed instead as property business income, whilst the interest is taxed as savings income.
- Amounts not charged in the accounts that are deductible from trading profits must be deducted when computing the taxable trading income. An example is capital allowances.
- Pre-trading expenditure incurred within the seven years prior to the commencement of trade is allowable if it would have been allowable had the trade already started.

Quick Quiz

1 List the traditional badges of trade.

2 What are the remoteness test and the duality test?

3 Is any adjustment required for the proprietor's salary?

4 What pre-trading expenditure is deductible?

Answers to Quick Quiz

1 The subject matter
The frequency of transactions
The length of ownership
Supplementary work and marketing
A profit motive
The way in which the goods were acquired

2 Expenditure is not deductible if it is not for trade purposes (the remoteness test), or if it reflects more than one purpose (the duality test).

3 The proprietor's salary must be added back as it is an appropriation of profits.

4 Pre-trading expenditure is deductible if it is incurred within seven years of the start of the trade and is of a type that would have been deductible if the trade had already started.

Now try the questions below from the Exam Question Bank

Number	Level	Marks	Time
Q9	Examination	15	27 mins

Capital allowances

Topic list	Syllabus reference
1 Capital allowances in general	B3(g)
2 Plant and machinery – qualifying expenditure	B3(g)(i)
3 Allowances on plant and machinery	B3(g)(ii)-(iv)
4 Short-life assets	B3(g)(v)
5 Long life assets	B3(g)(vi)
6 Industrial buildings – types	B3(g)(vii)
7 Allowances on industrial buildings	B3(g)(viii),(ix)

Introduction

We saw in the last chapter that depreciation cannot be deducted in computing taxable trade profits and that capital allowances are given instead. In this chapter, we look at the rules for calculating capital allowances, starting with plant and machinery.

Our study of plant and machinery falls into three parts. Firstly, we look at what qualifies for allowances: many business assets obtain no allowances at all. Secondly, we see how to compute the allowances and lastly, we look at special rules for assets with short and long lives.

We then look at industrial buildings. Again, we start off by looking at what qualifies for the allowances and then how to compute the allowances.

You may wish to return to this chapter while you are studying Chapter 19 on companies.

Study guide

		Intellectual level
B3	**Income from self-employment**	
(g)	Capital allowances	
(i)	Define plant and machinery for capital allowances purposes.	1
(ii)	Compute writing down allowances and first year allowances.	2
(iii)	Compute capital allowances for motor cars.	2
(iv)	Compute balancing allowances and balancing charges.	2
(v)	Recognise the treatment of short life assets.	2
(vi)	Explain the treatment of long life assets.	2
(vii)	Define an industrial building for industrial buildings allowance purposes.	1
(viii)	Compute industrial buildings allowance for new and second-hand buildings.	2
(ix)	Compute the balancing adjustment on the disposal of an industrial building.	2

Exam guide

You may have to answer a whole question on capital allowances or a capital allowances computation may be included as a working in a computation of taxable trading profits. The computation may be for either income tax or corporation tax purposes; the principle is basically the same. Look out for private use assets; only restrict the capital allowances if there is private use by **proprietors**, never restrict capital allowances for private use by **employees**. Also watch out for the length of the period of account; you may need to scale WDAs up (income tax only) or down (income tax or corporation tax).

1 Capital allowances in general

FAST FORWARD

Capital allowances are available to give tax relief for certain capital expenditure.

Capital expenditure may not be deducted in computing taxable trade profits, but it *may* attract capital allowances. Capital allowances are treated as a trading expense and are deducted in arriving at taxable trade profits. Balancing charges, effectively negative allowances, are added in arriving at those profits.

Capital expenditure on plant and machinery qualifies for capital allowances. Expenditure on industrial buildings may also qualify for allowances.

Both in incorporated businesses and companies are entitled to capital allowances. For completeness, in this chapter we will look at the rules for companies alongside those for unincorporated businesses. We will look at companies in more detail later in this Text.

For unincorporated businesses, capital allowances are calculated for periods of account. These are simply the periods for which the trader chooses to make up accounts. For companies, capital allowances are calculated for accounting periods. (See later in this Text.)

For capital allowances purposes, expenditure is generally deemed to be incurred when the obligation to pay becomes unconditional. This will often be the date of a contract, but if for example payment is due a month after delivery of a machine, it would be the date of delivery. However, amounts due more than four months after the obligation becomes unconditional are deemed to be incurred when they fall due.

2 Plant and machinery – qualifying expenditure

FAST FORWARD

Statutory rules generally exclude specified items from treatment as plant, rather than include specified items as plant.

2.1 Definition of plant and machinery

Capital expenditure on plant and machinery qualifies for capital allowances if the plant or machinery is used for a qualifying activity, such as a trade. 'Plant' is not defined by the legislation, although some specific exclusions and inclusions are given. The word 'machinery' may be taken to have its normal everyday meaning.

2.2 The statutory exclusions

2.2.1 Buildings

Expenditure on a building and on any asset which is incorporated in a building or is of a kind normally incorporated into buildings does not qualify as expenditure on plant, but see below for exceptions.

In addition to complete buildings, **the following assets count as 'buildings', and are therefore not plant**.

- Walls, floors, ceilings, doors, gates, shutters, windows and stairs
- Mains services, and systems, of water, electricity and gas
- Waste disposal, sewerage and drainage systems
- Shafts or other structures for lifts etc

2.2.2 Structures

Expenditure on structures and on works involving the alteration of land **does not qualify as expenditure on plant**, but see below for exceptions.

A 'structure' is a fixed structure of any kind, other than a building.

2.2.3 Exceptions

Over the years a large body of case law has been built up under which plant and machinery allowances have been given on certain types of expenditure which might be thought to be expenditure on a building or structure. Statute therefore gives a list of various assets which *may* still be plant. These include:

- Any machinery not within any other item in this list
- Electrical (including lighting), cold water, gas and sewerage systems:
  - Provided mainly to meet the particular requirements of the trade, or
  - Provided mainly to serve particular machinery or plant used for the purposes of the trade
- Space or water heating systems and powered systems of ventilation
- Manufacturing and display equipment
- Cookers, washing machines, refrigeration or cooling equipment, sanitary ware and furniture and furnishings
- Lifts etc
- Sound insulation provided mainly to meet the particular requirements of the trade
- Computer, telecommunication and surveillance systems

- Sprinkler equipment, fire alarm and burglar alarm systems
- Partition walls, where movable and intended to be moved
- Decorative assets provided for the enjoyment of the public in the hotel, restaurant or similar trades; advertising hoardings
- Movable buildings intended to be moved in the course of the trade
- Expenditure on altering land for the purpose only of installing machinery or plant

Items falling within the above list of exclusions will only qualify as plant if they fall within the meaning of plant as established by case law. This is discussed below.

2.2.4 Land

Land or an interest in land does not qualify as plant and machinery. For this purpose 'land' excludes buildings, structures and assets which are installed or fixed to land in such a way as to become part of the land for general legal purposes.

2.2.5 Computer software

Capital expenditure on computer software (both programs and data) **normally qualifies as expenditure on plant and machinery**.

2.3 Case law

FAST FORWARD

There are several cases on the definition of plant. To help you to absorb them, try to see the function/setting theme running through them.

Exam focus point

In this chapter we mention the names of cases where it was decided what was or wasn't 'plant'. You are **not** expected to know the names of cases for your examination. We have included them for your information only.

The original case law **definition of plant** (applied in this case to a horse) is **'whatever apparatus is used by a businessman for carrying on his business: not his stock in trade which he buys or makes for sale; but all goods and chattels, fixed or movable, live or dead, which he keeps for permanent employment in the business'** (*Yarmouth v France 1887*).

Subsequent cases have refined the original definition and have largely been concerned with the **distinction between plant actively used in the business (qualifying) and the setting in which the business is carried on (non-qualifying). This is the 'functional' test**. Some of the decisions have now been enacted as part of statute law, but they are still relevant as examples of the principles involved.

A barrister succeeded in his claim for his law library: 'Plant includes a man's tools of his trade. It extends to what he uses day by day in the course of his profession. It is not confined to physical things like the dentist's chair or the architect's table' (*Munby v Furlong 1977*).

Office partitioning was allowed. Because it was movable it was not regarded as part of the setting in which the business was carried on (*Jarrold v John Good and Sons Ltd 1963*) (actual item now covered by statute).

At a motorway service station, false ceilings contained conduits, ducts and lighting apparatus. **They did not qualify because they did not perform a function in the business. They were merely part of the setting in which the business was conducted** (*Hampton v Fortes Autogrill Ltd 1979*).

Similarly, it has been held that when an attractive floor is provided in a restaurant, the fact that the floor performs the function of making the restaurant attractive to customers is not enough to make it plant. It functions as premises, and the cost therefore does not qualify for capital allowances (*Wimpy International Ltd v Warland 1988*).

Conversely, light fittings, decor and murals can be plant. A company carried on business as hoteliers and operators of licensed premises. The function of the items was the creation of an atmosphere conducive to the comfort and well being of its customers (*CIR v Scottish and Newcastle Breweries Ltd 1982*) (decorative assets used in hotels etc, now covered by statute).

General lighting in a department store is not plant, as it is merely setting. Special display lighting, however, can be plant (*Cole Brothers Ltd v Phillips 1982*).

3 Allowances on plant and machinery

3.1 Pooling expenditure

Most expenditure on plant and machinery is put into a pool of expenditure on which capital allowances may be claimed. An addition increases the pool whilst a disposal decreases it.

Exceptionally the following items are not pooled.

(a) cars costing more than £12,000
(b) assets with private use by the proprietor
(c) short life assets where an election has been made.

Each of these items is dealt with in further detail below.

3.2 Writing down allowances

FAST FORWARD

Most expenditure on plant and machinery qualifies for a WDA at 25% every 12 months.

Key term

A **writing down allowance (WDA)** is given on pooled expenditure **at the rate of 25% a year** (on a reducing balance basis). The WDA is calculated on the tax written down value (TWDV) of pooled plant, after adding the current period's additions and taking out the current period's disposals.

When plant is sold, proceeds (but **limited to a maximum of the original cost**) are taken out of the pool. Provided that the trade is still being carried on, the pool balance remaining is written down in the future by WDAs, even if there are no assets left.

3.3 Example

Elizabeth has a balance of unrelieved expenditure on her general pool of plant and machinery of £16,000 on 1.4.07. In the year to 31.3.08 she bought a car for £8,000 and she disposed of plant which originally cost £4,000 for £6,000.

Calculate the capital allowances available for the year.

	£
Pool value b/f	16,000
Addition	8,000
Less disposal (limited to cost)	(4,000)
	20,000
WDA @ 25%	(5,000)
TWDV c/f	15,000

WDAs are 25% × number of months/12:

(a) For unincorporated businesses where the period of account is longer or shorter than 12 months

(b) For companies where the accounting period is shorter than 12 months (a company's accounting period for tax purposes is never longer than 12 months), or where the trade concerned started in the accounting period and was therefore carried on for fewer than 12 months. Remember that we will be studying companies in detail later in this Text.

Expenditure on plant and machinery by a person about to begin a trade is treated as incurred on the first day of trading. Assets previously owned by a trader and then brought into the trade (at the start of trading or later) are treated as bought for their market values at the times when they are brought in.

3.4 First year allowances

FAST FORWARD

Small and medium sized businesses are entitled to first year allowances (FYA) on certain expenditure. FYAs are available to all businesses for expenditure on low emission cars. FYAs are never pro-rated in short periods of account.

3.4.1 Spending by medium sized enterprises

Expenditure incurred on plant and machinery (other than leased assets, cars, sea going ships, railway assets or long life assets) by **medium sized enterprises qualifies for a first year allowance (FYA) of 40%.**

Exam focus point

The rates of FYAs will be given to you on the exam paper.

Key term

A **medium sized enterprise** is a company that either satisfies at least two of the following conditions in the period of account in which the expenditure is incurred.

(a) **Turnover not more than £22.8 million**
(b) **Assets not more than £11.4 million**
(c) **Not more than 250 employees**

or which was medium sized in the previous period. A company must not be a member of a large group when the expenditure is incurred.

3.4.2 Spending by small sized enterprises

Expenditure incurred on plant and machinery by small sized enterprises **qualifies for a FYA of 40%** in the same way as for medium sized enterprises. This rate has been **increased from 40% to 50% for expenditure on or after 1 April 2006 for two years.**

Key term

A **small enterprise** is a company which satisfies at least two of the following conditions in the period of account in which the expenditure is incurred:

(a) **Turnover not more than £5.6 million**
(b) **Assets not more than £2.8 million**
(c) **Not more than 50 employees**

or which was small in the previous period. If a company is a member of a group, the group must also be small when the expenditure is incurred.

3.4.3 100% FYAs

A 100% FYA is available to all businesses for expenditure incurred on low emission motor cars registered between 17 April 2002 and 31 March 2008. These cars are included in the general pool of expenditure.

Exam focus point

In exam questions you should only treat motor cars as low emission cars if they are specifically described as such. The fact that a car is low emission will always be stated in an exam question.

3.4.4 Calculation

FAST FORWARD

With capital allowances computations, the main thing is to get the layout right. Having done that, you will find that the figures tend to drop into place.

For FYA purposes, the provisions which treat capital expenditure incurred prior to the commencement of trading as incurred on the first day of trading do not apply except insofar as they require the FYAs to be given in the first period of account (or accounting period for companies). The availability and rate of FYA depend on the date on which the expenditure was actually incurred.

First year allowances are given in the place of writing down allowances. For subsequent years a WDA is given on the balance of expenditure at the normal rate. You should therefore transfer the balance of the expenditure to the pool at the end of the first period.

FYAs are given for incurring expenditure. It is irrelevant whether the basis period of expenditure is twelve months or not. **FYAs are never scaled up or down by reference to the length of the period.**

Question

Capital allowances

Walton starts a trade on 1 March 2005, and has the following results (before capital allowances).

Period of account	*Profits*
	£
1.3.05 – 31.7.05	42,500
1.8.05 – 31.7.06	36,800
1.8.06 – 31.7.07	32,000

Plant (none of which is eligible for 100% FYAs) is bought as follows.

Date	*Cost*
	£
1.5.05	13,000
1.6.05	9,500
1.5.06	4,000
1.6.07	1,600

On 1 May 2006, plant which cost £7,000 is sold for £4,000.

Walton's business is a small enterprise for FYA purposes.

Show the taxable trade profits arising in the above periods of account.

Answer

The capital allowances are as follows.

	FYA £	*Pool* £	*Allowances* £
1.3.05 – 31.7.05			
Additions (1.5.05 and 1.6.05)	22,500		
FYA 40%	(9,000)		9,000
		13,500	
1.8.05 – 31.7.06			
Disposals (1.5.06)		(4,000)	
		9,500	
WDA 25%		(2,375)	2,375
		7,125	
Addition (1.5.06)	4,000		
FYA 50%	(2,000)		2,000
		2,000	4,375
		9,125	
1.8.06 – 31.7.07			
WDA 25%		(2,281)	2,281
		6,844	
Addition (1.6.07)	1,600		
FYA 50%	(800)		800
		800	
TWDV c/f		7,644	
			3,081

Note. First year allowances are not pro-rated in a short period of account.

The profits of the first three periods of account are as follows.

Period of account	*Working*	*Profits* £
1.3.05 – 31.7.05	£(42,500 – 9,000)	33,500
1.8.05 – 31.7.06	£(36,800 – 4,375)	32,425
1.8.06 – 31.7.07	£(32,000 – 3,081)	28,919

Exam focus point

Note the tax planning opportunities available. It may be important to buy plant just before an accounting date, so that allowances become available as soon as possible. Alternatively, it may be desirable to claim less than the maximum allowances to even out annual taxable profits and avoid higher rate tax in later years.

3.5 The disposal value of assets

The most common disposal value at which assets are entered in a capital allowances computation is the sale proceeds.

There is an overriding rule that the capital allowances **disposal value cannot exceed the original purchase price.**

When a building is sold, the vendor and purchaser can make a joint election to determine how the sale proceeds are apportioned between the building and its fixtures. There are anti-avoidance provisions that ensure capital allowances given overall on a fixture do not exceed the original cost of the fixture.

3.6 Balancing charges and allowances

Balancing charges occur when the disposal value deducted exceeds the balance remaining in the pool. The charge equals the excess and is effectively a negative capital allowance, increasing profits. Most commonly this happens when the trade ceases and the remaining assets are sold. It may also occur, however, whilst the trade is still in progress.

Balancing allowances on the capital allowance pools of expenditure arise only when the trade ceases. The balancing allowance is equal to the remaining unrelieved expenditure after deducting the disposal value of all the assets. Balancing allowances may also arise on items which are not pooled (see below) whenever those items are disposed of.

3.7 Motor cars

FAST FORWARD

Motor cars costing more than £12,000 are not pooled, and the maximum WDA is £3,000 for a 12 month period.

Motor cars costing more than £12,000 are not pooled (whereas motor cars costing £12,000 or less are included in the general pool of expenditure). A separate record of allowances and WDV must be kept for each such car, and when it is sold a balancing allowance or charge arises.

The maximum WDA on an 'expensive' motor car is £3,000 a year. The limit is £3,000 × months/12 in periods of account which are not 12 months long.

FYAs are not available on cars (except for certain low emission cars which are included in the general pool – see above).

3.8 Private use assets

FAST FORWARD

Assets which are used privately by proprietors are not pooled and the capital allowances are restricted.

An asset (for example, a car) which is used partly for private purposes by a sole trader or a partner is not pooled.

Capital allowances must be calculated on the full cost but only the business use proportion of the allowances is allowed as a deduction from trading profits. This restriction applies to FYAs, WDAs, balancing allowances and balancing charges.

An asset with some private use by an employee (not a proprietor), however, suffers no such restriction. The employee may be taxed under the benefits code (see earlier in this Text) so the business receives capital allowances on the full cost of the asset.

Exam focus point

Capital allowances on assets with some private use is a common exam topic. Check carefully whether the private use is by the proprietor or by an employee.

Question — **Capital allowances on a car**

Quodos started to trade on 1 July 2004, making up accounts to 31 December 2004 and each 31 December thereafter. On 1 August 2004 he bought a car for £15,500 for business use. The private use proportion is 10%. The car was sold in July 2007 for £4,000. What are the capital allowances, assuming:

(a) The car was used by an employee, or
(b) The car was used by Quodos.

Answer

(a)

	Car	Allowances
	£	£
1.7.04 – 31.12.04		
Purchase price	15,500	
WDA 25% × 6/12 of £15,500 = £1,938, Limited to £3,000 × 6/12 = £1,500	(1,500)	1,500
	14,000	
1.1.05 – 31.12.05		
WDA 25% of £14,000 = £3,500, Limited to £3,000	(3,000)	3,000
	11,000	
1.1.06 – 31.12.06		
WDA 25% of £11,000	(2,750)	2,750
	8,250	
1.1.07 – 31.12.07		
Proceeds	(4,000)	
Balancing allowance	4,250	4,250

The private use of the car by the employee has no effect on the capital allowances due to Quodos.

(b)

	Car	Allowances
		90%
	£	£
1.7.04– 31.12.04		
Purchase price	15,500	
WDA 25% × 6/12 of £15,500 = £1,938 Limited to £3,000 × 6/12 = £1,500	(1,500)	1,350
	14,000	
1.1.05 – 31.12.05		
WDA 25% of £14,000 = £3,500, Limited to £3,000	(3,000)	2,700
	11,000	
1.1.06 – 31.12.06		
WDA 25% of £11,000	(2,750)	2,475
	8,250	
1.1.07 – 31.12.07		
Proceeds	(4,000)	
Balancing allowance	4,250	3,825

As the private use is by the proprietor, Quodos, only 90% of the WDAs and balancing allowance are available. Note that the private use restriction is made **after** the restriction of the WDA to £3,000pa for an expensive car.

3.9 The cessation of a trade

When a company ceases to trade no FYAs or WDAs are given in the final accounting period. Each asset is deemed to be disposed of on the date the trade ceased (usually at the then market value). Additions in the relevant period are brought in and then the disposal proceeds (limited to cost) are deducted from the balance of qualifying expenditure. If the proceeds exceed the balance then a balancing charge arises. If the balance of qualifying expenditure exceeds the proceeds then a balancing allowance is given.

4 Short-life assets

FAST FORWARD

Short life asset elections can bring forward the allowances due on an asset.

A trader can elect that specific items of plant be kept separately from the general pool. The election is irrevocable. For an unincorporated business, the time limit for electing is the 31 January which is 22 months after the end of the tax year in which the period of account of the expenditure ends. (For a company, it is two years after the end of the accounting period of the expenditure.) **Any asset subject to this election is known as a 'short-life asset', and the election is known as a 'de-pooling election'.**

Key term

Provided that the asset is disposed of within four years of the end of the accounting period in which it was bought, it is a **short life asset** and a balancing charge or allowance arises on its disposal.

If the asset is not disposed of in the correct time period, its tax written down value is added to the general pool at the end of that time.

The election should be made for assets likely to be sold for less than their tax written down values within four years. It should not be made for assets likely to be sold within four years for more than their tax written down values. (These are, of course, only general guidelines based on the assumption that a trader will want to obtain allowances as quickly as possible. There may be other considerations, such as a desire to even out annual taxable profits.)

Question — Short life assets

Caithlin bought an asset on 1 May 2003 for £12,000 and elected for de-pooling. Her accounting year end is 30 April. Calculate the capital allowances due if:

(a) The asset is scrapped for £300 in August 2007.
(b) The asset is scrapped for £200 in August 2008.

Answer

(a)

	£
Year to 30.4.04	
Cost	12,000
WDA 25%	(3,000)
	9,000
Year to 30.4.05	
WDA 25%	(2,250)
	6,750
Year to 30.4.06	
WDA 25%	(1,688)
	5,062
Year to 30.4.07	
WDA 25%	(1,266)
	3,796
Year to 30.4.08	
Disposal proceeds	(300)
Balancing allowance	3,496

(b) If the asset is still in use at 30 April 2008, a WDA of 25% × £3,796 = £949 would be claimable in the year to 30 April 2008. The tax written down value of £3,796 – £949 = £2,847 would be added to the general pool at the beginning of the next period of account. The disposal proceeds of £200 would be deducted from the general pool in that period's capital allowances computation. No balancing allowance will arise and the general pool will continue.

Short-life asset treatment cannot be claimed for motor cars or plant used partly for non-trade purposes.

Where a short-life asset is disposed of within the four year period to a connected person (broadly spouses/civil partners and their relatives, relatives and their spouses/civil partners, business partners and their spouses/civil partners and companies under the same control):

(a) The original owner receives a balancing allowance calculated as normal and the new owner receives WDAs on the cost to him, but

(b) **If both parties so elect, the asset is treated as being sold for its tax written down value at the start of the chargeable period in which the transfer takes place, so there is no balancing charge or allowance for the vendor.**

In both situations, the acquiring party will continue to 'de-pool' the asset up to the same date as the original owner would have done.

5 Long life assets

Key term

Long life assets are assets with an expected working life of 25 years or more.

The writing down allowance available on such assets is 6% per annum on a reducing balance basis. Expenditure on such assets must be kept in a pool that is separate from the general pool.

The following are not **treated as long life assets:**

(a) **Plant and machinery in dwelling houses, retail shops, showrooms, hotels and offices**
(b) **Motor cars**

The **long life asset rules do not apply to businesses whose total expenditure on long life assets in a chargeable period is £100,000**, or less. If the expenditure exceeds £100,000, the whole of the expenditure qualifies for allowances at 6% per annum only. For this purpose all expenditure incurred under a contract is treated as incurred in the first chargeable period to which that contract relates.

The £100,000 limit is reduced or increased proportionately in the case of a chargeable period of less or more than 12 months. In the case of groups of companies, the limit must be divided between the number of associated companies in the group (see later in this Text).

The £100,000 exclusion is not available in respect of leased assets, second-hand assets where the vendor was only able to claim allowances of 6%, or assets where the trader has only bought a share.

6 Industrial buildings – types

FAST FORWARD

Industrial buildings allowances broadly equal to the fall in value of the building whilst it was being used industrially are available to the trader.

Exam focus point

Remember, you do not need to know the case names below. They are included for information only.

6.1 General definition

A special type of capital allowance (an **industrial buildings allowance** or IBA) is available in respect of **expenditure on industrial buildings**. It is being phased out over the next few years and will be abolished from 2010/11.

The allowance is available to:

- Traders
- Landlords who let qualifying buildings to traders.

Traders can choose whether to segregate expenditure on long life assets in buildings and claim plant and machinery allowances (see above) or whether to claim industrial buildings allowances on the expenditure. Since the industrial buildings allowance is being phased out it will be better to claim plant and machinery allowances in such a case.

Key term

Industrial buildings include:

(a) All factories and ancillary premises used in:

  (i) A manufacturing business
  (ii) A trade in which goods and materials are subject to any process
  (iii) A trade in which goods or raw materials are stored

(b) Staff welfare buildings (such as workplace nurseries and canteens, but not directors' restaurants) where the trade is qualifying

(c) Sports pavilions in any trade

(d) Buildings in use for a transport undertaking, agricultural contracting, mining or fishing

(e) Roads operated under highway concessions. The operation of such roads is treated as a trade for capital allowances purposes. The operator is treated as occupying the roads.

The key term in (a) (ii) above is 'the subjection of goods to any process'.

- The unpacking, repacking and relabelling of goods in a wholesale cash and carry supermarket did not amount to a 'process' but was a mere preliminary to sale (*Bestway Holdings Ltd v Luff 1998*).
- The mechanical processing of cheques and other banking documents was a process but pieces of paper carrying information were not 'goods' and thus the building housing the machinery did not qualify (*Girobank plc v Clarke 1998*).

Estate roads on industrial estates qualify, provided that the estate buildings are used wholly or mainly for a qualifying purpose.

Dwelling houses, retail shops, showrooms and offices are not industrial buildings.

Warehouses used for storage often cause problems in practice. A warehouse used for storage which is merely a transitory and necessary incident of the conduct of the business is not an industrial building. Storage is only a qualifying purpose if it is an end in itself.

Any building is an industrial building if it is constructed for the welfare of employees of a trader whose trade is a qualifying one (that is, the premises in which the trade is carried on are industrial buildings).

Sports pavilions provided for the welfare of employees qualify as industrial buildings. In this case, it does not matter whether the taxpayer is carrying on a trade in a qualifying building or not. Thus a retailer's sports pavilion would qualify for IBAs.

Drawing offices (is those used for technical product and manufacturing planning) which serve an industrial building are regarded as industrial buildings themselves (*CIR v Lambhill Ironworks Ltd 1950*).

6.2 Hotels

Allowances on hotels are given as though they were industrial buildings.

Key term

For a building to qualify as a '**hotel**' for industrial buildings allowance purposes:

(a) It must have at least ten letting bedrooms

(b) It must have letting bedrooms as the whole or main part of the sleeping accommodation

(c) It must offer ancillary services including at least:

 (i) Breakfast
 (ii) Evening meals
 (iii) The cleaning of rooms
 (iv) The making of beds

(d) It must be open for at least four months during the April to October season.

6.3 Eligible expenditure

Allowances are computed on the amount of eligible expenditure incurred on qualifying buildings. The eligible expenditure is:

- The original cost of a building if built by the trader, or
- The purchase price if the building was acquired from a person trading as a builder.

If the building was acquired other than from a person trading as a builder, the eligible expenditure is the lower of the purchase price and the original cost incurred by the person incurring the construction expenditure.

If a building is sold more than once before being brought into use, the last buyer before the building is brought into use obtains the allowances. If, in such cases, the building was first sold by someone trading as a builder, the eligible expenditure is the lower of the price paid by the first buyer and the price paid by the last buyer.

In all cases where a building is sold before use and artificial arrangements have increased the purchase price, it is reduced to what it would have been without those arrangements.

Where part of a building qualifies as an industrial building and part does not, the whole cost qualifies for IBAs, provided that the cost of the non-qualifying part is not more than 25% of the total expenditure. If the non-qualifying part of the building does cost more than 25% of the total, its cost must be excluded from the capital allowances computation.

Difficulties arise where non-qualifying buildings (particularly offices and administration blocks) are joined to manufacturing areas. In *Abbott Laboratories Ltd v Carmody 1968* a covered walkway linking manufacturing and administrative areas was not regarded as creating a single building. The administrative area was treated as a separate, non-qualifying building.

The cost of land is disallowed but expenditure incurred in preparing land for building does qualify. The cost of items which would not be included in a normal commercial lease (such as rental guarantees) also does not qualify.

Professional fees, for example architects' fees, incurred in connection with the construction of an industrial building qualify. The cost of repairs to industrial buildings also qualifies, provided that the expenditure is not deductible as a trading expense.

IBAs: eligible expenditure

Sue purchased an industrial building for £2,500,000. This cost was made up of:

	£
Factory	2,100,000
Land	400,000
	2,500,000

The costs attributable to showrooms and offices within the factory were £400,000 and £200,000 respectively.

What is the expenditure qualifying for industrial buildings allowances?

Answer

The showrooms and offices are non-qualifying parts of the building. As the cost of the non qualifying parts, £600,000, is more than 25% of the total expenditure on the building (£2,100,000), industrial buildings allowances are not available on it. The cost of the land is not qualifying expenditure.

The qualifying expenditure for industrial buildings allowance purposes is therefore £1,500,000 (£2,100,000 – £600,000).

7 Allowances on industrial buildings

FAST FORWARD

An allowance, normally at the rate of 4% per annum, is given if a building is in industrial use on the last day of the period of account concerned.

7.1 Writing down allowances

A writing down allowance (WDA) is given to the person holding the 'relevant interest'. Broadly, the relevant interest is the interest of the first acquirer of the industrial building and may be a freehold or leasehold interest.

Where a long lease (more than 50 years) has been granted on an industrial building, the grant may be treated as a sale so that allowances may be claimed by the lessee rather than the lessor. A claim must be made by the lessor and lessee jointly, within two years of the start of the lease. The election allows allowances to be claimed on industrial buildings where the lessor is not subject to tax (as with local authorities).

The WDA is given for a period provided that the industrial building was in use as such on the last day of the period concerned.

If the building was not in use as an industrial building at the end of the relevant period it may have been:

- **Unused** for any purpose, or
- **Used for a non-industrial purpose.**

The distinction is important in ascertaining whether WDAs are due to the taxpayer. **If any disuse is temporary and previously the building had been in industrial use, WDAs may be claimed in exactly the same way as if the building were in industrial use.** The legislation does not define 'temporary' but in practice, any subsequent qualifying use of the building will usually enable the period of disuse to be regarded as temporary.

Non-industrial use has different consequences. If this occurs a notional WDA is deducted from the balance of unrelieved expenditure but no WDA may be claimed by the taxpayer.

The WDA is 4% of the eligible expenditure incurred by the taxpayer.

The allowance is calculated on a straight line basis (in contrast to WDAs on plant and machinery which are calculated on the reducing balance), starting when the building is brought into use.

The WDA is 4% × months/12 if the period concerned is not 12 months long.

Buildings always have a **separate computation for each building**. They are never pooled.

7.2 Sales of industrial buildings

7.2.1 First users – position on sale

Until 21 March 2007, the disposal of an industrial building gave rise to a balancing adjustment (ie a balancing change or a balancing allowance).

In preparation for the eventual abolition of industrial buildings allowance, **no balancing adjustments apply for disposals from 21 March 2007 onwards**.

Exam focus point

From the June 2008 sitting onwards the examiner has stated that questions will not be set involving a balancing adjustment on the sale of an industrial building, the calculation of the writing down allowance for the purchaser of a second-hand industrial building prior to 21 March 2007 or the calculation of the writing down allowance following a period of non-industrial use.

7.2.2 Second-hand users

The buyer obtains annual straight line WDAs for the remainder of the building's tax life (25 years after it is first used). This life is calculated to the nearest month. The allowances are granted on the residue before sale which is computed thus.

	£
Cost	X
Less allowances previously given	(X)
Residue before sale (ie WDV)	X

7.2.3 Example

Lipatti Ltd bought an industrial building for £180,000 on 1 November 2000 and brought it into use immediately. It sold the building on 1 November 2007 for £150,000 to Kapell plc who brought the building into industrial use immediately. Both companies make up accounts to 31 March each year. The IBA available to Kapell plc for the year ending 31 March 2008 is calculated as follows:

	£
Cost 1.11.00	180,000
Y/e 31.3.01 to y/e 31.3.07	
WDA £180,000 × 4% = £7,200 × 7	(50,400)
Residue before sale	129,600

Tax life of the building ends on 1.11.00 + 25 years = 31.10.25

The date of Kapell plc's purchase is 1.11.07

The unexpired life is therefore 18 years

Kapell plc's WDA for y/e 31 March 2008 is therefore

£129,600 / 18	7,200

You will see that the WDA for Kapell plc is the same as for Lipatti Ltd. This is because there is a whole number of years of the tax life remaining at the date of sale.

Question

Calculation of IBAs

Frankie started to trade in 2002 preparing accounts to 31 December and bought an industrial building for £100,000 (excluding land) on 1 October 2003. He brought it into use as a factory immediately. On 1 September 2007 he sells it for £120,000 to Holly, whose accounting date is 30 September and who brought the building into industrial use immediately. Show the IBA available to Holly for the year to 30 September 2007.

Answer

	£
Cost 1.10.03	100,000
Y/e 31.12.03 to y/e 31.12.06 WDA 4 × 4%	(16,000)
Residue before sale	84,000

The tax life of the building ends on 1.10.03 + 25 years = 30.9.2028
The date of Holly's purchase is 1.9.07
The unexpired life is therefore 21 years 1 month

Y/e 30.9.07 WDA £84,000/21.083333	£3,984

Chapter Roundup

- Capital allowances are available to give tax relief for certain capital expenditure.
- Statutory rules generally exclude specified items from treatment as plant, rather than include specified items as plant.
- There are several cases on the definition of plant. To help you to absorb them, try to see the function/setting theme running through them.
- Most expenditure on plant and machinery qualifies for a WDA at 25% every 12 months.
- Small and medium sized businesses are entitled to first year allowances (FYA) on certain expenditure. FYA are available to all businesses for expenditure on low emission cars. FYAs are never pro-rated in short periods of account.
- With capital allowances computations, the main thing is to get the layout right. Having done that, you will find that the figures tend to drop into place.
- Motor cars costing more than £12,000 are not pooled, and the maximum WDA is £3,000 for a 12 month period.
- Assets which are used privately by proprietors are not pooled and the capital allowances are restricted.
- Short life asset elections can bring forward the allowances due on an asset.
- Industrial buildings allowances broadly equal to the fall in value of the building whilst it was being used industrially are available to the trader.
- An allowance, normally at the rate of 4% per annum, is given if a building is in industrial use on the last day of the period of account concerned.

Quick Quiz

1. Are writing down allowances pro-rated in a six month period of account?
2. Are first year allowances pro-rated in a six month period of account?
3. When may balancing allowances arise?
4. Within what period must an asset be disposed of if it is to be treated as a short life asset?
5. List four types of building which do not usually qualify for industrial buildings allowance.
6. When are drawing offices industrial buildings?
7. What are the conditions for a hotel to qualify for allowances?
8. When must a 'notional allowance' be deducted from the qualifying cost of an industrial building?
9. Marcus acquires a second hand industrial building during his accounting period ending 31 December 2007. The residue before sale is £160,000 and the unexpired tax life is 20 years. What WDA is Marcus entitled to for y/e 31.12.07?

Answers to Quick Quiz

1 Yes. In a six month period, writing down allowance are pro-rated by multiplying by 6/12.

2 No. First year allowances are given in full in a short period of account.

3 Balancing allowances may arise in respect of pooled expenditure only when the trade ceases. Balancing allowances may arise on non-pooled items whenever those items are disposed of.

4 Within four years of the end of the period of account (or accounting period) in which it was bought.

5 Dwelling houses, retail shops, showrooms and offices.

6 Drawing offices which serve an industrial building are industrial buildings.

7 (a) It must have ten letting bedrooms

(b) It must have letting bedrooms as the whole or main part of the sleeping accommodation

(c) It must offer ancillary services including at least

(i) Breakfast
(ii) Evening meals
(iii) The cleaning of rooms
(iv) The making of beds

(d) It must be open for at least four months during the April to October letting season.

8 A notional allowance will be given if a building was in non-industrial use at the end of the period of account (accounting period) concerned.

9 £160,000/20 = £8,000.

Now try the questions below from the Exam Question Bank

Number	Level	Marks	Time
Q10	Examination	15	27 mins
Q11	Examination	15	27 mins

Assessable trading income

Topic list	Syllabus reference
1 Recognise the basis of assessment	B3(a)
2 Commencement and cessation	B3(e)
3 Change of accounting date	B3(f)(i)-(iii)

Introduction

In the previous two chapters we have seen how to calculate the taxable trading profits after capital allowances. We are now going to look at how these are taxed in the proprietor's hands.

Businesses do not normally prepare accounts for tax years so we look at the basis of assessment which is the method by which the taxable trading profits of periods of account are allocated to tax years. As well as the normal rules for a continuing business we need special rules for the opening years of a trade, and again in the closing years.

Special rules are also needed if the business changes its accounting date.

In the next chapter we will look at the tax reliefs available should the business make a loss.

Study guide

		Intellectual level
B3	**Income from self-employment**	
(a)	Recognise the basis of assessment for self employment income.	2
(e)	Compute the assessable profits on commencement and on cessation.	2
(f)	Change of accounting date	
(i)	Recognise the factors that will influence the choice of accounting date.	2
(ii)	State the conditions that must be met for a change of accounting date to be valid.	1
(iii)	Compute the assessable profits on a change of accounting date.	2

Exam guide

You are likely to have to deal with a tax computation for an unincorporated business at some point in the exam. It may be a simple computation for a continuing business, or you may have to deal with a business in its opening or closing years, including computing taxable trading profits and allocating them to tax years. You must be totally familiar with the rules and be able to apply them in the exam.

1 Recognise the basis of assessment

FAST FORWARD

Basis periods are used to link periods of account to tax years. Broadly, the profits of a period of account ending in a tax year are taxed in that year.

1.1 Basis periods and tax years

A tax year runs from 6 April to 5 April, but most businesses do not have periods of account ending on 5 April. **Thus there must be a link between a period of account of a business and a tax year.** The procedure is to **find a period to act as the basis period for a tax year. The profits for a basis period are taxed in the corresponding tax year**. If a basis period is not identical to a period of account, the profits of periods of account are time-apportioned as required on the assumption that profits accrue evenly over a period of account. We will apportion to the nearest month for exam purposes.

The general rule is that **the basis period is the year of account ending in the tax year**. This is known as the **current year basis of assessment**.

This general rule does not apply in the opening or closing years of a business. This is because in the first few years the business has not normally established a pattern of annual accounts, and very few businesses cease trading on the annual accounting date.

Special rules are also needed when the trader changes his accounting date.

We will look at these rules in the next sections.

2 Commencement and cessation

FAST FORWARD

In the first tax year of trade actual profits of the tax year are taxed. In the second tax year, the basis period is either the first 12 months, the 12 months to the accounting date ending in year two or the actual profits from April to April. Profits of the twelve months to the accounting date are taxed in year three.

2.1 The first tax year

The first tax year is the year during which the trade commences. For example, if a trade commences on 1 June 2007 the first tax year is 2007/08.

The **basis period for the first tax year runs from the date the trade starts to the next 5 April** (or to the date of cessation if the trade does not last until the end of the tax year).

So continuing the above example a trader commencing in business on 1 June 2007 will be taxed on profits arising form 1 June 2007 to 5 April 2008 in 2007/08, their first tax year.

2.2 The second tax year

(a) **If the accounting date falling in the second tax year is at least 12 months after the start of trading, the basis period is the 12 months to that accounting date.**

(b) **If the accounting date falling in the second tax year is less than 12 months after the start of trading, the basis period is the first 12 months of trading.**

(c) **If there is no accounting date falling in the second tax year**, because the first period of account is a very long one which does not end until a date in the third tax year, **the basis period for the second tax year is the year itself (from 6 April to 5 April).**

The following flowchart may help you determine the basis period for the second tax year.

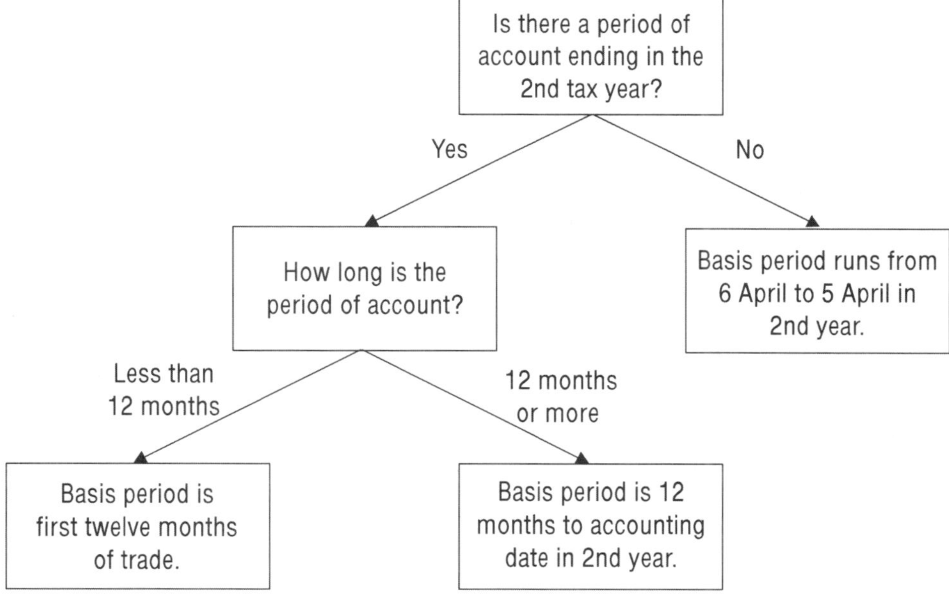

2.3 Example: period of twelve months or more ending in second year

John starts to trade on 1 January 2008 making up accounts to 31 December 2008.

1st tax year: 2007/08 – tax profits 1 January 2008 to 5 April 2008, ie 3/12 × year ended 31 December 2008

2nd tax year: 2008/09

- Is there a period of account ending in 2008/09?

  Yes – Year ended 31 December 2008 ends in 2008/09.

- How long is the period of account?

  12 months or more, ie 12 months (exactly) to 31 December 2008.

- So in 2008/09 tax profits of 12 months to 31 December 2008.

2.4 Example: short period ending in second year

Janet starts to trade on 1 January 2008 making up accounts as follows:

- 6 months to 30 June 2008
- 12 months to 30 June 2009.

1st tax year: 2007/08 – tax profits 1 January 2008 to 5 April 2008, ie 3/6 × 6 months ended 30 June 2008

2nd tax year: 2008/09.

- Is there a period of account ending in 2008/09?

  Yes – period ended 30 June 2008 ends in 2008/09.

- How long is the period of account?

  Less than 12 months.

- So in 2008/09 tax profits of first 12 months of trade ie 1 January 2008 to 31 December 2008, ie period ended 30 June 2008 profits plus 6/12 of year ended 30 June 2009 profits

2.5 Example: No period ending in second year

Jodie starts to trade on 1 March 2008 making up a 14 month set of accounts to 30 April 2009.

1st tax year: 2007/08 – tax profits 1 March 2008 to 5 April 2008, ie 1/14 × 14 months ended 30 April 2009

2nd tax year: 2008/09

- Is there a period of account ending in 2008/09?

  No (period ended 30 April 2009 ends in 2009/10)

- So in 2008/09 tax profits of 6 April 2008 to 5 April 2009, ie 12/14 × 14 months ended 30 April 2009

2.6 The third tax year

(a) **If there is an accounting date falling in the second tax year, the basis period for the third tax year is the period of account ending in the third tax year.**

(b) If there is no accounting date falling in the second tax year, the basis period for the third tax year is the 12 months to the accounting date falling in the third tax year.

2.7 Example: Accounting date in second year

Wilma starts to trade on 1 October 2007. She made taxable profits of £9,000 for the first 9 months to 30 June 2008 and £30,000 for the year to 30 June 2009.

The taxable profits for the first three tax years are as follows:

Year	*Basis period*	*Working*	*Taxable profits* £
2007/08	1.10.07 – 5.4.08	£9,000 × 6/9	6,000
2008/09	1.10.07 – 30.9.08	£9,000 + £30,000 × 3/12	16,500
2009/10	1.7.08 – 30.6.09 (period of account ending in 3rd year)		30,000

2.8 Example: No accounting date in the second year

Thelma starts to trade on 1 March 2008. Her first accounts, covering the 16 months to 30 June 2009, show a profit of £36,000. The taxable profits for the first three tax years are as follows.

Year	*Basis period*	*Working*	*Taxable profits* £
2007/08	1.3.08 – 5.4.08	£36,000 × 1/16	2,250
2008/09	6.4.08 – 5.4.09	£36,000 × 12/16	27,000
2009/10	1.7.08 – 30.6.09	£36,000 × 12/16	27,000

2.9 Later tax years

For later tax years, except the year in which the trade ceases, the normal current year basis of assessment applies, ie the basis period is the period of account ending in the tax year (see above).

Question

Basis periods

Peter commenced trading on 1 September 2003 preparing accounts to 30 April each year with the following results.

Period	*Profit* £
1.9.03 – 30.4.04	8,000
1.5.04 – 30.4.05	15,000
1.5.05 – 30.4.06	9,000
1.5.06 – 30.4.07	10,500

Show the profits to be taxed in each year from 2003/04 to 2007/08.

Answer

Year	*Basis period*	*Working*	*Taxable profits* £
2003/04	1.9.03 – 5.4.04	£8,000 × 7/8	7,000
2004/05	1.9.03 – 31.8.04	£8,000 + (£15,000 × 4/12)	13,000
2005/06	1.5.04 – 30.4.05		15,000
2006/07	1.5.05 – 30.4.06		9,000
2007/08	1.5.06 – 30.4.07		10,500

2.10 The choice of an accounting date

A new trader should consider which accounting date would be best. There are **three factors to consider** from the point of view of taxation.

- **If profits are expected to rise, a date early in the tax year** (such as 30 April) will delay the time when rising accounts profits feed through into rising taxable profits, whereas a date late in the tax year (such as 31 March) will accelerate the taxation of rising profits. This is because with an accounting date of 30 April, the taxable profits for each tax year are mainly the profits earned in the previous tax year. With an accounting date of 31 March the taxable profits are almost entirely profits earned in the current year.
- If the accounting date in the second tax year is less than 12 months after the start of trading, the taxable profits for that year will be the profits earned in the first 12 months. If the accounting date is at least 12 months from the start of trading, they will be the profits earned in the 12 months to that date. **Different profits may thus be taxed twice**, and if profits are fluctuating this can make a considerable difference to the taxable profits in the first few years. (See below for the relief given where profits are taxed twice – 'overlap relief'.)
- **The choice of an accounting date affects the profits shown in each set of accounts**, and this may affect the taxable profits.

Question — The choice of an accounting date

Christine starts to trade on 1 December 2005. Her monthly profits are £1,000 for the first seven months, and £2,000 thereafter. Show the taxable profits for the first three tax years with each of the following accounting dates (in all cases starting with a period of account of less than 12 months).

(a) 31 March
(b) 30 April
(c) 31 December

Answer

(a) *31 March*

Period of account	*Working*	*Profits*
		£
1.12.05 – 31.3.06	£1,000 × 4	4,000
1.4.06 – 31.3.07	£1,000 × 3 + £2,000 × 9	21,000
1.4.07 – 31.3.08	£2,000 × 12	24,000

Year	*Basis period*	*Taxable profits*
		£
2005/06	1.12.05 – 5.4.06	4,000
2006/07	1.4.06 – 31.3.07	21,000
2007/08	1.4.07 – 31.3.08	24,000

(b) *30 April*

Period of account	*Working*	*Profits*
		£
1.12.05 – 30.4.06	£1,000 × 5	5,000
1.5.06 – 30.4.07	£1,000 × 2 + £2,000 ×10	22,000

Year	Basis period	Working	Taxable profits
			£
2005/06	1.12.05 – 5.4.06	£5,000 × 4/5	4,000
2006/07	1.12.05 – 30.11.06	£5,000 + £22,000 × 7/12	17,833
2007/08	1.5.06 – 30.4.07		22,000

(c) *31 December*

Period of account	Working	Profits
		£
1.12.05 – 31.12.05	£1,000 × 1	1,000
1.1.06 – 31.12.06	£1,000 × 6 + £2,000 × 6	18,000
1.1.07 – 31.12.07	£2,000 × 12	24,000

Year	Basis period	Working	Taxable profits
			£
2005/06	1.12.05 – 5.4.06	£1,000 + £18,000 × 3/12	5,500
2006/07	1.1.06 – 31.12.06		18,000
2007/08	1.1.07 – 31.12.07		24,000

2.11 The final year

FAST FORWARD

On a cessation the basis period runs from the end of the basis period for the previous tax year.

(a) If a trade starts and ceases in the same tax year, the basis period for that year is the whole lifespan of the trade.

(b) If the final year is the second year, the basis period runs from 6 April at the start of the second year to the date of cessation. This rule overrides the rules that normally apply for the second year.

(c) If the final year is the third year or a later year, **the basis period runs from the end of the basis period for the previous year to the date of cessation**. This rule overrides the rules that normally apply in the third and later years.

Question — **Ceasing to trade**

Harriet, who has been trading since 1997, ceases her trade on 31 March 2008.

Her results for recent years were:

Year ended 31 December	£
2005	10,000
2006	14,000
2007	21,000
Period ended 31 March 2008	4,000

Show the taxable trade profits for the last three tax years of trading.

Answer

Trade ceases in 2007/08.

Year	*Basis period*	*Working*	*Assessment*
			£
2005/06	Y/e 31.12.05		10,000
2006/07	Y/e 31.12.06		14,000
2007/08	1.1.07 – 31.3.08	Y/e 31.12.07 plus p/e 31.3.08	25,000

2.12 Overlap profits

Key term

Profits which have been taxed more than once are called **overlap profits**.

When a business starts, some profits may be taxed twice because the basis period for the second year includes some or all of the period of trading in the first year or because the basis period for the third year overlaps with that for the second year, or both.

Overlap profits may be deducted on a change of accounting date (see below). Any overlap profits unrelieved when the trade ceases are deducted from the final year's taxable profits. Any deduction of overlap profits may create or increase a loss. The usual loss reliefs (covered later in this Text) are then available.

Exam focus point

A business with a 31 March year end will have no overlap profits as its accounting year coincides with the tax year. A business with a 31 December year end, for example, will have 3 months of overlap profit as its accounting year ends three months before the end of the tax year. Use this rule of thumb to check your calculation of overlap profits.

2.13 Examples: overlap profits

(a) John starts to trade on 1 January 2008 making up accounts to 31 December 2008. Show the overlap period.

Tax year	*Basis period*
2007/08	1.1.08 – 5.4.08
2008/09	1.1.08 – 31.12.08
2009/10	1.1.09 – 31.12.09

Overlap period: 1.1.08 – 5.4.08 (3 months)

(b) Janet starts to trade on 1 January 2008 making up accounts as follows:

6m to 30 June 2008
12m to 30 June 2009

Show the overlap period.

Tax year	*Basis period*
2007/08	1.1.08 – 5.4.08
2008/09	1.1.08 – 31.12.08
2009/10	1.7.08 – 30.6.09

Overlap period: 1.1.08 – 5.4.08 plus 1.7.08 – 31.12.08 (9 months)

(c) Jodie starts to trade on 1 March 2008 making up a 14 month set of accounts to 30 April 2009. Show the overlap period.

Tax year	*Basis period*
2007/08	1.3.08 – 5.4.08
2008/09	6.4.08 – 5.4.09
2009/10	1.5.08 – 30.4.09

Overlap period: 1.5.08 – 5.4.09 (11 months)

Question

Ceasing to trade and overlap profits

Jenny trades from 1 July 2002 to 31 December 2007, with the following results.

Period	*Profit*
	£
1.7.02 – 31.8.03	7,000
1.9.03 – 31.8.04	12,000
1.9.04 – 31.8.05	15,000
1.9.05 – 31.8.06	21,000
1.9.06 – 31.8.07	18,000
1.9.07 – 31.12.07	5,600
	78,600

Calculate the taxable trade profits to be taxed from 2002/03 to 2007/08, the overlap profits and state when these overlap profits can be relieved.

Answer

The profits to be taxed in each tax year from 2002/03 to 2007/08, and the total of these taxable profits are calculated as follows.

Year	*Basis period*	*Working*	*Taxable profit*
			£
2002/03	1.7.02 – 5.4.03	£7,000 × 9/14	4,500
2003/04	1.9.02 – 31.8.03	£7,000 × 12/14	6,000
2004/05	1.9.03 – 31.8.04		12,000
2005/06	1.9.04 – 31.8.05		15,000
2006/07	1.9.05 – 31.8.06		21,000
2007/08	1.9.06 – 31.12.07	£(18,000 + 5,600 – 3,500)	20,100
			78,600

The overlap profits are those in the period 1 September 2002 to 5 April 2003, a period of seven months. They are £7,000 × 7/14 = £3,500. Overlap profits are either relieved on a change of accounting date (see below) or are deducted from the final year's taxable profit when the business ceases. In this case the overlap profits are deducted when the business ceases.

Exam focus point

Over the life of the business, the total taxable profits equal the total actual profits.

3 Change of accounting date

FAST FORWARD

On a change of accounting date, special rules may apply for fixing basis periods. Overlap profits may either be created or relieved on a change of accounting date. Overlap profits may be relieved if more than 12 months worth of profits would otherwise be taxed in a year following a change of accounting date. On cessation any remaining overlap profits are relieved.

3.1 Need for special rules

A trader may change the date to which he prepares his annual accounts for a variety of reasons. For example, he may wish to move to a calendar year end or to fit in with seasonal variations of his trade. Special rules normally apply for fixing basis periods when a trader changes his accounting date.

On a change of accounting date there may be

- One set of accounts covering a period of less than twelve months, or
- One set of accounts covering a period of more than twelve months,

ending in a tax year. In each case, the basis period for the year relates to the new accounting date. We will look at each of the cases in turn.

3.2 One short period of account

When a change of accounting date results in one short period of account ending in a tax year, the basis period for that year is always the 12 months to the new accounting date.

3.3 Example: change of accounting date – short period

Sue prepares accounts to 31 December each year until she changes her accounting date to 30 June by preparing accounts for the six months to 30 June 2007.

There is one short period of account ending during 2007/08. This means the basis period for 2007/08 is the twelve months to 30 June 2007.

Sue's basis period for 2006/07 was the twelve months to 31 December 2006. This means the profits of the six months to 31 December 2006 are overlap profits that have been taxed twice. These overlap profits must be added to any overlap profits that arose when the business began. The total is either relieved when the business ceases or is relieved on a subsequent change of accounting date.

3.4 One long period of account

When a change of accounting date results in one long period of account ending in a tax year, the basis period for that year ends on the new accounting date. It begins immediately after the basis period for the previous year ends. This means the basis period will exceed 12 months.

No overlap profits arise in this situation. However, more than twelve months worth of profits are taxed in one income tax year and to compensate for this, relief is available for brought forward overlap profits. The overlap relief cannot reduce the number of months worth of profits taxed in the year to below twelve. So, if you have a fourteen month basis period you can give relief for up to two months worth of overlap profits.

3.5 Example: change of accounting date – long period

Zoe started trading on 1 October 2004 and prepared accounts to 30 September until she changed her accounting date by preparing accounts for the fifteen months to 31 December 2007. Her results were as follows

	£
Year to 30 September 2005	24,000
Year to 30 September 2006	48,000
Fifteen months to 31 December 2007	75,000

Profits for the first three tax years of the business are:

	£
2004/05 (1.10.04 – 5.4.05) 6/12 × £24,000	12,000
2005/06 (1.10.04 – 30.9.05)	24,000
2006/07 (1.10.05 – 30.9.06)	48,000

Overlap profits are £12,000. These arose in the six months to 5.4.05.

The change in accounting date results in one long period of account ending during 2007/08 which means the basis period for 2007/08 is the fifteen months to 31 December 2007. Three months worth of the brought forward overlap profits can be relieved.

	£
2007/08 (1.10.06 – 31.12.07)	75,000
Less overlap profits 3/6 × £12,000	(6,000)
	69,000

The unrelieved overlap profits of £6,000 (£12,000 – £6,000) are carried forward for relief either when the business ceases or on a further change of accounting date.

3.6 Conditions

The above changes in basis period automatically occur if the trader changes his accounting date during the first three tax years of his business.

In other cases **the following conditions must be met before a change in basis periods can occur**:

- The trader must notify HMRC of the change by the 31 January, following the tax year in which the change is made (by 31 January 2009 for a change made during 2007/08.)
- The period of account resulting from the change must not exceed 18 months.
- In general, there must have been no previous change of accounting date in the last 5 tax years. However, a second change can be made within this period if the later change is for genuine commercial reasons. If HMRC do not respond to a notification of a change of accounting date within 60 days of receiving it, the trader can assume that they are satisfied that the reasons for making the change are genuine commercial ones.

If the above conditions are not satisfied because the first period of account ending on the new date exceeds 18 months or the change of accounting date was not notified in time, but the 'five year gap or commercial reasons' condition is satisfied, then the basis period for the year of change is the 12 months to the *old* accounting date in the year of change. The basis period for the next year is then found using rules above as if it were the year of change.

If the 'five year gap or commercial reasons' test is not satisfied, the old accounting date remains in force for tax purposes (with the profits of accounts made up to the new date being time-apportioned as necessary) until there have been five consecutive tax years which were not years of change. The sixth tax year is then treated as the year of change to the new accounting date, and the rules above apply.

Chapter Roundup

- Basis periods are used to link periods of account to tax years. Broadly, the profits of a period of account ending in a tax year are taxed in that year.
- In the first tax year of trade actual profits of the tax year are taxed. In the second tax year, the basis period is either the first 12 months, the 12 months to the accounting date ending in year two or the actual profits from April to April. Profits of the twelve months to the accounting date are taxed in year three.
- On a cessation the basis period runs from the end of the basis period for the previous tax year.
- On a change of accounting date, special rules may apply for fixing basis periods. Overlap profits may either be created or relieved on a change of accounting date. Overlap profits may be relieved if more than 12 months worth of profits would otherwise be taxed in a year following a change of accounting date. On cessation any remaining overlap profits are relieved.

Quick Quiz

1. What is the normal basis of assessment?
2. What is the basis period for the tax year in which a trade commences?
3. On what two occasions can overlap profits potentially be relieved?

Answers to Quick Quiz

1. The normal basis of assessment is that the profits for a tax year are those of the 12 month accounting period ending in the tax year.
2. Date of commencement to 5 April in that year ie the actual tax year.
3. On a change of accounting date where a basis period resulting from the change exceeds 12 months or on the cessation of a business.

Now try the questions below from the Exam Question Bank

Number	Level	Marks	Time
Q12	Examination	15	27 mins
Q13	Examination	15	27 mins
Q14	Examination	15	27 mins

10

Trading losses

Topic list	Syllabus reference
1 Losses	B3(h)
2 Carry forward trade loss relief	B3h(i)
3 Trade transferred to company	B3h(ii)
4 Trade loss relief against general income	B3h(iii)
5 Losses in the early years of a trade	B3h(iv)
6 Terminal trade loss relief	B3h(v)

Introduction

We have seen how to calculate taxable trading profits and how to allocate them to tax years so that they can be slotted into the income tax computation.

Traders sometimes make losses rather than profits. In this chapter we consider the reliefs available for losses. A loss does not in itself lead to getting tax back from HMRC. Relief is obtained by setting a loss against trading profits, against general income or against capital gains (which are covered later in this Text), so that tax need not be paid on them. An important consideration is the choice between different reliefs. The aim is to use a loss to save as much tax as possible, as quickly as possible.

In the next chapter we will see how the rules for sole traders are extended to those trading in partnership.

Study guide

		Intellectual level
B3	**Income from self-employment**	
(h)	Relief for trading losses	
h(i)	Understand how trading losses can be carried forward.	2
h(ii)	Explain how trading losses can be carried forward following the incorporation of a business.	2
h(iii)	Understand how trading losses can be claimed against total income and chargeable gains.	2
h(iv)	Explain and compute the relief for trading losses in the early years of a trade.	1
h(v)	Explain and compute terminal loss relief.	1

Exam guide

Losses are likely to be included to some degree in the exam. The focus may, however, be on corporation tax losses, and you may not have to deal with trading losses for income tax purposes at all. Alternatively you could have a detailed computational question involving the carry back and carry forward of losses. Ensure you know the rules for ongoing trades and the additional relief in the early years of trading. On a cessation carry forward is only possible if the business is incorporated, but terminal loss relief may be due instead. Once you have established the reliefs available look to see which is most beneficial.

1 Losses

Trade losses may be relieved against future profits of the same trade, against general income and against capital gains.

1.1 Introduction

When computing taxable trade profits, profits may turn out to be negative, that is a loss has been made in the basis period. **A loss is computed in exactly the same way as a profit**, making the same adjustments to the accounts profit or loss.

If there is a loss in a basis period, the taxable trade profits for the tax year based on that basis period are nil.

This chapter considers how losses are calculated and how a loss-suffering taxpayer can use a loss to reduce his tax liability.

The rules in this chapter apply only to individuals, trading alone or in partnership. Loss reliefs for companies are completely different and are covered later in this Text.

1.2 The computation of the loss

The trade loss for a tax year is the trade loss in the basis period for that tax year.

1.3 Example: computation of trade loss

Here is an example of a trader with a 31 December year end who has been trading for many years.

Period of account	*Loss*
	£
Y/e 31.12.2007	9,000
Y/e 31.12.2008	24,000

Tax year	*Basis period*	*Trade loss for the tax year*
		£
2007/08	Y/e 31.12.07	9,000
2008/09	Y/3 31.12.08	24,000

1.4 How loss relief is given

Loss relief is given by deducting the loss from total income to calculate net income. Carry forward loss relief and terminal loss relief can only be set against the trading income of the same trade component of total income. Other loss reliefs may be set against general income (ie any component of total income).

2 Carry forward trade loss relief

Trading losses may be relieved against future profits of the same trade. The relief is against the first available profits of the same trade.

2.1 The relief

A trade loss not relieved in any other way will be **carried forward to set against the first available trade profits of the same trade** in the calculation of net trading income. Losses may be carried forward for any number of years.

2.2 Example: carrying forward losses

Brian has the following results.

Year ending	£
31 December 2005	(6,000)
31 December 2006	5,000
31 December 2007	11,000

Brian's net trading income, assuming that he claims carry forward loss relief only are:

	2005/06		*2006/07*		*2007/08*
	£		£		£
Trade profits	0		5,000		11,000
Less carry forward loss relief	(0)	(i)	(5,000)	(ii)	(1,000)
Net trading income	0		0		10,000

Loss memorandum		£
Trading loss, y/e 31.12.05		6,000
Less: claim in y/e 31.12.06	(i)	(5,000)
claim in y/e 31.12.07 (balance of loss)	(ii)	(1,000)
		0

3 Trade transferred to company

FAST FORWARD

Where a business is transferred to a company, loss relief is available for any remaining unrelieved losses of the unincorporated business against income received from the company.

Although carry forward loss relief is restricted to future profits of the same business, this is extended to cover income received from a company to which the business is transferred.

The amount carried forward is the total unrelieved trading losses of the business.

The set off is against income derived from the company including dividends, interest and salary.

Set off the loss against non-savings income, then against savings income and finally against dividend income.

The consideration for the sale must be wholly or mainly shares, which must be retained by the vendor throughout any tax year in which the loss is relieved; HMRC treat this condition as being satisfied if 80% or more of the consideration consists of shares.

4 Trade loss relief against general income

FAST FORWARD

A trading loss may be set against general income in the year of the loss and/or the preceding year. Personal allowances may be lost as a result of a claim. Once a claim has been made in any year, the remaining loss can be set against net chargeable gains.

4.1 The relief

Instead of carrying a trade loss forward against future trade profits, a claim may be made to relieve it against general income.

4.2 Relieving the loss

Relief is against the income of the tax year in which the loss arose. In addition or instead, relief may be claimed **against the income of the preceding year**.

If there are losses in two successive years, and relief is claimed against the first year's income both for the first year's loss and for the second year's loss, relief is given for the first year's loss before the second year's loss.

A claim for a loss must be made by the 31 January which is 22 months after the end of the tax year of the loss: thus by 31 January 2010 for a loss in 2007/08.

The taxpayer cannot choose the amount of loss to relieve: thus the loss may have to be set against income part of which would have been covered by the personal allowance. However, the taxpayer can choose whether to claim full relief in the current year and then relief in the preceding year for any remaining loss, or the other way round.

Set the loss against non-savings income then against savings income and finally against dividend income.

Relief is available by carry forward for any loss not relieved against general income.

Question

Loss relief against general income

Janet has a loss in her period of account ending 31 December 2007 of £25,000. Her other income is £18,000 part time employment income a year, and she wishes to claim loss relief for the year of loss and then for the preceding year. Her trading income in the previous year was £nil. Show her taxable income for each year, and comment on the effectiveness of the loss relief. Assume that tax rates and allowances for 2007/08 have always applied.

Answer

The loss-making period ends in 2007/08, so the year of the loss is 2007/08.

	2006/07	*2007/08*
	£	£
Total income	18,000	18,000
Less loss relief against general income	(7,000)	(18,000)
Net income	11,000	0
Less personal allowance	(5,225)	(5,225)
Taxable income	5,775	0

In 2007/08, £5,225 of the loss has been wasted because that amount of income would have been covered by the personal allowance. If Janet claims loss relief against general income, there is nothing she can do about this waste of loss relief.

4.3 Capital allowances

The trader may adjust the size of the loss relief claim by not claiming all the capital allowances he is entitled to: a reduced claim will increase the balance carried forward to the next year's capital allowances computation. This may be a useful **tax planning point where the effective rate of relief for capital allowances in future periods will be greater than the rate of tax relief for the loss relief**.

4.4 Trading losses relieved against capital gains

Where relief is claimed against general income of a given year, the taxpayer may include **a further claim to set the loss against his chargeable gains for the year** less any allowable capital losses for the same year or for previous years. This amount of net gains is computed ignoring taper relief and the annual exempt amount (see later in this Text).

The trading loss is first set against general income of the year of the claim, and only any excess loss is set against capital gains. The taxpayer cannot specify the amount to be set against capital gains, so the annual exempt amount may be wasted. We include an example here for completeness. You will study chargeable gains later in this Text and we suggest that you come back to this example at that point.

Question

Loss relief against income and gains

Sibyl had the following results for 2007/08.

	£
Loss available for relief against general income	27,000
Income	19,500
Capital gains less current year capital losses	10,000
Annual exemption for capital gains tax purposes	9,200
Capital losses brought forward	4,000

Assume no taper relief is due.

Show how the loss would be relieved against income and gains.

Answer

	£
Income	19,500
Less loss relief against general income	(19,500)
Net income	0
Capital gains	10,000
Less loss relief: lower of £(27,000 – 19,500) = £7,500 (note 1) and £(10,000 – 4,000) = £6,000 (note 2)	(6,000)
	4,000
Less annual exemption (restricted)	(4,000)
	0

Notes

1 This equals the loss left after the loss relief claim against general income

2 This equals the gains left after losses b/fwd but ignoring taper relief and the annual exemption.

A trading loss of £(7,500 – 6,000) = £1,500 is carried forward. Sibyl's personal allowance and £(9,200 – 4,000) = £5,200 of her capital gains tax annual exemption are wasted. Her capital losses brought forward of £4,000 are carried forward to 2008/09. Although we deducted this £4,000 in working out how much trading loss we were allowed to use in the claim, we do not actually need to use any of the £4,000.

4.5 Restrictions on trade loss relief against general income

Relief cannot be claimed against general income unless a business is conducted on a commercial basis with a view to the realisation of profits throughout the basis period for the tax year; this condition applies to all types of business.

4.6 The choice between loss reliefs

FAST FORWARD

It is important for a trader to choose the right loss relief, so as to save tax at the highest possible rate and so as to obtain relief reasonably quickly.

When a trader has a choice between loss reliefs, he should aim to obtain relief both quickly and at the highest possible tax rate. However, do consider that losses relieved against income which would otherwise be covered by the personal allowance are wasted.

Another consideration is that a trading loss cannot be set against the capital gains of a year unless relief is first claimed against general income of the same year. It may be worth making the claim against income and wasting the personal allowance in order to avoid a CGT liability.

Question — The choice between loss reliefs

Felicity's trading results are as follows.

Year ended 30 September	*Trading profit/(loss)*
	£
2005	1,900
2006	(21,000)
2007	13,000

Her other income (all non-savings income) is as follows.

	£
2005/06	2,200
2006/07	26,500
2007/08	15,000

Show the most efficient use of Felicity's trading loss. Assume that the personal allowance has been £5,225 throughout.

Answer

Relief could be claimed against general income for 2005/06 and/or 2006/07, with any unused loss being carried forward. Relief in 2005/06 would be against general income of £(1,900 + 2,200) = £4,100, all of which would be covered by the personal allowance anyway, so this claim should not be made. A claim against general income should be made for 2006/07 as this saves tax quicker than a claim in 2007/08 would. The final results will be as follows:

	2005/06	*2006/07*	*2007/08*
	£	£	£
Trading income	1,900	0	13,000
Less carry forward loss relief	(0)	(0)	(0)
	1,900	0	13,000
Other income	2,200	26,500	15,000
	4,100	26,500	28,000
Less loss relief against general income	(0)	(21,000)	(0)
Net income	4,100	5,500	28,000
Less personal allowance	(5,225)	(5,225)	(5,225)
Taxable income	0	275	22,775

Exam focus point

Before recommending loss relief against general income consider whether it will result in the waste of the personal allowance. Such waste is to be avoided if at all possible.

5 Losses in the early years of a trade

5.1 The computation of the loss

Under the rules determining the basis period for the first three tax years of trading, there may be periods where the basis periods overlap. If profits arise in these periods, they are taxed twice but are relieved later (on cessation or on a change of accounting date). However, a loss in an overlap period can only be relieved once. It must not be double counted.

If basis periods overlap, a loss in the overlap period is treated as a loss for the earlier tax year only.

5.2 Example: losses in early years

Here is an example of a trader who starts to trade on 1 July 2007 and makes losses in opening periods.

Period of account	*Loss*
	£
P/e 31.12.2007	9,000
Y/e 31.12.2008	24,000

Tax year	*Basis period*	*Working*	*Trade loss for the tax year*
			£
2007/08	1.7.07 – 5.4.08	£9,000 + (£24,000 × 3/12)	15,000
2008/09	1.1.08 – 31.12.08	£24,000 – (£24,000 × 3/12)	18,000

5.3 Example: losses and profits in early years

The rule against using losses twice also applies when losses are netted off against profits in the same basis period. Here is an example, with a commencement on 1 July 2007.

Period of account	*(Loss)/profit*
	£
1.7.07 – 30.4.08	(10,000)
1.5.08 – 30.4.09	24,000

Tax year	*Basis period*	*Working*	*Trade (Loss)/Profit*
			£
2007/08	1.7.07 – 5.4.08	£(10,000) × 9/10	(9,000)
2008/09	1.7.07 – 30.6.08	£24,000 × 2/12 + £(10,000) × 1/10	3,000

5.4 Early trade losses relief

FAST FORWARD

In opening years, a special relief involving the carry back of losses against general income is available. Losses arising in the first four tax years of a trade may be set against general income in the three years preceding the loss making year, taking the earliest year first.

Early trade losses relief is available for **trading losses incurred in the first four tax years of a trade**.

Relief is obtained by **setting the allowable loss against general income in the three years preceding the year of loss**, applying the loss to the earliest year first. Thus a loss arising in 2007/08 may be set off against income in 2004/05, 2005/06 and 2006/07 in that order.

A claim for early trade losses relief applies to all three years automatically, provided that the loss is large enough. The taxpayer cannot choose to relieve the loss against just one or two of the years, or to relieve only part of the loss. However, the taxpayer could reduce the size of the loss by not claiming the full capital allowances available to him. This will result in higher capital allowances in future years.

Claims for the relief must be made by the 31 January which is 22 months after the end of the tax year in which the loss is incurred.

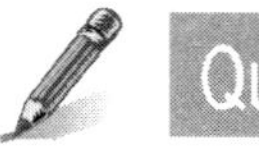

Question

Early trade losses relief

Mr A is employed as a dustman until 1 January 2006. On that date he starts up his own business as a scrap metal merchant, making up his accounts to 30 June each year. His earnings as a dustman are:

	£
2002/03	5,000
2003/04	6,000
2004/05	7,000
2005/06 (nine months)	6,000

His trading results as a scrap metal merchant are:

	Profit/ (Loss) £
Six months to 30 June 2006	(3,000)
Year to 30 June 2007	(1,500)
Year to 30 June 2008	(1,200)

Assuming that loss relief is claimed as early as possible, show the net income before personal allowances for each of the years 2002/03 to 2008/09 inclusive.

Answer

Since reliefs are to be claimed as early as possible, early trade loss relief is applied. The losses available for relief are as follows.

	£	£	*Years against which relief is available*
2005/06 (basis period 1.1.06 – 5.4.06)			
3 months to 5.4.06 £(3,000) × 3/6		(1,500)	2002/03 to 2004/05
2006/07 (basis period 1.1.06 – 31.12.06)			
3 months to 30.6.06			
(omit 1.1.06 – 5.4.06: overlap) £(3,000) × 3/6	(1,500)		
6 months to 31.12.06 £(1,500) × 6/12	(750)		
		(2,250)	2003/04 to 2005/06
2007/08 (basis period 1.7.06 – 30.6.07)			
6 months to 30.6.07			
(omit 1.7.06 – 31.12.06: overlap) £(1,500) × 6/12		(750)	2004/05 to 2006/07
2008/09 (basis period 1.7.07 – 30.6.08)			
12 months to 30.6.08		(1,200)	2005/06 to 2007/08

The net income is as follows.

	£	£
2002/03		
Original	5,000	
Less 2005/06 loss	(1,500)	
		3,500
2003/04		
Original	6,000	
Less 2006/07 loss	(2,250)	
		3,750
2004/05		
Original	7,000	
Less 2007/08 loss	(750)	
		6,250
2005/06		
Original	6,000	
Less 2008/09 loss	(1,200)	
		4,800

The taxable trade profits for 2005/06 to 2008/09 are zero. There were losses in the basis periods.

6 Terminal trade loss relief

FAST FORWARD

On the cessation of trade, a loss arising in the last 12 months of trading may be set against trade profits of the tax year of cessation and the previous 3 years, taking the latest year first.

6.1 The relief

Trade loss relief against general income will often be insufficient on its own to deal with a loss incurred in the last months of trading. For this reason there is a special relief, **terminal trade loss relief, which allows a loss on cessation to be carried back for relief against taxable trading profits in previous years.**

6.2 Computing the terminal loss

A terminal loss is **the loss of the last 12 months of trading**.

It is built up as follows.

		£
(a)	The actual trade loss for the tax year of cessation (calculated from 6 April to the date of cessation)	X
(b)	The actual trade loss for the period from 12 months before cessation until the end of the penultimate tax year	X
	Total terminal trade loss	X

If the result of either (a) or (b) is a profit rather than a loss, it is treated as zero.

Any unrelieved overlap profits are included within (a) above.

If any loss cannot be included in the terminal loss (eg because it is matched with a profit) it can be relieved instead against general income.

6.3 Relieving the terminal loss

The loss is relieved against trade profits only.

Relief is given in the tax year of cessation and the three preceding years, later years first.

Question — **Terminal loss relief**

Set out below are the results of a business up to its cessation on 30 September 2007.

	Profit/(loss)
	£
Year to 31 December 2004	2,000
Year to 31 December 2005	400
Year to 31 December 2006	300
Nine months to 30 September 2007	(1,950)

Overlap profits on commencement were £450. These were all unrelieved on cessation.

Show the available terminal loss relief, and suggest an alternative claim if the trader had had other non-savings income of £10,000 in each of 2006/07 and 2007/08. Assume that 2007/08 tax rates and allowances apply to all years.

Answer

The terminal loss comes in the last 12 months, the period 1 October 2006 to 30 September 2007. This period is split as follows.

2006/07 Six months to 5 April 2007
2007/08 Six months to 30 September 2007

The terminal loss is made up as follows.

Unrelieved trading losses		£	£
2007/08			
6 months to 30.9.07	£(1,950) × 6/9		(1,300)
Overlap relief	£(450)		(450)
2006/07			
3 months to 31.12.06	£300 × 3/12	75	
3 months to 5.4.07	£(1,950) × 3/9	(650)	
			(575)
			(2,325)

Taxable trade profits will be as follows.

Year	*Basis period*	*Profits*	*Terminal loss relief*	*Final taxable profits*
		£	£	£
2004/05	Y/e 31.12.04	2,000	1,625	375
2005/06	Y/e 31.12.05	400	400	0
2006/07	Y/e 31.12.06	300	300	0
2007/08	1.10.06 – 30.9.07	0	0	0
			2,325	

If the trader had had £10,000 of other income in 2006/07 and 2007/08, we could consider loss relief claims against general income for these two years, using the loss of £(1,950 + 450) = £2,400 for 2007/08.

The final results would be as follows. (We could alternatively claim loss relief in 2006/07.)

	2004/05	*2005/06*	*2006/07*	*2007/08*
	£	£	£	£
Trade profits	2,000	400	300	0
Other income	0	0	10,000	10,000
	2,000	400	10,300	10,000
Less loss relief against general income	0	0	0	(2,400)
Net income	2,000	400	10,300	7,600

Another option would be to make a claim against general income for the balance of the loss not relieved as a terminal loss £(2,400 – 2,325) = £75 in either 2006/07 or 2007/08.

However, as there is only taxable income in 2006/07 and 2007/08 the full claim against general income is more tax efficient.

Chapter Roundup

- Trade losses may be relieved against future profits of the same trade, against general income and against capital gains.
- Trading losses may be relieved against future profits of the same trade. The relief is against the first available profits of the same trade.
- Where a business is transferred to a company, loss relief is available for any remaining unrelieved losses of the unincorporated business against income received from the company.
- A trading loss may be set against general income in the year of the loss and/or the preceding year. Personal allowances may be lost as a result of the claim. Once a claim has been made in any year, the remaining loss can be set against net chargeable gains.
- It is important for a trader to choose the right loss relief, so as to save tax at the highest possible rate and so as to obtain relief reasonably quickly.
- In opening years, a special relief involving the carry back of losses against general income is available. Losses arising in the first four tax years of a trade may be set against general income in the three years preceding the loss making year, taking the earliest year first.
- On the cessation of trade, a loss arising in the last 12 months of trading may be set against trade profits of the tax year of cessation and the previous 3 years, taking the latest year first.

Quick Quiz

1. Against what income can trade losses carried forward be set off?
2. When a loss is to be relieved against general income, how are losses linked to particular tax years?
3. Against which years' general income may a loss be relieved, for a continuing business which has traded for many years?
4. Joe starts trading on 6 April 2007. He makes a loss in his first year of trading. Against income of which years can he set the loss under early trade loss relief?
5. In which years may relief for a terminal loss be given?

Answers to Quick Quiz

1 Against trade profits from the same trade.

2 The loss for a tax year is the loss in the basis period for that tax year. However, if basis periods overlap, a loss in the overlap period is a loss of the earlier tax year only.

3 The year in which the loss arose and/or the preceding year.

4 Loss incurred 2007/08: set against general income of 2004/05, 2005/06 and 2006/07 in that order.

5 In the year of cessation and then in the three preceding years, later years first.

Now try the question below from the Exam Question Bank

Number	Level	Marks	Time
Q15	Examination	15	27 mins

11 Partnerships and limited liability partnerships

Topic list	Syllabus reference
1 Partnerships	B3(i)(i)-(iii)
2 Loss reliefs	B3(i)(iv)
3 Limited liability partnerships	B3(i)(v)

Introduction

We have covered sole traders, learning how to calculate taxable trading profits after capital allowances and allocate them to tax years and how to deal with losses.

We now see how the income tax rules for traders are adapted to deal with business partnerships. On the one hand, a partnership is a single trading entity, making profits as a whole. On the other hand, each partner has a personal tax computation, so the profits must be apportioned to the partners. The general approach is to work out the profits of the partnership, then tax each partner as if he were a sole trader running a business equal to his slice of the partnership (for example 25% of the partnership).

This chapter concludes our study of the income tax computation. In the next chapter we will turn our attention to national insurance.

Study guide

		Intellectual level
B3	**Income from self-employment**	
(i)	Partnerships and limited liability partnerships	
(i)(i)	Explain how a partnership is assessed to tax.	2
(i)(ii)	Compute the assessable profits for each partner following a change in the profit sharing ratio.	2
(i)(iii)	Compute the assessable profits for each partner following a change in the membership of the partnership.	2
(i)(iv)	Describe the alternative loss relief claims that are available to partners.	1
(i)(v)	Explain the loss relief restriction that applies to the partners of a limited liability partnership.	1

Exam guide

Although partnerships are an important topic you are not guaranteed to get a question on them in your exam. This does not mean that you can ignore them. As long as you remember to allocate the profits between the partners according to their profit sharing arrangements for the period of account you should be able to cope with any aspect of partnership tax. Remember that each partner is taxed as a sole trader, and you should apply the opening and closing year rules and loss reliefs as appropriate to that partner.

1 Partnerships

FAST FORWARD

A partnership is simply treated as a source of profits and losses for trades being carried on by the individual partners. Divide profits or losses between the partners according to the profit sharing arrangements in the period of account concerned. If any of the partners are entitled to a salary or interest on capital, apportion this first, not forgetting to pro-rate in periods of less than 12 months.

1.1 Introduction

A partnership is a group of individuals who are trading together. They will agree amongst themselves how the business should be run and how profits and losses should be shared. It is not treated as a separate entity for tax purposes (in contrast to a company).

1.2 Basis of assessment

A business partnership is treated like a sole trader for the purposes of computing its profits. (As usual, 'trade' in this chapter includes professions and vocations.) Partners' salaries and interest on capital are not deductible expenses and must be added back in computing profits, because they are a form of drawings.

Once the partnership's profits for a period of account have been computed, they are shared between the partners according to the profit sharing arrangements for that period of account.

Question — Allocating profits

Steve and Tanya have been in partnership for many years. For the year ended 31 October 2007, taxable trading profits were £70,000.

Steve is allocated an annual salary of £12,000 and Tanya's salary is £28,000.

The profit sharing ratio is 2:1.

Allocate the trade profit to each partner for the year ended 31 October 2007.

Answer

Allocate the profits for the year ended 31 October 2007.

	Total	*Steve*	*Tanya*
	£	£	£
Profit	70,000		
Salaries	40,000	12,000	28,000
Balance (2:1)	30,000	20,000	10,000
Total	70,000	32,000	38,000

1.3 Change in profit sharing arrangements

If the profit sharing arrangements change part way through the period of account, the profits, salaries and interest for the period of account must be pro-rated accordingly.

Question — Change in profit sharing arrangements

Sue and Tim have been in partnership for many years. For the year ended 31 December 2007, taxable trading profits were £50,000.

Sue is allocated an annual salary of £10,000 and Tim's salary is £15,000.

The profit sharing ratio was 1:1 until 31 August 2007 when it changed to 1:2 with no provision for salaries.

Allocate the trade profit to each partner for the year ended 31 December 2007.

Answer

Allocate the profits for the year ended 31 December 2007.

	Total	*Sue*	*Tim*
	£	£	£
Profit	50,000		
1 January – 31 August (8 months)	33,333		
Salaries (8/12 × £10,000/£15,000)	16,667	6,667	10,000
Balance (1:1)	16,666	8,333	8,333
	33,333		
1 September – 31 December (4 months)	16,667		
Salaries	Nil	–	–
Balance (1:2)	16,667	5,556	11,111
	16,667		
Total	50,000	20,556	29,444

Note. Since the profit sharing arrangements changed part way through the period of account, the profits and salaries for the period of account must be pro-rated accordingly.

1.4 The tax positions of individual partners

Each partner is taxed like a sole trader who runs a business which:

- Starts when he joins the partnership
- Finishes when he leaves the partnership
- Has the same periods of account as the partnership (except that a partner who joins or leaves during a period will have a period which starts or ends part way through the partnership's period)
- Makes profits or losses equal to the partner's share of the partnership's profits or losses

1.5 Assets owned individually

Where the partners own assets (such as their cars) individually, a capital allowances computation must be prepared for each partner in respect of the assets he owns (not forgetting any adjustment for private use). **The capital allowances must go into the partnership's tax computation.**

1.6 Changes in membership

FAST FORWARD

Commencement and cessation rules apply to partners individually when they join or leave.

When a trade continues but partners join or leave (including cases when a sole trader takes in partners or a partnership breaks up leaving only one partner as a sole trader), **the special rules for basis periods in opening and closing years do not apply to the people who were carrying on the trade both before and after the change. They carry on using the period of account ending in each tax year as the basis period for the tax year (ie the current year basis). The commencement rules only affect joiners, and the cessation rules only affect leavers.**

However, when no-one carries on the trade both before and after the change, as when a partnership transfers its trade to a completely new owner or set of owners, the cessation rules apply to the old owners and the commencement rules apply to the new owners.

1.7 Example: a comprehensive partnership example

Alice and Bertrand start a partnership on 1 July 2004, making up accounts to 31 December each year. On 1 May 2006, Charles joins the partnership. On 1 November 2007, Charles leaves. On 1 January 2008, Deborah joins. The profit sharing arrangements are as follows.

	Alice	*Bertrand*	*Charles*	*Deborah*
1.7.04 – 31.1.05				
Salaries (per annum)	£3,000	£4,500		
Balance	3/5	2/5		
1.2.05 – 30.4.06				
Salaries (per annum)	£3,000	£6,000		
Balance	4/5	1/5		
1.5.06 – 31.10.07				
Salaries (per annum)	£2,400	£3,600	£1,800	
Balance	2/5	2/5	1/5	
1.11.07 – 31.12.07				
Salaries (per annum)	£1,500	£2,700		
Balance	3/5	2/5		
1.1.08 onwards				
Salaries (per annum)	£1,500	£2,700		£600
Balance	3/5	1/5		1/5

Profits and losses as adjusted for tax purposes are as follows.

Period	*Profit(loss)*
	£
1.7.04 – 31.12.04	22,000
1.1.05 – 31.12.05	51,000
1.1.06 – 31.12.06	39,000
1.1.07 – 31.12.07	15,000
1.1.08 – 31.12.08	18,000

When approaching the question, we must first share the trade profits for the periods of account between the partners, remembering to adjust the salaries for periods of less than a year.

	Total	*Alice*	*Bertrand*	*Charles*	*Deborah*
	£	£	£	£	£
1.7.04 – 31.12.04					
Salaries	3,750	1,500	2,250		
Balance	18,250	10,950	7,300		
Total (P/e 31.12.04)	22,000	12,450	9,550		
1.1.05 – 31.12.05					
January					
Salaries	625	250	375		
Balance	3,625	2,175	1,450		
Total	4,250	2,425	1,825		
February to December					
Salaries	8,250	2,750	5,500		
Balance	38,500	30,800	7,700		
Total	46,750	33,550	13,200		
Total for y/e 31.12.05	51,000	35,975	15,025		
1.1.06 – 31.12.06					
January to April					
Salaries	3,000	1,000	2,000		
Balance	10,000	8,000	2,000		
Total	13,000	9,000	4,000		
May to December					
Salaries	5,200	1,600	2,400	1,200	
Balance	20,800	8,320	8,320	4,160	
Total	26,000	9,920	10,720	5,360	
Total for y/e 31.12.06	39,000	18,920	14,720	5,360	
1.1.07 – 31.12.07					
January to October					
Salaries	6,500	2,000	3,000	1,500	
Balance	6,000	2,400	2,400	1,200	
Total	12,500	4,400	5,400	2,700	
November and December					
Salaries	700	250	450		
Balance	1,800	1,080	720		
Total	2,500	1,330	1,170		
Total for y/e 31.12.07	15,000	5,730	6,570	2,700	
1.1.08 – 31.12.08					
Salaries	4,800	1,500	2,700		600
Balance	13,200	7,920	2,640		2,640
Total for y/e 31.12.08	18,000	9,420	5,340		3,240

The next stage is to work out the basis periods and hence the taxable trade profits for the partners. All of them are treated as making up accounts to 31 December, but Alice and Bertrand are treated as starting to trade on 1 July 2004, Charles as trading only from 1 May 2006 to 31 October 2007 and Deborah as starting to trade on 1 January 2008. Applying the usual rules gives the following basis periods and taxable profits.

Alice

Year	*Basis period*	*Working*	*Taxable profits*
			£
2004/05	1.7.04 – 5.4.05	£12,450 + (£35,975 × 3/12)	21,444
2005/06	1.1.05 – 31.12.05		35,975
2006/07	1.1.06 – 31.12.06		18,920
2007/08	1.1.07 – 31.12.07		5,730

Note that for 2004/05 we take Alice's total for the year ended 2005 and apportion that, because the partnership's period of account runs from 1 January to 31 December 2005. Alice's profits for 2004/05 are *not* £12,450 + £2,425 + (£33,550 × 2/11) = £20,975.

Alice will have overlap profits for the period 1 January to 5 April 2005 (£35,975 × 3/12 = £8,994) to deduct when she ceases to trade.

Bertrand

Year	*Basis period*	*Working*	*Taxable profits*
			£
2004/05	1.7.04 – 5.4.05	£9,550 + (£15,025 × 3/12)	13,306
2005/06	1.1.05 – 31.12.05		15,025
2006/07	1.1.06 – 31.12.06		14,720
2007/08	1.1.07 – 31.12.07		6,570

Bertrand's overlap profits are £15,025 × 3/12 = £3,756.

Charles

Year	*Basis period*	*Working*	*Taxable profits*
			£
2006/07	1.5.06 – 5.4.07	£5,360 + (£2,700 × 3/10)	6,170
2007/08	6.4.07 – 31.10.07	£2,700 × 7/10	1,890

Because Charles ceased to trade in his second tax year of trading, his basis period for the second year starts on 6 April and he has no overlap profits.

Deborah

Year	*Basis period*	*Working*	*Taxable profits*
			£
2007/08	1.1.08 – 5.4.08	£3,240 × 3/12	810

Exam focus point

Partners are effectively taxed in the same way as sole traders with just one difference. Before you tax the partner you need to take each set of accounts (as adjusted for tax purposes) and divide the trade profit (or loss) between each partner.

Then carry on as normal for a sole trader – each partner is that sole trader in respect of his trade profits for each accounting period.

2 Loss reliefs

FAST FORWARD

Partners are entitled to loss relief in exactly the same way as sole traders.

Partners are entitled to the same loss reliefs as sole traders. The reliefs are:

(a) **Carry forward against future trading profits**. If the business is transferred to a company this is extended to carry forward against future income from the company.

(b) **Set off against general income of the same and/or preceding year**. This claim can be extended to set off against capital gains.

(c) **For a new partner, losses in the first four tax years of trade can be set off against other income of the three preceding years**. This is so even if the actual trade commenced many years before the partner joined.

(d) **For a ceasing partner terminal loss relief is available** when he is treated as ceasing to trade. This is so even if the partnership continues to trades after he leaves.

Different partners may claim loss reliefs in different ways.

Question

Partnership losses

Mary and Natalie have been trading for many years sharing profits equally. On 1 January 2008 Mary retired and Oliver joined the partnership. Natalie and Oliver share profits in the ratio of 2:1. Although the partnership had previously been profitable it made a loss of £24,000 for the year to 31 March 2008. The partnership is expected to be profitable in the future.

Calculate the loss accruing to each partner for 2007/08 and explain what reliefs are available.

Answer

We must first share the loss for the period of account between the partners, remembering to adjust the salaries for periods of less than a year.

	Total	*Mary*	*Natalie*	*Oliver*
	£	£	£	£
1.04.07 – 31.03.08				
1.04.07 – 31.12.07				
Total £24,000 × 9/12	(18,000)	(9,000)	(9,000)	
1.01.08 – 31.03.08				
Total £24,000 × 3/12	(6,000)		(4,000)	(2,000)
Total for y/e 31.03.08	(24,000)	(9,000)	(13,000)	(2,000)

Mary

For 2007/08, Mary has a loss of £9,000. She may claim relief against general income of 2007/08 and/or 2006/07, and may extend the claim to capital gains.

Mary has ceased trading, and may claim terminal loss relief. The terminal loss will be £9,000 (a profit arose in the period 1.01.07 – 31.03.07 which would be treated as zero) and this may be set against her taxable trade profits for 2007/08 (£nil), 2006/07, 2005/06 and 2004/05.

Natalie

For 2007/08, Natalie has a loss of £13,000. She may claim relief against general income of 2007/08 and/or 2006/07, and may extend the claim to capital gains. Any loss remaining unrelieved may be carried forward against future income from the same trade.

Oliver

Oliver's loss for 2007/08 is £2,000. He may claim relief for the loss against other income (and gains) of 2007/08 and/or 2006/07. As he has just started to trade he may claim relief for the loss against other income of 2004/05, 2005/06 and 2006/07. Any loss remaining unrelieved may be carried forward against future income from the same trade.

3 Limited liability partnerships

FAST FORWARD

Limited liability partnerships are taxed on virtually the same basis as normal partnerships except that loss relief is restricted for all partners.

It is possible to form a limited liability partnership. The difference between a limited liability partnership (LLP) and a normal partnership is that **in a LLP the liability of the partners is limited to the capital they contributed.**

The partners of a LLP are taxed on virtually the same basis as the partners of a normal partnership (see above). However, the amount of loss relief that a partner can claim against general income when the claim is against non-partnership income is restricted to the capital he contributed subject to an overall cap of £25,000.

Chapter Roundup

- A partnership is simply treated as a source of profits and losses for trades being carried on by the individual partners. Divide profits or losses between the partners according to the profit sharing arrangements in the period of account concerned. If any of the partners are entitled to a salary or interest on capital, apportion this first, not forgetting to pro-rate in periods of less than 12 months.
- Commencement and cessation rules apply to partners individually when they join or leave.
- Partners are entitled to loss relief in exactly the same way as sole traders.
- Limited liability partnerships are taxed on virtually the same basis as normal partnerships except that loss relief is restricted for all partners.

Quick Quiz

1 How are partnership trading profits divided between the individual partners?

2 What loss reliefs are partners entitled to?

3 Janet and John are partners sharing profits 60:40. For the years ended 30 June 2007 and 2008 the partnership made profits of £100,000 and £150,000 respectively. What are John's taxable trading profits in 2007/08?

4 Yolanda and Yan are in partnership sharing profits 80:20. For the year ended 31 December 2007 the business makes a loss of £40,000. If Yan decides to use his share of the loss against general income what loss relief(s) can Yolanda claim?

5 Pete and Doug have been partners for many years, sharing profits equally. On 1 January 2007 Dave joins the partnership and it is agreed to share profits 40:40:20. For the year ended 30 June 2007 profits are £100,000.

What is Doug's share of these profits?

Answers to Quick Quiz

1 Profits are divided in accordance with the profit sharing arrangements that existed during the period of account in which the profits arose.

2 Partners are entitled to the same loss reliefs as sole traders as appropriate.

3 £40,000.

2007/08: ye 30 June 2007

£100,000 × 40% = £40,000.

4 Yolanda has a choice of loss reliefs:

Loss relief against general income or carry forward loss relief.

Her loss relief claim is unaffected by Yan's.

5 £45,000

	Pete	*Doug*	*Dave*
Ye 30 June 2007	£	£	£
1.7.06 – 31.12.06			
6m × £100,000			
£50,000 50:50	25,000	25,000	
1.1.07 – 30.6.07			
6m × £100,000			
£50,000 40:40:20	20,000	20,000	10,000
	45,000	45,000	10,000

Now try the questions below from the Exam Question Bank

Number	Level	Marks	Time
Q16	Examination	15	27 mins
Q17	Examination	15	27 mins

12

National insurance contributions

Topic list	Syllabus reference
1 Scope of national insurance contributions (NICs)	E1(a)
2 Class 1 and Class 1A NICs for employed persons	E2(a), (b)
3 Class 2 and class 4 NICs for self-employed persons	E3(a), (b)

Introduction

In the previous chapters we have covered income tax for employees and for the self employed.

We look at the national insurance contributions payable under Classes 1 and 1A in respect of employment and under Classes 2 and 4 in respect of self employment.

In the next chapter we will turn our attention to the taxation of chargeable gains.

Study guide

		Intellectual level
E1	**The scope of national insurance**	
(a)	Describe the scope of national insurance.	1
E2	**Class 1 and Class 1A contributions for employed persons**	
(a)	Compute Class 1 NIC.	2
(b)	Compute Class 1A NIC.	2
E3	**Class 2 and Class 4 contributions for self employed persons**	
(a)	Compute Class 2 NIC.	2
(b)	Compute Class 4 NIC.	2

Exam guide

You will not find a complete question on national insurance but it is likely to form part of a larger question on the taxation of employees or the self employed. You must be absolutely clear who is liable for which class of contributions; only employers, for example, pay Class 1A.

1 Scope of national insurance contributions (NICs)

Four classes of national insurance contribution (NIC) exist, as set out below.

(a) **Class 1**. This is divided into:

  (i) **Primary**, paid by employees
  (ii) **Secondary, Class 1A and Class 1B** paid by employers

(b) **Class 2**. Paid by the self-employed

(c) **Class 3**. Voluntary contributions (paid to maintain rights to certain state benefits)

(d) **Class 4**. Paid by the self-employed

Exam focus point

Class 1B and Class 3 contributions are outside the scope of your syllabus.

The National Insurance Contributions Office (NICO), which is part of HM Revenue and Customs, examines employers' records and procedures to ensure that the correct amounts of NICs are collected.

2 Class 1 and Class 1A NICs for employed persons

2.1 Class 1 NICs

FAST FORWARD

Class 1 NICs are payable by employees and employers on earnings.

Both **employees** and **employers pay NICs** related to the employee's earnings. NICs are not deductible from an employee's gross salary for income tax purposes. However, employers' contributions are deductible trade expenses.

2.1.1 Earnings

'Earnings' broadly comprise gross pay, excluding benefits which cannot be turned into cash by surrender (eg holidays). It also includes payments for use of the employees own car on business over the approved amount of 40p per mile (irrespective of total mileage.) Therefore, where an employer reimburses an employee using his own car for business mileage, the earnings element is the excess of the mileage rate paid over 40 per mile. This applies even where business mileage exceeds 10,000 pa.

Certain payments are exempt. In general the income tax and NIC exemptions mirror one another. For example, payment of personal incidental expenses covered by the £5/£10 a night income tax de minimis exemption are excluded from NIC earnings. Relocation expenses of a type exempt from income tax are also excluded from NIC earnings but without the income tax £8,000 upper limit (although expenses exceeding £8,000 are subject to Class 1A NICs as described below).

An expense with a business purpose is not treated as earnings. For example, if an employee is reimbursed for business travel or for staying in a hotel on the employer's business this is not normally 'earnings'. Again the NIC rules for travel expenses follow the income tax rules.

One commonly met expenses payment is telephone calls. If an employee is reimbursed for his own telephone charges the reimbursed cost of private calls (and all reimbursed rental) is earnings.

In general, non cash vouchers are subject to Class 1 NICs. However, the following are exempt.

- Childcare vouchers up to £55 per week
- Any other voucher which is exempt from income tax

An employer's contribution to an employee's occupational or private registered pension scheme is excluded from the definition of 'earnings'.

2.1.2 Rates of Class 1 NICs

The rates of contribution for 2007/08, and the income bands to which they apply, are set out in the Rates and Allowance Tables in this Text.

Employees pay main primary contributions of 11% of earnings between the earnings threshold of £5,225 and the upper earnings limit of £34,840 or the equivalent monthly or weekly limit (see below). They also pay additional primary contributions of 1% on earnings above the upper earning limit.

Employers pay secondary contributions of 12.8% on earnings above the earnings threshold of £5,225 or the equivalent monthly or weekly limit. There is no upper limit.

If an individual has more than one job then NIC is calculated on the earnings from each job separately and independently. However there is an overall annual maximum amount of Class 1 NIC any individual will be due to pay. If the total NIC paid from those different jobs exceeds the maximum that individual can claim a refund of the excess.

2.1.3 Earnings period

NICs are calculated in relation to an earnings period. This is the period to which earnings paid to an employee are deemed to relate. Where earnings are paid at regular intervals, the earnings period will generally be equated with the payment interval, for example a week or a month. An earnings period cannot usually be less than seven days long.

Exam focus point

> In the exam NIC will generally be calculated on an annual basis.

Question — **Class 1 contributions**

Sally works for Red plc. She is paid £3,000 per month.

Show Sally's primary contributions and the secondary contributions paid by Red plc for 2007/08.

Answer

Earnings threshold £5,225
Upper earnings limit £34,840
Annual salary £3,000 × 12 = £36,000

Sally	
Primary contributions	£
£(34,840 – 5,225) = £29,615 × 11% (main)	3,258
£(36,000 – 34,840) = £1,160 × 1% (additional)	12
Total primary contributions	3,270
Red plc	£
Secondary contributions	
£(36,000 – 5,225) = £30,775 × 12.8%	3,939

Special rules apply to company directors, regardless of whether they are paid at regular intervals or not. Where a person is a director at the beginning of the tax year, his earnings period is the tax year, even if he ceases to be director during the year. **The annual limits as shown in the Tax Tables apply**.

Question — **Employees and directors**

Bill and Ben work for Weed Ltd. Bill is a monthly paid employee. Ben who is a director of Weed Ltd, is also paid monthly. Each are paid an annual salary of £33,000 in 2007/08 and received a bonus of £3,000 in December 2007.

Show the primary and secondary contributions for both Bill and Ben, using a monthly earnings period for Bill.

Answer

Bill

Earnings threshold £5,225/12 = £435
Upper earnings limit £34,840/12 = £2,904
Regular monthly earnings £33,000/12 = £2,750

Primary contributions

	£
11 months	
£(2,750 – 435) = £2,315 ×11% × 11 (main only)	2,801
1 month (December)	
£(2,904 – 435) = £2,469 × 11% (main)	272
£(5,750 – 2,904) = £2,846 × 1% (additional)	28
Total primary contributions	3,101

Secondary contributions

	£
11 months	
£(2,750 – 435) = £2,315 × 12.8% × 11	3,260
1 month (December)	
£(2,750 + £3,000 – 435) = £5,315 ×12.8%	680
Total secondary contributions	3,940

Ben

Total earnings £(33,000 + 3,000) = £36,000

Primary contributions

	£
Total earnings exceed UEL	
£(34,840 – 5,225) = £29,615 × 11% (main)	3,258
£(36,000 – 34,840) = £1,160 × 1% (additional)	12
Total primary	3,270

Secondary contributions

£(36,000 – 5,225) = £30,775 × 12.8%	3,939

Because Ben is a director an annual earnings period applies. The effect of this is that increased primary contributions are due.

2.2 Class 1A NICs

FAST FORWARD

Class 1A NICs are payable by employers on benefits provided for employees.

Employers must pay Class 1A NIC at 12.8% in respect of most taxable benefits. Taxable benefits are calculated in accordance with income tax rules. There is no Class 1A in respect of any benefits already treated as earnings for Class 1 purposes (eg non cash vouchers). Tax exempt benefits are not liable to Class 1A NIC.

No contributions are levied when an employee is earning less than £8,500 a year.

Question — Class IA NIC

James has the following benefits for income tax purposes

	£
Company car	5,200
Living accommodation	10,000
Medical insurance	800

Calculate the Class 1A NICs that the employer will have to pay.

Answer

Total benefits are £16,000 (£10,000 + £5,200 + £800)

Class 1A NICs:

12.8% × £16,000 = £2,048

2.3 Miscellaneous points

Class 1 contributions are collected under the PAYE system described earlier in this Text. Class 1A contributions are collected annually in arrears, and are due by 19 July following the tax year.

Class 1 and 1A contributions broadly apply to amounts which are taxable as employment income. They do not apply to dividends paid to directors and employees who are also shareholders in the company.

3 Class 2 and Class 4 NICs for self-employed persons

FAST FORWARD

The self employed pay Class 2 and Class 4 NICs. Class 2 NICs are paid at a flat weekly rate. Class 4 NICs are based on the level of the individual's profits.

3.1 Class 2 contributions

The self employed (sole traders and partners) **pay NICs in two ways. Class 2 contributions are payable at a flat rate. The Class 2 rate for 2007/08 is £2.20 a week.**

Self employed people must register with HMRC for Class 2 contributions within three months of the end of the month in which they start self employment. People who fail to register may incur a £100 penalty.

3.2 Class 2 contributions

Additionally, **the self employed pay Class 4 NICs,** based on the level of the individual's taxable business profits.

Main rate Class 4 NICs are calculated by applying a fixed percentage (8% for 2007/08) to the individual's profits between the lower limit (£5,225 for 2007/08) and the upper limit (£34,840 for 2007/08). Additional rate contributions are 1% (for 2007/08) on profits above that limit.

3.3 Example: Class 4 contributions

If a sole trader had profits of £14,080 for 2007/08 his Class 4 NIC liability would be as follows.

	£
Profits	14,080
Less lower limit	(5,225)
	8,855

Class 4 NICs = 8% × £8,855 = £708.40 (main only)

3.4 Example: additional Class 4 contributions

If an individual's profits are £36,000, additional Class 4 NICs are due on the excess over the upper limit. Thus the amount payable in 2007/08 is as follows.

	£
Profits (upper limit)	34,840
Less lower limit	(5,225)
	29,615
Main rate Class 4 NICs 8% × £29,615	2,369
Additional rate Class 4 NICs £(36,000 – 34,840) = £1,160 × 1%	12
	2,381

For Class 4 NIC purposes, profits are the trade profits taxable for income tax purposes, less trading losses.

There is no deduction for personal pension premiums.

Class 4 NICs are collected by HMRC. They are paid at the same time as the associated income tax liability. Interest is charged on overdue contributions. The administration of tax is covered later in this Text.

Chapter Roundup

- Class 1 NICs are payable by employees and employers on earnings.
- Class 1A NICs are payable by employers on benefits provided for employees.
- The self employed pay Class 2 and Class 4 NICs. Class 2 NICs are paid at a flat weekly rate. Class 4 NICs are based on the level of the individual's profits.

Quick Quiz

1 What national insurance contributions are payable by employers and employees?

2 On what are Class 1A NICs based?

3 How are Class 4 NICs calculated?

Answers to Quick Quiz

1 Employees – Class 1 primary contributions

Employers – Class 1 secondary contributions
Class 1A contributions

2 Class 1A NICs are based on taxable benefits paid to P11D employees.

3 The main rate is a fixed percentage (8% in 2007/08) of an individual's tax profits between an upper limit and lower limit. The additional rate applies above the upper limit.

Now try the questions below from the Exam Question Bank

Number	Level	Marks	Time
Q18	Examination	10	18 mins
Q19	Examination	15	27 mins

Part B
Taxation of chargeable gains

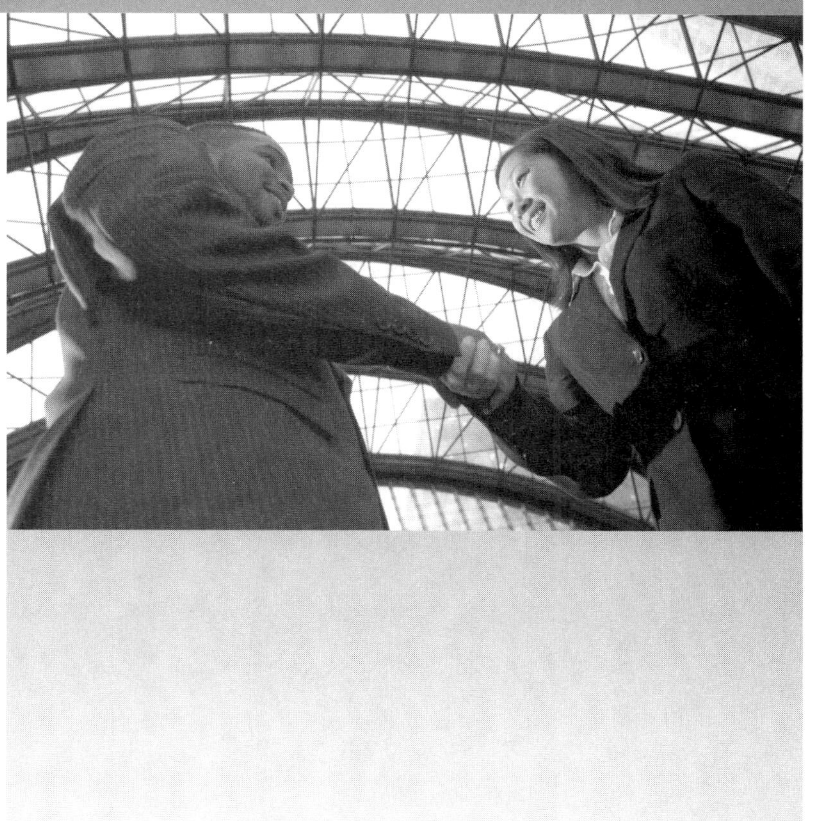

13

Computing chargeable gains

Topic list	Syllabus reference
1 Chargeable persons, disposals and assets	D1(a)-(c)
2 The annual exemption	D5(c)
3 Capital losses	D2(c)
4 Taper relief	D5(a), (b)
5 CGT payable by individuals	D5(c)

Introduction

Now that we have completed our study of the income tax and national insurance liabilities we turn our attention to the capital gains tax computation.

We look at the circumstances in which a chargeable gain may arise and then we look at how an individual's CGT liability is computed.

First we consider the annual exemption and then we look at the relief for capital losses, including the interaction between capital losses brought forward and the annual exemption.

We next study taper relief noting how it is applied to net capital gains after loss reliefs but before the annual exemption.

Finally, we look at the computation of the CGT liability.

In the next chapters we will see how chargeable gains are computed and look at the available reliefs.

Study guide

		Intellectual level
D1	**The scope of the taxation of capital gains**	
(a)	Describe the scope of capital gains tax.	2
(b)	Explain how the residence and ordinary residence of an individual is determined.	2
(c)	List those assets which are exempt.	1
D2	**The basic principles of computing gains and losses**	
(c)	Explain the treatment of capital losses for both individuals and companies.	1
D5	**The computation of capital gains tax payable by individuals**	
(a)	Recognise a business asset for the purposes of taper relief.	2
(b)	Compute taper relief for business and non business assets.	2
(c)	Compute the amount of capital gains tax payable.	2

Exam guide

Question 3 of the exam will always be a 20 mark question on capital gains, and there may also be an element of capital gains in questions 1 and/or 2. Question 3 may, however, involve either an individual or a company, so you may not have to deal with taper relief, the annual exemption or the computation of CGT payable. These are however all fundamental to your studies and cannot be overlooked.

1 Chargeable persons, disposals and assets

FAST FORWARD

A gain is chargeable if there is a chargeable disposal of a chargeable asset by a chargeable person.

Key term

For a chargeable gain to arise there must be:

- A **chargeable person**; and
- A **chargeable disposal**; and
- A **chargeable asset**

otherwise no charge to tax occurs.

1.1 Chargeable persons

FAST FORWARD

Capital gains are chargeable on individuals and companies.

The following are chargeable persons.

- **Individuals**
- **Companies**

We will look at the taxation of chargeable gains on companies later in this Text.

1.2 Chargeable disposals

The following are chargeable disposals.

- **Sales of assets or parts of assets**
- **Gifts of assets or parts of assets**
- **The loss or destruction of assets**

A chargeable disposal occurs on the date of the contract (where there is one, whether written or oral), or the date of a conditional contract becoming unconditional. This may differ from the date of transfer of the asset. However, when a capital sum is received for example on the loss or destruction of an asset, the disposal takes place on the day the sum is received.

Where a disposal involves an acquisition by someone else, the date of acquisition for that person is the same as the date of disposal.

Transfers of assets on death are exempt disposals.

1.3 Chargeable assets

All forms of property, wherever in the world they are situated, are chargeable assets unless they are specifically designated as exempt.

1.4 Overseas aspects of CGT

FAST FORWARD

CGT applies primarily to persons resident or ordinarily resident in the UK.

Individuals are liable to CGT on the disposal of assets situated anywhere in the world if for any part of the tax year in which the disposal occurs they are resident or ordinarily resident in the UK. By concession, when a person first becomes resident in the UK, he is normally charged to CGT only on those gains which arise after his arrival provided he has not been resident or ordinarily resident in the UK for four out of the last seven years.

Exam focus point

The computation of capital gains arising on overseas assets is outside the scope of your syllabus.

1.5 Exempt assets

The following are exempt assets.

- **Motor vehicles** suitable for private use
- **National Savings and Investments certificates** and **premium bonds**
- Foreign currency for private use
- Decorations for bravery where awarded, not purchased
- Damages for personal or professional injury
- **Gilt-edged securities (treasury stock)**
- **Qualifying corporate bonds (QCBs)**
- **Certain chattels**
- Debts (except debts on a security)
- Investments held in individual savings accounts

If an asset is an exempt asset any gain is not taxable and any loss is not allowable.

1.6 Chargeable gain or loss

The computation of chargeable gains and allowable losses will be covered in the following sessions.

2 The annual exemption

FAST FORWARD

An individual is entitled to an annual exemption for each tax year.

There is an annual exemption for each tax year. For each individual for 2007/08 it is £9,200. The annual exemption is deducted from the chargeable gains for the year after the deductions of losses and other reliefs.

Thus if Susie has chargeable gains for 2007/08 of £15,000 her taxable gains are £15,000 – £9,200 = £5,800.

Companies are not entitled to the annual exemption.

3 Capital losses

FAST FORWARD

Losses are set off against gains of the same year (or accounting period) and any excess carried forward. Losses of individuals are set off before taper relief. For individuals, brought forward losses are only set off to reduce net gains down to the amount of the annual exemption.

3.1 Calculation of losses

Losses are, in general, calculated in the same way as gains.

The indexation allowance (see next chapter) **cannot create or increase an allowable loss**. If there is a gain before the indexation allowance, the allowance can reduce that gain to zero, but no further. If there is a loss before the indexation allowance, there is no indexation allowance. (A gain remaining after the indexation allowance is called an **indexed gain**.)

3.2 Allowable losses of the same year

Allowable capital losses arising in a tax year are deducted from indexed gains arising in the same tax year.

Any loss which cannot be set off is carried forward to set against future indexed gains. Losses must be used as soon as possible (but see below).

Losses are offset against gains before taper relief (see below).

3.3 Allowable losses brought forward

Allowable losses brought forward are only set off to reduce current year gains less current year allowable losses to the annual exempt amount. No set-off is made if net chargeable gains for the current year do not exceed the annual exempt amount.

Losses are offset against gains before taper relief (see below).

3.4 Example: the use of losses

(a) George has gains for 2007/08 of £10,000 and allowable losses of £6,000. As the losses are *current year losses* they must be fully relieved against the £10,000 of gains to produce net gains before taper relief of £4,000, despite the fact that net gains are below the annual exemption.

(b) Bob has gains of £13,100 for 2007/08 and allowable losses brought forward of £6,000. Bob restricts his loss relief to £3,900 so as to leave net gains before taper relief of £(13,100 – 3,900) = £9,200, which will be exactly covered by his annual exemption for 2007/08. The remaining £2,100 of losses will be carried forward to 2008/09.

(c) Tom has gains of £5,000 for 2007/08 and losses brought forward from 2006/07 of £4,000. He will leapfrog 2007/08 and carry forward all of his losses to 2008/09. His gains of £5,000 are covered by his annual exemption for 2007/08.

3.5 Capital losses for companies

Companies are not eligible for taper relief and do not have an annual exemption. Losses of the current accounting period must be deducted from the gains of the current accounting period. Excess losses are carried forward and deducted from net gains in future accounting periods (see later in this Text).

4 Taper relief

Individuals are also entitled to taper relief, depending on the length of ownership of the asset. There is more generous taper relief for business assets than non-business assets.

4.1 Rates of relief

Taper relief may be available to reduce gains realised after 5 April 1998 by individuals. Taper relief does not apply to companies.

Taper relief reduces the percentage of the gain chargeable according to how many complete years the asset has been held since acquisition or 6 April 1998 if later. Taper relief is more generous for business assets than for non-business assets.

The percentages of gains which remain chargeable after taper relief are set out below.

Number of complete years after 5.4.98 for which asset held	*Gain on business assets % of gain chargeable*	*Gain on non business assets % of gain chargeable*
0	100	100
1	50	100
2	25	100
3	25	95
4	25	90
5	25	85
6	25	80
7	25	75
8	25	70
9	25	65
10	25	60

Exam focus point

You will be given the above percentages in your exam.

Non-business assets acquired before 17 March 1998 qualify for an additional 1 year (a 'bonus year') of taper relief. For disposals of non-business assets during 2007/08, taper relief will be based on ten complete years of ownership where the asset was owned prior to 17 March 1998. Only 60% of the gain will be chargeable.

4.2 Example: complete years held for taper relief

Peter buys a non business asset on 1 January 1998 and sells it on 1 July 2007. For taper relief purposes Peter is treated as if he had held the asset for 10 complete years (nine complete years after 5 April 1998 plus one additional year).

If the asset had been a business asset, Peter holds the asset for nine years only but in any case has maximum taper relief after two years ownership.

4.3 Application of taper relief

Taper relief is applied to net gains after the deduction of current year and brought forward losses to give chargeable gains for the year.

The annual exemption is then deducted from the chargeable gains to give the taxable gains.

Key terms

Chargeable gain: The capital gain after deducting the indexation allowance and taper relief, but before deducting the annual exemption.

Taxable gain: The chargeable gain less the annual exemption.

4.4 Example: use of losses and taper relief

Ruby sold a business asset in July 2007 which she had purchased in January 2006. She realised a gain (before taper relief) of £18,400. She also sold a painting in 2007/08 realising an allowable loss of £6,000. She has a capital loss brought forward from 2006/07 of £10,000.

Losses are dealt with **before** taper relief. However losses brought forward are only deducted from net current gains to the extent that the gains exceed the CGT annual exemption:

	£
Gain	18,400
Loss	(6,000)
Current net gains	12,400
Less brought forward loss	(3,200)
Net gains before taper relief	9,200
Chargeable gains (after taper relief) (1 year ownership) £9,200 × 50%	4,600
Less annual exemption	(9,200)
Taxable gains	Nil

Note that the benefit of the taper relief is effectively wasted since the brought forward loss reduces the gain down to the annual exemption amount but taper is then applied to that amount reducing it further.

The loss carried forward is £6,800 (£10,000 – £3,200).

Allocate losses to gains in the way that produces the lowest tax charge. **Losses should therefore be deducted from the gains attracting the lowest rate of taper** (ie where the highest percentage of the gain remains chargeable).

4.5 Example: allocation of losses to gains

Alastair made the following capital losses and gains in 2007/08:

	£
Loss	10,000
Gains (before taper relief)	
Asset A (non-business asset)	25,000
Asset B (business asset)	18,000

Asset A was purchased in December 1997 and sold in January 2008. Taper relief reduces the gain to 60% of the original gain (10 years including additional year; non-business asset). Asset B was purchased on 5 November 2004 and sold on 17 December 2007. Taper relief reduces the gain to 25% of the original gain (3 years; business asset).

The best use of the loss is to offset it against the gain on the non-business asset:

	£	£
Gain – Asset A	25,000	
Less loss	(10,000)	
Net gain before taper relief	15,000	
Gain after taper relief (£15,000 × 60%)		9,000
Gain – Asset B	18,000	
Gain after taper relief £18,000 × 25%		4,500
Chargeable gains		13,500
Less annual exemption		(9,200)
Taxable gains		4,300

4.6 Business assets

A business asset is:

- An asset **used for the purposes of a trade** carried on by any individual or partnership (whether or not the owner of the asset is involved in carrying on the trade concerned) or by a qualifying company.
- An asset **held for the purposes of any office or employment** held by the individual owner with a person carrying on a trade.
- **Shares in a qualifying company** held by an individual.

A **trading company** (or holding company of a trading group) is a qualifying company if:

(a) It is **not listed** on a recognised stock exchange nor a 51% subsidiary of a listed company (companies listed on the Alternative Investment Market (AIM) are unlisted for this purpose), or

(b) The individual shareholder is an **officer or employee** of the company, or

(c) The individual holds at least **5% of the voting rights** in the company.

A **non-trading company** (or holding company of a non-trading group) is also a qualifying company if:

(a) The individual is an **officer or employee** of the company, **and**

(b) The individual did not have a **material interest** in the company or in any other company which at that time had control of the company.

A **material interest** is defined as possession or the ability to control more than 10% of the issued shares or voting in the company, or an entitlement to more than 10% of the income or the assets of the company available for distribution. It is necessary to look at the combined rights of the individual and of any person connected with him.

A taxpayer is broadly **connected** with his own or his spouse's/civil partner's close relatives and their spouses/civil partners and with his business partners (and their spouses/civil partners). A company is connected with the persons controlling them and with other companies under the same control.

4.7 Miscellaneous points

There are certain special situations which will affect the operation of taper relief and will be covered later in this Text:

(a) Where there has been a transfer of assets between spouses or civil partners (a no loss/no gain transfer) the taper on a subsequent disposal will be based on the combined period of holding by the spouses or civil partners

(b) Where gains have been relieved under a provision which reduces the cost of the asset in the hands of a new owner (such as gift relief) the taper will operate by reference to the holding period of the new owner.

5 CGT payable by individuals

FAST FORWARD

Individuals pay CGT on gains arising in a tax year at 10%, 20%, or 40%.

Taxable gains are chargeable to capital gains tax as if the gains were an extra slice of savings income for the year of assessment concerned. This means that CGT may be due at 10%, 20% or 40%.

The rate bands are used first to cover income and then gains. If a gift aid payment and/or personal pension contribution is made, the basic rate can be extended, as for income tax calculations (see earlier).

Exam focus point

Taxable gains are never included in the income tax computation. The amount of taxable income is used only to determine the tax rates which apply to the taxable gains.

Question — **Rates of CGT**

In 2007/08, Carol, a single woman, has the following income, gains and losses.

	£
Salary	37,540
Chargeable gains (not eligible for taper relief)	27,100
Allowable capital losses	7,700

Calculate the CGT payable.

Answer

(a) Carol's taxable income is as follows.

	£
Salary	37,540
Less personal allowance	(5,225)
Taxable income	32,315

(b) The gains to be taxed are as follows.

	£
Gains	27,100
Less losses	(7,700)
	19,400
Less annual exemption	(9,200)
Taxable gains	10,200

(c) The tax bands are allocated as follows.

	Total	*Income*	*Gains*
Starting rate	2,230	2,230	0
Basic rate	32,370	30,085	2,285
Higher rate	7,915	0	7,915
		32,315	10,200

(d) The CGT payable is as follows.

	£
£2,285 × 20%	457
£7,915 × 40%	3,166
Total CGT payable	3,623

Chapter Roundup

- A gain is chargeable if there is a chargeable disposal of a chargeable asset by a chargeable person.
- Capital gains are chargeable on individuals and companies.
- CGT applies primarily to persons resident or ordinarily resident in the UK.
- An individual is entitled to an annual exemption for each tax year.
- Losses are set off against gains of the same year (or accounting period) and any excess carried forward. Losses of individuals are set off before taper relief. For individuals, brought forward losses are only set off to reduce net gains down to the amount of the annual exemption.
- Individuals are also entitled to taper relief, depending on the length of ownership of the asset. There is more generous taper relief for business assets than non-business assets.
- Individuals pay CGT on gains arising in a tax year at 10%, 20%, or 40%.

Quick Quiz

1 Give some examples of chargeable disposals.

2 On what assets does a UK resident pay CGT?

3 To what extent must allowable losses be set against chargeable gains?

4 Mike owned a business asset for two and a half years. His gain on sale is £20,000. What is his gain after taper relief?

5 At what rate or rates do individuals pay CGT?

Answers to Quick Quiz

1 The following are chargeable disposals

- Sales of assets or parts of assets
- Gifts of assets or parts of assets
- Receipts of capital sums following the loss or destruction of an asset

2 All assets, whether situated in the UK or abroad, unless specifically exempt.

3 Current year losses must be set off against gains in full, even if this reduces net gains below the annual exemption. Losses brought forward are set off to bring down untapered gains to the level of the annual exemption

4 Two complete years ownership

$25\% \times £20,000 = £5,000$

5 10% (gains within starting rate band), 20% (gains within basic rate band) or 40%.

Now try the questions below from the Exam Question Bank

Number	Level	Marks	Time
Q20	Introductory	11	20 mins

14 Computing chargeable gains – further aspects

Topic list	Syllabus reference
1 Computing a gain or loss	D2(a)
2 The indexation allowance	D2(b)
3 Transfers between spouses/civil partners	D2(d) B6(c)
4 Part disposals	D2(e)
5 The damage, loss or destruction of an asset	D2(f)

Introduction

In the previous chapter we saw how to calculate an individual's taxable gains for the year after losses, taper relief and the annual exemption. We now look at the detailed calculation of the gain on a disposal of an asset, (including the indexation allowance where appropriate).

Next we consider the special rules for transfers between spouses or civil partners.

We then look at part disposals. If only part of an asset has been disposed of we need to know how to allocate the cost between the part disposed of and the part retained.

Finally, we consider the damage or destruction of an asset and the receipt of compensation or insurance proceeds, and look at the reliefs available where the proceeds are applied in restoring or replacing the asset.

In the following chapters we look at further rules, including those for disposals of shares, and various CGT reliefs that may be available.

Study guide

		Intellectual level
D2	**The basic principles of computing gains and losses**	
(a)	Compute capital gains for both individuals and companies.	2
(b)	Calculate the indexation allowance available to companies, and identify the indexation allowance available to individuals.	2
(d)	Explain the treatment of transfers between a husband and wife or between a couple in a civil partnership.	2
(e)	Compute the amount of allowable expenditure for a part disposal.	2
(f)	Explain the treatment where an asset is damaged, lost or destroyed, and the implications of receiving insurance proceeds and reinvesting such proceeds.	2

Exam guide

Since question three will always be a 20 mark question on capital gains you are almost certain to have to prepare a detailed capital gains computation, whether for an individual or company. Learn the basic layout, so that slotting in the figures becomes automatic. Then in the exam you will be able to turn your attention to the particular points raised in the question. The A/(A+B) formula for part disposals must be learnt. The rules for damage or destruction of an asset are less likely to be examined in detail, but try to remember the objective of the reliefs available where the proceeds are used for restoration or replacement and they will seem more straightforward.

1 Computing a gain or loss

FAST FORWARD

An indexed gain is computed by taking the proceeds and deducting both the cost and the indexation allowance. Incidental costs of acquisition and disposal may be deducted together with any enhancement expenditure reflected in the state and nature of the asset at the date of disposal.

1.1 Basic calculation

An indexed gain (or an allowable loss) is generally calculated as follows.

	£
Disposal consideration	45,000
Less incidental costs of disposal	(400)
Net proceeds	44,600
Less allowable costs	(21,000)
Unindexed gain	23,600
Less indexation allowance (if available)	(8,800)
Indexed gain	14,800

For individuals, taper relief may then apply (see earlier in this Text).

Usually the disposal consideration is the proceeds of sale of the asset, but a disposal is deemed to take place at market value:

- where the disposal is **not a bargain at arm's length**
- where the disposal is made for a **consideration which cannot be valued**
- where the disposal is by way of a **gift**.

Special valuation rules apply for shares (see later in this Text).

Incidental costs of disposal may include:

- valuation fees
- estate agency fees
- advertising costs
- legal costs

These costs should be deducted separately from any other allowable costs (because they do not qualify for any indexation allowance if it is available on that disposal).

Allowable costs include:

- the original cost of acquisition
- incidental costs of acquisition
- capital expenditure incurred in enhancing the asset

Incidental costs of acquisition may include the types of cost listed above as incidental costs of disposal, but acquisition costs do qualify for indexation allowance (from the month of acquisition) if it is available on the disposal.

Enhancement expenditure is capital expenditure which enhances the value of the asset and is reflected in the state or nature of the asset at the time of disposal, or expenditure incurred in establishing, preserving or defending title to, or a right over, the asset. Excluded from this category are:

- costs of repairs and maintenance
- costs of insurance
- any expenditure deductible from trading profits
- any expenditure met by public funds (for example council grants)

Enhancement expenditure may qualify for indexation allowance from the month in which it becomes due and payable. Taper relief, however, will apply to the whole gain from April 1998 or the date of acquisition, if later, regardless of the date of the enhancement expenditure.

Question — Calculating the gain

Joanne bought a piece of land as an investment on 1 October 2005 for £20,000. The legal costs of purchase were £250.

Joanne sold the land on 12 December 2007 for £35,000. She incurred estate agency fees of £700 and legal costs of £500 on the sale.

Calculate Joanne's gain on sale.

Answer

	£
Proceeds of sale	35,000
Less costs of disposal £(700 + 500)	(1,200)
	33,800
Less costs of acquisition £(20,000 + 250)	(20,250)
Gain	13,550

2 The indexation allowance

FAST FORWARD

The indexation allowance gives relief for the inflationary element of a gain but, for individuals, is only available up to April 1998.

The purpose of having an indexation allowance is to remove the inflationary element of a gain from taxation. It is calculated by reference to the movement in the Retail Prices Index (RPI).

Individuals are entitled to an indexation allowance from the date of acquisition of an asset until April 1998. From April 1998 the indexation allowance has been replaced by taper relief.

Exam focus point

For an individual you will be given the indexation factor from acquisition to April 1998 in the exam. You may also be given the indexation factor from acquisition to the date of sale, and you must be careful only to use the factor to April 1998.

The indexation factor is multiplied by the cost of the asset to calculate the indexation allowance. If the RPI has fallen, the indexation allowance is zero: it is not negative.

Question — The indexation allowance

Tracey acquired an asset on 15 February 1983 at a cost of £5,000. Enhancement expenditure of £2,000 was incurred on 10 April 1984. The asset is sold for £25,500 on 20 December 2007. Incidental costs of sale are £500. The indexation factor from February 1983 to April 1998 is 0.949 and from April 1984 to April 1998 is 0.835. The indexation factor from February 1983 to December 2007 is 1.532 and from April 1984 to December 2007 is 1.370. Calculate the indexed gain arising.

Answer

The indexation allowance is available until April 1998 and is computed as follows.

	£
0.949 × £5,000	4,745
0.835 × £2,000	1,670
	6,415

The computation of the indexed gain is as follows.

	£
Proceeds	25,500
Less incidental costs of sale	(500)
Net proceeds	25,000
Less allowable costs £(5,000 + 2,000)	(7,000)
Unindexed gain	18,000
Less indexation allowance (see above)	(6,415)
Indexed gain	11,585

The indexation allowance cannot create or increase an allowable loss. If there is a gain before the indexation allowance, the allowance can reduce that gain to zero, but no further. If there is a loss before the indexation allowance, there is no indexation allowance.

3 Transfers between spouses/civil partners

Disposals between spouses or members of a civil partnership are made on a no gain no loss basis and do not give rise to a chargeable gain or allowable loss.

Spouses and civil partners are taxed as separate individuals. Each has his own annual exemption, and losses of one spouse or civil partner cannot be set against gains of the other spouse or civil partner.

Disposals between spouses or civil partners living together give rise to no gain no loss, whatever actual price (if any) was charged by the transferor. **This means that there is no chargeable gain or allowable loss, and the transferee takes over the transferor's indexed cost.**

For taper relief purposes disposals by the transferee will be based on the combined period of ownership. For assets other than shares, business use by the transferor will be treated as business use by the transferee. Shares will only be treated as business assets whilst the company is a qualifying company for the transferee.

Question

Inter spouse transfer

Harry bought an office block on 11 May 1996 for £150,000. He gave it to his wife Margaret on 18 June 2005 when it was worth £350,000. Margaret sold it on 27 August 2007 for £400,000.

The indexation factor from May 1996 to April 1998 is 0.063, and from May 1996 to June 2005 is 0.176.

Calculate any chargeable gains arising to Harry and Margaret, assuming that Harry has used the premises for business purposes throughout the whole period, but Margaret did not.

Answer

The disposal from Harry to Margaret is a no gain no loss disposal. Harry has no chargeable gain, and the base cost for Margaret is cost plus indexation:

	£
Cost	150,000
Indexation May 1996 – April 1998	
£150,000 × 0.063	9,450
Base cost for Margaret	159,450

The chargeable gain on the sale by Margaret is:

	£
Proceeds of sale	400,000
Less cost	(159,450)
Gain	240,550

The asset is a business asset for Margaret as it was a business asset for Harry throughout. Gain after taper relief (business asset > 2 years)

25% × £240,550 = £60,138

4 Part disposals

FAST FORWARD

On a part disposal, the cost must be apportioned between the part disposed of and the part retained.

The disposal of part of a chargeable asset is a chargeable event. The chargeable gain (or allowable loss) is computed by deducting a fraction of the original cost of the whole asset from the disposal value. The balance of the cost is carried forward until the eventual disposal of the asset.

Exam formula

The fraction is:

$$\text{Cost} \times \frac{A}{A+B} = \frac{\text{value of the part disposed of}}{\text{value of the part disposed of} + \text{market value of the remainder}}$$

In this fraction, A is the proceeds *before* deducting incidental costs of disposal.

The part disposal fraction should not be applied indiscriminately. Any expenditure incurred wholly in respect of a particular part of an asset should be treated as an allowable deduction in full for that part and not apportioned. An example of this is incidental selling expenses, which are wholly attributable to the part disposed of.

Question

Part disposal

Mr Heal owns a painting which originally cost him £27,000 in March 1984 and had an indexed cost at April 1998 of £50,166. He sold a quarter interest in the painting in July 2007 for £18,000. The market value of the three-quarter share remaining is estimated to be £36,000. What is the chargeable gain after taper relief?

Answer

The amount of the indexed cost attributable to the part sold is

$$\frac{18{,}000}{18{,}000+36{,}000} \times £50{,}166 = £16{,}722$$

	£
Proceeds	18,000
Less indexed cost (see above)	(16,722)
Gain before taper relief	1,278

Gain after taper relief (6.4.98 – 5.4.07 = 9 years plus additional year = 10 years)

60% × £1,278 = £767

5 The damage, loss or destruction of an asset

FAST FORWARD

The gain which would otherwise arise on the receipt of insurance proceeds may, subject to certain conditions, be deferred.

5.1 Destruction or loss of an asset

If an asset is destroyed any compensation or insurance monies received will normally be brought into an ordinary CGT disposal computation as proceeds.

If all the proceeds are applied for the replacement of the asset within 12 months, any gain can be deducted from the cost of the replacement asset.

If only part of the proceeds are used, the gain immediately chargeable can be limited to the amount not used. The rest of the gain is then deducted from the cost of the replacement.

Question — **Asset destroyed**

Fiona bought a non-business asset for £25,000 in June 2004. It was destroyed in July 2007. Insurance proceeds were £34,000, and Fiona spent £30,500 on a replacement asset in January 2008. Compute the chargeable gain and the base cost of the new asset.

Answer

	£
Proceeds	34,000
Less cost	(25,000)
	9,000
Gain immediately chargeable £(34,000 – 30,500)	(3,500)
Deduction from base cost	5,500

The base cost of the new asset is £(30,500 – 5,500) = £25,000.

The gain chargeable of £3,500 qualifies for taper relief (3 complete years of ownership of a non-business asset). 95% of the gain is charged to tax ie £3,325.

5.2 Damage to an asset

If an asset is damaged then the receipt of any compensation or insurance monies received will normally be treated as a part disposal.

If all the proceeds are applied in restoring the asset the taxpayer can elect to disregard the part disposal. The proceeds will instead be deducted from the cost of the asset.

Question — **Asset damaged**

Frank bought an investment property for £100,000 in May 2007. It was damaged two and a half months later. Insurance proceeds of £20,000 were received in November 2007, and Frank spent a total of £25,000 on restoring the property. Prior to restoration the property was worth £120,000. Compute the chargeable gain, if any, and the base cost of the restored property assuming Frank elects for there to be no part disposal.

How would your answer differ if no election were made?

Answer

As the proceeds have been applied in restoring the property Frank has elected to disregard the part disposal.

The base cost of the restored property is £(100,000 – 20,000 + 25,000) = £105,000.

If no election were made, the receipt of the proceeds would be a part disposal in November 2007. The gain would be:

	£
Proceeds	20,000
Less cost £100,000 × 20,000/(20,000 + 120,000)	(14,286)
Gain	5,714

No taper relief is available as the asset is a non-business asset held for less than three years.

The base cost of the restored asset is £(100,000 – 14,286) + £25,000 = £110,714.

Assuming this is Frank's only disposal in the tax year, the gain is covered by the annual exemption. It may therefore be preferable not to make the election.

Chapter Roundup

- An indexed gain is computed by taking the proceeds and deducting both the cost and the indexation allowance. Incidental costs of acquisition and disposal may be deducted together with any enhancement expenditure reflected in the state and nature of the asset at the date of disposal.
- The indexation allowance gives relief for the inflationary element of a gain but, for individuals, is only available up to April 1998.
- Disposals between spouses or members of a civil partnership are made on a no gain no loss basis and do not give rise to a chargeable gain or allowable loss.
- On a part disposal, the cost must be apportioned between the part disposed of and the part retained.
- The gain which would otherwise arise on the receipt of insurance proceeds may, subject to certain conditions, be deferred.

Quick Quiz

1. What is enhancement expenditure?
2. 10 acres of land are sold for £15,000 out of 25 acres. Original cost in 1999 was £9,000. Costs of sale are £2,000. Rest of land valued at £30,000. What is the total amount deductible from proceeds?
3. Emma drops and destroys a vase. She receives compensation for £2,000 from her insurance company. How can she avoid a charge to CGT arising?

Answers to Quick Quiz

1 Enhancement expenditure is capital expenditure enhancing the value of the asset and reflected in the state/nature of the asset at disposal, or expenditure incurred in establishing, preserving or defending title to asset.

2 $\frac{15{,}000}{15{,}000 + 30{,}000} \times$ £9,000 = £3,000 + £2,000 (costs of disposal) = £5,000

3 Emma can avoid a charge to CGT on receipt of the compensation by investing at least £2,000 in a replacement asset within 12 months.

Now try the questions below from the Exam Question Bank

Number	Level	Marks	Time
Q21	Examination	10	18 mins

15

Chattels and the principal private residence exemption

Topic list	Syllabus reference
1 Chattels	D3(a), (b)
2 Wasting assets	D3(a), (c)
3 Private residences	D3(d)-(f)

Introduction

In the previous two chapters we have considered the basic rules for the capital gains computation and the calculation of CGT payable by an individual, together with the rules for part disposals.

We now turn our attention to specific assets, starting with chattels. Where there is a disposal of low value assets, the chattels rules may apply to restrict the gain or allowable loss. The gain may even be exempt in certain circumstances. We look at the detailed rules.

The highest value item that an individual is likely to sell is his home. We look at the rules to see when the gain may be wholly or partly exempt.

In the next chapter we will consider the reliefs specifically available on business assets, and later we will turn our attention to the special rules for shares.

Study guide

		Intellectual level
D3	**Gains and losses on the disposal of movable and immovable property**	
(a)	Identify when chattels and wasting assets are exempt.	1
(b)	Compute the chargeable gain when a chattel is disposed of.	2
(c)	Calculate the chargeable gain when a wasting asset is disposed of.	2
(d)	Compute the exemption when a principal private residence is disposed of.	2
(e)	Calculate the chargeable gain when a principal private residence has been used for business purposes.	2
(f)	Identify the amount of letting relief available when a principal private residence has been let out.	2

Exam guide

As at least 20% of the marks for the exam will be for capital gains, you are quite likely to come across a question on either chattels or the reliefs available on the disposal of a principal private residence.

With chattels always look for the exemption for wasting chattels, a restriction of the gain if proceeds exceed £6,000, or a restriction of loss relief if proceeds are less than £6,000. The rules for chattels apply to companies as well as individuals, but watch out for assets on which capital allowances have been given.

On the disposal of a principal private residence if there has been any non-occupation or business use schedule out the relevant dates before you start to calculate the gain in case it turns out to be wholly exempt.

1 Chattels

FAST FORWARD

Gains on most wasting chattels are exempt and losses are not allowable.

When a non-wasting chattel is sold for less than £6,000, any gain is exempt. There is marginal relief for gains where sale proceeds exceed £6,000. Losses are restricted where sales proceeds exceed £6,000.

1.1 What is a chattel?

Key term

A **chattel** is tangible moveable property.

A **wasting asset** is an asset with an estimated remaining useful life of 50 years or less.

Plant and machinery, whose predictable useful life is always deemed to be less than 50 years, is an example of a wasting chattel (unless it is immoveable, in which case it will be wasting but not a chattel). Machinery includes, in addition to its ordinary meaning, motor vehicles (unless exempt as cars), railway and traction engines, engine-powered boats and clocks.

1.2 Wasting chattels

Wasting chattels are exempt (so that there are no chargeable gains and no allowable losses).

There is one exception to this: assets used for the purpose of a trade, profession or vocation in respect of which capital allowances have been or could have been claimed. This means that items of plant and machinery used in a trade are not exempt merely on the ground that they are wasting. (However, cars are always exempt.)

1.3 Gains

If a chattel is not exempt under the wasting chattels rule, any gain arising on its disposal will still be exempt if the asset is sold for gross proceeds of £6,000 or less, even if capital allowances were claimed on it.

If sale proceeds exceed £6,000, any gain is limited to a maximum of 5/3 × (gross proceeds – £6,000).

Question — **Chattels: gains**

Adam purchased a Chippendale chair on 1 June 1984. Its indexed cost at 5 April 1998 was £1,458. On 10 October 2007 he sold the chair at auction for £6,300 (which was net of the auctioneer's 10% commission). What is the chargeable gain?

Answer

	£
Proceeds (£6,300 × 100/90)	7,000
Less incidental costs of sale	(700)
Net proceeds	6,300
Less indexed cost	(1,458)
Indexed gain	4,842

The maximum gain is 5/3 × £(7,000 – 6,000) = £1,667

The chargeable gain before taper relief is the lower of £4,842 and £1,667, so it is £1,667.

Gain after taper relief £1,667 × 60% = £1,000

Note. Non-business asset taper relief is available for ten years' ownership post 5.4.98 (including the additional year).

1.4 Losses

Where a chattel which is not exempt under the wasting chattels rule is sold for less than £6,000 and a loss arises, the allowable loss is restricted by assuming that the chattel was sold for £6,000. This rule cannot turn a loss into a gain, only reduce the loss, perhaps to zero.

Question — **Chattels: losses**

Eve purchased a rare first edition on 1 July 1999 for £8,000 which she sold in October 2007 at auction for £2,700 (which was net of 10% commission). Compute the gain or loss.

Answer

	£
Proceeds (assumed)	6,000
Less incidental costs of disposal (£2,700 × 10/90)	(300)
	5,700
Less cost	(8,000)
Allowable loss	(2,300)

1.5 Chattels and capital allowances

FAST FORWARD

The CGT rules are modified for assets eligible for capital allowances.

The wasting chattels exemption does not apply to chattels on which capital allowances have been claimed or could have been claimed. The chattels rules based on £6,000 do apply.

Where a chattel on which capital allowances have been obtained is sold at a loss, the allowable cost for chargeable gains purposes is reduced by the lower of the loss and the net amount of allowances given (taking into account any balancing allowances or charges). The result is no gain and no loss. This is because relief for the loss has already been given through the capital allowances computation.

If the chattel is sold at a gain the cost is not adjusted for capital allowances.

2 Wasting assets

FAST FORWARD

When a wasting asset is disposed of its cost must be depreciated over its estimated useful life.

2.1 Introduction

A wasting asset is one which has an estimated remaining useful life of 50 years or less and whose original value will depreciate over time. Examples of such assets are copyrights and registered designs.

2.2 The computation

The normal capital gains computation is amended to reflect the anticipated depreciation over the life of the asset.

The cost is written down on a straight line basis, and it is this depreciated cost which is deducted in the computation. **The indexation allowance is also based on the depreciated cost**.

Thus if a taxpayer acquires a wasting asset with a remaining life of 40 years and disposes of it after 15 years, so that 25 years of useful life remain, only 25/40 of the cost is deducted in the computation.

Any enhancement expenditure must be separately depreciated.

2.3 Example: wasting asset

Harry bought a copyright on 1 May 2003 for £20,000. The copyright is due to expire in May 2023. He sold it on 1 May 2007 for £22,000.

Harry's chargeable gain is:

	£
Proceeds of sale	22,000
Less depreciated cost £20,000 × 16/20	(16,000)
Gain	6,000

2.4 Capital allowances

If capital allowances have been given on a wasting asset its cost is not depreciated over time.

3 Private residences

There is an exemption for gains on principal private residences, but the exemption may be restricted because of periods of non-occupation or because of business use.

3.1 General principles

A gain arising on the sale of an individual's only or main private residence (his principal private residence or PPR) is exempt from CGT. The exemption also covers grounds of up to half a hectare. The grounds can exceed half a hectare if the house is large enough to warrant it, but if not, the gain on the excess grounds is taxable.

For the exemption to be available the taxpayer must have occupied the property as a residence rather than just as temporary accommodation.

3.2 Occupation

The gain is wholly exempt where the owner has occupied the whole of the residence throughout his period of ownership. Where occupation has been for only part of the period, the proportion of the gain exempted is

$$\text{Total gain} \times \frac{\text{Period of occupation}}{\text{Total period of ownership}}$$

The **last 36 months of ownership are always** treated as **a period of occupation**, if at some time the residence has been the taxpayer's main residence, even if within those last 36 months the taxpayer also has another house which is his principal private residence.

Where a loss arises and all, or a proportion of, any gain would have been exempt, all or the same proportion of the loss is not allowable.

3.3 Deemed occupation

The **period of occupation is also deemed to include certain periods of absence, provided the individual had no other exempt residence at the time and the period of absence was at some time both preceded and followed by a period of actual occupation.** The last 36 months rule (see above) takes precedence over this rule.

These periods of **deemed occupation** are:

(a) **Any period** (or periods taken together) of absence, **for any reason**, **up to three years**, and

(b) **Any periods** during which the owner was **required by his employment (ie employed taxpayer) to live abroad**, and

(c) **Any period** (or periods taken together) **up to four years** during which the owner was **required to live elsewhere due to his work** (ie both employed and self employed taxpayer) so that he could not occupy his private residence.

It does not matter if the residence is let during the absence.

Exempt periods of absence must normally be preceded and followed by periods of actual occupation. An extra-statutory concession relaxes this where an individual who has been required to work abroad or elsewhere (ie (b) and (c) above) is unable to resume residence in his home because the terms of his employment require him to work elsewhere.

Question

Principal private residence relief

Mr A purchased a house on 1 April 1983 for £50,000. He lived in the house until 30 June 1983. He then worked abroad for two years before returning to the UK to live in the house again on 1 July 1985. He stayed in the house until 31 December 2000 before retiring and moving out to live with friends in Spain until the house was sold on 28 December 2007 for £150,000.

Calculate any chargeable gain arising. Assume an indexation factor March 1983 to April 1998 = 0.956

Answer

	£
Proceeds	150,000
Less cost	(50,000)
Unindexed gain	100,000
Less indexation allowance (March 1983 to April 1998)	
0.956 × £50,000	(47,800)
Indexed gain	52,200
Less exempt under PPR rules (working)	
$\frac{249}{297}$ × £52,200	(43,764)
Chargeable gain	8,436
Gain after taper relief (10 years including additional year) 60% × £8,436	£5,062

Working

Exempt and chargeable periods

Period		*Total months*	*Exempt months*	*Chargeable months*
(ii)	April 1983 – June 1983 (occupied)	3	3	0
(iii)	July 1983 – June 1985 (working abroad)	24	24	0
(iv)	July 1985 – December 2000 (occupied)	186	186	0
(v)	January 2001 – December 2004 (see below)	48	0	48
(vi)	January 2005 – December 2007 (last 36 months)	36	36	0
		297	249	48

No part of the period from January 2001 to December 2004 can be covered by the exemption for three years of absence for any reason because it is not followed at any time by actual occupation.

Exam focus point

To help you to answer questions such as that above it is useful to draw up a table showing the period of ownership, exempt months (real/deemed occupation) and chargeable months (non-occupation) similar to that in the working.

3.4 Business use

Where part of a residence is used exclusively for business purposes throughout the period of ownership, the gain attributable to use of that part is taxable. The 'last 36 months always exempt' rule does not apply to that part.

Question — **Business use of PPR**

Mr Smail purchased a property for £35,000 on 31 May 2002 and began operating a dental practice from that date in one quarter of the house. He closed the dental practice on 31 December 2007, selling the house on that date for £130,000.

Compute the chargeable gain, if any, arising before taper relief.

Answer

	£
Proceeds	130,000
Less: cost	(35,000)
Gain	95,000
Less PPR exemption 0.75 × £95,000	(71,250)
Chargeable gain before taper relief	23,750

Exemption is lost on one quarter throughout the period of ownership (including the last 36 months) because of the use of that fraction for business purposes.

If part of a residence was used for business purposes for only part of the period of ownership, the gain is apportioned between chargeable and exempt parts. If the business part was *at some time* used as part of the residence, the gain apportioned to that part *will* qualify for the last 36 months exemption.

3.5 Letting relief

The principal private residence exemption is extended to any gain accruing while the property is let, up to a certain limit. The two main circumstances in which the letting exemption applies are:

(a) When the owner is absent and lets the property, where the absence is not a deemed period of occupation.

(b) When the owner lets part of the property while still occupying the rest of it. The absence from the let part cannot be a deemed period of occupation, because the owner has another residence (the rest of the property). However, the let part will qualify for the last 36 months exemption *if* the let part has *at some time* been part of the only or main residence.

In both cases the letting must be for residential use. **The extra exemption is restricted to the lowest of:**

(a) The amount of the total **gain** which is already **exempt under the PPR provisions**
(b) The gain accruing during the letting period (the **letting part of the gain**)
(c) **£40,000** (maximum)

Letting relief cannot convert a gain into an allowable loss.

If a lodger lives as a member of the owner's family, sharing their living accommodation and eating with them, the **whole** property is regarded as the owner's main residence.

Question — **Letting relief (1)**

Mr Ovett purchased a house on 5 October 1993 and sold it on 5 April 2008 making an indexed gain of £290,000.

On 5 January 1995 he had been sent to work in Edinburgh, and he did not return to his own house until 6 July 2004. The property was let out during his absence, and he lived in a flat provided for him by his employer. What is the chargeable gain on the disposal?

Answer

	£
Indexed gain	290,000
Less PPR exemption (working)	
$£290,000 \times \frac{144}{174}$	(240,000)
	50,000
Less letting exemption: Lowest of:	
(a) gain exempt under PPR rules: £240,000	
(b) gain attributable to letting: $£290,000 \times \frac{30}{174} = £50,000$	
(c) £40,000 (maximum)	(40,000)
Chargeable gain before taper relief	10,000

Gain after taper relief (10 years including additional year) 60% × £10,000 = £6,000

Working

Period	*Notes*	*Total ownership months*	*Exempt month*	*Chargeable months*
5.10.93 – 4.1.95	Actual occupation	15	15	0
5.1.95 – 4.1.99	4 years absence working in the UK	48	48	0
5.1.99 – 4.1.02	3 year of absence for any reason	36	36	0
5.1.02 – 5.7.04	Absent – let	30	0	30
6.7.04 – 5.4.08	Occupied (includes last 36 months)	45	45	0
		174	144	30

Question

Letting relief (2)

Miss Coe purchased a house on 31 March 1993 for £90,000. She sold it on 31 August 2007 for £340,000. In 1996 the house was redecorated and Miss Coe began to live on the top floor renting out the balance of the house (constituting 60% of the total house) to tenants between 1 January 1997 and 31 December 2006. On 2 January 2007 Miss Coe put the whole house on the market but continued to live only on the top floor until the house was sold. What is the chargeable gain? Assume an indexation factor March 1993 to April 1998 = 0.167.

Answer

	£
Proceeds	340,000
Less: cost	(90,000)
Unindexed gain	250,000
Less indexation allowance (March 1993 to April 1998)	
0.167 × £90,000	(15,030)
Indexed gain	234,970
Less PPR exemption (working)	
$£234,970 \times \frac{117.8}{173}$	(159,997)
	74,973
Less letting exemption: Lowest of:	
(a) gain exempt under PPR rules: £159,997	
(b) gain attributable to letting: $£234,970 \times \frac{55.2}{173} = £74,973$	
(c) £40,000 (maximum)	(40,000)
Chargeable gain before taper relief	34,973

Gain after taper relief (10 years including additional year) 60% × £34,973 = £20,984

Working

Period	*Notes*	*Total ownership months*	*Exempt months*	*Chargeable months*
1.4.93 – 31.12.96	100% of house occupied	45	45	0
1.1.97 – 31.8.04	40% of house occupied 60% of house let	92	36.8	55.2
1.9.04 – 31.8.07	Last 36 months treated as 100% of house occupied	36	36	0
		173	117.8	55.2

Note. The gain on the 40% of the house always occupied by Miss Coe is fully covered by PPR relief. The other 60% of the house has not always been occupied by Miss Coe and thus any gain on this part of the house is taxable where it relates to periods of time when Miss Coe was not actually (or deemed to be) living in it.

As a further point if Miss Coe had reoccupied the lower floors (60% part) of the house prior to the sale then 3 years worth of the non-occupation period between 1.1.97 and 31.8.04 could have been treated as deemed occupation under the special '3 years absence for any reason' rule.

Chapter Roundup

- Gains on most wasting chattels are exempt and losses are not allowable.

  When a non-wasting chattel is sold for less than £6,000, any gain is exempt. There is marginal relief for gains where sale proceeds exceed £6,000. Losses are restricted where proceeds are less than £6,000.
- The CGT rules are modified for assets eligible for capital allowances.
- When a wasting asset is disposed of its cost must be depreciated over its estimated useful life.
- There is an exemption for gains on principal private residences, but the exemption may be restricted because of periods of non-occupation or because of business use.

Quick Quiz

1 How are gains on non-wasting chattels sold for more than £6,000 restricted?

2 How are losses on non-wasting chattels sold for less than £6,000 restricted?

3 For what periods may an individual be deemed to occupy his principal private residence?

4 What is the maximum letting exemption?

Answers to Quick Quiz

1 Gain restricted to 5/3 × (gross proceeds – £6,000)

2 Allowable loss restricted by deeming proceeds to be £6,000

3 Periods of deemed occupation are:

- last 36 months of ownership, and
- any period of absence up to three years, and
- any period during which the owner was required by his employment to work abroad, and
- any period up to four years during which the owner was required to live elsewhere due to his work (employed or self employed) or that he could not occupy his private residence.

4 £40,000.

Now try the questions below from the Exam Question Bank

Number	Level	Marks	Time
Q22	Examination	10	18 mins

Business reliefs

Topic list	Syllabus reference
1 The replacement of business assets (rollover relief)	D6(a)
2 Gift relief (holdover relief)	D6(b)
3 Incorporation relief	D6(c)

Introduction

Having discussed the general rules for capital gains we now turn our attention to specific reliefs for businesses.

The most important relief is rollover relief, which enables a gain on the disposal of a business asset to be rolled over if a new asset is purchased for business use. This enables the payment of tax to be deferred until the business has actually retained the proceeds of sale uninvested so that it can meet the liability. This is the only relief that is available to both individuals and companies.

Next we consider the relief for gifts of business assets. This generous relief allows an entrepreneur to give away his business during his lifetime and pass any gains to the donee.

The final relief, incorporation relief, enables an individual to transfer his sole trade or partnership business into a company without crystallising a tax charge. The gain is deferred until the eventual disposal of the shares in the company.

In the next chapter we will cover the computation of capital gains on the disposal of shares.

Study guide

		Intellectual level
D6	**The use of exemptions and reliefs in deferring and minimising tax liabilities arising on the disposal of capital assets**	
(a)	Explain and apply rollover relief as it applies to individuals and companies.	2
(b)	Explain and apply holdover relief for the gift of business assets.	2
(c)	Explain and apply the incorporation relief that is available upon the transfer of a business to a company.	2

Exam guide

Capital gains form at least 20% of your exam, and may be found in the context of corporation tax or CGT. Rollover relief may be met in either context, and as it is an extremely important relief for all businesses it is likely to be examined. If you are required to compute a gain on a business asset look out for the purchase of a new asset, but carefully check the date and cost of the acquisition. Do not be caught out by the purchase of an investment property.

The relief for gifts of assets is only available to individuals, and effectively passes the gain to the donee. You may need to comment on the resetting of the taper relief clock. Incorporation relief is again only available to individuals. Note that it can be disclaimed. It is unlikely that these reliefs would form a whole question.

1 The replacement of business assets (rollover relief)

FAST FORWARD

Rollover relief is available to all businesses that reinvest in qualifying assets in the period commencing one year before and ending 36 months after the disposal concerned.

1.1 Conditions

A gain may be 'rolled over' (deferred) where the proceeds received on the disposal of a business asset are spent on a replacement business asset. This is **rollover relief**. A claim cannot specify that only part of a gain is to be rolled over.

All the following conditions must be met.

(a) **The old asset sold and the new asset bought are both used only in the trade** or trades carried on **by the person claiming rollover relief**. Where part of a building is in non-trade use for all or a substantial part of the period of ownership, the building (and the land on which it stands) is treated as two separate assets, the trade part (qualifying) and the non-trade part (non-qualifying). This split cannot be made for other assets.

(b) **The old asset and the new asset both fall within one** (but not necessarily the same one) **of the following classes.**

  (i) Land and buildings (including parts of buildings) occupied as well as used only for the purpose of the trade

  (ii) Fixed (that is, immovable) plant and machinery

  (iii) Goodwill.

(c) **Reinvestment of the proceeds received on the disposal of the old asset takes place in a period beginning one year before and ending three years after the date of the disposal.**

(d) **The new asset is brought into use in the trade on its acquisition** (not necessarily immediately, but not after any significant and unnecessary delay).

Goodwill is not a qualifying asset for the purposes of corporation tax (ie for companies). Companies are covered later in this Text.

The new asset can be used in a different trade from the old asset.

A rollover claim is not allowed when a taxpayer buys premises, sells part of the premises at a profit and then claims to roll over the gain into the part retained. However, a rollover claim is allowed (by concession) when the proceeds of the old asset are spent on improving a qualifying asset which the taxpayer already owns. The improved asset must already be in use for a trade, or be brought into trade use immediately the improvement work is finished.

1.2 Operation of relief

FAST FORWARD

A rolled over gain is deducted from the base cost of the replacement asset acquired.

Deferral is obtained by deducting the chargeable gain from the cost of the new asset. For full relief, the whole of the proceeds must be reinvested. Where only part is reinvested, a gain equal to the amount not reinvested or the full gain, if lower, will be chargeable to tax immediately.

The new asset will have a base cost for chargeable gains purposes of its purchase price less the gain rolled over.

Question — **Rollover relief**

A freehold factory was purchased by Zoë for business use in August 2000. It was sold in December 2007 for £70,000, giving rise to a gain of £17,950. A replacement factory was purchased in June 2008 for £60,000. Compute the base cost of the replacement factory, taking into account any possible rollover of the gain from the disposal in December 2007. Ignore taper relief.

Answer

	£
Total gain	17,950
Less: rollover relief (balancing figure)	(7,950)
Chargeable gain: amount not reinvested £(70,000 – 60,000)	10,000
Cost of new factory	60,000
Less rolled over gain	(7,950)
Base cost of new factory	52,050

1.3 Interaction with taper relief

Rollover relief applies to the untapered gain. Any gain left in charge will then be eligible for taper relief. When the replacement asset is sold taper relief on that sale is given by reference to the holding period for that asset as normal (assuming further rollover relief is not claimed on this disposal). **Effectively, taper relief on the rolled over gain, for the period of ownership of the original asset, is lost.**

Question — **Rollover relief and taper relief interaction**

Karen is a sole trader who bought a business asset for £204,579 on 5 November 2001 and sold it on 31 December 2007 for £491,400. A replacement business asset was acquired on 1 November 2007 at a cost of £546,000. The new asset was sold on 3 September 2009 for £914,550. Karen made a claim for rollover relief on the first asset sale.

Calculate the taxable gains for each asset disposal.

Answer

31 December 2007 disposal

	£
Sale proceeds	491,400
Cost (5.11.2001)	(204,579)
Gain before taper relief	286,821
Less: rollover relief (note)	(286,821)
Chargeable gain	NIL

Note. Since the asset was sold for £491,400 and within the required time period a replacement asset was purchased for £546,000 there was a full reinvestment of the sale proceeds. Thus the full gain before taper relief of £286,821 is rolled over against the cost of the new asset.

3 September 2009 disposal

	£	£
Sale proceeds		914,550
Cost (1 November 2007)	546,000	
Less rollover relief	(286,821)	
		(259,179)
Gain		655,371
Ownership period is 1 November 2007 to 3 September 2009		
= 1 complete year of ownership		
Gain after taper relief (50%)		£327,686

1.4 Non-business use

Where the old asset has not been used in the trade for a fraction of its period of ownership, the amount of the gain that can be rolled over is reduced by the same fraction. When considering proceeds not reinvested the restriction on rollover relief is based on the proportion of proceeds relating to the part of the asset used in the trade or the proportion relating to the period of trade use.

Exam focus point

Look out for both the old and the new asset having some non-business use. You must compare the proceeds of the business use proportion with the amount reinvested in the business use portion of the new asset.

Question — **Assets with non-business use**

John bought a factory for £150,000 on 11 November 2002, for use in his business. From 11 November 2003, he let the factory out to a quoted company, for a period of two years. He then used the factory for his own business again, until he sold it on 10 May 2007 for £225,000. On 13 December 2006, he purchased another factory for use in his business. This second factory cost £100,000.

Calculate the chargeable gain before taper relief, on the sale of the first factory and the base cost of the second factory.

Answer

Gain on first factory

	Non business	*Business*
	£	£
Proceeds of sale (24:30) (W1)	100,000	125,000
Less: cost (24:30)	(66,667)	(83,333)
Gain (no indexation allowance)	33,333	41,667
Less: rollover relief		(16,667)
Chargeable gain before taper relief (W2)	33,333	25,000

Base cost of second factory

	£
Cost	100,000
Less gain rolled over	(16,667)
Base cost c/f	83,333

Workings

1 *Use of factory*

Total ownership period:

11.11.02 – 10.05.07 = 54 months

Attributable to non business use:

11.11.03 – 10.11.05 = 24 months

Attributable to business use (balance: 54m – 24m) = 30 months

2 *Proceeds not reinvested*

	£
Proceeds of business element	125,000
Less: cost of new factory	(100,000)
Not reinvested	25,000

1.5 Depreciating assets

FAST FORWARD

When the replacement asset is a depreciating asset, the gain on the old asset is 'frozen' rather than rolled over.

Where the replacement asset is a depreciating asset, the gain is not rolled over by reducing the cost of the replacement asset. Rather it is deferred until it crystallises on the earliest of:

(a) The disposal of the replacement asset.

(b) The date the replacement asset ceases to be used in the trade (but the gain does not crystallise on the taxpayer's death).

(c) Ten years after the acquisition of the replacement asset (maximum).

Key term

An asset is a **depreciating asset** if it is, or within the next ten years will become, a wasting asset. Thus, any asset with an expected life of 60 years or less is covered by this definition. Plant and machinery is always treated as depreciating.

Taper relief is applied to the original gain **before** it is deferred, in relation to the ownership of the original asset. No further relief is given for the time that the gain is deferred. Taper relief applies on the depreciating asset from the date of purchase in the normal way.

Question

Gain deferred into depreciating asset

Norma bought a freehold shop for use in her business in June 2006 for £125,000. She sold it for £140,000 on 1 August 2007. On 10 July 2007, Norma bought some fixed plant and machinery to use in her business, costing £150,000. She then sells the plant and machinery for £167,000 on 19 November 2009. Show Norma's CGT position.

Answer

Gain deferred

	£
Proceeds of shop	140,000
Less cost	(125,000)
Gain	15,000

Gain after taper relief (1 year)

50% × £15,000 = £7,500

This gain is deferred in relation to the purchase of the plant and machinery.

Sale of plant and machinery

	£
Proceeds	167,000
Less cost	(150,000)
Gain	17,000

Gain on plant and machinery after taper relief (2 years)
£17,000 × 25% = £4,250

Total gain chargeable on sale (gain on plant and machinery plus deferred gain)
£(4,250 + 7,500) = £11,750

Where a gain on disposal is deferred against a replacement depreciating asset it is possible to transfer the deferred gain to a non-depreciating asset provided the non-depreciating asset is bought before the deferred gain has crystallised.

2 Gift relief (holdover relief)

FAST FORWARD

Gift relief can be claimed on gifts of business assets.

2.1 The relief

If an individual gives away a qualifying asset, the transferor and the transferee can jointly elect by 31 January nearly six years after the end of the tax year of the transfer, **that the transferor's gain be reduced to nil. The transferee is then deemed to acquire the asset for market value at the date of transfer less the transferor's deferred gain** (no taper relief given). The transferee will qualify for further indexation allowance (if available) on that reduced base cost from the date of the transfer and will start a new period for taper relief from the date of his acquisition.

If a disposal involves actual consideration rather than being an outright gift, but is still not a bargain made at arm's length (so that the proceeds are deemed to be the market value of the asset), this is known as a sale at undervalue. **Any excess of actual consideration over actual costs** (excluding indexation allowance) **is chargeable immediately and only the balance of the gain is deferred**. The amount chargeable immediately is limited to the full gain after indexation allowance.

Exam focus point

> The asset need only be a business asset in the hands of the donor. It is immaterial if the donee does not use it for business purposes.

2.2 Qualifying assets

Gift relief can be claimed on gifts or sales at undervalue on transfers of **business assets**. The definition of a business asset for gift relief is **not** the same as for taper relief.

Business assets are:

(a) Assets used in a trade, profession or vocation carried on:

(1) by the donor

(2) by the donor's personal company (ie one where the individual holds at least 5% of the voting rights).

If the asset was used for the purposes of the trade, profession or vocation for only part of its period of ownership, the gain to be held over is the gain otherwise eligible × period of such use/total period of ownership.

If the asset was a building or structure only partly used for trade, professional or vocational purposes, only the **part of the gain attributable to the part so used is eligible for gift relief**.

(b) **Shares and securities in trading companies**

(1) the shares or securities are **not listed on a recognised stock exchange** (but they may be on the AIM); or

(2) if the donor is an individual, the company concerned is his **personal company** (defined as above);

If the company has chargeable non-business assets at the time of the gift, and (2) applied at any time in the last 12 months, **the gain to be held over is:**

Exam formula

$$\text{Gain} \times \frac{\text{the value of the chargeable business assets (CBA)}}{\text{the value of the chargeable assets (CA)}}$$

Question — Gift relief

On 6 December 2007 Angelo sold to his son Michael a freehold shop valued at £200,000 for £50,000, and claimed gift relief. Angelo had originally purchased the shop from which he had run his business in July 2003 for £30,000. Michael continued to run a business from the shop premises but decided to sell the shop in May 2009 for £195,000. Compute any chargeable gains arising. Assume the rules of CGT in 2007/08 continue to apply in May 2009.

Answer

(a) *Angelo's CGT position (2007/08)*

	£
Proceeds (market value)	200,000
Less cost	(30,000)
Gain	170,000
Less gain deferred	(150,000)
Gain left in charge £(50,000 – 30,000)	20,000

Gain after taper relief (note) = £5,000

(b) *Michael's CGT position (2009/10)*

	£
Proceeds	195,000
Less cost £(200,000 – 150,000)	(50,000)
Gain	145,000

Gain after taper relief (note) = £72,500

Note. Taper relief is available for Angelo since the asset disposed of in December 2007 is a business asset. The period of ownership is four complete years. Only 25% of the gain will be taxable.

Michael acquired the asset on 6 December 2007 and sold it in May 2009. He therefore owned the asset for one complete year. 50% of the gain is taxable.

Question

Gift of shares – CBA/CA restriction

Morris gifts shares in his personal company to his son Minor realising a gain of £100,000. The company balance sheet at the date of the gift shows:

	£
Freehold factory and offices	150,000
Leasehold warehouse	80,000
Investments	120,000
Other net assets	200,000
	550,000

You are required to show the gain qualifying for hold-over relief and the chargeable gain before taper relief.

Answer

Gain qualifying for hold-over relief:

$$£100{,}000 \times \frac{\text{Chargeable business assets (CBA)}}{\text{Chargeable assets (CA)}} = £100{,}000 \times \frac{150+80}{150+80+120}$$

$$= £100{,}000 \times \frac{230}{350}$$

$$= £65{,}714$$

The gain which is not held-over is £100,000 – £65,714 = £34,286, before taper relief.

3 Incorporation relief

FAST FORWARD

A gain arising on the incorporation of a business is automatically deferred into the base cost of the shares acquired by incorporation relief. However, an individual can elect for the relief not to apply.

If a person transfers his business to a company this is a disposal of the business assets for CGT purposes and he realises net chargeable gains (chargeable gains less allowable losses) on those assets. It is, however, clearly undesirable to discourage entrepreneurs from incorporating their businesses and so relief is available.

The relief (incorporation relief) is automatic (so no claim need be made). **All, or some, of the gains are held over if all the following conditions are met.**

(a) The **business is transferred as a going concern**
(b) **All its assets** (other than cash) **are transferred**
(c) **The consideration is wholly or partly in shares**.

Exam formula

The amount held over is found by applying the fraction:

$$\text{Gain before taper relief} \times \frac{\text{Value of shares received from the company}}{\text{Total value of consideration from the company}}$$

This amount is then deducted from the base cost of the shares received. The company is deemed to acquire assets transferred at their market values.

Question

Incorporation relief

Mr P transferred his business to a company in May 2007, realising an indexed gain of £24,000 on the only business asset transferred (a factory). The consideration comprised cash of £15,000 and shares at a market value of £75,000.

(a) What is the gain on the transfer before taper relief?
(b) What is the base cost of the shares for any future disposal?

Answer

(a)

	£
Gain	24,000
Less held over $\frac{75,000}{15,000 + 75,000} \times £24,000$	(20,000)
Gain before taper relief	4,000

(b)

	£
Market value	75,000
Less gain held over	(20,000)
Base cost of shares	55,000

An individual can elect not to receive incorporation relief. He might do this, for example, to keep his entitlement to taper relief on the gain arising on incorporation if the shares are sold within two years of the incorporation (ie before the maximum business asset taper relief is available).

Chapter Roundup

- Rollover relief is available to all businesses that reinvest in qualifying assets in the period commencing one year before and ending 36 months after the disposal concerned.
- A rolled over gain is deducted from the base cost of the replacement asset acquired.
- When the replacement asset is a depreciating asset, the gain on the old asset is 'frozen' rather than rolled over.
- Gift relief can be claimed on gifts of business assets.
- A gain arising on the incorporation of a business is automatically deferred into the base cost of the shares acquired by incorporation relief. However, an individual can elect for the relief not to apply.

Quick Quiz

1. Alice sells a factory for £500,000 realising a gain of £100,000. She acquires a factory two months later for £480,000. How much rollover relief is available?
2. What deferral relief is available when a business asset is replaced with a depreciating business asset?
3. Which disposals of shares qualify for gift relief?
4. What are the conditions for deferring gains on the incorporation of a business?

Answers to Quick Quiz

1. Amount not reinvested £(500,000 – 480,000) = £20,000. Rollover relief £(100,000 – 20,000) = £80,000.
2. Gain is frozen on acquisition of depreciating asset until earlier of: disposal of that asset; asset no longer used in trade; 10 years after acquisition of replacement asset.
3. Shares which qualify for gift relief are those in trading companies
   - which are not listed on a recognised stock exchange, or
   - which are in the individual's personal company ie the individual holds at least 5% of the voting rights
4. The conditions for incorporation relief are:
   - the business is transferred as a going concern
   - all of its assets (other than cash) are transferred
   - the consideration is wholly or partly in shares

Now try the question below from the Exam Question Bank

Number	Level	Marks	Time
Q23	Examination	20	27 mins
Q24	Introductory	5	9 mins

17

Shares and securities

Topic list	Syllabus reference
1 Valuing quoted shares	D4(a)
2 The matching rules for individuals	D4(b)
3 Post April 1998 acquisitions and disposals	D4(b)
4 The FA 1985 pool	D4(c)
5 Bonus and rights issues	D4(d)
6 Reorganisations and takeovers	D4(d)
7 Gilts and qualifying corporate bonds	D4(e)

Introduction

We have now covered most aspects of the capital gains computation apart from shares and securities.

Shares and securities need special rules because an individual may hold several shares or securities in the same company, bought at different times for different prices but otherwise identical. We need to identify the shares disposed of, not only to compute the gain but also to establish the holding period for taper relief purposes.

We also discuss the rules for bonus and rights issues, takeovers and reorganisations.

In the next chapter we will conclude our study of personal taxation by considering administration.

Study guide

		Intellectual level
D4	**Gains and losses on the disposal of shares and securities**	
(a)	Calculate the value of quoted shares where they are disposed of by way of a gift.	2
(b)	Explain and apply the identification rules as they apply to individuals and to companies, including the same day, nine day, and thirty day matching rules.	2
(c)	Explain the pooling provisions.	2
(d)	Explain the treatment of bonus issues, rights issues, takeovers and reorganisations.	2
(e)	Explain the exemption available for gilt-edged securities and qualifying corporate bonds.	1

Exam guide

Shares and securities are likely to form at least part of a question on capital gains. You must learn the identification rules as they are crucial in calculating the gain correctly. The identification rules for companies are covered later in this Text.

The rules for bonus and rights issues are important – these are the only occasions now where shares can be added to an FA 1985 pool for individuals. Takeovers and reorganisations are also important; remember to apportion the cost (and indexed cost) across the new holding.

1 Valuing quoted shares

Quoted shares and securities are valued using prices in The Stock Exchange Daily Official List, taking the lower of:

- lower quoted price + $^{1}/_{4}$ × (higher quoted price – lower quoted price)('quarter-up' rule)
- the average of the highest and lowest marked bargains (ignoring bargains marked at special prices)

Question — CGT value of shares

Shares in A plc are quoted at 100-110p. The highest and lowest marked bargains were 99p and 110p. What would be the market value for CGT purposes?

Answer

The value will be the lower of:

(a) $100 + \frac{1}{4} \times (110 - 100) = 102.5$;

(b) $\frac{110 + 99}{2} = 104.5$.

The market value for CGT purposes will therefore be 102.5p per share.

2 The matching rules for individuals

FAST FORWARD

There are special rules for matching shares sold with shares purchased. We need to consider shares acquired from 6 April 1998 onwards and then the FA 1985 pool as at 5 April 1998.

Quoted and unquoted shares and securities present special problems when attempting to compute gains or losses on disposal. For instance, suppose that an individual buys some quoted shares in X plc as follows.

Date	*Number of shares*	*Cost*
		£
5 May 1983	100	150
17 January 1999	100	375

On 15 June 2007, he sells 120 of the shares for £1,450. To determine the chargeable gain, we need to be able to work out which shares out of the two original holdings were actually sold.

We therefore need **matching rules**. These **allow us to decide which shares have been sold and so work out what the allowable cost on disposal should be.**

At any one time, we will only be concerned with shares or securities of the same class in the same company. If an individual owns both ordinary shares and preference shares in X plc, we will deal with the two classes of share entirely separately, because they are distinguishable.

Below 'shares' refers to both shares and securities.

For individuals, share disposals are matched with acquisitions in the following order.

(a) **Same day acquisitions**.

(b) **Acquisitions within the following 30 days** (known as the 'bed and breakfast rule').

(c) **Previous acquisitions after 5 April 1998 identifying the most recent acquisition first (LIFO basis)**.

(d) **Any shares in the FA 1985 pool at 5 April 1998** (see below).

The 'bed and breakfast' rule stops shares being sold to crystallise a capital gain or loss, usually to use the annual exemption and then being repurchased a day or so later. Without the rule a gain or loss would arise on the sale since it would be 'matched' to the original acquisition.

Exam focus point

Learn the 'matching rules' because a crucial first step to getting a shares question right is to correctly match the shares sold to the original shares purchased.

3 Post April 1998 acquisitions and disposals

3.1 Introduction

No indexation applies to shares acquired after April 1998. However, taper relief (see earlier in this Text) may be available to reduce the amount of the gain arising.

3.2 Example: Post April 1998 disposals for individuals

Ron acquired the following shares in First plc:

Date of acquisition	*No of shares*	*Cost*
9.11.03	15,000	25,000
4.8.06	5,000	19,400
15.7.07	5,000	19,000

He disposed of 20,000 of the shares on 10 July 2007 for £80,000. The shares are not business assets for the purposes of taper relief. Calculate the chargeable gain arising.

Solution

Matching of shares

(a) Acquisition in 30 days after disposal:

	£
Proceeds $\frac{5,000}{20,000} \times £80,000$	20,000
Less cost (15.7.07)	(19,000)
Gain	1,000

(b) Post 5.4.98 acquisitions

(i) 5,000 shares acquired 4.8.06

	£
Proceeds $\frac{5,000}{20,000} \times £80,000$	20,000
Less cost (4.8.06)	(19,400)
Gain	600

Note. No taper relief is due as owned for only 11 months.

(ii) 10,000 shares acquired 9.11.03

	£
Proceeds $\frac{10,000}{20,000} \times £80,000$	40,000
Less cost (9.11.03) 10,000/15,000 × £25,000	(16,667)
Gain	23,333

Gain after taper relief (9.11.03 – 9.11.06 = 3 years)

95% × £23,333 = £22,167

Total gains £(1,000 + 600 + 22,167) = £23,767

4 The FA 1985 pool

4.1 Composition of pool

We treat shares acquired before 6 April 1998 as a 'pool' which grew as new shares were acquired and shrunk as they were sold. **This FA 1985 pool** (introduced by the Finance Act 1985) **comprises the following**.

- **Shares held by an individual on 5 April 1985 and acquired by that individual on or after 6 April 1982.**
- **Shares acquired by that individual on or after 6 April 1985, but before 6 April 1998.**

In making computations which use the FA 1985 pool, we must keep track of:

(a) The **number** of shares
(b) The **cost** of the shares ignoring indexation
(c) The **indexed cost** of the shares

Exam focus point

The examiner has stated that you will be given the indexed cost of the FA 1985 pool as at 6 April 1998 in the exam when dealing with shares disposed of by an individual. He has also stated that there will not be a detailed question on the pooling provisions for shares.

A more detailed discussion of the FA 1985 pool is given later in this Text when considering capital gains made by a company.

4.2 Disposals from the FA 1985 pool after 5 April 1998

In the case of a disposal the cost and the indexed cost attributable to the shares disposed of are deducted from the amounts within the FA 1985 pool. The proportions of the cost and indexed cost to take out of the pool should be computed using the A/(A + B) fraction that is used for any other part disposal. However, we are not usually given the value of the remaining shares (B in the fraction). We just use numbers of shares.

The indexation allowance is the indexed cost taken out of the pool minus the cost taken out. As usual, the indexation allowance cannot create or increase a loss.

Question — **The FA 1985 pool**

At 6 April 1998 Oliver's FA 1985 pool of shares in Twist plc comprised 4,000 shares, cost £10,000, indexed cost £17,461. Oliver sold 3,000 shares on 10 July 2007 for £17,000. Compute the gain before taper relief, and the value of the FA 1985 pool following the disposal.

Answer

The gain is computed as follows:

	£
Proceeds	17,000
Less cost (working)	(7,500)
	9,500
Less indexation allowance £(13,096 – 7,500)	(5,596)
Chargeable gain before taper relief	3,904

Taper relief will then apply.

Working – FA85 pool

	No of shares	*Cost*	*Indexed cost*
		£	£
Value at 6.4.98	4,000	10,000	17,461
Disposal	(3,000)		
Cost and indexed cost $\frac{3,000}{4,000}$ × £10,000 and £17,461		(7,500)	(13,096)
	1,000	2,500	4,365

5 Bonus and rights issues

FAST FORWARD: Bonus and rights issues are attached to the holdings to which they relate.

5.1 Bonus issues

When a company issues bonus shares all that happens is that the size of the original holding is increased. Since bonus shares are issued at no cost there is no need to adjust the original cost. Instead the numbers purchased at particular times are increased by the bonus. The normal matching rules then apply.

5.2 Example: bonus issue

The following transactions in the ordinary shares of X plc would be matched as shown below

6.4.98	FA 1985 pool contains 1,000 shares
5.12.03	Purchase of 1,200 shares
6.10.04	Bonus issue of one for four
6.5.07	Sale of 2,250 shares

(a) *December 2003 holding*

	No of shares
5.12.03	1,200
6.10.04 Bonus issue one for four	300
	1,500
Disposal 6.5.07	(1,500)

(b) *The FA 1985 pool*

	No of shares
6.4.98	1,000
6.10.04 Bonus issue one for four	250
	1,250
Disposal 6.5.07 (balance)	(750)
Remaining shares	500

5.3 Rights issues

The difference between a bonus issue and a rights issue is that in a rights issue the new shares are paid for and this results in an adjustment to the original cost. For the purposes of calculating the **indexation allowance**, **expenditure** on a rights issue is taken as being **incurred on the date of the issue** and not on the date of acquisition of the original holding.

For **taper relief** purposes, treat the rights expenditure in the same way as any other enhancement expenditure ie taper relief applies from the date the **original** holding was acquired (or 6 April 1998 if later).

As with bonus issues, rights shares derived from the 1985 pool shares go into that pool and those derived from post 5.4.98 holdings attach to those holdings. The cost of the holdings are increased by the amount paid, as is the indexed cost of the FA 1985 pool.

Question — Rights issue

Simon had the following transactions in S Ltd.

1.10.95	Bought 10,000 shares (10%) holding for £15,000; indexed cost at 5.4.98 was £16,282
11.9.06	Bought 2,000 shares for £5,000
1.2.07	Took up rights issue 1 for 2 at £2.75 per share
14.10.07	Sold 5,000 shares for £15,000

Compute the chargeable gain arising in October 2007, after taper relief (if applicable). The shares have always been a business asset for taper relief purposes.

Answer

(a) *Post 5.4.98 holding*

	Number	*Cost*
		£
Shares acquired 11.9.06	2,000	5,000
Shares acquired 1.2.07 (rights) 1:2 @ £2.75	1,000	2,750
	3,000	7,750

Gain

	£
Proceeds $\frac{3,000}{5,000} \times £15,000$	9,000
Less cost	(7,750)
Gain	1,250

Taper relief (based on ownership of **original** holding 11.9.06 – 10.9.07)

50% (One year: business asset) × £1,250 = £625

(b) *FA 1985 pool*

	Number	*Cost*	*Indexed cost*
		£	£
Pool at 5.4.98	10,000	15,000	16,282
Rights issue 1.2.07	5,000	13,750	13,750
	15,000	28,750	30,032
14.10.07 Sale	(2,000)	(3,833)	(4,004)
c/f	13,000	24,917	26,028

Gain

	£
Proceeds $\frac{2,000}{5,000} \times £15,000$	6,000
Less cost	(3,833)
Unindexed gain	2,167
Less indexation £(4,004 – 3,833)	(171)
Indexed gain	1,996

Taper relief (based on **original** holding 6.4.98 – 5.4.07)

25% (Nine years: business asset) × £1,996 = £499

(c) Total gains (after taper relief)

£(625 + 499) = £1,124

6 Reorganisations and takeovers

FAST FORWARD

The costs (and indexed cost where relevant) of the original holding are allocated to the new holdings pro rata to their values on a takeover or reorganisation.

6.1 Reorganisations

A reorganisation takes place where new shares or a mixture of new shares and debentures are issued in exchange for the original shareholdings. The new shares take the place of the old shares. The problem is how to apportion the original cost between the different types of capital issued on the reorganisation.

If the new shares and securities are quoted, then the cost is apportioned by reference to the market values of the new types of capital on the first day of quotation after the reorganisation.

Question — Reorganisations

An original quoted shareholding is made up of ordinary shares purchased as follows.

6.4.98 FA 1985 pool: 3,000 shares costing £13,250, indexed cost £14,800
3.2.02 2,000 shares costing £9,000

In 2007 there is a reorganisation whereby each ordinary share is exchanged for two 'A' ordinary shares (quoted at £2 each) and one preference share (quoted at £1 each). Show how the original costs will be apportioned.

Answer

Original holdings

	Original	*New ords*	*MV £2*	*New prefs*	*MV £1*
		2:1	£	1:1	£
FA85 Pool	3,000	6,000	12,000	3,000	3,000
3.2.02 holding	2,000	4,000	8,000	2,000	2,000
Total	5,000	10,000	20,000	5,000	5,000

FA85 holding

	New holding	*MV*	*Cost*	*Indexed cost*
		£	£	£
Ords	6,000	12,000	10,600	11,840
Prefs	3,000	3,000	2,650	2,960
Total	9,000	15,000	13,250	14,800

Original cost/indexed cost is split 12,000:3,000

3.2.02 holding

	New holding	*MV*	*Cost*
		£	£
Ords	4,000	8,000	7,200
Prefs	2,000	2,000	1,800
Total	6,000	10,000	9,000

Original cost is split 8,000:2,000

6.2 Takeovers

A chargeable gain does not arise on a 'paper for paper' takeover. The cost of the original holding is passed on to the new holding which takes the place of the original holding. **If part of the takeover consideration is cash then a gain must be computed**: the normal part disposal rules will apply.

The takeover rules apply where the company issuing the new shares ends up with more than 25% of the ordinary share capital of the old company or the majority of the voting power in the old company, or the company issuing the new shares makes a general offer to shareholders in the other company which is initially made subject to a condition which, if satisfied, would give the first company control of the second company.

The exchange must take place for bona fide commercial reasons and does not have as its main purpose, or one of its main purposes, the avoidance of CGT or corporation tax.

Question — Takeover

Mr Le Bon held 20,000 £1 shares in Duran plc out of a total number of issued shares of one million. They were bought in 2002 for £2 each. In 2007 the board of Duran plc agreed to a takeover bid by Spandau plc under which shareholders in Duran plc received three ordinary Spandau plc shares plus one preference share for every four shares held in Duran plc. Immediately following the takeover, the ordinary shares in Spandau plc were quoted at £5 each and the preferences shares at 90p. Show the base costs of the ordinary shares and the preference shares.

Answer

The total value due to Mr Le Bon on the takeover is as follows.

		£
Ordinary	20,000 × 3/4 × £5	75,000
Preference	20,000 × 1/4 × 90p	4,500
		79,500

The base costs are therefore:

	£
Ordinary shares: 75,000/79,500 × 20,000 × £2	37,736
Preference shares: 4,500/79,500 × 20,000 × £2	2,264
	40,000

7 Gilts and qualifying corporate bonds

FAST FORWARD

Gilts and Qualifying Corporate bonds held by individuals are exempt from CGT. You should never waste time computing gains and losses on them.

Key term

Gilts are UK Government securities issued by HM Treasury as shown on the Treasury list. You may assume that the list includes all issues of Treasury Loan, Treasury Stock, Exchequer Loan, Exchequer Stock and War Loan.

Disposals of gilt edged securities (gilts) and qualifying corporate bonds by individuals are exempt from CGT.

Key term

A **qualifying corporate bond (QCB)** is a security (whether or not secured on assets) which:

(a) represents a **'normal commercial loan'**. This excludes any bonds which are convertible into shares (although bonds convertible into other bonds which would be QCBs are not excluded), or which carry the right to excessive interest or interest which depends on the results of the issuer's business;

(b) is **expressed in sterling** and for which no provision is made for conversion into or redemption in another currency;

(c) was **acquired** by the person now disposing of it **after 13 March 1984**; and

(d) does not have a redemption value which depends on a published index of share prices on a stock exchange.

Permanent interest bearing shares issued by building societies which meet condition (b) above are also QCBs.

Chapter Roundup

- There are special rules for matching shares sold with shares purchased. We need to consider shares acquired from 6 April 1998 onwards and then the FA 1985 pool as at 5 April 1998.
- Bonus and rights issues are attached to the holdings to which they relate.
- The costs (and indexed cost where relevant) of the original holding are allocated to the new holdings pro rata to their values on a takeover or reorganisation.
- Gilts and Qualifying Corporate bonds held by individuals are exempt from CGT. You should never waste time computing gains and losses on them.

Quick Quiz

1 In what order are acquisitions of shares matched with disposals for individuals?

2 At 6 April 1998 an individual held 1,000 shares. He acquired 1,000 more shares on each of 15 January 2004 and 15 January 2008 in X plc. He sells 2,500 shares on 10 January 2008. How are the shares matched on sale?

3 Sharon acquired 10,000 share in Z plc in 1986. She takes up a 1 for 2 rights offer in 2007. How are the rights issue shares dealt with?

4 What is a qualifying corporate bond?

Answers to Quick Quiz

1 The matching of shares sold is in the following order.

(a) Same day acquisitions.
(b) Acquisitions within the following 30 days.
(c) Previous acquisitions after 5.4.98 identifying the most recent acquisition first (LIFO basis).
(d) Any shares in the FA 1985 pool at 5.4.98.

2 January 2008 1,000 shares (following 30 days)
January 2004 1,000 shares (after 5 April 1998)
FA 1985 pool 500 shares

3 The rights issue shares are added to the FA 1985 pool holding (1986 acquisition).

4 A qualifying corporate bond is a security which:

- represents a normal commercial loan
- is expressed in sterling
- was acquired after 13 March 1984
- is not redeemable in relation to share prices on a stock exchange

Now try the questions below from the Exam Question Bank

Number	Level	Marks	Time
Q25	Examination	15	27 mins
Q42	Examination	20	36 mins

Q42 has been analysed to give you guidance on how to answer exam questions.

18

Self assessment and payment of tax by individuals

Topic list	Syllabus reference
1 The self assessment system	G1(a)
2 Tax returns and keeping records	G2(a), (e)
3 Self-assessment and claims	G2(a)
4 Payments of income tax and capital gains tax	G2(b), (c)
5 Enquiries, determinations and discovery assessments	G3(a), (b)
6 Penalties	G4(a), (b)

Introduction

In the earlier chapters we have learned how to calculate an individual's liability to income tax, capital gains tax and national insurance.

In this chapter we see how individuals (including partners) must 'self assess' their liability to income tax, capital gains tax and Class 4 NICs.

In the remaining chapters we will consider the remaining taxes within the syllabus: corporation tax and VAT.

Study guide

		Intellectual level
G1	**The systems for self-assessment and the making of returns**	
(a)	Explain and apply the features of the self assessment system as it applies to individuals.	2
G2	**The time limits for the submission of information, claims and payment of tax, including payments on account**	
(a)	Recognise the time limits that apply to the filing of returns and the making of claims.	2
(b)	Recognise the due dates for the payment of tax under the self-assessment system.	2
(c)	Compute payments on account and balancing payments/repayments for individuals.	2
(e)	List the information and records that taxpayers need to retain for tax purposes.	1
G3	**The procedures relating to enquiries, appeals and disputes**	
(a)	Explain the circumstances in which HM Revenue & Customs can enquire into a self assessment tax return.	2
(b)	Explain the procedures for dealing with appeals and disputes.	1
G4	**Penalties for non-compliance**	
(a)	Calculate interest on overdue tax.	2
(b)	State the penalties that can be charged.	2

Exam guide

Question 1 of the exam will always be on income tax and question 3 on CGT. Either of these could include a part on the self assessment system, be it the filing of a return, the payment of tax or the opening of an enquiry by HMRC, or it could be included in questions 4 or 5. Your knowledge should include the penalties used to enforce the self assessment system.

1 The self assessment system

1.1 Introduction

The self assessment system relies upon the taxpayer completing and filing a tax return and paying the tax due. The system is enforced by a system of penalties for failure to comply within the set time limits, and by interest for late payment of tax.

Many taxpayers have very simple affairs: receiving a salary under deduction of tax through PAYE, with a small amount of investment income which can be dealt with through the PAYE code. These individuals will not normally have to complete a tax return. Self-employed taxpayers, company directors and individuals with complicated affairs will have to.

Once a taxpayer is within the self assessment system he will be required to complete and file a return every year unless HMRC recognise that his affairs have become sufficiently straightforward for no return to be required.

Conversely, individuals whose affairs become more complicated so that they are likely to owe tax must notify HMRC that they should be brought within the self assessment system.

1.2 Notification of liability to income tax and CGT

FAST FORWARD

Individuals who do not receive a tax return must notify their chargeability to income tax or CGT.

Individuals who are chargeable to income tax or CGT for any tax year and who have not received a notice to file a return are required to give notice of chargeability to an Officer of the Revenue and Customs within six months from the end of the year ie by 5 October 2008 for 2007/08.

A person who has no chargeable gains and who is not liable to higher rate tax does not have to give notice of chargeability if all his income:

(a) Is taken into account under PAYE
(b) Is from a source of income not subject to tax under a self-assessment
(c) Has had (or is treated as having had) income tax deducted at source, or
(d) Is UK dividends.

2 Tax returns and keeping records

FAST FORWARD

Tax returns must usually be filed by 31 October (non-electronic) or 31 January (electronic) following the end of the tax year.

2.1 Tax returns

The tax return comprises a Tax Form, together with supplementary pages for particular sources of income. Taxpayers are sent a Tax Form and a number of supplementary pages depending on their known sources of income, together with a Tax Return Guide and various notes relating to the supplementary pages. Taxpayers with new sources of income may have to ask the orderline for further supplementary pages. Taxpayers with simple tax returns may be asked to complete a short four page tax return.

If a return for the previous year was filed electronically the taxpayer may be sent a notice to file a return, rather than the official HMRC form.

Partnerships must file a separate return which includes 'a partnership statement' showing the firm's profits, losses, proceeds from the sale of assets, tax suffered, tax credits, charges on income and the division of all these amounts between partners.

A partnership return must include a declaration of the name, residence and tax reference of each partner, as well as the usual declaration that the return is correct and complete to the best of the signatory's knowledge.

Each partner must then include his share of partnership profits on his personal tax return.

2.2 Time limit for submission of tax returns

Key term

The latest filing date for a personal tax return for a tax year (Year 1) is:

- 31 October in the next tax year (Year 2), for a non-electronic return (eg a paper return).
- 31 January in Year 2, for an electronic return (eg made via the internet).

This rule applies where **Year 1 is the tax year 2007/08 and for subsequent years.**

There are **two exceptions to this general rule**.

The **first exception applies if the notice to file a tax return is issued by HMRC to the taxpayer after 31 July in Year 2, but on or before 31 October in Year 2**. In this case, the **latest filing date is**:

- **the end of 3 months following the notice, for a non-electronic return.**
- **31 January in Year 2, for an electronic return.**

The second exception applies **if the notice to file the tax return is issued to the taxpayer after 31 October in Year 2**. In this case, **the latest filing date is the end of 3 months following the notice.**

Question

Submission of tax returns

Advise the following clients of the latest filing date for her personal tax return for 2007/08 if the return is:

(a) non-electronic; or
(b) electronic.

Norma Notice to file tax return issued by HMRC on 6 April 2008
Melanie Notice to file tax return issued by HMRC on 10 August 2008
Olga Notice to file tax return issued by HMRC on 12 December 2008

Answer

	Non-electronic	*Electronic*
Norma	31 October 2008	31 January 2009
Melanie	9 November 2008	31 January 2009
Olga	11 March 2009	11 March 2009

A partnership return may be filed as a non-electronic return or an electronic return. **The general rule and the exceptions to the general rule for personal returns apply also to partnership returns**.

2.3 Standard accounting information

'Three line' accounts (ie income less expenses equals profit) only need be included on the tax return of businesses with a turnover (or gross rents from property) of less than £15,000 pa. This is not as helpful as it might appear, as underlying records must still be kept for tax purposes (disallowable items etc) when producing three line accounts.

The tax return requires trading results to be presented in a standard format. Although there is no requirement to submit accounts with the return, accounts may be filed. If accounts accompany the return, HMRC's power to raise a discovery assessment (see below) is restricted.

2.4 Keeping records

All taxpayers must retain all records required to enable them to make and deliver a correct tax return.

Records must be retained until the later of:

(a) (i) **5 years after the 31 January following the tax year where the taxpayer is in business** (as a sole trader or partner or letting property). Note that this applies to all of the records, not only the business records, or

(ii) **1 year after the 31 January following the tax year otherwise, or**

(b) Provided notice to deliver a return is given before the date in (a):

(i) **The time after which enquiries by HMRC into the return can no longer be commenced**, or

(ii) **The date any such enquiries have been completed.**

Where a person receives a notice to deliver a tax return after the normal record keeping period has expired, he must keep all records in his possession at that time until no enquiries can be raised in respect of the return or until such enquiries have been completed.

The duty to preserve records can generally be satisfied by retaining copies of original documents except that for documents which show domestic (or foreign) tax deducted or creditable, the originals (eg. dividend certificates) must be kept.

Examples of records which must be kept are:

- Dividend vouchers and interest notifications
- P60, P45, P11D
- Statements of rental income
- Business records for preparing accounts (receipts, invoices, accounting books)
- Contract notes for share acquisitions and sales
- Details of other capital acquisitions and disposals.

3 Self-assessment and claims

If a return is filed non-electronically the taxpayer can ask HMRC to compute the tax due. Electronic returns have tax calculated automatically.

3.1 Self-assessment

Key term

A **self-assessment** is a calculation of the amount of taxable income and gains after deducting reliefs and allowances, a calculation of income tax and CGT payable after taking into account tax deducted at source and tax credits on dividends.

If the taxpayer is filing a **non-electronic return (other than a Short Tax Return), he may make the tax calculation on his return or ask HMRC to do so on his behalf**.

If the taxpayer wishes HMRC to make the calculation for Year 1, a non-electronic return must be filed:

- **on or before 31 October in Year 2 or**,
- **if the notice to file the tax return is issued after 31 August in Year 2, within 2 months of the notice**.

A Short Tax Return filed non-electronically must be filed by these dates.

If the taxpayer is filing an **electronic return, the calculation of tax liability is made automatically when the return is made online**.

3.2 Amending the self-assessment

The taxpayer may amend his return (including the tax calculation) for Year 1 within twelve months after the filing date. For this purpose the filing date means:

- **31 January of Year 2**; or
- **where the notice to file a return was issued after 31 October in Year 2, the last day of the three month period starting with the issue**.

A return may be amended by the taxpayer at a time when an enquiry is in progress into the return. The amendment does not restrict the scope of an enquiry into the return but may be taken into account in that enquiry. If the amendment made during an enquiry is the amount of tax payable, the amendment does not take effect while the enquiry is in progress.

A return may be amended by HMRC to correct any obvious error or omission in the return (such as errors of principle and arithmetical mistakes). The correction must be usually be made within nine months after the day on which the return was actually filed. The taxpayer can object to the correction but must do so within 30 days of receiving notice of it.

Similar rules apply to the amendment and correction of partnership returns.

3.3 Claims

All claims and elections which can be made in a tax return must be made in this manner if a return has been issued. A claim for any relief, allowance or repayment of tax must be quantified at the time it is made. These rules do not apply to claims involving two or more years.

Certain claims have a time limit that is longer than the time limit for filing or amending a tax return. A claim may therefore be made after the time limit for amending the tax return has expired. Claims not made on the tax return are referred to as **'stand alone' claims**.

Claims made on a tax return are subject to the administrative rules governing returns, for the making of corrections, enquiries etc.

3.3.1 Claims involving more than one year

Self-assessment is intended to avoid the need to reopen earlier years, so relief should be given for the year of the claim. This rule can best be explained by considering a claim to carry back a trade loss to an earlier year of assessment:

(a) The claim for relief is treated as made in relation to the year in which the loss was actually incurred

(b) The amount of any tax repayment due is calculated in terms of tax of the earlier year to which the loss is being carried back, and

(c) Any tax repayment etc is treated as relating to the later year in which the loss was actually incurred. A repayment supplement may accrue from the later year.

3.3.2 Time limits

In general the time limit for making a claim is 5 years from 31 January following the tax year. Where different time limits apply these have been mentioned throughout this Text.

3.3.3 Error or mistake claims

An error or mistake claim may be made for errors in a return or partnership statement where tax would otherwise be overcharged. The claim may not be made where the tax liability was computed in accordance with practice prevailing at the time the return or statement was made.

An error or mistake claim may not be made in respect of a claim. If a taxpayer makes an error or mistake in a claim, he may make a supplementary claim within the time limits allowed for the original claim.

The taxpayer may appeal to the Special Commissioners against any refusal of an error or mistake claim.

4 Payment of income tax and capital gains tax

Two payments on account and a final balancing payment of income tax and Class 4 NICs are due. All capital gains tax is due on 31 January following the end of the tax year.

4.1 Payments on account and final payment

4.1.1 Introduction

The self-assessment system may result in the taxpayer making three payments of income tax and Class 4 NICs.

Date	Payment
31 January in the tax year	1st payment on account
31 July after the tax year	2nd payment on account
31 January after the tax year	Final payment to settle the remaining liability

HMRC issue payslips/demand notes in a credit card type 'Statement of Account' format, but there is no statutory obligation for it to do so and **the onus is on the taxpayer to pay the correct amount of tax on the due date.**

4.1.2 Payments on account

Key term

Payments on account are usually required where the income tax and Class 4 NICs due in the previous year exceeded the amount of income tax deducted at source; this excess is known as **'the relevant amount'**. Income tax deducted at source includes tax suffered, PAYE deductions and tax credits on dividends.

The payments on account are each equal to 50% of the relevant amount for the previous year.

Exam focus point

Payments on account of CGT are never required.

Question — Payments on account

Sue is a self employed writer who paid tax for 2007/08 as follows:

		£
Total amount of income tax charged		9,200
This included:	Tax deducted on savings income	3,200
She also paid:	Class 4 NIC	1,900
	Class 2 NIC	114
	Capital gains tax	4,800

How much are the payments on account for 2008/09?

Answer

		£
Income tax:		
Total income tax charged for 2007/08		9,200
Less tax deducted for 2007/08		(3,200)
		6,000
Class 4 NIC		1,900
'Relevant amount'		7,900
Payments on account for 2008/09:		
31 January 2008	£7,900 × ½	3,950
31 July 2008	As before	3,950

There is no requirement to make payments on account of capital gains tax nor Class 2 NIC.

Payments on account are not required if the relevant amount falls below a de minimis limit of £500. Also, payments on account are not required from taxpayers who paid 80% or more of their tax liability for the previous year through PAYE or other deduction at source arrangements.

If the previous year's liability increases following an amendment to a self-assessment, or the raising of a discovery assessment, an adjustment is made to the payments on account due.

4.1.3 Reducing payments on account

Payments on account are normally fixed by reference to the previous year's tax liability but if a taxpayer expects his liability to be lower than this **he may claim to reduce his payments on account to:**

(a) **A stated amount**, or
(b) **Nil**.

The claim must state the reason why he believes his tax liability will be lower, or nil.

If the taxpayer's eventual liability is higher than he estimated he will have reduced the payments on account too far. Although the payments on account will not be adjusted, the taxpayer will suffer an interest charge on late payment.

A penalty of the difference between the reduced payment on account and the correct payment on account may be levied if the reduction was claimed fraudulently or negligently.

4.1.4 Balancing payment

The balance of any income tax and Class 4 NICs together with all CGT due for a year, is normally payable on or before the 31 January following the year.

Question

Payment of tax

Giles made payments on account for 2007/08 of £6,500 each on 31 January 2008 and 31 July 2008, based on his 2006/07 liability. He then calculates his total income tax and Class 4 NIC liability for 2007/08 at £18,000 of which £2,750 was deducted at source. In addition he calculated that his CGT liability for disposals in 2007/08 is £5,120.

What is the final payment due for 2007/08?

Answer

Income tax and Class 4 NIC: £18,000 – £2,750 – £6,500 – £6,500 = £2,250. CGT = £5,120.

Final payment due on 31 January 2009 for 2007/2008 £2,250 + £5,120 = £7,370

In one case the due date for the final payment is later than 31 January following the end of the year. **If a taxpayer has notified chargeability by 5 October but the notice to file a tax return is not issued before 31 October, then the due date for the payment is three months after the issue of the notice.**

Tax charged in an amended self-assessment is usually payable on the later of:

(a) The normal due date, generally 31 January following the end of the tax year, and
(b) The day following 30 days after the making of the revised self-assessment.

Tax charged on a discovery assessment (see below) is due thirty days after the issue of the assessment.

4.2 Surcharges

Key term

Surcharges are normally imposed in respect of amounts paid late:

	Paid	*Surcharge*
(a)	Within 28 days of due date:	none
(b)	More than 28 days but not more than six months after the due date:	5%
(c)	More than six months after the due date:	10%

Surcharges apply to:

(a) Balancing payments of income tax and Class 4 NICs and any CGT under self-assessment or a determination

(b) Tax due on the amendment of a self-assessment

(c) Tax due on a discovery assessment

The surcharge rules do not apply to late payments on account.

No surcharge will be applied where the late paid tax liability has attracted a tax-geared penalty on the failure to notify chargeability to tax, or the failure to submit a return, or on the making of an incorrect return (including a partnership return).

4.3 Interest on late paid tax

Interest is chargeable on late payment of both payments on account and balancing payments. In both cases interest runs from the due date until the day before the actual date of payment.

Exam focus point

You will be given the rate of interest to use in the exam.

Interest is charged from 31 January following the tax year (or the normal due date for the balancing payment, in the rare event that this is later), even if this is before the due date for payment on:

(a) Tax payable following an amendment to a self-assessment
(b) Tax payable in a discovery assessment, and
(c) Tax postponed under an appeal which becomes payable.

Since a determination (see below) is treated as if it were a self-assessment, interest runs from 31 January following the tax year.

If a taxpayer claims to reduce his payments on account and there is still a final payment to be made, interest is normally charged on the payments on account as if each of those payments had been the lower of:

(a) the reduced amount, plus 50% of the final income tax liability; and
(b) the amount which would have been payable had no claim for reduction been made.

Question

Interest

Herbert's payments on account for 2007/08 based on his income tax liability for 2006/07 were £4,500 each. However when he submitted his 2006/07 income tax return in January 2007 he made a claim to reduce the payments on account for 2007/08 to £3,500 each. The first payment on account was made on 29 January 2008, and the second on 12 August 2008.

Herbert filed his 2007/08 tax return in December 2008. The return showed that his tax liabilities for 2007/08 (before deducting payments on account) were income tax and Class 4 NIC: £10,000, capital gains tax: £2,500. Herbert paid the balance of tax due of £5,500 on 19 February 2009.

For what periods and in respect of what amounts will Herbert be charged interest?

Answer

Herbert made an excessive claim to reduce his payments on account, and will therefore be charged interest on the reduction. The payments on account should have been £4,500 each based on the original 2006/07 liability (not £5,000 each based on the 2007/08 liability). Interest will be charged as follows:

(a) First payment on account

  (i) On £3,500 – nil – paid on time
  (ii) On £1,000 from due date of 31 January 2008 to day before payment, 18 February 2009

(b) Second payment on account

  (i) On £3,500 from due date of 31 July 2008 to day before payment, 11 August 2008
  (ii) On £1,000 from due date of 31 July 2008 to day before payment, 18 February 2009

(c) Balancing payment

  (i) On £3,500 from due date of 31 January 2009 to day before payment, 18 February 2009

Where interest has been charged on late payments on account but the final balancing settlement for the year produces a repayment, all or part of the original interest is repaid.

4.4 Repayment of tax and repayment supplement

Tax is repaid when claimed unless a greater payment of tax is due in the following 30 days, in which case it is set-off against that payment.

Interest is paid on overpayments of:

(a) Payments on account

(b) Final payments of income tax and Class 4 NICs and CGT, including tax deducted at source or tax credits on dividends, and

(c) Penalties and surcharges.

Repayment supplement runs from the original date of payment (even if this was prior to the due date), until the day before the date the repayment is made. Income tax deducted at source and tax credits are treated as if they were paid on the 31 January following the tax year concerned.

Repayment supplement paid to individuals is tax free.

5 Enquiries, determinations and discovery assessments

5.1 Enquiries into returns

FAST FORWARD

HMRC can enquire into tax returns but strict procedural rules govern enquiries.

5.1.1 Opening an enquiry

An officer of the Revenue and Customs has a limited period within which to commence enquiries into a return or amendment. For an enquiry into a return for 2007/08 or a subsequent year the officer must give written notice of his intention by:

(a) The **first anniversary of the actual filing date (if the return was delivered on or before the due filing date)**, or

(b) **If the return is filed after the due filing date, the quarter day following the first anniversary of the actual filing date. The quarter days are 31 January, 30 April, 31 July and 31 October.**

If the taxpayer amended the return after the due filing date, the enquiry 'window' extends to the quarter day following the first anniversary of the date the amendment was filed. Where the enquiry was not raised within the limit which would have applied had no amendment been filed, the enquiry is restricted to matters contained in the amendment.

The officer does not have to have, or give, any reason for raising an enquiry. In particular the taxpayer will not be advised whether he has been selected at random for an audit. Enquiries may be full enquiries, or may be limited to 'aspect' enquiries.

5.1.2 During the enquiry

In the course of his enquiries **the officer may require the taxpayer to produce documents, accounts or any other information required. The taxpayer can appeal to the Commissioners.**

During the course of his enquiries an officer may amend a self-assessment if it appears that insufficient tax has been charged and an immediate amendment is necessary to prevent a loss to the Crown. This might apply if, for example, there is a possibility that the taxpayer will emigrate.

If a return is under enquiry HMRC may postpone any repayment due as shown in the return until the enquiry is complete. HMRC have discretion to make a provisional repayment but there is no facility to appeal if the repayment is withheld.

At any time during the course of an enquiry, the taxpayer may apply to the Commissioners to require the officer to notify the taxpayer within a specified period that the enquiries are complete, unless the officer can demonstrate that he has reasonable grounds for continuing the enquiry.

If both sides agree, disputes concerning a point of law can be resolved through litigation without having to wait until the whole enquiry is complete.

5.1.3 Closing an enquiry

An officer must issue a notice that the enquiries are complete, state his conclusions and amend the self-assessment, partnership statement or claim accordingly.

If the taxpayer is not satisfied with the officer's amendment he may, within 30 days, appeal to the Commissioners.

Once an enquiry is complete the officer cannot make further enquiries. HMRC may, in limited circumstances, raise a discovery assessment if they believe that there has been a loss of tax (see below).

5.2 Determinations

HMRC may only raise enquiries if a return has been submitted.

If notice has been served on a taxpayer to submit a return but the return is not submitted by the due filing date, an officer of HMRC may make a determination of the amounts liable to income tax and CGT tax and of the tax due. Such a determination must be made to the best of the officer's information and belief, and is then treated as if it were a self-assessment. This enables the officer to seek payment of tax, including payments on account for the following year and to charge interest.

The determination must be made within the period ending 5 years after 31 January following the tax year. It may be superseded by a self-assessment made within the same period or, if later, within 12 months of the date of the determination.

5.3 Discovery assessments

If an officer of HMRC discovers that profits have been omitted from assessment, that any assessment has become insufficient, or that any relief given is, or has become excessive, an assessment may be raised to recover the tax lost.

If the tax lost results from an error in the taxpayer's return but the return was made in accordance with prevailing practice at the time, no discovery assessment may be made.

A discovery assessment may only be raised where a return has been made if:

(a) There has been **fraudulent or negligent conduct** by the taxpayer or his agent, or

(b) At the time that enquiries into the return were completed, or could no longer be made, the officer **did not have information** to make him aware of the loss of tax.

Information is treated as available to an officer if it is contained in the taxpayer's return or claim for the year or either of the two preceding years, or it has been provided as a result of an enquiry covering those years, or it has been specifically provided.

These rules do not prevent HMRC from raising assessments in cases of genuine discoveries, but prevent assessments from being raised due to HMRC's failure to make timely use of information or to a change of opinion on information made available.

5.4 Appeals and postponement of payment of tax

A taxpayer may appeal against an amendment to a self-assessment or partnership statement, or an amendment to or disallowance of a claim, following an enquiry, or against an assessment which is not a self-assessment, such as a discovery assessment.

The appeal must normally be made within 30 days of the amendment or self-assessment.

The notice of appeal must state the **grounds** of appeal. These may be stated in general terms. At the hearing the Commissioners may allow the appellant to put forward grounds not stated in his notice if they are satisfied that his omission was not wilful or unreasonable.

In some cases it may be possible to agree the point at issue by negotiation with HMRC, in which case the appeal may be settled by agreement. If the appeal cannot be agreed, it will be heard by the General or Special Commissioners.

An appeal does not relieve the taxpayer of liability to pay tax on the normal due date unless he obtains a 'determination' of the Commissioners or agreement of the Inspector that payment of all or some of the tax may be postponed pending determination of the appeal. The amount not postponed is due 30 days after the determination or agreement is issued, if that is later than the normal due date.

If any part of the postponed tax becomes due a notice of the amount payable is issued and the amount is payable 30 days after the issue of the notice. Interest, however, is still payable from the normal due date.

6 Penalties

Self-assessment is enforced through a system of automatic surcharges, penalties and interest.

6.1 Penalties for late notification of chargeability

The maximum mitigable penalty where notice of chargeability is not given is 100% of the tax assessed which is not paid on or before 31 January following the tax year.

6.2 Penalties for late filing

6.2.1 Individual returns

The maximum penalties for delivering a tax return after the filing due date are:

(a)	**Return up to 6 months late:**	**£100**
(b)	**Return more than 6 months but not more than 12 months late:**	**£200**
(c)	**Return more than 12 months late:**	**£200 + 100% of the tax liability**

In addition, the General or Special Commissioners can direct that a maximum penalty of £60 per day be imposed where failure to deliver a tax return continues after notice of the direction has been given to the taxpayer. In this case the additional £100 penalty, imposed under (b) if the return is more than six months late, is not charged.

The fixed penalties of £100/£200 can be set aside by the Commissioners if they are satisfied that the taxpayer had a reasonable excuse for not delivering the return. If the tax liability shown on the return is less than the fixed penalties, the fixed penalty is reduced to the amount of the tax liability. The tax geared penalty is mitigable by HMRC or the Commissioners.

6.2.2 Reasonable excuse

A taxpayer only has a reasonable excuse for a late filing if a default occurred because of a factor outside his control. This might be non-receipt of the return by the taxpayer, an industrial dispute in the post office after the return was posted, serious illness of the taxpayer or a close relative, or destruction of records through fire and flood. Illness etc is only accepted as a reasonable excuse if the taxpayer was taking timeous steps to complete the return, and if the return is filed as soon as possible after the illness etc.

6.3 Penalties for failure to keep records

The maximum (mitigable) penalty for each failure to keep and retain records is £3,000 per tax year/accounting period.

Record keeping failures are taken into account in considering the mitigation of other penalties. Where the record keeping failure is taken into account in this way, a penalty will normally only be sought in serious and exceptional cases where, for example, records have been destroyed deliberately to obstruct an enquiry or there has been a history of serious record keeping failures.

Chapter Roundup

- Individuals who do not receive a tax return must notify their chargeability to income tax or CGT.
- Tax returns must usually be filed by 31 October (non-electronic) or 31 January (electronic) following the end of the tax year.
- If a return is filed non-electronically the taxpayer can ask HMRC to compute the tax due. Electronic returns have tax calculated automatically.
- Two payments on account and a final balancing payment of income tax and Class 4 NICs are due. All capital gains tax is due on 31 January following the end of the tax year.
- HMRC can enquire into tax returns but strict procedural rules govern enquiries.
- Self assessment is enforced through a system of automatic surcharges, penalties and interest.

Quick Quiz

1. By when must a taxpayer who has not received a tax return give notice of his chargeability to capital gains tax due in 2007/08?
2. By when must a taxpayer file a non-electronic tax return for 2007/08?
3. What are the normal payment dates for income tax?
4. What surcharges are due in respect of income tax payments on account that are paid two months after the due date?

Answers to Quick Quiz

1. Within six months of the end of the year, ie by 5 October 2008.
2. 31 October 2008.
3. Two payments on account of income tax are due on 31 January in the tax year and on 31 July following. A final balancing payment is due on 31 January following the tax year.
4. None. Surcharges do not apply to late payment of payments on account.

Now try the question below from the Exam Question Bank

Number	Level	Marks	Time
Q26	Introductory	8	15 mins
Q27	Examination	25	45 mins

Part C
Taxation of companies

19 Computing profits chargeable to corporation tax

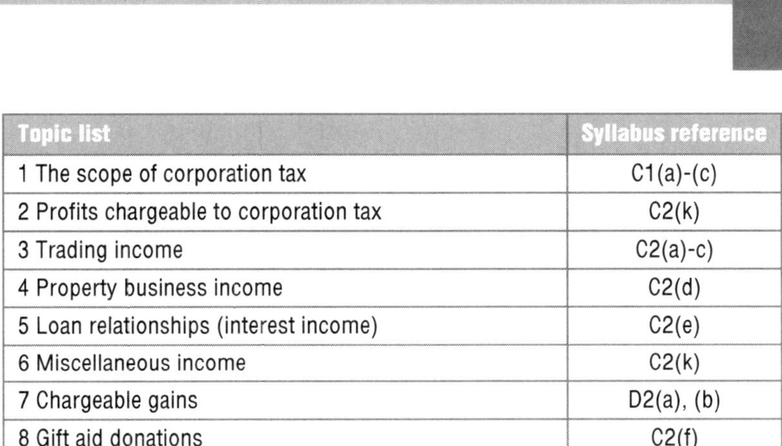

Topic list	Syllabus reference
1 The scope of corporation tax	C1(a)-(c)
2 Profits chargeable to corporation tax	C2(k)
3 Trading income	C2(a)-c)
4 Property business income	C2(d)
5 Loan relationships (interest income)	C2(e)
6 Miscellaneous income	C2(k)
7 Chargeable gains	D2(a), (b)
8 Gift aid donations	C2(f)
9 Long periods of account	C2(k)

Introduction

Now that we have completed our study of personal tax we turn our attention to corporation tax, ie the tax that a company must pay on its profits.

First we consider the scope of corporation tax and we see that a company must pay tax for an 'accounting period' which may be different from its period of account.

We then learn how to calculate the profits chargeable to corporation tax. This involves calculating income from different sources, such as trading income, interest and property income, adding capital gains and deducting gift aid donations. You have learnt the general rules for calculating income and gains in your earlier studies, but here we see where there are special rules for companies.

In the next chapter you will learn how to compute the corporation tax liability on those profits.

Study guide

		Intellectual level
C1	**The scope of corporation tax**	
(a)	Define the terms 'period of account', 'accounting period', and 'financial year'.	1
(b)	Recognise when an accounting period starts and when an accounting period finishes.	1
(c)	Explain how the residence of a company is determined.	2
C2	**Profits chargeable to corporation tax**	
(a)	Recognise the expenditure that is allowable in calculating the tax-adjusted trading profit.	2
(b)	Explain how relief can be obtained for pre-trading expenditure.	1
(c)	Compute capital allowances (as for income tax).	2
(d)	Compute property business profits.	2
(e)	Explain the treatment of interest paid and received under the loan relationship rules.	1
(f)	Explain the treatment of gift aid donations.	2
(k)	Compute profits chargeable to corporation tax.	2

Exam guide

Question 2 in the exam will focus on corporation tax. Corporation tax may also feature in other questions (apart from question 1 on income tax). Question 3, for example, is on capital gains, and could test capital gains of a company. When dealing with a corporation tax question you must first be able to identify the accounting period(s) involved; watch out for long periods of account. You must also be able to calculate the profits chargeable to corporation tax; learn the standard layout so that you can easily slot in figures from your workings.

1 The scope of corporation tax

FAST FORWARD

Companies pay corporation tax on their profits chargeable to corporation tax (PCTCT).

1.1 Companies

Companies must pay corporation tax on their **profits chargeable to corporation tax** for each **accounting period.** We look at the meaning of these terms below.

Key term

A '**company**' is any corporate body (limited or unlimited) or unincorporated association, eg sports club.

1.2 Accounting periods

FAST FORWARD

An accounting period cannot exceed 12 months in length so a long period of account must be split into two accounting periods. The first accounting period is always twelve months in length.

Corporation tax is chargeable in respect of accounting periods. It is important to understand the difference between an accounting period and a period of account.

Key term

A **period of account** is any period for which a company prepares accounts; usually this will be 12 months in length but it may be longer or shorter than this.

Key term

An **accounting period** is the period for which corporation tax is charged and cannot exceed 12 months. Special rules determine when an accounting period starts and ends.

An accounting period starts when a company starts to trade, or otherwise becomes liable to corporation tax, or immediately after the previous accounting period finishes. An accounting period finishes on the earliest of:

- 12 months after its start
- the end of the company's period of account
- the commencement of the company's winding up
- the company's ceasing to be resident in the UK
- the company's ceasing to be liable to corporation tax

If a company has a period of account exceeding 12 months (a long period), it is split into two accounting periods: the first 12 months and the remainder. For example, if a company prepares accounts for the sixteen months to 30 April 2007, the two accounting periods for which the company will pay corporation tax will be the twelve months to 31 December 2006 and the four months to 30 April 2007.

1.3 Financial year

FAST FORWARD

Tax rates are set for financial years.

The rates of corporation tax are fixed for financial years.

Key term

A financial year runs from 1 April to the following 31 March and is identified by the calendar year in which it begins. For example, the year ended 31 March 2008 is the Financial year 2007 (FY 2007). This should not be confused with a tax year, which runs from 6 April to the following 5 April.

1.4 Residence of companies

FAST FORWARD

A company is UK resident if it is incorporated in the UK or if it is incorporated abroad and its central management and control are exercised in the UK.

A company incorporated in the UK is resident in the UK. A company incorporated abroad is resident in the UK if its central management and control are exercised here. Central management and control are usually treated as exercised where the board of directors meet.

Question — Residence of a company

Supraville SARL is a company incorporated in France. It has its head office in London where the board of directors meet monthly. It trades throughout the European Union.

Is Supraville SARL resident in the UK?

Answer

Yes.

The central management and control of Supraville SARL is in London (ie the UK) where the board of directors meet.

2 Profits chargeable to corporation tax

FAST FORWARD

PCTCT comprises the company's income and chargeable gains, less gift aid donations. It does not include dividends received from other UK resident companies.

2.1 Proforma computation

FAST FORWARD

Income includes trading income, property income, income from-non trading loan relationships (interest) and miscellaneous income.

A company may have both income and gains. As a general rule income arises from receipts which are expected to recur regularly (such as the profits from a trade) whereas chargeable gains arise on the sale of capital assets which have been owned for several years (such as the sale of a factory used in the trade).

A company pays corporation tax on its profits chargeable to corporation tax (PCTCT). A company may receive income from various sources. All income received must be classified according to the nature of the income as different computational rules apply to different types of income. The main types of income for a company are:

- Profits of a trade
- Profits of a property business
- Investment income
- Miscellaneous income

For unincorporated businesses and all other income tax purposes (see earlier in this Text) these classes of income have replaced the old classification system under which the different types of income were known as **Schedules**, some of which were divided into **Cases**. These old rules still apply for corporation tax purposes, for example trading profits are strictly known as Schedule D Case I profits and the profits of a property business are called Schedule A profits. However, the plain English terminology above will also be used for corporation tax purposes in your exam and therefore only this new terminology is used in this Text.

A company's profits chargeable to corporation tax are arrived at by aggregating its various sources of income and its chargeable gains and then deducting gift aid donations. Here is a pro forma computation. All items are explained later in this chapter.

	£
Trading profits	X
Investment income	X
Foreign income	X
Miscellaneous income	X
Property business profits	X
Chargeable gains	X
Total profits	X
Less gift aid donations	(X)
Profits chargeable to corporation tax (PCTCT) for an accounting period	X

Exam focus point

It would be of great help in the exam if you could learn the above proforma. When answering a corporation tax question you could immediately reproduce the proforma and insert the appropriate numbers as you are given the information in the question.

Dividends received from UK resident companies are not included in the profits chargeable to corporation tax.

3 Trading income

3.1 Adjustment of profits

FAST FORWARD

The adjustment of profits computation for companies broadly follows that for computing business profits subject to income tax. There are, however, some minor differences.

The trading income of companies is derived from the net profit figure in the accounts, just as for individuals, adjusted as follows.

	£	£
Net profit per accounts		X
Add expenditure not allowed for taxation purposes		X
		X
Less: income not taxable as trading income	X	
expenditure not charged in the accounts but allowable for the purposes of taxation	X	
capital allowances	X	
		(X)
Trading income		X

The adjustment of profits computation for companies broadly follows that for computing business profits subject to income tax. There are, however, some minor differences. There is no disallowance for 'private use' for companies; instead the director or employee will be taxed on the benefit received.

Gift aid donations are added back in the calculation of adjusted profit. They are treated instead as a deduction from total profits.

Investment income including rents is deducted from net profit in arriving at trading income but brought in again further down in the computation (see below).

Exam focus point

When adjusting profits as supplied in a profit and loss account confusion can arise as regards whether figures are net or gross. Properly drawn up company accounts should normally include all income gross. However, some examination questions include items 'net'. Read the question carefully.

3.2 Pre-trading expenditure

Pre-trading expenditure incurred by the company within the 7 years before trade commences is treated as an allowable expense incurred on the first day of trading provided it would have been allowable had the company been trading when the expense was actually incurred.

3.3 Capital allowances

The calculation of capital allowances follows income tax principles.

For companies, however, there is never any reduction of allowances to take account of any private use of an asset. The director or employee suffers a taxable benefit instead. As shown above capital allowances must be deducted in arriving at taxable trading income.

A company's accounting period can never exceed 12 months. If the period of account is longer than 12 months it is **divided into two**; one for the first 12 months and one for the balance. **The capital allowances computation must be carried out for each period separately**.

4 Property business income

Rental income is deducted in arriving at trading income but brought in again further down in the computation as property business income.

The calculation of property business income follows income tax principles.

The income tax rules for property businesses were set out earlier in this Text. In summary all UK rental activities are treated as a single source of income calculated in the same way as trading income.

However there are certain differences for companies:

(a) **Property business losses** are:

- **first set off against non-property business income and gains of the company for the current period**; and any excess is
- **carried forward for set off against future income (of all descriptions)**.

(b) **Interest paid by a company on a loan to buy or improve property is not a property business expense**. The **loan relationship rules apply** instead (see below).

5 Loan relationships (interest income)

5.1 General principle

If a company borrows or lends money, including issuing or investing in debentures or buying gilts, **it has a loan relationship. This can be a creditor relationship** (where the company lends or invests money) **or a debtor relationship** (where the company borrows money or issues securities).

5.2 Treatment of trading loan relationships

If the company is a party to a **loan relationship for trade purposes, any debits – ie interest paid or other debt costs – charged through its accounts are allowed as a trading expense** and are therefore deductible in computing trading income.

Similarly **if any credits – ie interest income or other debt returns – arise on a trading loan these are treated as a trading receipt and are taxable as trading income.** This is not likely to arise unless the trade is one of money lending.

5.3 Treatment of non-trading loan relationships

If a loan relationship is not one to which the company is a party for trade purposes any debits or credits must be pooled. A net credit on the pool is chargeable as interest income.

Interest charged on underpaid tax is allowable and interest received on overpaid tax is assessable under the rules for non-trading loan relationships.

Exam focus point

You will not be expected to deal with net deficits (ie losses) on non-trading loan relationships in your exam.

5.4 Accounting methods

Debits and credits must be brought into account using the UK generally accepted accounting practice (GAAP) or using the International Accounting Standards (IAS). This will usually be the accruals basis.

5.5 Incidental costs of loan finance

Under the loan relationship rules expenses ('debits') are allowed if incurred directly:

(a) to bring a loan relationship into existence

(b) entering into or giving effect to any related transactions

(c) making payment under a loan relationship or related transactions or

(d) taking steps to ensure the receipt of payments under the loan relationship or related transaction.

A related transaction means 'any disposal or acquisition (in whole or in part) of rights or liabilities under the relationship, including any arising from a security issue in relation to the money debt in question'.

The above categories of incidental costs are also allowable even if the company does not enter into the loan relationship (ie abortive costs). Costs directly incurred in varying the terms of a loan relationship are also allowed.

5.6 Other matters

It is not only the interest costs of borrowing that are allowable or taxable. The capital costs are treated similarly. Thus if a company issues a loan at a discount and repays it eventually at par, the capital cost is usually allowed on redemption (if the accruals basis is adopted).

6 Miscellaneous income

Patent royalties received which do not relate to the trade are taxed as miscellaneous income. Patent royalties which relate to the trade are included in trading income normally on an accruals basis.

7 Chargeable gains

FAST FORWARD

Chargeable gains for companies are computed in broadly the same way as for individuals, but indexation allowance continues up to the date of sale and there is no taper relief or annual exemption.

7.1 Introduction

Companies do not pay capital gains tax. Instead their chargeable gains are included in the profits chargeable to corporation tax. A company's capital gains or allowable losses are computed in a similar way to individuals but with a few major differences:

- Indexation allowance continues after 6 April 1998
- Taper relief does not apply
- No annual exemption is available
- The FA 1985 pool for shares does not stop at 5 April 1998 and different matching rules for shares apply if the shareholder is a company.

7.2 Indexation

Companies are entitled to indexation allowance from the date of acquisition until the date of disposal of an asset.

For example, if J Ltd bought a painting on 2 January 1987 and sold it on 19 November 2007 the indexation allowance is available from January 1987 until November 2007, not just until April 1998.

Exam formula

The indexation factor is:

$$\frac{\text{RPI for month of disposal} - \text{RPI for month of acquisition}}{\text{RPI for month of acquisition}}$$

The calculation is expressed as a decimal and is rounded to three decimal places.

Question — **The indexation allowance**

An asset is acquired by a company on 15 February 1983 (RPI = 83.0) at a cost of £5,000. Enhancement expenditure of £2,000 is incurred on 10 April 1984 (RPI = 88.6). The asset is sold for £25,500 on 20 December 2007 (RPI = 210.1). Incidental costs of sale are £500. Calculate the chargeable gain arising.

Answer

The indexation allowance is available until December 2007 and is computed as follows.

	£
$\frac{210.1 - 83.0}{83.0} = 1.531 \times £5,000$	7,655
$\frac{210.1 - 88.6}{88.6} = 1.371 \times £2,000$	2,742
	10,397

The computation of the chargeable gain is as follows.

	£
Proceeds	25,500
Less incidental costs of sale	(500)
Net proceeds	25,000
Less allowable costs £(5,000 + 2,000)	(7,000)
Unindexed gain	18,000
Less indexation allowance (see above)	(10,397)
Chargeable gain	7,603

7.3 Disposals of shares by companies

7.3.1 The matching rules

We have discussed the share matching rules for individuals earlier in this Text. We also need special rules for companies, but these are simpler as we do not need to distinguish between pre and post 5 April 1998 acquisitions as the FA 1985 pool continues to run for companies.

For companies the matching of shares sold is in the following order.

(a) Shares acquired on the **same day**
(b) Shares acquired in the **previous nine days**
(c) Shares from the **FA 1985 pool**

The composition of the FA 1985 pool is explained below.

Exam focus point

Learn the 'matching rules' because a crucial first step to getting a shares question right is to correctly match the shares sold to the original shares purchased.

7.3.2 Example: share matching rules for companies

Nor Ltd acquired the following shares in Last plc:

Date of acquisition	*No of shares*
9.11.02	15,000
15.12.04	15,000
11.7.07	5,000
15.7.07	5,000

Nor Ltd disposed of 20,000 of the shares on 15 July 2007.

We match the shares as follows:

(a) Acquisition on same day: 5,000 shares acquired 15 July 2007.
(b) Acquisitions in previous 9 days: 5,000 shares acquired 11 July 2007.
(c) FA 1985 pool: 10,000 shares out of 30,000 shares in FA 1985 pool (9.11.02 + 15.12.04).

7.3.3 The FA 1985 pool

Exam focus point

The examiner has stated that a detailed question will not be set on the pooling provisions. However, work through the examples below as you are expected to understand how the pool works.

The FA 1985 pool comprises the following shares of the same class in the same company.

- **Shares held by a company on 1 April 1985 and acquired by that company on or after 1 April 1982**.
- **Shares acquired by that company on or after 1 April 1985**.

As for individuals, we must keep track of:

(a) the **number** of shares
(b) the **cost** of the shares ignoring indexation
(c) the **indexed cost** of the shares

7.3.4 Example: the FA 1985 pool

Oliver Ltd bought 1,000 shares in Judith plc for £2,750 in August 1984 and another 1,000 for £3,250 in December 1984. RPIs are August 1984 = 89.9, December 1984 = 90.9 and April 1985 = 94.8. The FA 1985 pool at 1 April 1985 is as follows.

	No of shares	*Cost* £	*Indexed cost* £
August 1984 (a)	1,000	2,750	2,750
December 1984 (b)	1,000	3,250	3,250
	2,000	6,000	6,000
Indexation allowance			
$\frac{94.8-89.9}{89.9} = 0.055 \times £2{,}750$			151
$\frac{94.8-90.9}{90.9} = 0.043 \times £3{,}250$			140
Indexed cost of the pool at 1 April 1985			6,291

Disposals and acquisitions of shares which affect the indexed value of the FA 1985 pool are termed **'operative events'. Prior to reflecting each such operative event within the FA 1985 share pool, a further indexation allowance (an 'indexed rise') must be computed up to the date of the operative event concerned from the date of the last such operative event** (or from the later of the first acquisition and April 1985 if the operative event in question is the first one).

Indexation calculations within the FA 1985 pool (after its April 1985 value has been calculated) **are not rounded to three decimal places**. This is because rounding errors would accumulate and have a serious effect after several operative events.

If there are several operative events between 1 April 1985 and the date of a disposal, the indexation procedure described above will have to be performed several times over.

Question — **Value of FA 1985 pool**

Following on from the above example, assume that Oliver Ltd acquired 2,000 more shares on 10 July 1986 at a cost of £4,000. Recalculate the value of the FA 1985 pool on 10 July 1986 following the acquisition. Assume the RPI in July 1986 = 97.5.

Answer

	No of shares	*Cost* £	*Indexed cost* £
Value at 1.4.85 b/f	2,000	6,000	6,291
Indexed rise $\frac{97.5-94.8}{94.8} \times £6{,}291$			179
	2,000	6,000	6,470
Acquisition	2,000	4,000	4,000
Value at 10.7.86	4,000	10,000	10,470

In the case of a disposal, following the calculation of the indexed rise to the date of disposal, the cost and the indexed cost attributable to the shares disposed of are deducted from the amounts within the FA 1985 pool. The proportions of the cost and indexed cost to take out of the pool should be computed by using the proportion of cost that the shares disposed of bear to the total number of shares held.

The indexation allowance is the indexed cost taken out of the pool minus the cost taken out. As usual, the indexation allowance cannot create or increase a loss.

Question — **Disposals from the FA 1985 pool**

Continuing the above exercise, suppose that Oliver Ltd sold 3,000 shares on 10 July 2007 for £19,000. Compute the gain, and the value of the FA 1985 pool following the disposal. Assume RPI July 2007 = 206.6.

Answer

	No of shares	*Cost*	*Indexed cost*
		£	£
Value at 10.7.86	4,000	10,000	10,470
Indexed rise			
$\frac{206.6-97.5}{97.5} \times$ £10,470			11,716
	4,000	10,000	22,186
Disposal	(3,000)		
Cost and indexed cost $\frac{3{,}000}{4{,}000} \times$ £10,000 and £22,186		(7,500)	(16,640)
Value at 10.7.07	1,000	2,500	5,546

The gain is computed as follows:

	£
Proceeds	19,000
Less cost	(7,500)
	11,500
Less indexation allowance £(16,640 – 7,500)	(9,140)
Chargeable gain	2,360

8 Gift aid donations

FAST FORWARD: Gift aid donations are paid gross by a company and deducted when computing PCTCT.

Gift aid donations are deductible in computing PCTCT.

Almost all donations of money to charity can be made under the **gift aid scheme** whether they are one off donations or are regular donations. **Gift aid donations are paid gross.**

Donations to local charities which are incurred wholly and exclusively for the purposes of a trade are deducted in the calculation of the tax adjusted trading profits.

9 Long periods of account

As we saw above, if a company has a long period of account exceeding 12 months, it is split into two accounting periods: the first 12 months and the remainder.

Where the period of account differs from the corporation tax accounting periods, profits are **allocated to the relevant periods** as follows:

- **Trading income** before capital allowances is apportioned on a **time basis.**
- **Capital allowances** and balancing charges are **calculated for each accounting period.**

- **Other income is allocated to the period to which it relates** (eg rents to the period when accrued). Miscellaneous income, however, is apportioned on a time basis.
- **Chargeable gains and losses** are allocated to the **period in which they are realised.**
- **Gift aid donations** are deducted in the accounting **period in which they are paid.**

Question — Long period of account

Xenon Ltd makes up an 18 month set of accounts to 30 September 2008 with the following results.

	£
Trading profits	180,000
Property income	
18 months @ £500 accruing per month	9,000
Capital gain (1 August 2008 disposal)	250,000
Less: Gift aid donation (paid 31 March 2008)	(50,000)
	389,000

What are the profits chargeable to corporation tax for each of the accounting periods based on the above accounts?

Answer

The 18 month period of account is divided into:

Year ending 31 March 2008
6 months to 30 September 2008

Results are allocated:

	Y/e 31.3.08	*6m to 30.9.08*
	£	£
Trading profits 12:6	120,000	60,000
Property Income		
12 × £500	6,000	
6 × £500		3,000
Capital gain (1.8.08)		250,000
Less: Gift aid donation (31.3.08)	(50,000)	
PCTCT (profits chargeable to corporation tax)	76,000	313,000

Chapter Roundup

- Companies pay corporation tax on their profits chargeable to corporation tax (PCTCT).
- An accounting period cannot exceed 12 months in length so a long period of account must be split into two accounting periods. The first accounting period is always twelve months in length.
- Tax rates are set for financial years.
- A company is UK resident if it is incorporated in the UK or if it is incorporated abroad and its central management and control are exercised in the UK.
- PCTCT comprises the company's income and chargeable gains, less gift aid donations. It does not include dividends received from other UK resident companies.
- Income includes trading income, property income, income from-non trading loan relationships (interest) and miscellaneous income.
- The adjustment of profits computation for companies broadly follows that for computing business profits subject to income tax. There are, however, some minor differences.
- Chargeable gains for companies are computed in broadly the same way as for individuals, but indexation allowance continues up to the date of sale and there is no taper relief or annual exemption.
- Gift aid donations are paid gross by a company and deducted when computing PCTCT.

Quick Quiz

1. When does an accounting period end?
2. What is the difference between a period of account and an accounting period?
3. Should interest paid on a trading loan be adjusted in the trading income computation?
4. What are the matching rules for shares disposed of by a company?
5. How are trading profits (before capital allowances) of a long period of account divided between accounting periods?

Answers to Quick Quiz

1 An accounting period ends on the earliest of:

(a) 12 months after its start
(b) the end of the company's period of account
(c) the commencement of the company's winding up
(d) the company ceasing to be resident in the UK
(e) the company ceasing to be liable to corporation tax

2 A period of account is the period for which a company prepares accounts. An accounting period is the period for which corporation tax is charged. If a company prepares annual accounts the two will coincide.

3 Interest paid on a trading loan should not be adjusted in the trading income computation as it is an allowable expense, computed on the accruals basis.

4 The matching rules for shares disposed of by a company are:

(a) Shares acquired on the **same day**
(b) Shares acquired in the **previous nine days**,
(c) Shares from the **FA 1985 pool**

5 Trading income (before capital allowances) is apportioned on a time basis.

Now try the question below from the Exam Question Bank

Number	Level	Marks	Time
Q28	Introductory	10	18 mins
Q29	Introductory	5	9 mins
Q30	Examination	15	27 mins

Computing the corporation tax liability

Topic list	Syllabus reference
1 Charge to corporation tax	C3(a)-(c)
2 Associated companies	C3(a), C4(a)

Introduction

In the previous chapter you learnt how to identify a company's accounting period and how to compute the profits chargeable to corporation tax for that accounting period.

In this chapter you will learn how to compute the corporation tax liability on those profits.

In the next chapters we will deal with losses, groups and overseas matters.

Study guide

		Intellectual level
C3	**The comprehensive computation of corporation tax liability**	
(a)	Compute the corporation tax liability and apply marginal relief.	2
(b)	Explain the implications of receiving franked investment income.	2
(c)	Explain how exemptions and reliefs can defer or minimise corporation tax liabilities.	2
C4	**The effect of a group corporate structure for corporation tax purposes**	
(a)	Define an associated company and recognise the effect of being an associated company for corporation tax purposes.	2

Exam guide

Question 2 of the exam will always be on corporation tax, and corporation tax may also be the subject of questions 3, 4 or 5. Computing the corporation tax is usually an integral part of at least one question, and you must be sure that you understand the rules for marginal relief. Note in particular the consequences of short accounting periods and of having associated companies. It will be crucial for you to know the marginal rate of corporation tax for a company when you are dealing with loss relief and group relief later in your studies.

1 Charge to corporation tax

FAST FORWARD: A company pays corporation tax on its profits chargeable to corporation tax (PCTCT).

1.1 'Profits'

FAST FORWARD: 'Profits' is PCTCT plus franked investment income (FII).

Although we tax PCTCT another figure needs to be calculated ('profits') to determine the rate of corporation tax to use to tax PCTCT.

'Profits' means profits chargeable to corporation tax plus the grossed-up amount of dividends received from UK companies other than those in the same group. The grossed-up amount of UK dividends is the dividend received multiplied by 100/90. This is because dividends are treated as paid net of a 10% tax credit (see earlier in this Text). You may see the grossed up amount of dividend received referred to as **franked investment income (FII)**.

Do not include overseas dividends in the computation of 'profits'. These will have been included as foreign income when calculating PCTCT (see later in this Text).

Exam focus point

Be careful to charge corporation tax on PCTCT, not on profits.

1.2 The full rate

The rates of corporation tax are fixed for financial years. The full rate of corporation tax is 30% for FY 2007, and applies to companies with 'profits' of £1,500,000 or more, having remained unchanged since FY 1999. A company with PCTCT of, say, £2 million, will pay £600,000 corporation tax.

1.3 The small companies' rate (SCR)

FAST FORWARD

Companies may be taxed at the small companies' rate (SCR) or obtain marginal relief, depending on their 'profits'.

The SCR of corporation tax of 20% for FY 2007 (FY 2006 and FY 2005 19%) applies to the profits chargeable to corporation tax of UK resident companies whose 'profits' are not more than £300,000.

Question — The small companies' rate

B Ltd had the following results for the year ended 31 March 2008.

	£
Trading profits	42,000
Dividend received 1 May 2007	9,000

Compute the corporation tax payable.

Answer

	£
Trading profits	42,000
Dividend plus tax credit £9,000 × 100/90	10,000
'Profits' (less than £300,000 limit)	52,000
Corporation tax payable	
£42,000 × 20%	£8,400

1.4 Marginal relief

Small companies' marginal relief applies where the 'profits' of an accounting period of a UK resident company are over £300,000 but under £1,500,000.

We first calculate the corporation tax at the full rate and then deduct:

(M – P) × I/P × marginal relief fraction

where M = upper limit (currently £1,500,000)
P = 'profits' (see above)
I = PCTCT

The marginal relief fraction is 1/40 for FY 2007 (FY 2006 and FY 2005 11/400).

This information is given in the rates and allowances section of the exam paper.

Question — Small companies' marginal relief

Lenox Ltd has the following results for the year ended 31 March 2008.

	£
PCTCT	296,000
Dividend received 1 December 2007	12,600

Calculate the corporation tax liability.

Answer

	£
PCTCT	296,000
Dividend plus tax credit £12,600 × 100/90	14,000
'Profits'	310,000

'Profits' are above £300,000 but below £1,500,000, so marginal relief applies.

	£
Corporation tax on PCTCT £296,000 × 30%	88,800
Less small companies' marginal relief	
£(1,500,000 – 310,000) × 296,000/310,000 × 1/40	(28,406)
	60,394

FAST FORWARD

The marginal rate of corporation tax between the small companies' limits is 32.5% (FY 2007). The marginal tax rate is an effective rate; it is never actually used in working out corporation tax.

In exam questions you often need to be aware that there is a **marginal rate of 32.5 %** which applies to any PCTCT that lies in between the small companies' limits.

This is calculated as follows:

	£			£
Upper limit	1,500,000	@	30%	450,000
Lower limit	(300,000)	@	20%	(60,000)
Difference	1,200,000			390,000

$$\frac{390,000}{1,200,000} = 32.5\%$$

Effectively the band of profits (here £1,200,000) falling between the upper and lower limits are taxed at a rate of 32.5%

1.5 Example: effective marginal rate of tax

A Ltd has PCTCT of £350,000 for the year ended 31 March 2008. Its corporation tax liability is

	£
£350,000 × 30%	105,000
Less small companies' marginal relief	
£(1,500,000 – 350,000) × $^{1}/_{40}$	(28,750)
	76,250

This is the same as calculating tax at 20% × £300,000 + 32.5% × £50,000 = £60,000 + £16,250 = £76,250.

Consequently tax is charged at an effective rate of 32.5% on PCTCT that exceeds the small companies' lower limit.

Note that although there is an effective corporation tax charge of 32.5%, this rate of tax is never used in actually calculating corporation tax. The rate is just an effective marginal rate that you must be aware of. It will be particularly important when considering loss relief and group relief (see later in this Text).

The marginal rate of corporation tax for FY 2006 and FY 2005 was 32.75%.

1.6 Accounting period in more than one Financial Year

An accounting period **may fall within more than one Financial Year. If the rates and limits for corporation tax are the same in both Financial Years, tax can be computed for the accounting period as if it fell within one Financial Year**.

However, **if the rates and/or limits for corporation tax are different in the Financial Years, PCTCT and 'profits' are time apportioned between the Financial Years**. This will be the case where a company is a small company (or marginal relief company) with an accounting period partly in FY 2006 and partly in FY 2007. **It is also necessary to adjust the upper and lower limits**.

1.7 Example

Wentworth Ltd makes up its accounts to 31 December each year. For the year to 31 December 2007, it has PCTCT of £174,000. It receives a dividend of £5,400 on 1 December 2007.

The corporation tax payable by Wentworth Ltd is calculated as follows.

	£
PCTCT	174,000
Dividend plus tax credit £5,400 × 100/90	6,000
'Profits'	180,000

	FY 2006 3 months to 31.3.07	*FY 2007 9 months to 31.12.07*
	£	£
PCTCT (3:9)	43,500	130,500
'Profits' (3:9)	45,000	135,000
Lower limit:		
£300,000 × 3/12	75,000	
£300,000 × 9/12		225,000
Small companies rate applies in both FYs		
FY 2006 £43,500 × 19%	8,265	
FY 2007 £130,500 × 20%		26,100
Total corporation tax payable £(8,265 + 26,100)		£34,365

Question — Accounting period in more than one financial year

Elliot Ltd has the following results for the year to 30 September 2007.

	£
PCTCT	360,000
Dividend received 15 July 2007	8,100

Calculate the corporation tax payable by Elliot Ltd.

Answer

	£
PCTCT	360,000
Add: FII £8,100 × 100/90	9,000
'Profits'	369,000

	FY 2006 6 months to 31.3.07 £	FY 2007 6 months 30.9.07 £
PCTCT (6:6)	180,000	180,000
'Profits' (6:6)	184,500	184,500
Lower limit: £300,000 × 6/12	150,000	150,000
Upper limit: £1,500,000 × 6/12	750,000	750,000
Marginal relief applies in both FYs		
FY 2006		
£180,000 × 30%	54,000	
Less: marginal relief $£(750{,}000 - 184{,}500) \times \frac{180{,}000}{184{,}500} \times 11/400$	(15,172)	
	38,828	
FY 2007		
£180,000 × 30%		54,000
Less: marginal relief $£(750{,}000 - 184{,}500) \times \frac{180{,}000}{184{,}500} \times 1/40$		(13,793)
		40,207
Total corporation tax payable £(38,828 + 40,207)		£79,035

1.8 Short accounting periods

FAST FORWARD

The upper and lower limits which are used to be determine tax rates are pro-rated on a time basis if an accounting period lasts for less than 12 months.

Question — **Short accounting period**

Ink Ltd prepared accounts for the six months to 31 March 2008. Profits chargeable to corporation tax for the period were £200,000. No dividends were received. Calculate the corporation tax payable for the period.

Answer

Upper limit £1,500,000 × 6/12 = £750,000

Lower limit £300,000 × 6/12 = £150,000

As 'profits' fall between the limits small companies' marginal relief applies.

	£
Corporation tax (FY 07)	
£200,000 × 30%	60,000
Less small companies' marginal relief 1/40 × (£750,000 – £200,000)	(13,750)
Corporation tax	46,250

1.9 Long periods of account

Remember than an accounting period cannot be more than 12 months long. If the period of account exceeds 12 months it must be split into two accounting periods, the first of 12 months and the second of the balance.

Exam focus point

If you have to deal with a long period of account remember to pro-rate the upper and lower limits on a time basis for the second (short) accounting period.

Question

Long period of account

Xenon Ltd in the previous chapter made up an 18 month set of accounts to 30 September 2008.

The 18 month period of account is divided into:

Year ending 31 March 2008
6 months to 30 September 2008

Results were allocated:

	Y/e 31.3.08	*6m to 30.9.08*
	£	£
Trading profits 12:6	120,000	60,000
Property income	6,000	3,000
Capital gain (1.8.08)		250,000
Less: Gift aid donation (31.3.08)	(50,000)	
PCTCT	76,000	313,000

Assuming Xenon Ltd received FII of £27,000 on 31 August 2008 calculate the corporation tax payable for each accounting period. Assume the rates of corporation tax for FY 2007 apply in FY 2008.

Answer

	Y/e 31.3.08	*6m to 30.9.08*
	£	£
PCTCT	76,000	313,000
FII	0	27,000
Profits	76,000	340,000
Small companies lower limit	300,000	150,000
Small companies upper limit	1,500,000	750,000
	Small company	Marginal relief
CT payable		
£76,000 × 20%	15,200	
£313,000 × 30%		93,900
Less marginal relief £(750,000 – 340,000) × 313,000/340,000 × 1/40		(9,436)
		84,464
Total corporation tax payable £(15,200 + 84,464)		99,664

2 Associated companies

FAST FORWARD

The upper and lower limits which are used to determine tax rates are divided by the total number of associated companies. Broadly, associated companies are worldwide trading companies under common control.

2.1 What is an associated company?

Key term

The expression **'associated companies'** in tax has no connection with financial accounting. For tax purposes a company is associated with another company if either controls the other or if both are under the control of the same person or persons (individuals, partnerships or companies). Whether such a company is UK resident or not is irrelevant. Control is given by holding over 50% of the share capital or the voting power or being entitled to over 50% of the distributable income or of the net assets in a winding up.

2.2 Effects of associated companies

If a company has one or more 'associated companies', then the profit limits for small companies rate purposes are divided by the number of associated companies + 1 (for the company itself).

Companies which have only been associated for part of an accounting period are deemed to have been associated for the whole period for the purpose of determining the profit limits.

2.3 Exception

An associated company is ignored for these purposes if it has not carried on any trade or business at any time in the accounting period (or the part of the period during which it was associated) ie it is 'dormant'.

Question — **Associated companies**

For the year to 31 March 2008 a company with two other associated companies had PCTCT of £200,000 and no dividends paid or received. Compute the corporation tax payable.

Answer

(a) Reduction in the lower limit for SCR

Divide by number of associated companies + 1 = 3

£300,000 ÷ 3 = £100,000

(b) Reduction in the upper limit for SCR

£1,500,000 ÷ 3 = £500,000

(c) 'Profits' = £200,000

As 'profits' fall between the lower and upper limits for SCR purposes, the full rate less small companies' marginal relief applies:

(d) Corporation tax

	£
£200,000 × 30%	60,000
Less marginal relief £(500,000 – 200,000) × 1/40	(7,500)
Corporation tax	52,500

2.4 Associated companies and short accounting periods

If a company has associated companies and also a short accounting period, first reduce the upper and lower limits for the associated companies and then prorate them for the short accounting period.

2.5 Example: small company limits

Alpha plc, a company with one subsidiary, prepares accounts for the 9 months to 31 December 2008.

The small companies limit will be multiplied by ½ as there is one associated company, and by 9/12 as the accounting period is only 9 months long.

The small companies lower limit will be £300,000 × ½ × 9/12 = £112,500

The small companies upper limit will be £1,500,000 × ½ × 9/12 = £562,500

Chapter Roundup

- A company pays corporation tax on its profits chargeable to corporation tax (PCTCT).
- 'Profits' is PCTCT plus franked investment income (FII).
- Companies may be taxed at the small companies' rate (SCR) or obtain marginal relief, depending on their 'profits'.
- The marginal rate of corporation tax between the small companies' limits is 32.5%. The marginal tax rate is an effective rate; it is never actually used in working out corporation tax.
- The upper and lower limits which are used to be determine tax rates are pro-rated on a time basis if an accounting period lasts for less than 12 months.
- The upper and lower limits which are used to determine tax rates are divided by the total number of associated companies. Broadly, associated companies are worldwide trading companies under common control.

Quick Quiz

1 Which companies are entitled to the small companies' rate of corporation tax?

2 What is the marginal relief formula?

3 What is an associated company?

4 What effect do associated companies have on the corporation tax computation?

Answers to Quick Quiz

1 Companies with profits of up to £300,000

2 $(M - P) \times I/P \times$ marginal relief fraction

where:

M = upper limit
P = 'profits'
I = PCTCT

3 A company is associated with another company if either controls the other or if both are under the control of the same person or persons (Individual, partnership or companies).

4 If a company has associated companies the small companies lower and upper limits are divided by the number of associated companies + 1.

Now try the question below from the Exam Question Bank

Number	Level	Marks	Time
Q31	Examination	15	27 mins
Q32	Examination	15	27 mins

Losses

Topic list	Syllabus reference
1 Trading losses	C2
2 Carry forward trade loss relief	C2(g)
3 Trade loss relief against total profits	C2(h)
4 Choosing loss reliefs and other planning points	C2(i)
5 Other losses	C2(j), D2(c)

Introduction

In the previous two chapters we have seen how a company calculates its profits chargeable to corporation tax and the corporation tax payable.

We now look at how a company may obtain relief for losses. An important factor in deciding what relief to claim is the **marginal rate** of tax, which may be 20%, 30% or 32.5% as seen earlier.

In the next chapter we will look at groups, and in particular how losses can be relieved by group relief.

Study guide

		Intellectual level
C2	**Profits chargeable to corporation tax**	
(g)	Understand how trading losses can be carried forward.	2
(h)	Understand how trading losses can be claimed against income of the current or previous accounting periods.	2
(i)	Recognise the factors that will influence the choice of loss relief claim.	2
(j)	Explain how relief for a property business loss is given.	1

Exam guide

Losses could form part of question 2 on corporation tax in the exam, they may also be included in questions 3, 4 or 5, or they may not be examined at all. If they do appear, they may be a significant part of the question. Dealing with losses involves a methodical approach: first establish what loss is available for relief, second identify the different reliefs available, and third evaluate the options. Do check the question for specific instructions; you may be told that loss relief should be taken as early as possible.

1 Trading losses

FAST FORWARD

Trading losses may be relieved against current total profits, against total profits of earlier periods or against future trading income.

In summary, the following reliefs are available for trading losses incurred by a company.

(a) **Set-off against current profits**
(b) **Carry back against earlier profits**
(c) **Carry forward against future trading profits**

Reliefs (a) and (b) must be claimed, and are given in the order shown. Relief (c) is given automatically for any loss for which the other reliefs are not claimed.

2 Carry forward trade loss relief

FAST FORWARD

Trading losses carried forward can only be set against future trading profits arising from the same trade.

A company must set off a trading loss against income from the same trade in future accounting periods (unless it has been otherwise relieved see below). **Relief is against the first available profits.**

Question — Carry forward trade loss relief

A Ltd has the following results for the three years to 31 March 2008.

	Year ended		
	31.3.06	*31.3.07*	*31.3.08*
	£	£	£
Trading profit/(loss)	(8,550)	3,000	6,000
Property income	0	1,000	1,000
Gift aid donation	300	1,400	1,700

Calculate the profits chargeable to corporation tax for all three years showing any losses available to carry forward at 1 April 2008.

Answer

	Year ended		
	31.3.06	*31.3.07*	*31.3.08*
	£	£	£
Trading profits	0	3,000	6,000
Less: carry forward loss relief		(3,000)	(5,550)
	0	0	450
Property income	0	1,000	1,000
Less: Gift aid donation	0	(1,000)	(1,450)
PCTCT	0	0	0
Unrelieved gift aid donation	300	400	250

Note that the trading loss carried forward is set only against the trading profit in future years. It cannot be set against the property income.

The gift aid donations that become unrelieved remain unrelieved as they cannot be carried forward.

Loss memorandum

	£
Loss for y/e 31.3.06	8,550
Less used y/e 31.3.07	(3,000)
Loss carried forward at 1.4.07	5,550
Less used y/e 31.3.08	(5,550)
Loss carried forward at 1.4.08	0

3 Trade loss relief against total profits

Loss relief against total profits is given before gift aid donations. Gift aid donations may be unrelieved as a result.

3.1 Current year relief

A company may claim to set a trading loss incurred in an accounting period against total profits before deducting gift aid donations of the same accounting period.

3.2 Carry back relief

FAST FORWARD

Loss relief against total profits may be given against current period profits and against profits of the previous 12 months.

A claim for current period loss relief can be made without a claim for carryback. However, if a loss is to be carried back a claim for current period relief must have been made first.

Such a loss may then be carried back and set against total profits before deducting gift aid donations of an accounting period falling wholly or partly within the 12 months of the start of the period in which the loss was incurred.

If a period falls partly outside the 12 months, loss relief is limited to the proportion of the period's profits (before gift aid donations) equal to the proportion of the period which falls within the 12 months.

Any possible loss relief claim for the period of the loss must be made before any excess loss can be carried back to a previous period.

Any carry-back is to more recent periods before earlier periods. Relief for earlier losses is given before relief for later losses.

3.3 Claims

A claim for relief against current or prior period profits must be made within two years of the end of the accounting period in which the loss arose. Any claim must be for the *whole* loss (to the extent that profits are available to relieve it). The loss can however be reduced by not claiming full capital allowances, so that higher capital allowances are given (on higher tax written down values) in future years.

Question — Loss relief against total profits

Helix Ltd has the following results.

		Year ended	
	30.9.05	*30.9.06*	*30.9.07*
	£	£	£
Trading profit/(loss)	10,500	10,000	(35,000)
Bank interest	500	500	500
Chargeable gains	0	0	4,000
Gift Aid donation	250	250	250

Show the PCTCT for all the years affected assuming that loss relief against total profits is claimed.

Answer

The loss of the year to 30 September 2007 is relieved against current year profits and against profits of the previous twelve months.

		Year ended	
	30.9.05	*30.9.06*	*30.9.07*
	£	£	£
Trading profit	10,500	10,000	0
Investment income	500	500	500
Chargeable gains	0	0	4,000
	11,000	10,500	4,500
Less current period loss relief	0	0	(4,500)
	11,000	10,500	0
Less carry back loss relief	0	(10,500)	0
	11,000	0	0
Less gift aid donation	(250)	0	0
PCTCT	10,750	0	0
Unrelieved gift aid donation		250	250

Loss memorandum		£
Loss incurred in y/e 30.9.07		35,000
Less used:	y/e 30.9.07	(4,500)
	y/e 30.9.08	(10,500)
Loss available to carry forward		20,000

Any loss remaining unrelieved after any loss relief claims against total profits is carried forward to set against future profits of the same trade.

Question

Loss relief claims

Patagonia Ltd has the following results for the four accounting periods to 31 July 2007.

	Y/e	*3 months to*	*Y/e*	*Y/e*
	30.4.05	*31.7.05*	*31.7.06*	*31.7.07*
	£	£	£	£
Trading profit (loss)	20,000	15,000	(50,000)	35,000
Building society interest	1,000	400	1,800	1,000
Chargeable gains (loss)	(400)	–	1,900	2,000
Gift aid donations	600	500	–	600

Show the profits chargeable to corporation tax for all year affected. Assume loss relief is claimed against total profits where possible.

Answer

	Y/e 30.4.05	3 months to 31.7.05	Y/e 31.7.06	Y/e 31.7.07
	£	£	£	£
Trading profit	20,000	15,000	–	35,000
Less carry forward loss relief	–	–	–	(15,550)
	20,000	15,000	–	19,450
Interest income	1,000	400	1,800	1,000
Chargeable gains £(1,900 – 400)	–	–	1,500	2,000
	21,000	15,400	3,300	22,450
Less current period loss relief			(3,300)	
	21,000	15,400	–	22,450
Less carry back loss relief	(15,750)	(15,400)		
	5,250	–	–	22,450
Less gift aid donations	(600)			(600)
PCTCT	4,650	–	–	21,850
Unrelieved gift aid donations	–	500	–	–

Loss memorandum		£
Loss incurred in Y/e 31.7.06		50,000
Less used y/e 31.7.06		(3,300)
		46,700
Less used 3 months to 31.7.05	15,400	
Y/e 30.4.05		
9/12 × £21,000 (before gift aid donations)	15,750	(31,150)
		15,550
Less: Loss carried forward used y/e 31.7.07		(15,550)
C/f		Nil

Notes

1 The loss can be carried back to set against profits of the previous **12 months**. This means profits in the y/e 30.4.05 must be time apportioned by multiplying by 9/12.

2 Losses remaining after the loss relief claims against total profits are carried forward to set against **future trading profits**.

3.4 Interaction with losses brought forward

A trading loss carried back is relieved after any trading losses brought forward have been offset.

Question — Losses carried forward and back

Chile Ltd has the following results.

	Year ended 30.9.06	30.9.07	30.9.08
	£	£	£
Trading profit/(loss)	21,000	(20,000)	40,000
Bank interest	1,000	1,500	500
Chargeable gains	0	2,000	
Gift Aid donations	500	500	500

Chile Ltd had a trading loss of £16,000 carried forward at 1 October 2005.

Show the PCTCT for all the years affected assuming that loss relief against total profits is claimed.

Answer

The loss of the year to 30.9.07 is relieved against current year profits and against profits of the previous twelve months. The trading loss brought forward at 1 October 2005 is relieved in the year ended 30 September 2006 before the loss brought back.

		Year ended	
	30.9.06	*30.9.07*	*30.9.08*
	£	£	£
Trading profit	21,000	0	40,000
Less carry forward loss relief	(16,000)	0	(10,500)
	5,000	0	29,500
Investment income	1,000	1,500	500
Chargeable gains	0	2,000	0
	6,000	3,500	30,000
Less current period loss relief	0	(3,500)	0
	6,000	0	30,000
Less carry back loss relief	(6,000)	0	0
	0	0	30,000
Less gift aid donation	0	0	(500)
PCTCT	0	0	29,500
Unrelieved gift aid donations	500	500	

Loss memorandum	£
Loss brought forward at 1 October 2005	16,000
Less used y/e 30.9.06	(16,000)
	0

	£
Loss incurred in y/e 30.9.07	20,000
Less used: y/e 30.9.07	(3,500)
y/e 30.9.06	(6,000)
	10,500
Less used: y/e 30.9.08	(10,500)
C/f	Nil

3.5 Terminal trade loss relief

FAST FORWARD

Trading losses in the last 12 months of trading can be carried back and set against profits of the previous 36 months.

For trading losses incurred in the twelve months up to the cessation of trade the carry back period is extended from twelve months to three years, later years first.

Question

Terminal losses

Brazil Ltd had the following results for the accounting periods up to the cessation of trade on 30 September 2007.

	Y/e 30.9.04	*Y/e 30.9.05*	*Y/e 30.9.06*	*Y/e 30.9.07*
	£	£	£	£
Trading profits	60,000	40,000	15,000	(180,000)
Gains	–	10,000	–	6,000
Rental income	12,000	12,000	12,000	12,000

You are required to show how the losses are relieved assuming the maximum use is made of loss relief against total profits.

Answer

	Y/e 30.9.04	*Y/e 30.9.05*	*Y/e 30.9.06*	*Y/e 30.9.07*
	£	£	£	£
Trading profits	60,000	40,000	15,000	–
Rental income	12,000	12,000	12,000	12,000
Gains	–	10,000	–	6,000
	72,000	62,000	27,000	18,000
Less current period loss relief Y/e 30.9.07				(18,000)
				–
Less carry back loss relief	(72,000)	(62,000)	(27,000)	
PCTCT	–	–	–	–

Loss memorandum

	£
Loss in y/e 30.9.07	180,000
Less used Y/e 30.9.07	(18,000)
Loss of y/e 30.9.07 available for 36 months carry back	162,000
Less used Y/e 30.9.06	(27,000)
	135,000
Less used y/e 30.9.05	(62,000)
	73,000
Less used y/e 30.9.04	(72,000)
Loss remaining unrelieved	1,000

4 Choosing loss reliefs and other planning points

When selecting a loss relief, firstly consider the rate at which relief is obtained and, secondly, the timing of the relief.

4.1 Making the choice

Several alternative loss reliefs may be available. In making a choice consider:

- **The rate at which relief will be obtained:**
  - 30% at the full rate (FY 2007, FY 2006 and FY 2005)
  - 20% at the small companies' rate (FY 2007); 19% at the small companies rate (FY 2006 and FY 2005)
  - 32.5% if the small companies' marginal relief applies (FY 2007); 32.75% if the small companies' marginal rate applies (FY 2006 and FY 2005)

  We previously outlined how the 32.5% marginal rate is calculated. Remember it is just a marginal rate of tax; it is never actually used in computing a company's corporation tax.
- **How quickly relief will be obtained**: loss relief against total profits is quicker than carry forward loss relief.
- **The extent to which relief for gift aid donations might be lost.**

Exam focus point

When choosing between loss relief claims **always** consider the rate of tax 'saved' by the loss first.

If in the current period the loss 'saves' 20% tax but if carried forward saves 30% tax then a carry forward is the better choice (even though the timing of loss relief is later).

If the tax saved now is 30% and in the future is the same (30%) **then** consider timing (in this example a current claim is better timing wise).

So, first – rate of tax saved, second – timing.

Question — **The choice between loss reliefs**

M Ltd has had the following results.

	Year ended 31 March			
	2005	*2006*	*2007*	*2008*
	£	£	£	£
Trading profit/(loss)	2,000	(1,000,000)	200,000	138,000
Chargeable gains	35,000	750,000	0	0
Gift aid donations paid	30,000	20,000	20,000	20,000

Recommend appropriate loss relief claims, and compute the corporation tax for all years based on your recommendations. Assume that future years' profits will be similar to those of the year ended 31 March 2008 and the rates of corporation tax in FY 2007 apply in later years.

Answer

A loss relief against total profits claim for the year ended 31 March 2006 will save tax partly in the small companies' marginal relief band and partly at the small companies rate. It will waste the gift aid donation of £20,000.

PCTCT in the previous year is £7,000 (£35,000 + £2,000 – £30,000) and falls in the small companies' band. Carry back would waste gift aid donations of £30,000 and would use £37,000 of loss to save tax on £7,000.

If no current period loss relief claim is made, £200,000 of the loss will save tax at the small companies' rate in the year ended 31 March 2007, with £20,000 of gift aid donations being wasted. The remaining £800,000 of the loss, would be carried forward to the year ended 31 March 2008 and later years to save tax at the small companies' rate.

To conclude a loss relief claim against total income should be made for the year of the loss but not in the previous year. £20,000 of gift aid donations would be wasted in the current year, but much of the loss would save tax at the small companies' marginal corporation tax rate and relief would be obtained quickly.

The final computations are as follows.

	Year ended 31 March			
	2005	*2006*	*2007*	*2008*
	£	£	£	£
Trading income	2,000	0	200,000	138,000
Less carry forward loss relief	0	0	(200,000)	(50,000)
	2,000	0	0	88,000
Chargeable gains	35,000	750,000	0	0
	37,000	750,000	0	88,000
Less current period loss relief	0	(750,000)	0	0
	37,000	0	0	88,000
Less gift aid donations	(30,000)	0	0	(20,000)
Profits chargeable to corporation tax	7,000	0	0	68,000
CT at 19%/20%	1,330	0	0	13,600
Unrelieved gift aid donations	0	20,000	20,000	0

4.2 Other tax planning points

A company must normally claim capital allowances on its tax return. A company with losses should consider claiming less than the maximum amount of capital allowances available. This will result in a higher tax written down value to carry forward and therefore higher capital allowances in future years.

Reducing capital allowances in the current period reduces the loss available for relief against total profits. As this relief, if claimed, must be claimed for all of a loss available, a reduced capital allowance claim could be advantageous where all of a loss would be relieved at a lower tax rate in the current (or previous) period than the effective rate of relief for capital allowances will be in future periods.

5 Other losses

5.1 Capital losses

Capital losses can only be set against capital gains in the same or future accounting periods, never against income. Capital losses must be set against the first available gains and cannot be carried back.

5.2 Property business losses

Property business losses are first set off against non-property business income and gains of the company for the current period. Any excess is then:

(a) **Carried forward** against future income (of all descriptions), or
(b) Available for surrender as group relief (see later in this Text).

Chapter Roundup

- Trading losses may be relieved against current total profits, against total profits of earlier periods or against future trading income.
- Trading losses carried forward can only be set against future trading profits arising from the same trade.
- Loss relief against total profits is given before gift aid donations. Gift aid donations remain unrelieved.
- Loss relief against total profits may be given against current period profits and against profits of the previous 12 months.

  A claim for current period loss relief can be made without a claim for carryback. However, if a loss is to be carried back a claim for current period relief must have been made first.
- Trading losses in the last 12 months of trading can be carried back and set against profits of the previous 36 months.
- When selecting a loss relief, firstly consider the rate at which relief is obtained and, secondly, the timing of the relief.

Quick Quiz

1 Against what profits may trading losses carried forward be set?

2 To what extent may losses be carried back?

3 Why might a company make a reduced capital allowances claim?

Answers to Quick Quiz

1 Profits from the same trade.

2 A loss may be carried back and set against total profits (before deducting gift aid donations) of the prior 12 months. A loss arising on the final 12 months of trading can be carried back to set against profits arising in the previous 36 months. The loss carried back is the trading loss left unrelieved after a claim against total profits (before deducting gift aid donations) of the loss making AP has been made.

3 Reducing capital allowances in the current AP reduces the loss available for relief against total profits. Such a loss relief claim demands that all of the available loss is utilised. Reducing capital allowances reduces the size of the available loss.

Now try the question below from the Exam Question Bank

Number	Level	Marks	Time
Q33	Examination	15	27 mins

Groups

Topic list	Syllabus reference
1 Types of group	C4(a)
2 Group relief	C4(b), C5
3 Capital gains group	C4(c), C5

Introduction

In the previous chapters in this section we have covered corporation tax on single companies, including the reliefs for losses.

In this chapter we consider the extent to which tax law recognises group relationships between companies. Companies in a group are still separate entities with their own tax liabilities, but tax law recognises the close relationship between group companies. They can, if they meet certain conditions, share their losses and also pass assets between each other without chargeable gains.

In the next chapter we consider overseas aspects of corporation tax.

Study guide

		Intellectual level
C4	**The effect of a group corporate structure for corporation tax purposes**	
(b)	Define a 75% group, and recognise the reliefs that are available to members of such a group.	2
(c)	Define a 75% capital gains group, and recognise the reliefs that are available to members of such a group.	2
C5	**The use of exemptions and reliefs in deferring and minimising corporation tax liabilities**	

Exam guide

Groups will only feature in your examination as part of question 2, which will always be on corporation tax. Your first step in dealing with any group question must be to establish the relationship between the companies and identify what group or groups exist. You may find it helpful to draw a diagram. You must be aware that 75% groups and capital gains groups do not always coincide. The next steps will be to identify the amounts eligible for relief and to work out your strategy for maximising tax relief. Always look out for companies receiving marginal relief; they will have the highest marginal tax rate of 32.5%.

1 Types of group

A group exists for taxation purposes where one company is a subsidiary of another. The percentage shareholding involved determines the taxation consequences of the fact that there is a group.

The three examinable types of relationship for tax purposes are:

- **Associated companies** (see earlier in this text)
- **75% subsidiaries**
- **Groups for chargeable gains purposes (capital gains groups)**

2 Group relief

FAST FORWARD

> Within a 75% group, current period trading losses, excess property business losses and excess gift aid donations can be surrendered between UK companies. Profits and losses of corresponding accounting periods must be matched up. Group relief is available where the existence of a group is established through companies resident anywhere in the world.

2.1 Group relief provisions

The group relief provisions enable companies within a 75% group to transfer trading losses to other companies within the group, in order to set these against taxable profits and reduce the group's overall corporation tax liability.

2.2 Definition of a 75% group

Key term

For one company to be a **75% subsidiary** of another, the holding company must have:

- At least 75% of the ordinary share capital of the subsidiary
- A right to at least 75% of the distributable income of the subsidiary, and
- A right to at least 75% of the net assets of the subsidiary were it to be wound up.

Two companies are members of a 75% group where one is a 75% subsidiary of the other, or both are 75% subsidiaries of a third company.

Two companies are in a 75% group only if there is a 75% effective interest. Thus an 80% subsidiary (T) of an 80% subsidiary (S) is not in a 75% group with the holding company (H), because the effective interest is only 80% × 80% = 64%. However, S and T are in a 75% group and can claim group relief from each other. S *cannot* claim group relief from T and pass it on to H; it can only claim group relief for its own use.

A 75% group may include non-UK resident companies. **However, losses may generally only be surrendered between UK resident companies.**

Exam focus point

Relief for trading losses incurred by an overseas subsidiary is not examinable in your paper.

Illustration of a 75% group:

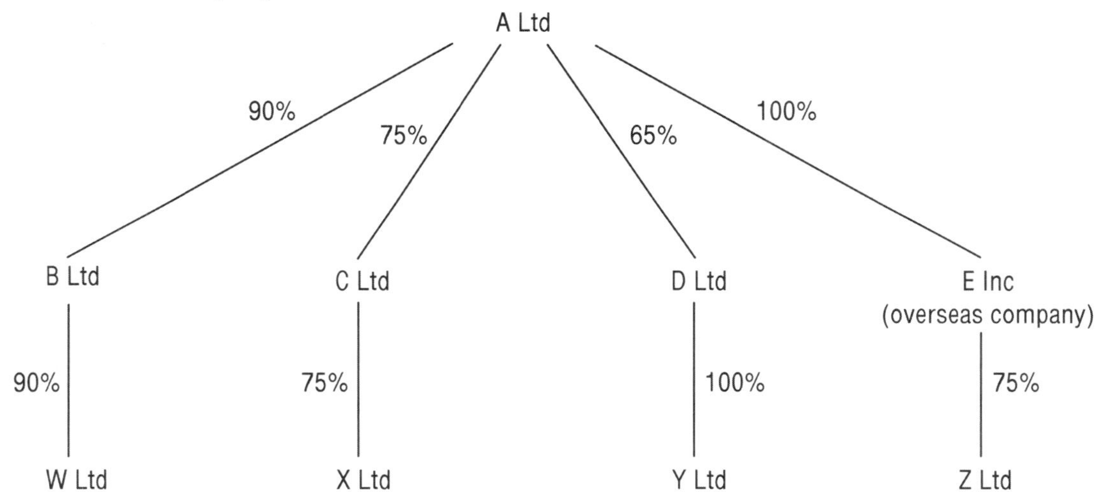

The companies in the 75% group are:

A Ltd
B Ltd
W Ltd (81% effective holding by A)
C Ltd
E Inc
Z Ltd (75% effective holding by A)

In addition C Ltd and X Ltd and also D Ltd and Y Ltd form their own separate mini-75% groups.

Note that a 75% group may also be called a 'group relief' group.

2.3 The relief

FAST FORWARD

A surrendering company can surrender any amount of its loss but a claimant company can only claim an amount up to its available profits. The best option is normally to surrender losses to set against profits of the company suffering the highest marginal rate of tax.

A company which has made a loss (the surrendering company) may transfer its loss to another member of the 75% group (the claimant company).

2.3.1 The claimant company

A **claimant company** is assumed to use its own current year losses or losses brought forward in working out the profits against which it may claim group relief, even if it does not in fact claim relief for current losses against total profits.

Furthermore, **group relief is against profits after all other reliefs for the current period or brought forward from earlier periods** including gift aid donations.

Group relief is given before relief for any amounts carried back from later periods.

2.3.2 The surrendering company

A surrendering company may group relieve a loss before setting it against its own profits for the period of the loss, and may specify any amount to be surrendered.

This is **important** for **tax planning as it enables the surrendering company to leave profits in its own computation to be charged to corporation tax at the small companies rate**, while surrendering its losses to other companies to cover profits which would otherwise fall into the marginal relief band or be taxed at the full rate. Remember that profits in the small companies' marginal relief band are taxed at the marginal rate of 32.5%.

Question — **Group relief of losses**

In a group relief group of four companies, the results for the year ended 31 March 2008 are as follows.

	Profit/(loss)
	£
A Ltd	52,000
B Ltd	212,500
C Ltd	1,000,000
D Ltd	(400,000)

How should the loss be allocated to save as much tax as possible? How much tax is saved?

Answer

The upper and lower limits for small companies' marginal relief are £1,500,000/4 = £375,000 and £300,000/4 = £75,000 respectively.

	A Ltd	*B Ltd*	*C Ltd*
	£	£	£
Profits before group relief	52,000	212,500	1,000,000
Less group relief (note)	0	(137,500)	(262,500)
PCTCT	52,000	75,000	737,500
Tax saved			
£137,500 × 32.5%		44,687	
£262,500 × 30%			78,750
Total £(44,687 + 78,750) = £123,437			

Note. We wish to save the most tax possible for the group.

Since A Ltd is in the small companies' band any loss given to it will save tax at the small companies rate of 20%.

B Ltd is in the marginal relief for small companies' rate band. Therefore, any loss given to B saves the effective marginal rate of 32.5% until the profits fall to £75,000 (the small companies' lower limit). After this only 20% is saved.

C Ltd is in the full rate band of 30% until profits fall to £375,000 (the small companies' upper limit).

So to conclude it is best to give B Ltd £137,500 of loss and save 32.5% tax on the profits in the marginal relief band. The balance of the loss is then given to C Ltd to save 30% tax.

2.4 Losses eligible for relief

A company may surrender to other group companies trading losses, excess property income losses and excess gift aid donations. Gift aid donations can only be group-relieved to the extent that they exceed profits before taking account of any losses of the current period or brought forward or back from other accounting periods. Excess gift aid donations must be surrendered before excess property income losses.

Only current period losses are available for group relief.

Capital losses cannot be group relieved. However, see later in this chapter for details of how a group may net off its gains and losses.

2.5 Corresponding accounting periods

Surrendered losses must be set against profits of a corresponding accounting period. If the accounting periods of a surrendering company and a claimant company are not the same this means that both the profits and losses must be apportioned so that only the results of the period of overlap may be set off. Apportionment is on a time basis. However, in the period when a company joins or leaves a group, an alternative method may be used if the result given by time-apportionment would be unjust or unreasonable.

Corresponding accounting periods

	£
S Ltd incurs a trading loss for the year to 30 September 2007	(150,000)
H Ltd makes taxable profits:	
for the year to 31 December 2006	200,000
for the year to 31 December 2007	100,000

What group relief can H Ltd claim from S Ltd?

Answer

H Ltd can claim group relief as follows.

	£
For the year ended 31 December 2006 profits of the corresponding accounting period (1.10.06 – 31.12.06) are £200,000 × 3/12	50,000
Losses of the corresponding accounting period are £150,000 × 3/12	37,500
A claim for £37,500 of group relief may be made against H Ltd's profits	
For the year ended 31 December 2007 profits of the corresponding accounting period (1.1.07 – 30.9.07) are £100,000 × 9/12	75,000
Losses of the corresponding accounting period are £150,000 × 9/12	112,500
A claim for £75,000 of group relief may be made against H Ltd's profits	

If a claimant company claims relief for losses surrendered by more than one company, the total relief that may be claimed for a period that overlaps is limited to the proportion of the claimant's profits attributable to that period. Similarly, if a company surrenders losses to more than one claimant, the total losses that may be surrendered in a period that overlaps is limited to the proportion of the surrendering company's losses attributable to that period.

2.6 Claims

A claim for group relief is normally made on the claimant company's tax return. It is ineffective unless a notice of consent is also given by the surrendering company.

Group wide claims/surrenders can be made as one person can act for two or more companies at once.

Any payment by the claimant company for group relief, up to the amount of the loss surrendered, is ignored for all corporation tax purposes.

2.7 Tax planning for group relief

This section outlines some tax planning points to bear in mind when dealing with a group.

Group relief should first be given in this order:

1st To companies in the small companies marginal relief band paying **32.5%** tax (FY 2007) (but only sufficient loss to bring profits down to the SCR limit)

2nd To companies paying the full rate of tax at **30%** (FY 2007)

3rd To companies paying SCR at **20%** (FY 2007)

Similarly, a company should make a claim to use a loss itself rather than surrender the loss to other group companies if the claim against its own profits would lead to a tax saving at a higher rate.

Companies with profits may benefit by reducing their claims for capital allowances in a particular year. This may leave sufficient profits to take advantage of group relief which may only be available for the current year. The amount on which writing-down allowances can be claimed in later years is increased accordingly.

3 Capital gains group

A capital gains group consists of the top company plus companies in which the top company has a 50% effective interest, provided there is a 75% holding at each level. Within a capital gains group, assets are transferred at no gain and no loss.

3.1 Definition

Companies are in a capital gains group if:

(a) At each level, there is a 75% holding, and
(b) The top company has an effective interest of over 50% in the group companies.

If A holds 75% of B, B holds 75% of C and C holds 75% of D, then A, B and C are in such a group, but D is outside the group because A's interest in D is only 75% × 75% × 75% = 42.1875%. Furthermore, D is not in a group with C, because the group must include the top company (A).

The definition of a capital gains group is wider than a that of a 75% group as only a effective 50% interest is needed compared to a 75% interest. However a company can only be in one capital gains group although it may be a member of more than one 75% group.

Illustration of a capital gains group:

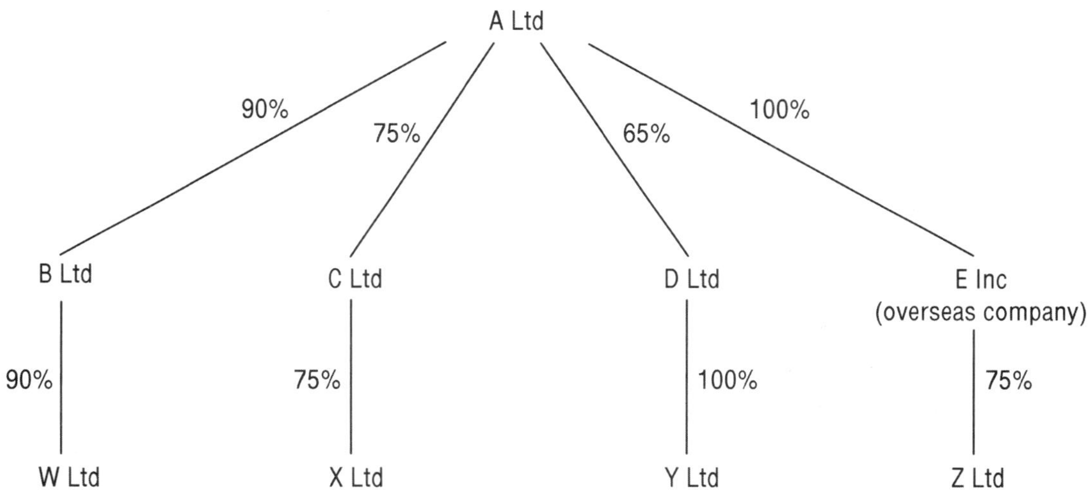

The companies in a group for capital gains purposes are:

A Ltd
B Ltd
W Ltd
C Ltd
X Ltd (75% subsidiary of 75% subsidiary, effective interest over 50%)
E Inc
Z Ltd

There is a separate capital gains group of D Ltd and Y Ltd.

3.2 Intra-group transfers

Companies in a capital gains group make intra-group transfers of chargeable assets without a chargeable gain or an allowable loss arising. No election is needed, as this relief is compulsory. The assets are deemed to be transferred at such a price as will give the transferor no gain and no loss.

3.3 Matching group gains and losses

FAST FORWARD

Gains and losses can be matched within a group. This can be done by electing that all or part of any asset disposed of outside the group is treated as transferred between group companies before disposal outside the group.

Capital losses cannot be included in a group relief claim. However, **two members of a capital gains group can elect that an asset that has been disposed of outside the group is treated as if it had been transferred between them immediately before disposal**. The deemed transferee company is then treated as having made the disposal. The election can be made for the whole or part of an asset. This election is to be made within two years of the end of the accounting period in which the disposal took place.

From a tax planning point of view, elections(s) should be made to match gains and losses and ensure that net taxable gains arise in the company subject to the lowest rate of corporation tax.

Question — Matching gains and losses

D plc group has had the following results for the year ended 30 June 2008.

	D plc	*A Ltd*	*B Ltd*	*C Ltd*
	£	£	£	£
Trading profit	400,000	46,000	20,000	220,000
Interest income	10,000	11,000	12,000	14,000
Chargeable gains/ (allowable losses)	18,000	(5,000)	6,000	(2,000)

Reliefs are always claimed as early as possible.

Required

Compute the PCTCT for all companies and show all amounts to be carried forward at 30 June 2008. Assume that the rates of corporation tax for FY 2007 also apply in FY 2008.

Answer

Year ended 30.6.08

	D plc	*A Ltd*	*B Ltd*	*C Ltd*
	£	£	£	£
Trading profit	400,000	46,000	20,000	220,000
Interest income	10,000	11,000	12,000	14,000
Income before gains	410,000	57,000	32,000	234,000

There are 4 companies in the group.

Upper limit 1,500,000/4 = £375,000
Lower limit 300,000/4 = £75,000

D plc is paying CT at 30%.

A Ltd and B Ltd are paying CT at 20%.

C Ltd is paying CT at a marginal rate of 32.5%

Since the election can be used to transfer all or part of any of the gains, the simplest way to achieve the optimum result is to identify where the resultant net gains should be taxed:

A Ltd up to the lower limit capacity = £75,000 – £57,000 = £18,000 of gains

B Ltd up to the lower limit capacity = £75,000 – £32,000 = £43,000 of gains

One way of achieving this would be to:

(a) deem D plc's gain to arise in A Ltd, offsetting A Ltd's loss, and
(b) deem C Ltd's loss to arise in B Ltd offsetting B Ltd's gain.

The PCTCT becomes:

	D plc	*A Ltd*	*B Ltd*	*C Ltd*
	£	£	£	£
Income before gains	410,000	57,000	32,000	234,000
Capital Gain				
(18,000 – 5,000)/(6,000 – 2,000)		13,000	4,000	
Income before gains	410,000	70,000	36,000	234,000

Note that there are other alternatives: all the gains and losses could have been deemed to arise in A Ltd, so that the total net gains of £17,000 resulted in A Ltd having a PCTCT of £74,000.

3.4 Rollover relief

FAST FORWARD

Rollover relief is available in a capital gains group.

If a member of a capital gains group disposes of an asset eligible for capital gains rollover relief it may treat all of the group companies as a single unit for the purpose of claiming such relief. Acquisitions by other group members within the qualifying period of one year before the disposal to three years afterwards may therefore **be matched with the disposal**. However, both the disposing company and the acquiring company must make the claim. If an asset is transferred at no gain and no loss between group members, that transfer does not count as the acquisition of an asset for rollover or holdover relief purpose.

Exam focus point

Try to remember the following summary – it will be of great help in the exam.

Parent Co **controls** over 50% of subsidiary

- associated companies for upper and lower limits

Parent Co **owns** 75% or more of subsidiary

- surrender trading losses, property business losses, excess gift aid donations to companies with some PCTCT for same time period

Parent Co **owns** 75% or more of subsidiary and subsidiary owns 75% or more of its subsidiaries

- transfer assets between companies automatically at no gain/no loss
- capital gains and losses can be matched between group member companies
- all companies treated as one for rollover relief purposes.

Chapter Roundup

- Within a 75% group, current period trading losses, excess property business losses and excess gift aid donations can be surrendered between UK companies. Profits and losses of corresponding accounting periods must be matched up. Group relief is available where the existence of a group is established through companies resident anywhere in the world.
- A surrendering company can surrender any amount of its loss but a claimant company can only claim an amount up to its available profits. The best option is normally to surrender losses to set against profits of the company suffering the highest marginal rate of tax.
- A capital gains group consists of the top company plus companies in which the top company has a 50% effective interest, provided there is a 75% holding at each level. Within a capital gains group, assets are transferred at no gain and no loss.
- Gains and losses can be matched within a group. This can be done by electing that all or part of any asset disposed of outside the group is treated as transferred between group companies before disposal outside the group.
- Rollover relief is available in a capital gains group.

Quick Quiz

1 List the types of losses which may be group relieved.

2 When may assets be transferred intra-group at no gain and no loss?

3 How can capital gains and losses within a group be matched with each other?

Answers to Quick Quiz

1 Trading losses, excess property business losses and excess gift aid donations.

2 No gain no loss asset transfers are mandatory between companies in a capital gains group.

3 Two members of a gains group can elect that all or part an asset which has been disposed of to a third party is treated as transferred between them prior to disposal. This election effectively allows the group to match its gains and losses in one company.

Now try the questions below from the Exam Question Bank

Number	Level	Marks	Time
Q34	Examination	15	27 mins
Q35	Examination	15	27 mins

Overseas matters for companies

Topic list	Syllabus reference
1 Branch or subsidiary abroad	C4
2 Double taxation relief (DTR)	C4(d)
3 Transfer pricing	C4(e)

Introduction

In the previous chapter we considered group relationships. We now turn our attention to UK companies trading abroad. We see how relief may be given for overseas taxes suffered and how the transfer pricing legislation applies.

We will conclude our corporation tax studies in the next chapter by considering the administration of corporation tax.

Study guide

		Intellectual level
C4	**The effect of a group corporate structure for corporation tax purposes**	
(d)	Calculate double taxation relief for withholding tax and underlying tax.	2
(e)	Explain the basic principles of the transfer pricing rules.	2

Exam guide

Overseas aspects of corporation tax will only be tested in question 2, ie as part of a larger question. Questions dealing with DTR need a methodical approach: first calculate the taxable foreign income and the amount of foreign tax available for relief, next compute the UK corporation tax payable, allocating it between UK income and foreign income, and finally apply DTR, which will be the lower of the foreign tax paid and the UK corporation tax payable. The transfer pricing rules are designed to stop profits being shifted abroad; the concept is straightforward – the UK profits must be increased by the shifted profits.

1 Branch or subsidiary abroad

FAST FORWARD

A UK resident company intending to do business abroad must choose between an overseas branch and an overseas subsidiary. A branch may be useful if losses are expected in the early years. If a subsidiary is chosen, the rules on trading at artificial prices must be considered.

1.1 Taxation of foreign income and gains

A UK resident company is subject to corporation tax on its worldwide profits. It is also (unlike a non-resident company) entitled to the small companies' rate of tax and to marginal relief.

If a UK resident company makes investments abroad it will be liable to corporation tax on the income made, the taxable amount being the gross amount, ie before the deduction of any foreign taxes.

In particular, a UK resident company may receive dividends from an overseas subsidiary. It may also receive interest from abroad. Overseas dividends and interest received by a company are included gross in the computation of a company's PCTCT and are taxed at normal corporation tax rates.

1.2 Taxation of foreign branches and foreign subsidiaries

An overseas branch of a UK company is effectively an extension of the UK trade, and 100% of the branch profits are assessed to UK corporation tax. Whether or not profits are remitted to the UK is irrelevant.

Question — **Overseas branch**

T Ltd is a UK company with an overseas branch. The results of T Ltd for the year ended 31 March 2008 are as follows:

	Total	*UK*	*Branch*
	£	£	£
Tax adjusted profit	1,000,000	800,000	200,000

The overseas branch is subject to tax overseas at the rate of 25%. Calculate the UK tax liability.

Answer

The corporation tax liability of T Ltd for the year ended 31 March 2008 is as follows.

	£
UK trading profit	800,000
Overseas trading profit	200,000
Trading profit/ PCTCT	1,000,000
Corporation tax at 30%	300,000
Marginal relief 1/40 (1,500,000 – 1,000,000)	(12,500)
	287,500
Double taxation relief (see below)	(50,000)
	237,500

(1) Double taxation relief is calculated as £50,000 (200,000 at 25%) being the amount of overseas tax paid.

(2) This is lower than the UK corporation tax on the branch profits of £57,500 (287,500 × 200,000/1,000,000). The UK corporation tax rate is 28.75%.

Note. Double tax relief is covered in more detail in Section 2.

It is important to appreciate the difference between operating overseas through a branch and operating overseas through a subsidiary.

(1) Relief is usually available in the UK for trading losses if incurred by an overseas branch but usually no UK relief is available for trading losses incurred by an overseas subsidiary.

(2) UK capital allowances will be available in respect of plant and machinery purchased by an overseas branch.

(3) An overseas subsidiary will be an associated company, and so the small companies lower and upper limits will be reduced. This may increase the rate of UK corporation tax.

(4) A non-UK resident subsidiary will only be assessed to UK corporation tax in respect of dividends remitted to the UK. The full profits of an overseas branch are, however, liable to corporation tax in the year that they are made, regardless of whether they are remitted to UK.

2 Double taxation relief (DTR)

A company may be subject to overseas taxes as well as to UK corporation tax on the same profits. Double taxation relief is available in respect of the foreign tax suffered.

2.1 Types of DTR

In the UK, relief for foreign tax suffered by a company is available in three ways:

(a) **Treaty relief**

Under a treaty entered into between the UK and the overseas country, a treaty may exempt certain profits from taxation in one of the countries involved, thus completely avoiding double taxation. More usually treaties provide for credit to be given for tax suffered in one of the countries against the tax liability in the other.

(b) **Unilateral credit relief**

Where no treaty relief is available, unilateral relief may be available in the UK giving credit for the foreign tax against the UK tax.

(c) **Unilateral expense relief**

Not examined in your syllabus.

2.2 Credit relief

FAST FORWARD

Double tax relief (DTR) is the lower of:

- the UK tax on a source of income
- the overseas tax on that income source (withholding and possibly underlying tax).

Relief is available for overseas tax suffered on branch profits, dividends and interest, up to the amount of the UK corporation tax (at the company's average rate) attributable to that income. The gross income including the overseas tax is included within the UK profits chargeable to corporation tax.

2.3 Withholding tax

Overseas tax may be deducted from foreign income arising to the UK company. This includes:

(a) Overseas tax paid on the profits of a foreign branch, and
(b) Overseas tax deducted from dividends paid by a foreign company.

This tax is called withholding tax.

Question

Unilateral credit relief

On 1 May 2007, AS plc receives a dividend from Bola Inc, an overseas company, of £80,000. This has been paid subject to 20% withholding tax. AS plc has UK trading income of £2,000,000 for the year to 31.3.08. Show that the foreign income is £100,000 and compute the corporation tax payable.

Answer

	Total	*UK*	*Overseas*
	£	£	£
Trading income	2,000,000	2,000,000	
Foreign income (W)	100,000		100,000
PCTCT	2,100,000	2,000,000	100,000
Corporation tax at 30%	630,000	600,000	30,000
Less DTR: lower of:			
(a) overseas tax: £20,000; or			
(b) UK tax on overseas income: £30,000	(20,000)		(20,000)
	610,000	600,000	10,000

Working: Foreign income

£80,000 × 100/(100 – 20) = £100,000.

2.4 Underlying tax relief

FAST FORWARD

A company may obtain double taxation relief for overseas withholding tax, and also (if it owns at least 10% of the voting power) for underlying tax.

In addition to the relief available for withholding tax shown above, relief is available for underlying tax relating to a dividend received from a foreign company in which the UK company owns at least 10% of the voting power, either directly or indirectly.

The underlying tax is the tax attributable to the relevant profits out of which the dividend was paid.

Exam formula

Underlying tax is calculated as:

$$\text{Gross dividend income} \times \frac{\text{Foreign tax paid}}{\text{after-tax accounting profits}}$$

FAST FORWARD

To calculate taxable foreign income gross up for withholding tax, and then, if appropriate, for underlying tax.

Question

Underlying tax relief

A Ltd, a UK company with no associated companies, holds 30,000 out of 90,000 voting ordinary shares in B Inc (resident in Lintonia).

The profit and loss account of B Inc for the year to 31 March 2008 is as follows (converted into sterling).

		£	£
Trading profit			1,000,000
Less taxation:	provided on profits	300,000	
	transfer to deferred tax account	100,000	
			(400,000)
Profits after tax			600,000
Less dividends:	Net	240,000	
	withholding tax (20%)	60,000	
			(300,000)
Retained profits			300,000

The actual tax paid on the profits for the year to 31 March 2008 was £270,000.

Apart from the net dividend of £80,000 received out of the above profits from B Inc on 31 May 2007 the only other taxable profit of A Ltd for its year to 31 March 2008 was £610,000 UK trading profit. A Ltd received no UK dividends during the year.

Calculate A Ltd's UK corporation tax liability after double taxation relief.

Answer

A LTD: UK CORPORATION TAX LIABILITY

	£	£
Trading income		610,000
Foreign income		
Net dividend	80,000	
Withholding tax at 20%		
£80,000 × 20/80	20,000	
Gross dividend	100,000	
Underlying tax		
$£100,000 \times \frac{270,000}{600,000}$	45,000	
Gross income		145,000
PCTCT		755,000

	Total	*UK*	*Overseas*
	£	£	£
Trading income	610,000	610,000	
Foreign income	145,000		145,000
PCTCT	755,000	610,000	145,000
Corporation tax £755,000 × 30%			226,500
Less small companies' marginal relief £(1,500,000 – 755,000) × 1/40			(18,625)
			207,875
The average rate of corporation tax is £207,875/£755,000 = 27.533%.			
Corporation tax at the average rate	207,875	167,952	39,923
Less DTR: lower of:			
(a) overseas tax £(20,000 + 45,000) = £65,000;			
(b) UK tax on overseas income £39,923	(39,923)		(39,923)
	167,952	167,952	0

Corporation tax of £167,952 is payable. £(65,000 – 39,923) = £25,077 of overseas tax is unrelieved (ie excess). It is possible to carry the unrelieved tax back or forward. The carry back or forward of unrelieved overseas tax is not examinable.

2.5 Allocation of losses and gift aid donations

FAST FORWARD

Gift aid donations and losses should initially be set against UK income. They should subsequently be set against the overseas income source that suffers the lowest rate of overseas tax.

One further factor affects the computation of UK tax on overseas income against which credit for overseas tax may be claimed. This is the allocation of Gift aid donations and losses relieved against total profits.

A company may allocate its gift aid donations and losses relieved against total profits in whatever manner it likes for the purpose of computing double taxation relief. It should set the maximum amount against any UK profits, thereby maximising the corporation tax attributable to the foreign profits and hence maximising the double taxation relief available.

If a company has several sources of overseas profits, then gift aid donations and losses should be allocated first to UK profits, and then to overseas sources which have suffered the **lowest** rates of overseas taxation.

Losses relieved by carry forward must in any case be set against the first available profits of the trade which gave rise to the loss.

A company with a choice of loss reliefs should consider the effect of its choice on double taxation relief. For example, a claim against total profits might lead to there being no UK tax liability, or a very small liability, so that foreign tax would go unrelieved. Carry forward loss relief might avoid this problem and still leave very little UK tax to pay for the period of the loss.

Question

Allocation of charges

Kairo plc is a UK resident company with four UK resident subsidiaries and a 100% subsidiary resident in Utopia. The company produced the following results for the year to 31 March 2008.

	£
UK trading profits	10,000
Profits from overseas branch (before overseas tax)	40,000
Dividend received from Utopian subsidiary	140,000
Gift aid donations	(15,000)

The dividend from the Utopian subsidiary, shown above, is the amount received. In addition, foreign taxes amounted to:

	£
Withholding tax	40,000
Underlying tax	70,000
	110,000

Overseas tax on the overseas branch profits amounted to £10,000.

Compute the UK corporation tax liability.

Answer

KAIRO PLC – CORPORATION TAX – YEAR TO 31 MARCH 2008

	Total	*UK*	*Branch*	*Utopia*
	£	£	£	£
Income	300,000	10,000	40,000	250,000
Less Gift aid donations (note)	(15,000)	(10,000)	(5,000)	
Taxable profits	285,000	Nil	35,000	250,000
Corporation tax @ 30%*	85,500	–	10,500	75,000
Less DTR (W)	(85,500)	–	(10,000)	(75,000)
MCT	500	–	500	–

* The full rate of corporation tax applies, since the upper limit for profits (£1,500,000 ÷ 6 = £250,000) is exceeded.

Working

The DTR is the lower of:

Branch: UK tax £10,500;
Overseas tax £10,000, ie £10,000
Rate of overseas tax = 25%

Utopia: UK tax £75,000;
Overseas tax £110,000, ie £75,000
Rate of overseas tax = 44%

Note. The branch profits suffer the lowest rate of overseas tax so the gift aid donations remaining after offset against the UK income are allocated against the branch income in preference to the Utopia income.

3 Transfer pricing

FAST FORWARD

> The transfer pricing legislation restricts the freedom of a company to buy and sell goods at whatever price it wishes between associated persons. A profit on such a transfer must be computed as though the transfer had been made at an arm's length price. The transfer pricing legislation does not apply to transactions between two UK resident persons unless they are large enterprises.

Companies under common control could structure their transactions in such a way that they can shift profit (or losses) from one company to another.

For example consider a company which wishes to sell goods valued at £20,000 to an independent third party.

Selling company —— Goods invoice value: £20,000 ——→ Buying company

In this case all the profit on the sale arises to the selling company. Alternatively the sale could be rearranged:

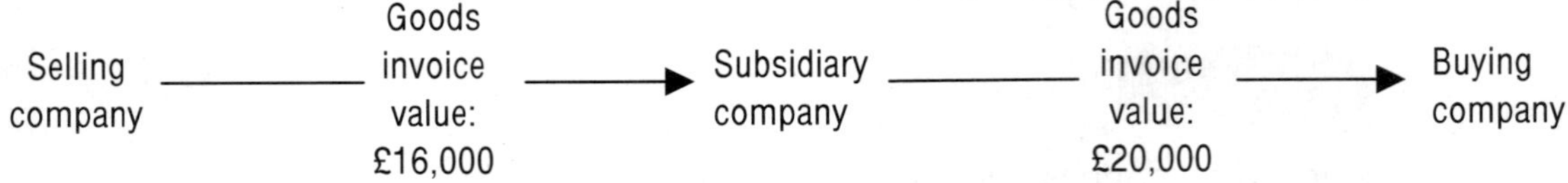

In this case £4,000 of the profit has been diverted to the subsidiary.

This technique could be used to direct profits to a company which will pay less tax on those profits.

This is a 'tax advantage' and there is **anti avoidance legislation** which **requires the profit to be computed as if the transactions had been carried out at arm's length and not at the prices actually used.**

The transfer pricing rules apply to transactions between two persons if either:

(a) one person directly or indirectly participates in the management, control or capital of the other; or

(b) a third party directly or indirectly participates in the management, control or capital of both.

Exam focus point

> You will only be expected to deal with situations where profits are being shifted to an overseas company in your exam.

Companies must self-assess their liability to tax under the transfer pricing rules and pay any corporation tax due. A statutory procedure exists for advance pricing arrangements (APAs) whereby a company can agree in advance that its transfer pricing policy is acceptable to HMRC – ie not requiring a self-assessment adjustment. The APA facility is voluntary but companies may feel the need to use the facility as it provides necessary advance confirmation that their approach to transfer pricing in their self-assessment is acceptable.

Chapter Roundup

- A UK resident company intending to do business abroad must choose between an overseas branch and an overseas subsidiary. A branch may be useful if losses are expected in the early years. If a subsidiary is chosen, the rules on trading at artificial prices must be considered.
- Double tax relief is the lower of:
  - the UK tax on a source of income
  - the overseas tax on that income source (withholding and possibly underlying tax).
- A company may obtain double taxation relief for overseas withholding tax, and also (if it owns at least 10% of the voting power) for underlying tax.
- To calculate taxable foreign income gross up for withholding tax and then, if appropriate, for underlying tax.
- Gift aid donations and losses should initially be set against UK income. They should subsequently be set against the overseas income source that suffers the lowest rate of overseas tax.
- The transfer pricing legislation restricts the freedom of a company to buy and sell goods at whatever price it wishes between associated persons. A profit on such a transfer must be computed as though the transfer had been made at an arms length price. The transfer pricing legislation does not apply to transactions between UK resident persons unless they are large enterprises.

Quick Quiz

1. A UK company is planning to set up a new operation in Australia that will initially be loss making. Should it set up as a branch or a subsidiary of the UK company?
2. How is underlying tax calculated?
3. How best should gift aid donations be allocated in computing credit relief for foreign tax?
4. What steps can be taken against the use of artificial transfer prices?

Answers to Quick Quiz

1 If losses are expected to arise then a branch operation is best since relief is usually available for losses of a foreign branch.

2 Underlying tax is calculated as

$$\text{Dividend plus withholding tax (ie gross dividend)} \times \frac{\text{foreign tax paid}}{\text{after} - \text{tax accounting profits}}$$

3 Gift aid donations should be set firstly against any UK profits, then against overseas income sources suffering the lowest rates of overseas taxation before those suffering at the higher rates.

4 Although a company may buy and sell goods at any price it wishes, the transfer pricing anti-avoidance legislation requires profit to be computed as if the transactions had been carried out at arm's length, in certain circumstances.

Now try the question below from the Exam Question Bank

Number	Level	Marks	Time
Q36	Examination	15	27 mins

Self assessment and payment of tax by companies

Topic list	Syllabus reference
1 Corporation tax self assessment	G1(b)
2 Returns, records and claims	G2(a), (e)
3 Enquiries and assessments	G3(a), (b)
4 Payment of corporation tax and interest	G2(b), (d), G4(a)
5 Penalties	G4(b)

Introduction

We now complete our corporation tax studies by looking at the self assessment system for corporation tax, under which companies must file returns and pay the tax due.

In the following chapters we will turn our attention to VAT, which applies to both incorporated and unincorporated businesses.

Study guide

		Intellectual level
G1	**The systems for self-assessment and the making of returns**	
(b)	Explain and apply the features of the self assessment system as it applies to companies.	2
G2	**The time limits for the submission of information, claims and payment of tax, including payments on account**	
(a)	Recognise the time limits that apply to the filing of returns and the making of claims.	2
(b)	Recognise the due dates for the payment of tax under the self-assessment system.	2
(d)	Explain how large companies are required to account for corporation tax on a quarterly basis.	2
(e)	List the information and records that taxpayers need to retain for tax purposes.	1
G3	**The procedures relating to enquiries, appeals and disputes**	
(a)	Explain the circumstances in which HM Revenue & Customs can enquire into a self assessment tax return.	2
(b)	Explain the procedures for dealing with appeals and disputes.	1
G4	**Penalties for non-compliance**	
(a)	Calculate interest on overdue tax.	2
(b)	State the penalties that can be charged.	2

Exam guide

Although question 2 of the exam will always be on corporation tax it will not necessarily include any of the administrative procedures of the self assessment system. They could, however, feature in either question 4 or 5. It is unlikely, but not impossible, that you will be tested on the administrative rules for companies and individuals in the same paper.

1 Corporation tax self assessment

FAST FORWARD

A company that does not receive a notice requiring a return to be filed must, if it is chargeable to tax, **notify HMRC within twelve months of the end of the accounting period**.

1.1 Introduction

The self assessment system relies upon the company completing and filing a tax return and paying the tax due. The system is enforced by a system of penalties for failure to comply within the set time limits, and by interest for late payment of tax.

Dormant companies and companies which have not yet started to trade may not be required to complete tax returns. Such companies have a duty to notify HMRC when they should be brought within the self assessment system.

1.2 Notification of first accounting period

A company must notify HMRC of the beginning of its first accounting period (ie usually when it starts to trade) and the beginning of any subsequent period that does not immediately follow the end of a previous accounting period. The notice must be in the prescribed form and submitted within three months of the relevant date.

1.3 Notification of chargeability

A company that does not receive a notice requiring a return to be filed must, if it is chargeable to tax, **notify HMRC within twelve months of the end of the accounting period**.

2 Returns, records and claims

A company must, in general, file a CT 600 tax return within twelve months of the end of an accounting period.

2.1 Returns

A company's tax return (CT 600 version 2) must include a self assessment of any tax payable.

An obligation to file a return arises only when the company receives a notice requiring a return. A return is required for each accounting period ending during or at the end of the period specified in the notice requiring a return. A company also has to file a return for certain other periods which are not accounting periods (eg for a period when the company is dormant).

A notice to file a return may also require other information, accounts and reports. For a UK resident company the requirement to deliver accounts normally extends only to the accounts required under the Companies Act.

A return is due on or before the filing date. This is normally the later of:

(a) **12 months after the end of the period to which the return relates**;
(b) **three months from the date on which the notice requiring the return was made**.

The relevant period of account is that in which the accounting period to which the return relates ends.

2.2 Amending a return

A company may amend a return within twelve months of the filing date.

HMRC may amend a return to correct obvious errors within nine months of the day the return was filed, or if the correction is to an amended return, within nine months of the filing of an amendment. The company may amend its return so as to reject the correction. If the time limit for amendments has expired, the company may reject the correction by giving notice within three months.

2.3 Records

Companies must keep records until the latest of:

(a) **six years from the end of the accounting period**;
(b) the date any enquiries are completed;
(c) the date after which enquiries may not be commenced.

All business records and accounts, including contracts and receipts, must be kept.

If a return is demanded more than six years after the end of the accounting period, any records which the company still has must be kept until the later of the end of any enquiry and the expiry of the right to start an enquiry.

2.4 Claims

Wherever possible claims must be made on a tax return or on an amendment to it and must be quantified at the time the return is made.

If a company believes that it has paid excessive tax because of an error in a return, an error or mistake claim may be made within six years from the end of the accounting period. An appeal against a decision on such a claim must be made within 30 days. An error or mistake claim may not be made if the return was made in accordance with a generally accepted practice which prevailed at the time.

Other claims must be made by six years after the end of the accounting period, unless a different time limit is specified. If an error or mistake is made in a claim, a supplementary claim may be made within the time limit for the original claim.

If HMRC amend a self assessment or issue a discovery assessment then the company has a further period to make, vary or withdraw a claim (unless the claim is irrevocable) even if this is outside the normal time limit. The period is one year from the end of the accounting period in which the amendment or assessment was made, or one year from the end of the accounting period in which the enquiry was closed if the amendment is the result of an enquiry. The relief is limited where there has been fraudulent or negligent conduct by the company or its agent.

3 Enquiries and assessments

FAST FORWARD

HMRC can enquire into returns.

3.1 Enquiries

3.1.1 Opening an enquiry

A return or an amendment need not be accepted at face value by HMRC. **They may enquire into it, provided that they first give written notice that they are going to enquire.** The notice must be given by a year after the later of:

(a) The filing date;

(b) The 31 January, 30 April, 31 July or 31 October next following the actual date of delivery of the return or amendment.

Only one enquiry may be made in respect of any one return or amendment.

3.1.2 During an enquiry

If a notice of an enquiry has been given, HMRC may demand that the company **produce documents** for inspection and copying. However, documents relating to an appeal need not be produced and the company may appeal against a notice requiring documents to be produced.

HMRC may amend a self assessment at any time during an enquiry if they believe there might otherwise be a loss of tax. The company may appeal against such an amendment within 30 days. The company may itself make amendments during an enquiry under the normal rules for amendments. No effect will be given to such amendments during the enquiry but they may be taken into account in the enquiry.

3.1.3 Closing an enquiry

An enquiry ends when HMRC give notice that it has been completed and notify what they believe to be the correct amount of tax payable. Before that time, the company may ask the Commissioners to order HMRC to notify the completion of its enquiry by a specified date. Such a direction will be given unless HMRC can demonstrate that they have reasonable grounds for continuing the enquiry.

The company has 30 days from the end of an enquiry to amend its self assessment in accordance with HMRC's conclusions. If HMRC are not satisfied with the company's amendments, they have a further 30 days to amend the self assessment. The company then has another 30 days in which it may appeal against HMRC's amendments.

3.2 Determinations

If a return is not delivered by the filing date, HMRC may issue a determination of the tax payable within the five years from the filing date. This is treated as a self assessment and there is no appeal against it. However, it is automatically replaced by any self assessment made by the company by the later of five years from the filing date and 12 months from the determination.

3.3 Discovery assessments

If HMRC believe that not enough tax has been assessed for an accounting period they can make a discovery assessment to collect the extra tax. However, when a tax return has been delivered this power is limited as outlined below.

No discovery assessment can be made on account of an error or mistake as to the basis on which the tax liability ought to be computed, if the basis generally prevailing at the time when the return was made was applied.

A discovery assessment can only be made if either:

(a) the loss of tax is due to **fraudulent or negligent conduct** by the company or by someone acting on its behalf; or

(b) **HMRC could not reasonably be expected to have been aware of the loss of tax, given the information so far supplied to them,** when their right to start an enquiry expired or when they notified the company that an enquiry had finished. The information supplied must be sufficiently detailed to draw HMRC's attention to contentious matters such as the use of a valuation or estimate.

The time limit for raising a discovery assessment is six years from the end of the accounting period but this is extended to 21 years if there has been fraudulent or negligent conduct. The company may appeal against a discovery assessment within 30 days of issue.

4 Payment of corporation tax and interest

In general, corporation tax is due nine months after the end of an accounting period but large companies must pay their corporation tax in four quarterly instalments.

4.1 Payment dates – small and medium companies

Corporation tax is due for payment by small and medium sized companies **nine months after the end of the accounting period**.

4.2 Payment dates – large companies

Large companies must pay their corporation tax in instalments. **Broadly, a large company is any company that pays corporation tax at the full rate**.

Instalments are due on the 14th day of the month, starting in the seventh month. Provided that the accounting period is twelve months long subsequent instalments are due in the tenth month during the accounting period and in the first and fourth months after the end of the accounting period.

Exam focus point

> In the exam you will only ever be expected to calculate tax due in instalments for 12 month accounting periods.

4.3 Example: quarterly instalments

X Ltd is a large company with a 31 December accounting year end. Instalments of corporation tax will be due to be paid by X Ltd on:

- 14 July and 14 October in the accounting period;
- 14 January and 14 April after the accounting period ends

Thus for the year ended 31 December 2007 instalment payments are due on 14 July 2007, 14 October 2007, 14 January 2008 and 14 April 2008.

4.4 Calculating the instalments

The amount of each instalment is 25% of the estimated amount due.

Instalments are based on the estimated corporation tax liability for the **current** period (not the previous period). A company is required to estimate its corporation tax liability before the end of the accounting period, and must revise its estimate each quarter. It is extremely important for companies to forecast their tax liabilities accurately. Large companies whose directors are poor at estimating may find their companies incurring significant interest charges.

Companies can have instalments repaid if they later conclude they ought not to have been paid.

4.5 Exceptions

A company is not required to pay instalments in the first year that it is 'large', unless its profits exceed £10 million. The £10 million limit is reduced proportionately if there are associated companies. For this purpose only, a company will be regarded as an associated company where it was an associated company at the **start** of an accounting period. (This differs from the normal approach in CT where being an associated company for any part of the AP affects the thresholds of both companies for the whole of the AP).

Any company whose liability does not exceed £10,000 need not pay by instalments.

4.6 Interest on late or overpaid tax

Interest runs from the due date on over/underpaid instalments. The position is looked at cumulatively after the due date for each instalment. HMRC calculate the interest position after the company submits its corporation tax return.

Small and medium companies are charged interest if they pay their corporation tax after the due date, and will receive interest if they overpay their tax or pay it early.

Interest paid/received on late payments or over payments of corporation tax is dealt with as investment income as interest paid/received on a non-trading loan relationship.

5 Penalties

Penalties may be levied for failure to notify the first accounting period, failure to notify chargeability, the late filing of returns, failure to keep records and failure to produce documents during an enquiry.

5.1 Notification of first accounting period

Failure to notify the first accounting period will mean a **maximum penalty of £3,000.**

5.2 Notification of chargeability

Failure to notify chargeability results in a **maximum penalty equal to the tax unpaid twelve months after the end of the accounting period**.

5.3 Late filing penalties

There is a £100 penalty for a failure to submit a return on time, rising to £200 if the delay exceeds three months. These penalties become £500 and £1,000 respectively when a return was late (or never submitted) for each of the preceding two accounting periods.

An additional tax geared penalty is applied if a return is more than six months late. The penalty is 10% of the tax unpaid six months after the return was due if the total delay is up to 12 months, and 20% of that tax if the return is over 12 months late.

There is a tax geared penalty for a fraudulent or negligent return and for failing to correct an innocent error without unreasonable delay. The maximum penalty is equal to the tax that would have been lost had the return been accepted as correct. HMRC can mitigate this penalty. If a company is liable to more than one tax geared penalty, the total penalty is limited to the maximum single penalty that could be charged.

5.4 Failure to keep records

Failure to keep records can lead to a **penalty of up to £3,000** for each accounting period affected. However, this penalty does not apply when the only records which have not been kept are ones which could only have been needed for the purposes of claims, elections or notices not included in the return.

5.5 Failure to produce documents during an enquiry

If HMRC demand documents, but the company does not produce them, there is a **penalty of £50**. There is also a **daily penalty**, which applies for each day from the day after the imposition of the £50 penalty until the documents are produced. The daily penalty may be imposed by HMRC, in which case it is £30. If, however, HMRC ask the Commissioners to impose the penalty, it is £150.

Chapter Roundup

- A company that does not receive a notice requiring a return to be filed must, if it is chargeable to tax, notify HMRC within twelve months of the end of the accounting period.
- A company must, in general, file a CT 600 tax return within twelve months of the end of an accounting period.
- HMRC can enquire into returns.
- In general, corporation tax is due nine months after the end of an accounting period but large companies must pay their corporation tax in four quarterly instalments.
- Penalties may be levied for failure to notify the first accountancy period, failure to notify chargeability, the late filing of returns, failure to keep records and failure to produce documents during an enquiry.

Quick Quiz

1. What are the fixed penalties for failure to deliver a corporation tax return on time?
2. When must HMRC give notice that it is going to start an enquiry if a return was filed on time?
3. Which companies must pay quarterly instalments of their corporation tax liability?
4. State the due dates for the payment of quarterly instalments of corporation tax for a 12 month accounting period.
5. What is the penalty if a company fails to keep records?

Answers to Quick Quiz

1. There is a £100 penalty for failure to submit a return on time rising to £200 if the delay exceeds three months. These penalties increase to £500 and £1,000 respectively when a return was late for each of the preceding two accounting periods.
2. Notice must be given by one year after the filing date.
3. 'Large' companies ie companies that pay corporation tax at the full rate.
4. 14th day of:

   (a) 7th month in AP
   (b) 10th month in AP
   (c) 1st month after AP ends
   (d) 4th month after AP ends

5. £3,000 for each accounting period affected.

Now try the questions below from the Exam Question Bank

Number	Level	Marks	Time
Q37	Introductory	5	9 mins
Q41	Examination	30	54 mins

Q41 has been analysed to give you guidance on how to answer exam questions.

Part D
Value added tax

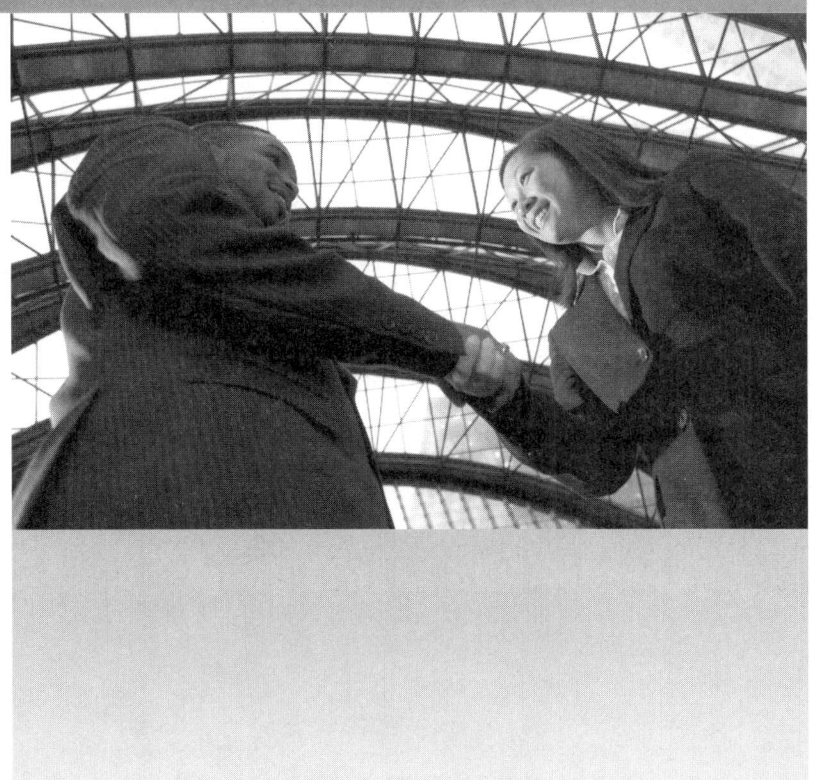

25

An introduction to VAT

Topic list	Syllabus reference
1 The scope of VAT	F1(a)
2 Zero-rated and exempt supplies	F1(b)
3 Registration	F2(a), (b)
4 Deregistration	F2(d)
5 Pre-registration input tax	F2(c)
6 Accounting for and administering VAT	F3(a)
7 The tax point	F3(b)
8 The valuation of supplies	F3(d)
9 The deduction of input tax	F3(e)
10 Relief for impairment losses (bad debts)	F3(f)

Introduction

The final topic in our studies is value added tax (VAT). We cover VAT in this and the next chapter.

VAT is a tax on turnover rather than on profits. As the name suggests, it is charged (usually at 17.5%) on the value added. The VAT is collected bit by bit along the chain of manufacturer, wholesaler, retailer, until it finally hits the consumer who does not add value, but uses up the goods.

In this chapter we look at the scope of VAT and then consider when a business must, or may, be registered for VAT. We also look at administration and accounting. VAT is a tax with simple computations but many detailed rules to ensure its enforcement. You may find it easier to absorb the detail if you ask yourself, in relation to each rule, exactly how it helps to enforce the tax.

Next we look at the rules regarding the deduction of input tax.

In the following chapter we will conclude our study of VAT and the F6 syllabus.

Study guide

		Intellectual level
F1	**The scope of value added tax (VAT)**	
(a)	Describe the scope of VAT.	2
(b)	List the principal zero-rated and exempt supplies.	1
F2	**The VAT registration requirements**	
(a)	Recognise the circumstances in which a person must register for VAT.	2
(b)	Explain the advantages of voluntary VAT registration.	2
(c)	Explain the circumstances in which preregistration input VAT can be recovered.	2
(d)	Explain how and when a person can deregister for VAT.	1
F3	**The computation of VAT liabilities**	
(a)	Explain how VAT is accounted for and administered.	2
(b)	Recognise the tax point when goods or services are supplied.	2
(d)	Explain and apply the principles regarding the valuation of supplies.	2
(e)	Recognise the circumstances in which input VAT is non-deductible.	2
(f)	Compute the relief that is available for impairment losses on trade debts.	2

Exam guide

There will always be at least 10% of the marks in the exam on VAT. Although this will usually be in question 1 or 2 there may be a separate question on VAT. The registration requirements are often examined; make sure that you know the difference between the historical test and the future test, and the dates by which HMRC must be notified and registration takes effect. Do not overlook pre-registration input VAT. You may be required to calculate the VAT due for a return period; watch out for non deductible input tax and check the dates if there are impairment losses.

1 The scope of VAT

FAST FORWARD

VAT is charged on turnover at each stage in a production process, but in such a way that the burden is borne by the final consumer.

1.1 The nature of VAT

VAT is a tax on turnover, not on profits. The basic principle is that the VAT should be borne by the final consumer. Registered traders may deduct the tax which they suffer on supplies to them (input tax) from the tax which they charge to their customers (output tax) at the time this is paid to HMRC. Thus, at each stage of the manufacturing or service process, the net VAT paid is on the value added at that stage.

1.2 Example: the VAT charge

A forester sells wood to a furniture maker for £100 plus VAT. The furniture maker uses this wood to make a table and sells the table to a shop for £150 plus VAT. The shop then sells the table to the final consumer for £300 plus VAT. VAT will be accounted for to HMRC as follows.

	Cost	Input tax 17.5%	Net sale price	Output tax 17.5%	Payable to HMRC
	£	£	£	£	£
Forester	0	0	100	17.50	17.50
Furniture maker	100	17.50	150	26.25	8.75
Shop	150	26.25	300	52.50	26.25
					52.50

Because the traders involved account to HMRC for VAT charged less VAT suffered, their profits for income tax or corporation tax purposes are based on sales and purchases net of VAT.

1.3 Taxable supplies

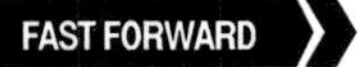

VAT is chargeable on taxable supplies made by a taxable person in the course or furtherance of any business carried on by him. Supplies may be of goods or services.

Key term

A **taxable supply** is a supply of goods or services made in the UK, other than an exempt supply.

A taxable supply is either standard-rated or zero-rated. The standard rate is 17.5% (although on certain supplies, for example the supply of domestic fuel, a lower rate is charged of 5%).

Zero-rated supplies are taxable at 0%. A taxable supplier whose outputs are zero-rated but whose inputs are standard-rated will obtain repayments of the VAT paid on purchases.

An exempt supply is not chargeable to VAT. A person making exempt supplies is unable to recover VAT on inputs.

The exempt supplier thus has to shoulder the burden of VAT. Of course, he may increase his prices to pass on the charge, but he cannot issue a VAT invoice which would enable a taxable customer to obtain a credit for VAT, since no VAT is chargeable on his supplies.

1.4 Example: standard-rated, zero-rated and exempt supplies

Here are figures for three traders, the first with standard-rated outputs, the second with zero-rated outputs and the third with exempt outputs. All their inputs are standard-rated.

	Standard-rated	Zero-rated	Exempt
	£	£	£
Inputs	20,000	20,000	20,000
VAT	3,500	3,500	3,500
	23,500	23,500	23,500
Outputs	30,000	30,000	30,000
VAT	5,250	0	0
	35,250	30,000	30,000
Pay/(reclaim)	1,750	(3,500)	0
Net profit	10,000	10,000	6,500

VAT legislation lists zero-rated, lower rate and exempt supplies. There is no list of standard-rated supplies.

We look at the main categories of zero-rated and exempt supplies later in this chapter.

1.5 Supplies of goods

Goods are supplied if exclusive ownership of the goods passes to another person.

The following are treated as supplies of goods.

- The supply of any form of power, heat, refrigeration or ventilation, or of water
- The grant, assignment or surrender of a major interest (the freehold or a lease for over 21 years) in land
- Taking goods permanently out of the business for the non-business use of a taxable person or for other private purposes including the supply of goods by an employer to an employee for his private use
- Transfers under an agreement contemplating a transfer of ownership, such as a hire purchase agreement

Gifts of goods are normally treated as sales at cost (so VAT is due). **However, business gifts are not supplies of goods if**:

(a) **The total cost of gifts made to the same person does not exceed £50 in any 12 month period**. If the £50 limit is exceeded, output tax will be due in full on the total of gifts made. Once the limit has been exceeded a new £50 limit and new 12 month period begins.

(b) **The gift is a sample**. However, if two or more identical samples are given to the same person, all but one of them are treated as supplies.

1.6 Supplies of services

Apart from a few specific exceptions, **any supply which is not a supply of goods and which is done for a consideration is a supply of services**. A consideration is any form of payment in money or in kind, including anything which is itself a supply.

A supply of services also takes place if:

- Goods are lent to someone for use outside the business
- Goods are hired to someone
- Services bought for business purposes are used for private purposes

The European Court of Justice has ruled that restaurants supply services rather than goods.

1.7 Taxable persons

The term 'person' includes individuals, partnerships (which are treated as single entities, ignoring the individual partners) and **companies. If a person is in business making taxable supplies, then the value of these supplies is called the taxable turnover. If a person's taxable turnover exceeds certain limits then he is a taxable person and should be registered for VAT** (see later in this Text).

2 Zero-rated and exempt supplies

FAST FORWARD

Some supplies are taxable (either standard-rated, reduced-rated or zero-rated). Others are exempt.

2.1 Types of supply

We have seen that a trader may make standard rated, reduced rated, zero rated or exempt supplies.

If a trader makes a supply we need to categorise that supply for VAT as follows:

Step 1 Consider the zero-rated list to see if it is zero-rated. If not:

Step 2 Consider the exempt list to see if it is exempt. If not:

Step 3 Consider the lower rate list to see if the reduced rate of VAT applies. If not:

Step 4 The supply is standard rated.

Exam focus point

In the exam students will not be expected to categorise all the zero-rated and exempt supplies. The main supplies in each group are highlighted below.

2.2 Zero-rated supplies

The following are items on the **zero-rated list**.

(a) Human and animal food

(b) Sewerage services and water

(c) Printed matter used for reading (eg books, newspapers)

(d) Construction work on new homes or the sale of the freehold of new homes by builders

(e) Transport of goods and passengers

(f) Drugs and medicines on prescription or provided in private hospitals

(g) Clothing and footwear for young children and certain protective clothing eg motor cyclists' crash helmets

2.3 Exempt supplies

The following are items on the **exempt** list.

(a) Financial services

(b) Insurance

(c) Postal services provided by the Post Office

(d) Betting and gaming

(e) Certain education and vocational training

(f) Health services

(g) Burial and cremation services

(h) Sale of freeholds of buildings (other than commercial buildings less than 3 years old) and leaseholds of land and buildings.

2.4 Exceptions to the general rule

The zero-rated, exempt and lower rate lists outline general categories of goods or services which are either zero-rated or exempt or charged at a lower rate of 5%. However, the VAT legislation then goes into great detail to outline exceptions to the general rule.

For example the zero-rated list states human food is zero-rated. However, the legislation then states that food supplied in the course of catering (eg restaurant meals, hot takeaways) is not zero-rated. Luxury items of food (eg crisps, peanuts, chocolate covered biscuits) are also not zero-rated.

In the exempt list we are told that financial services are exempt. However the legislation then goes on to state that credit management and processing services are not exempt. Investment advice is also not exempt.

Land and buildings is a complex topic. Broadly, sales of new homes are zero-rated, sales of new commercial buildings are standard rated and most other transactions are exempt.

Thus great care must be taken when categorising goods or services as zero-rated, exempt or standard-rated. It is not as straightforward as it may first appear.

3 Registration

FAST FORWARD

A trader becomes liable to register for VAT if the value of taxable supplies in any period up to 12 months exceeds £64,000 or if there are reasonable grounds for believing that the value of the taxable supplies will exceed £64,000 in the next 30 days. A trader may also register voluntarily.

3.1 Compulsory registration

3.1.1 Historical test

At the end of every month a trader must calculate his cumulative turnover of taxable supplies for the previous 12 months to date. **The trader becomes liable to register for VAT if the value of his cumulative taxable supplies** (excluding VAT) **exceeds £64,000** (from 1 April 2007 onwards). The person is required to notify HMRC within 30 days of the end of the month in which the £64,000 limit is exceeded. HMRC will then register the person with effect from the end of the month following the month in which the £64,000 was exceeded, or from an earlier date if they and the trader agree.

Registration under this rule is not required if HMRC are satisfied that the value of the trader's taxable supplies (excluding VAT) in the year then starting will not exceed £62,000 (from 1 April 2007 onwards).

Question — **VAT registration**

Fred started to trade cutlery on 1 January 2007. Sales (excluding VAT) were £5,625 a month for the first nine months and £7,700 a month thereafter. From what date should Fred be registered for VAT?

Answer

	£	
Sales to 31 October 2007	58,325	
Sales to 30 November 2007	66,025	(exceeds £64,000)

Fred must notify his liability to register by 30 December 2007 (not 31 December) and will be registered from 1 January 2008 or from an agreed earlier date.

3.1.2 Future test

A person is also liable to register at any time if there are reasonable grounds for believing that his taxable supplies (excluding VAT) in the following 30 days will exceed £64,000. Only taxable turnover of that 30 day period is considered **not** cumulative turnover. HMRC must be notified by the end of the 30 day period and registration will be with effect from the beginning of that period.

Exam focus point

Be sure you know the difference between the historic and future tests.

Question — **Future test**

Constant Ltd started to trade on 1 December 2006 with sales of goods as follows

	VAT status	*£ per month*
Goods A	standard rated	5,000
Goods B	zero rated	2,000

On 1 April 2007 Constant Ltd signed a contract to provide £40,000 of Goods A and £30,000 of Goods B to Unicorn plc by 25 April 2007. This is in addition to normal sales.

From which date should Constant Ltd be registered for VAT?

Answer

Goods A and B are taxable supplies.

Cumulative turnover at end of March 2007 is £28,000.

Cumulative turnover at end of April 2007 is £105,000.

But on 1 April 2007 the company signed a contract and hence 'knew' that within the next 30 days it would supply £77,000 of taxable supplies – this meets the future test conditions. Therefore the company needs to notify HMRC of their need to register within 30 days of 1 April 2007, ie by 30 April 2007.

HMRC will then register the company from 1 April 2007.

The historic test is met at the end of April 2007 (this would require notification by 30 May 2007 and registration by 1 June 2007).

However when a trader satisfies both tests HMRC will use the test that gives the earlier registration date.

In this case the future test gives the earliest date, 1 April 2007.

3.1.3 Other registration issues

When determining the value of a person's taxable supplies for the purposes of registration, supplies of goods and services that are *capital assets* of the business are to be disregarded, except for non zero-rated taxable supplies of interests in land.

When a person is liable to register in respect of a past period, it is his responsibility to pay VAT. If he is unable to collect it from those to whom he made taxable supplies, the VAT burden will fall on him. A person must start keeping VAT records and charging VAT to customers as soon as it is known that he is required to register. However, VAT should not be shown separately on any invoices until the registration number is known. The invoice should show the VAT inclusive price and customers should be informed that VAT invoices will be forwarded once the registration number is known. Formal VAT invoices should then be sent to such customers within 30 days of receiving the registration number.

Notification of liability to register must be made on form VAT 1. Simply writing to, or telephoning, a local VAT office is not enough. On registration the VAT office will send the trader a certificate of registration. This shows the VAT registration number, the date of registration, the end of the first VAT period and the length of the VAT periods.

If a trader makes a supply before becoming liable to register, but gets paid after registration, VAT is not due on that supply.

3.2 Voluntary registration

A person may decide to become registered even though his taxable turnover falls below the registration limit. Unless a person is registered he cannot recover the input tax he pays on purchases.

Voluntary registration is advantageous where a person wishes to recover input tax on purchases. For example, consider a trader who has one input during the year which cost £1,000 plus £175 VAT; he works on the input which becomes his sole output for the year and he decides to make a profit of £1,000.

(a) If he is not registered he will charge £2,175 and his customer will obtain no relief for any VAT.

(b) If he is registered he will charge £2,000 plus VAT of £350. His customer will have input tax of £350 which he will be able to recover if he, too, is registered.

If the customer is a non-taxable person he will prefer (a) as the cost to him is £2,175. If he is taxable he will prefer (b) as the net cost is £2,000. Thus, a decision whether or not to register voluntarily may depend upon the status of customers. It may also depend on the status of the outputs and the image of the business the trader wishes to project (registration may give the impression of a substantial business). The administrative burden of registration should also be considered.

4 Deregistration

FAST FORWARD

A trader may deregister voluntarily if he expects the value of his taxable supplies in the following one year period will not exceed £62,000. Alternatively, a trader who no longer makes taxable supplies may be compulsorily deregistered.

4.1 Voluntary deregistration

A person is eligible for voluntary deregistration if HMRC are satisfied that the value of his taxable supplies (net of VAT and excluding supplies of capital assets) **in the following one year period will not exceed £62,000 (from 1 April 2007).** However, voluntary deregistration will not be allowed if the reason for the expected fall in value of taxable supplies is the cessation of taxable supplies or the suspension of taxable supplies for a period of 30 days or more in that following year.

HMRC will cancel a person's registration from the date the request is made or from an agreed later date.

4.2 Compulsory deregistration

A trader may be compulsorily deregistered if HMRC are satisfied that he is no longer making nor intending to make taxable supplies. Failure to notify a requirement to deregister within 30 days may lead to a penalty. Compulsory deregistration may also lead to HMRC reclaiming input tax which has been wrongly recovered by the trader since the date on which he should have deregistered.

4.3 The consequences of deregistration

VAT is chargeable on all goods and services on hand at the date of deregistration.

On deregistration, VAT is chargeable on all stocks and capital assets in a business on which input tax was claimed, since the registered trader is in effect making a taxable supply to himself as a newly unregistered trader. If the VAT chargeable does not exceed £1,000, it need not be paid.

4.4 Transfer of a going concern

FAST FORWARD

The transfer of a business as a going concern is outside the scope of VAT.

There is no VAT charge if a business (or a separately viable part of it) **is sold as a going concern to another taxable person** (or a person who immediately becomes a taxable person as a result of the transfer). Such a sale is **outside the scope of VAT**.

If a transfer of a going concern (TOGC) is from a VAT registered trader to a new owner who is not VAT registered then it is possible to apply to transfer the registration number of the previous owner to the new owner. This would also transfer to the new owner the responsibility for the past VAT history of the old business. So, if the previous owner had committed any VAT misdemeanours the liability for those would transfer to the new owner of the business. As a result of this it may not be wise to apply to transfer the VAT registration number between old and new owners unless of course, it is a situation where there is a very close connection between the two.

If the VAT registration number is not transferred then the new owners do not have any responsibility for the VAT affairs of the previous owner of the business. This is probably a safer way to structure the transfer of a business.

5 Pre-registration input tax

5.1 Introduction

VAT incurred before registration can be treated as input tax and recovered from HMRC subject to certain conditions.

5.2 Pre-registration goods

If the claim is for input tax suffered on goods purchased prior to registration then the following conditions must be satisfied.

(a) The goods were acquired for the purpose of the business which either was carried on or was to be carried on by him at the time of supply.

(b) The goods have not been supplied onwards or consumed before the date of registration (although they may have been used to make other goods which are still held).

(c) The VAT must have been incurred in the three years prior to the effective date of registration.

5.3 Pre-registration services

If the claim is for input tax suffered on the supply of services prior to registration then the following conditions must be satisfied.

(a) The services were supplied for the purposes of a business which either was carried on or was to be carried on by him at the time of supply.

(b) The services were supplied within the six months prior to the date of registration.

Input tax attributable to supplies made before registration is not deductible even if the input tax concerned is treated as having been incurred after registration.

6 Accounting for and administering VAT

6.1 Administration

FAST FORWARD

VAT is administered by HMRC.

6.1.1 Introduction

The administration of VAT is dealt with by HM Revenue and Customs (HMRC).

Local offices are responsible for the local administration of VAT and for providing advice to registered persons whose principal place of business is in their area. They are controlled by regional collectors.

Completed VAT returns should be sent to the VAT Central Unit at Southend, not to a local office.

From time to time a registered person will be visited by staff from a local office (a control visit) to ensure that the law is understood and is being applied properly. If a trader disagrees with any decision as to the application of VAT given by HMRC he can ask his local office to reconsider the decision. It is not necessary to appeal formally while a case is being reviewed in this way. Where an appeal can be settled by agreement, a written settlement has the same force as a decision by the Revenue and Customs Prosecution Office.

6.1.2 Assessments

HMRC may issue assessments of VAT due to the best of their judgement if they believe that a trader has failed to make returns or if they believe those returns to be incorrect or incomplete. The time limit for making assessments is normally three years after the end of a VAT period, but this is extended to 20 years in the case of fraud, dishonest conduct, certain registration irregularities and the unauthorised issue of VAT invoices.

HMRC sometimes write to traders, setting out their calculations, before issuing assessments. The traders can then query the calculations.

6.1.3 Appeals

A trader may appeal to a VAT Tribunal. VAT Tribunals are administered by the Tribunals Service, part of the Ministry of Justice and are completely independent of HMRC. Provided that VAT returns and payments shown thereon have been made, appeals can be heard.

An appeal must be lodged with the VAT Tribunal (not the local office) within 30 days of the date of any decision by HMRC.

6.2 VAT periods

FAST FORWARD

VAT is accounted for on regular returns. Extensive records must be kept.

The VAT period (also known as the tax period) is the period covered by a VAT return. It is usually three calendar months. The return shows the total input and output tax for the tax period and must be submitted (along with any VAT due) within one month of the end of the period. (Businesses which pay VAT electronically automatically receive a seven day extension to this time limit.)

HMRC allocate VAT periods according to the class of trade carried on (ending in June, September, December and March; July, October, January and April; or August, November, February and May), to spread the flow of VAT returns evenly over the year. When applying for registration a trader can ask for VAT periods which fit in with his own accounting year. It is also possible to have VAT periods to cover accounting systems not based on calendar months.

A registered person whose input tax will regularly exceed his output tax can elect for a one month VAT period, but will have to balance the inconvenience of making 12 returns a year against the advantage of obtaining more rapid repayments of VAT.

Certain small businesses may submit an annual VAT return.

6.3 Substantial traders

If a trader does not make monthly returns, and the total VAT liability over 12 months to the end of a VAT period exceeds £2,000,000, he must make payments on account of each quarter's VAT liability during the quarter. Payments are due a month before the end of the quarter and at the end of the quarter, with the final payment due at the usual time, a month after the end of the quarter. An electronic payment system must be used, not a cheque through the post.

For a trader who exceeds the £2,000,000 limit in the 12 months to 30 September, 31 October or 30 November, the amount of each of the two payments on account is 1/24 of the total VAT liability of those 12 months. The obligation to pay on account starts with the first VAT period starting *after* 31 March.

6.4 Refunds of VAT

There is a three year time limit on the right to reclaim overpaid VAT. This time limit does not apply to input tax which a business could not have reclaimed earlier because the supplier only recently invoiced the VAT, even though it related to a purchase made some time ago. Nor does it apply to overpaid VAT penalties.

If a taxpayer has overpaid VAT and has overclaimed input tax by reason of the same mistake, HMRC can set off any tax, penalty, interest or surcharge due to them against any repayment due to the taxpayer and repay only the net amount. In such cases the normal three year time limit for recovering VAT, penalties, interest, etc by assessment does not apply.

HMRC can refuse to make any repayment which would unjustly enrich the claimant. They can also refuse a repayment of VAT where all or part of the tax has, for practical purposes, been borne by a person other than the taxpayer (eg by a customer of the taxpayer) except to the extent that the taxpayer can show loss or damage to any of his businesses as a result of mistaken assumptions about VAT.

7 The tax point

FAST FORWARD

The tax point is the deemed date of supply. The basic tax point is the date on which goods are removed or made available to the customer, or the date on which services are completed. If a VAT invoice is issued or payment is received before the basic tax point, the earlier of these dates becomes the tax point. If the earlier date rule does not apply, and the VAT invoice is issued within 14 days of the basic tax point, the invoice date becomes the actual tax point.

7.1 The basic tax point

The tax point of each supply is the deemed date of supply. The basic tax point is the date on which the goods are removed or made available to the customer, or the date on which services are completed.

The tax point determines the VAT period in which output tax must be accounted for and credit for input tax will be allowed. The tax point also determines which rate applies if the rate of VAT or a VAT category changes (for example when a supply ceases to be zero-rated and becomes standard-rated).

7.2 The actual tax point

If a VAT invoice is issued or payment is received before the basic tax point, the earlier of these dates automatically becomes the tax point. If the earlier date rule does not apply and if the VAT invoice is issued within 14 days after the basic tax point, the invoice date becomes the tax point (although the trader can elect to use the basic tax point for all his supplies if he wishes). This 14 day period may be extended to accommodate, for example, monthly invoicing; the tax point is then the VAT invoice date or the end of the month, whichever is applied consistently.

Question

Tax point

Julia sells a sculpture to the value of £1,000 net of VAT. She receives a payment on account of £250 plus VAT on 25 March 2008. The sculpture is delivered on 28 April 2008. Julia's VAT returns are made up to calendar quarters. She issues an invoice on 4 May 2008.

Outline the tax point(s) and amount(s) due.

Answer

A separate tax point arises in respect of the £250 deposit and the £750 balance payable.

Julia should account for VAT as follows.

(a) *Deposit*

25 March 2008: tax at 17.5% × £250 = £43.75. This is accounted for in her VAT return to 31 March 2008. The charge arises on 25 March 2008 because payment is received before the basic tax point (which is 28 April 2008 – date of delivery).

(b) *Balance*

4 May 2008: tax at 17.5% × £750 = £131.25. This is accounted for on the VAT return to 30 June 2008. The charge arises on 4 May because the invoice was issued within 14 days of the basic tax point of 28 April 2008 (delivery date).

7.3 Miscellaneous points

Goods supplied on sale or return are treated as supplied on the earlier of adoption by the customer or 12 months after despatch.

Continuous supplies of services paid for periodically normally have tax points on the earlier of the receipt of each payment and the issue of each VAT invoice, unless one invoice covering several payments is issued in advance for up to a year. The tax point is then the earlier of each due date or date of actual payment. However, for connected businesses the tax point will be created periodically, in most cases based on 12 month periods.

8 The valuation of supplies

FAST FORWARD

In order to ascertain the amount of VAT on a supply, the supply must be valued. If a discount is offered for prompt payment, VAT is chargeable on the net amount even if the discount is not taken up.

8.1 Value of supply

The value of a supply is the VAT-exclusive price on which VAT is charged. The consideration for a supply is the amount paid in money or money's worth. Thus with a standard rate of 17.5%:

Value + VAT = consideration
£100 + £17.50 = £117.50

The VAT proportion of the consideration is known as the 'VAT fraction'. It is

$$\frac{\text{rate of tax}}{100+\text{rate of tax}}=\frac{17.5}{100+17.5}=\frac{7}{47}$$

Provided the consideration for a bargain made at arm's length is paid in money, the value for VAT purposes is the VAT exclusive price charged by the trader. If it is paid in something other than money, as in a barter of some goods or services for others, it must be valued and VAT will be due on the value.

If the price of goods is effectively reduced with money off coupons, the value of the supply is the amount actually received by the taxpayer.

8.2 Discounts

Where a discount is offered for prompt payment, VAT is chargeable on the net amount, regardless of whether the discount is taken up.

When goods are sold to staff at a discount, VAT is only due on the discounted price.

8.3 Miscellaneous

For goods supplied under a hire purchase agreement VAT is chargeable on the cash selling price at the start of the contract.

When goods are permanently taken from a business for non-business purposes VAT must be accounted for on their market value. Where business goods are put to a private or non-business use, the value of the resulting supply of services is the cost to the taxable person of providing the services. If services bought for business purposes are used for non-business purposes (without charge), then VAT must be accounted for on their cost, but the VAT to be accounted for is not allowed to exceed the input tax deductible on the purchase of the services.

9 The deduction of input tax

9.1 Input tax recovery

FAST FORWARD

Not all input VAT is deductible, eg VAT on most motor cars.

For input tax to be deductible, the payer must be a taxable person, with the supply being to him in the course of his business. In addition a VAT invoice must be held (except for payments of up to £25 including VAT which are for telephone calls or car park fees or which are made through cash operated machines).

Input tax recovery can be denied to any business that does not hold a valid VAT invoice and cannot provide alternative evidence to prove the supply took place.

9.2 Capital items

The distinction between capital and revenue which is important in other areas of tax **does not apply to VAT**. Thus a manufacturer buying plant subject to VAT will be able to obtain a credit for all the VAT immediately. The plant must of course be used to make taxable supplies, and if it is only partly so used only part of the VAT can be reclaimed. Conversely, if plant is sold secondhand then VAT should be charged on the sale and is output tax in the normal way.

9.3 Non-deductible input tax

Exam focus point

> In the F6 exam students are not required to know actual cases where VAT decisions were made. They are included below for your information only.

The following input tax is not deductible even for a taxable person with taxable outputs.

(a) **VAT on motor cars** not used wholly for business purposes. VAT on cars is never reclaimable unless the car is acquired new for resale or is acquired for use in or leasing to a taxi business, a self-drive car hire business or a driving school (see further below).

(b) **VAT on business entertaining** where the cost of the entertaining is not a tax deductible trading expense. If the items bought are used partly for such entertaining and partly for other purposes, the proportion of the VAT relating to the entertainment is non-deductible.

In *Ernst & Young v CCE* the Tribunal held that staff entertaining was wholly for business purposes and a full input tax recovery was allowed. HMRC accept this decision in respect of staff entertainment but maintain that following the case *KPMG v CCE* input tax on entertaining guests at a staff party is non-deductible.

(c) **VAT on expenses incurred on domestic accommodation for directors.**

(d) **VAT on non-business items passed through the business accounts.** However, when goods are bought partly for business use, the purchaser may:

(i) Deduct all the input tax, and account for output tax in respect of the private use, or
(ii) Deduct only the business proportion of the input tax.

Where services are bought partly for business use, only method (ii) may be used. If services are initially bought for business use but the use then changes, a fair proportion of the input tax (relating to the private use) is reclaimed by HMRC by making the trader account for output tax.

(e) **VAT which does not relate to the** making of supplies by the buyer in the course of a **business**.

9.4 Irrecoverable VAT

Where all (as with many cars) or some (as for partial business use) of the input tax on a purchase is not deductible, the **non-deductible VAT is included in the cost for income tax, corporation tax, capital allowance or capital gains purposes. Deductible VAT is omitted from costs, so that only net amounts are included in accounts. Similarly, sales** (and proceeds in chargeable gains computations) **are shown net of VAT**, because the VAT is paid over to HMRC.

9.5 Motoring expenses

9.5.1 Cars

The VAT incurred on the purchase of a car not used wholly for business purposes is not recoverable (except as mentioned above). If accessories are fitted after the original purchase and a separate invoice is raised then the VAT on the accessories can be treated as input tax so long as the accessories are for business use.

If a car is used wholly for business purposes (including leasing, so long as the charges are at the open market rate), the input tax is recoverable but the buyer must account for VAT when he sells the car. **If a car is leased, the lessor recovered the input tax when the car was purchased and the lessee makes some private use of the car** (for example private use by employees), **the lessee can only recover 50% of the input tax on the lease charges. A hiring of five days or less is assumed to be for wholly business use.**

If a car is used for business purposes then any VAT charged on repair and maintenance costs can be treated as input tax. No apportionment has to be made for private use.

9.5.2 Fuel for business use

The VAT incurred on fuel used for business purposes is fully deductible as input tax. If the fuel is bought by employees who are reimbursed for the actual cost or by a mileage allowance, the employer may deduct the input tax provided he **holds a VAT invoice (or invoices) showing sufficient VAT to cover the input tax claim being made**. Normally there will not be an invoice showing the exact amount of input VAT reclaimed because some of the fuel may have been used by employees for private purposes and only business use is reimbursed (or a mileage allowance is used). It is sufficient to hold invoice(s) showing an amount of input tax on fuel at least equal to the input tax being recovered by the business.

9.5.3 Fuel for private use

FAST FORWARD

If fuel is supplied for private purposes all input VAT incurred on the fuel is allowed but the business must account for output VAT using a set of scale charges.

When fuel is supplied for an individual's private use at less than the cost of that fuel to the business, all input tax incurred on the fuel is allowed, but the business must account for output tax using set scale charges per VAT return period, based on the CO_2 emissions of the car (from 1 May 2007). As for income tax, the CO_2 emissions are rounded down to the nearest 5%. The scale figures will be stated in the exam if required. However, take care to note whether the examiner has given you the VAT inclusive or the VAT exclusive scale figure.

The output tax is the VAT inclusive scale charge × 7/47 or the VAT exclusive scale charge × 17.5%.

If the employee has to pay the full cost of fuel (or more than its cost) to the employer, the employer must account for VAT on the amount paid, rather than on the scale charge.

Question — **Fuel scale charge**

Iain is an employee of ABC Ltd. He has the use of a car with CO_2 emissions of 176 g/km for one month and a car with CO_2 emissions of 208 g/km for two months during the quarter ended 31 March 2008.

ABC Ltd pay all the petrol costs in respect of both cars without requiring Iain to make any reimbursement in respect of private fuel. Total petrol costs for the quarter amount to £300 (including VAT).

What is the VAT effect of the above on ABC Ltd?

VAT scale rates (VAT inclusive) for 3 month periods

CO_2 emissions	£
175	268
205	341

Answer

Value for the quarter:

	£
Car 1	
£268 × 1/3 =	89.33
Car 2	
£341 × 2/3 =	227.33
	316.66
Output tax:	
7/47 × £316.66	£47.16
Input tax	
7/47 × £300	£44.68

10 Relief for impairment losses (bad debts)

FAST FORWARD

Relief for VAT on impairment losses (bad debts) is available if the debt is over six months old (measured from when the payment is due) and has been written off in the trader's accounts.

Where a supplier of goods or services has accounted for VAT on the supply and the customer does not pay, the supplier may claim a refund of VAT on the amount unpaid. **Relief is available for VAT on impairment losses (bad debts) if the debt is over six months old (measured from when payment is due) and has been written off in the creditor's accounts.** Where payments on account have been received, they are attributed to debts in chronological order. If the debtor later pays all or part of the amount owed, a corresponding part of the VAT repaid must be paid back to HMRC.

Impairment loss relief claims must be made within three years of the time the debt became eligible for relief. The creditor must have a copy of the VAT invoice, and records to show that the VAT in question has been accounted for and that the debt has been written off. The VAT is reclaimed on the creditor's VAT return.

A business which has claimed input tax on a supply, but which has not paid the supplier of the goods or services within six months of date of supply (or the date on which the payment is due, if later), must repay the input tax, irrespective of whether the supplier has made a claim for bad debt relief. The input tax will be repaid by making an adjustment to the input tax on the VAT return for the accounting period in which the end of the six months falls.

Exam focus point

Watch out for the six month rule when claiming relief for impairment losses.

Chapter Roundup

- VAT is charged on turnover at each stage in a production process, but in such a way that the burden is borne by the final consumer.
- VAT is chargeable on taxable supplies made by a taxable person in the course or furtherance of any business carried on by him. Supplies may be of goods or services.
- Some supplies are taxable (either standard-rated, reduced-rated or zero-rated). Others are exempt.
- A trader becomes liable to register for VAT if the value of taxable supplies in any period up to 12 months exceeds £64,000 or if there are reasonable grounds for believing that the value of the taxable supplies will exceed £64,000 in the next 30 days. A trader may also register voluntarily.
- A trader may deregister voluntarily if he expects the value of his taxable supplies in the following one year period will not exceed £62,000. Alternatively, a trader who no longer makes taxable supplies may be compulsorily deregistered.
- VAT is chargeable on all goods and services on hand at the date of deregistration.
- The transfer of a business as a going concern is outside the scope of VAT.
- VAT is administered by HMRC.
- VAT is accounted for on regular returns. Extensive records must be kept.
- The tax point is the deemed date of supply. The basic tax point is the date on which goods are removed or made available to the customer, or the date on which services are completed. If a VAT invoice is issued or payment is received before the basic tax point, the earlier of these dates becomes the tax point. If the earlier date rule does not apply, and the VAT invoice is issued within 14 days of the basic tax point, the invoice date becomes the actual tax point.
- In order to ascertain the amount of VAT on a supply, the supply must be valued. If a discount is offered for prompt payment, VAT is chargeable on the net amount even if the discount is not taken up.
- Not all input VAT is deductible, eg VAT on most motor cars.
- If fuel is supplied for private purposes all input VAT incurred on the fuel is allowed but the business must account for output VAT using a set of scale charges.
- Relief for VAT on impairment losses (bad debts) is available if the debt is over six months old (measured from when the payment is due) and has been written off in the trader's accounts.

Quick Quiz

1. On what transactions will VAT be charged?
2. What is a taxable person?
3. When may a person choose to be deregistered?
4. What is the time limit in respect of claiming pre-registration input tax on goods?
5. On what amount is VAT charged if a discount is offered for prompt payment?
6. What input tax is never deductible?
7. What relief is available for bad debts?

Answers to Quick Quiz

1. VAT is charged on taxable supplies of goods and services made in the UK by a taxable person in the course or furtherance of any business carried on by him.
2. Any 'person' whose taxable turnover exceeds the registration limit. The term 'person' includes individuals, partnerships and companies.
3. A person is eligible for voluntary deregistration if HMRC are satisfied that the value of his taxable supplies in the following year will not exceed £62,000.
4. The VAT must have been incurred in the three years prior to the effective date of registration.
5. VAT is chargeable on the net price, regardless of whether the discount is taken up.
6. VAT on:
   - motor cars
   - business entertaining
   - expenses incurred on domestic accommodation for directors
   - non-business items passed through the accounts
   - items which do not relate to making business supplies
7. Where a supplier has accounted for VAT on a supply and the customer fails to pay, then the supplier may claim a refund of the VAT accounted for to HMRC but never actually collected from the customer.

Now try the question below from the Exam Question Bank

Number	Level	Marks	Time
Q38	Examination	10	18 mins

Further aspects of VAT

Topic list	Syllabus reference
1 VAT invoices and records	F3(c)
2 Penalties	F3(g)
3 Special schemes	F4(a)-(c)

Introduction

In the previous chapter we looked at the scope of VAT and when businesses must, or may, register for VAT.

In this chapter we consider the contents of a valid VAT invoice and the main penalties used to enforce the VAT system.

Finally we look at the three special schemes which are intended to reduce the administrative burden for small businesses.

This chapter concludes our study of UK taxation and the F6 syllabus.

Study guide

		Intellectual level
F3	**The computation of VAT liabilities**	
(c)	List the information that must be given on a VAT invoice.	1
(g)	Explain the circumstances in which the default surcharge, a serious misdeclaration penalty, and default interest will be applied.	1
F4	**The effect of special schemes**	
(a)	Describe the cash accounting scheme, and recognise when it will be advantageous to use the scheme.	2
(b)	Describe the annual accounting scheme, and recognise when it will be advantageous to use the scheme.	2
(c)	Describe the flat rate scheme, and recognise when it will be advantageous to use the scheme.	2

Exam guide

There will always be at least 10% of the marks in the exam on VAT. Although this may be in question 1 or 2 there may be a separate question on VAT. Penalties are an important topic as they are used to enforce the VAT system, but the special schemes are designed to make life simpler for small businesses. The flat rate scheme may also lead to a small extra profit for the business, depending on the flat rate percentage and the level of inputs.

1 VAT invoices and records

1.1 VAT invoices

FAST FORWARD

A taxable person making a taxable supply to another registered person must supply a VAT invoice within 30 days.

A taxable person making a taxable supply to another person registered for VAT must supply a *VAT* invoice within 30 days of the time of supply, and must keep a copy. The invoice must show:

(a) The supplier's name, address and registration number

(b) The date of issue, the tax point and an invoice number

(c) The name and address of the customer

(d) A description of the goods or services supplied, giving for each description the quantity, the unit price, the rate of VAT and the VAT exclusive amount

(e) The rate of any cash discount

(f) The total invoice price excluding VAT (with separate totals for zero-rated and exempt supplies)

(g) Each VAT rate applicable and the total amount of VAT

If an invoice is issued, and a change in price then alters the VAT due, a credit note or debit note to adjust the VAT must be issued.

Credit notes must give the reason for the credit (such as 'returned goods'), and the number and date of the original VAT invoice. If a credit note makes no VAT adjustment, it should state this.

A less detailed VAT invoice may be issued by a retailer where the invoice is for a total including VAT of up to £250. Such an invoice must show:

(a) The supplier's name, address and registration number
(b) The date of the supply
(c) A description of the goods or services supplied
(d) The rate of VAT chargeable
(e) The total amount chargeable including VAT

Zero-rated and exempt supplies must not be included in less detailed invoices.

VAT invoices are not required for payments of up to £25 including VAT which are for telephone calls or car park fees or are made through cash operated machines. In such cases, input tax can be claimed without a VAT invoice.

1.2 Records

FAST FORWARD

Every VAT registered trader must keep records for six years.

Every VAT registered trader must keep records for six years, although HMRC may sometimes grant permission for their earlier destruction. They may be kept on paper, on microfilm or microfiche or on computer. However, there must be adequate facilities for HMRC to inspect records.

All records must be kept up to date and in a way which allows:

- The calculation of VAT due
- Officers of HMRC to check the figures on VAT returns

The following records are needed.

- Copies of VAT invoices, credit notes and debit notes issued
- A summary of supplies made
- VAT invoices, credit notes and debit notes received
- A summary of supplies received
- A VAT account
- Order and delivery notes, correspondence, appointment books, job books, purchases and sales books, cash books, account books, records of takings (such as till rolls), bank paying-in slips, bank statements and annual accounts
- Records of zero-rated and exempt supplies, gifts or loans of goods, taxable self-supplies and any goods taken for non-business use

2 Penalties

2.1 The default surcharge

FAST FORWARD

A default occurs when a trader either submits his VAT return late, or submits the return on time but pays the VAT late. A default surcharge is applied if there is a default during a default surcharge period.

A default occurs when a trader either submits his VAT return late, or submits the return on time but pays the VAT late. If a trader defaults, HMRC will serve a surcharge liability notice on the trader. The notice specifies a surcharge period running from the date of the notice to the anniversary of the end of the period for which the trader is in default.

If a further default occurs in respect of a return period ending during the specified surcharge period, the original surcharge period will be extended to the anniversary of the end of the period to which the new default relates. In addition, if the default involves the late payment of VAT (as opposed to simply a late return) **a surcharge is levied.**

The surcharge depends on the number of defaults involving late payment of VAT which have occurred in respect of periods ending in the surcharge period, as follows.

Default involving late payment of VAT in the surcharge period	Surcharge as a percentage of the VAT outstanding at the due date
First	2%
Second	5%
Third	10%
Fourth or more	15%

Surcharges at the 2% and 5% rates are not normally demanded unless the amount due would be at least £400 but for surcharges calculated using the 10% or 15% rates there is a minimum amount of £30 payable.

A trader must submit one year's returns on time and pay the VAT shown on them on time in order to break out of the surcharge liability period and the escalation of surcharge percentages.

Question

Default surcharge

Peter Popper has an annual turnover of around £300,000. His VAT return for the quarter to 31.12.06 is late. He then submits returns for the quarters to 30.9.07 and 31.3.08 late as well as making late payment of the tax due of £12,000 and £500 respectively.

Peter's VAT return to 31.3.09 is also late and the VAT due of £1,100 is also paid late. All other VAT returns and VAT payments are made on time. Outline Peter Popper's exposure to default surcharge.

Answer

A surcharge liability notice will be issued after the late filing on the 31.12.06 return outlining a surcharge period extending to 31.12.07.

The late 30.9.07 return is in the surcharge period so the period is extended to 30.9.08. The late VAT payment triggers a 2% penalty. 2% × £12,000 = £240. Since £240 is less than the £400 de minimis limit it is not collected by HMRC.

The late 31.3.08 return is in the surcharge period so the period is now extended to 31.3.09. The late payment triggers a 5% penalty. 5% × £500 = £25. Since £25 is less than the £400 de minimis limit it is not collected by HMRC.

The late 31.03.09 return is in the surcharge period. The period is extended to 31.03.10. The late payment triggers a 10% penalty 10% × £1,100 = £110. This is collected by HMRC since the £400 de minimis does not apply to penalties calculated at the 10% (and 15%) rate.

Peter will have to submit all four quarterly VAT returns to 31.3.10 on time and pay the VAT on time to 'escape' the default surcharge regime.

A default will be ignored for all default surcharge purposes if the trader can show that the return or payment was sent at such a time, and in such a manner, that it was reasonable to expect that HMRC would receive it by the due date. Posting the return and payment first class the day before the due date is generally accepted as meeting this requirement. A default will also be ignored if the trader can demonstrate a reasonable excuse for the late submission or payment.

The application of the default surcharge regime to small businesses is modified. **A small business is one with a turnover below £150,000**. When a small business is late submitting a VAT return or paying VAT it will receive a letter from HMRC offering help. No penalty will be charged. If a further default occurs within 12 months a surcharge liability notice will be issued.

2.2 The misdeclaration penalty: very large errors

The making of a return which understates a person's true liability or overstates the repayment due to him incurs a penalty of 15% of the VAT which would have been lost if the return had been accepted as correct. The same penalty applies when HMRC issue an assessment which is too low and the trader fails to notify the error within 30 days from the issue of the assessment.

These penalties apply only where the VAT which would have been lost equals or exceeds the lower of

(a) **£1,000,000 or**

(b) **30% of the sum of the true input tax and the true output tax**. This sum is known as the gross amount of tax (GAT). In the case of an incorrect assessment 30% of the true amount of tax (TAT), the VAT actually due from the trader, is used instead of 30% of the GAT.

The penalty may be mitigated.

Question — **Misdeclaration penalty**

A trader declares output tax of £100,000 and claims input tax of £30,000 on the VAT return for the quarter ended 31 March 2008. It is subsequently discovered that output tax is understated by £28,000.

Does a misdeclaration penalty arise?

Answer

The test for misdeclaration penalty is the lower of:

- 30% of GAT (Gross Amount of Tax)
  30% × £(100,000 + 28,000 + 30,000) = £47,400
- £1,000,000

ie £47,400

Since the error of £28,000 is less than £47,400 the error is not 'large' and hence no penalty arises.

Errors on a VAT return of up to £2,000 (net: underdeclaration minus overdeclaration) may be corrected on the next return without giving rise to a misdeclaration penalty or interest (see below for details on interest). Note that errors over £2,000 cannot be corrected in this way and should be notified to HMRC on form VAT 652 or by letter. The misdeclaration penalty may apply.

This penalty does not apply if the trader can show reasonable excuse for his conduct, or if he made a full disclosure when he had no reason to suppose that HMRC were enquiring into his affairs.

If his conduct leads to a conviction for fraud, or to a penalty for conduct involving dishonesty, it cannot also lead to a misdeclaration penalty.

2.3 Interest on unpaid VAT

Interest (not deductible in computing taxable profits) **is charged on VAT which is the subject of an assessment** (where returns were not made or were incorrect), **or which could have been the subject of an assessment but was paid before the assessment was raised. It runs from the reckonable date until the date of payment.** This interest is sometimes called 'default interest'.

The reckonable date is when the VAT should have been paid (one month from the end of the return period), or in the case of VAT repayments, seven days from the issue of the repayment order. However, where VAT is charged by an assessment, interest does not run from more than three years before the date of the assessment; where the VAT was paid before an assessment was raised, interest does not run for more than three years before the date of payment.

In practice, interest is only charged when there would otherwise be a loss to the Exchequer. It is not, for example, charged when a company failed to charge VAT but if it had done so another company would have been able to recover the VAT.

3 Special schemes

Special schemes include the cash accounting scheme, the annual accounting scheme and the optional flat rate scheme. These schemes make VAT accounting easier for certain types of trader.

3.1 The cash accounting scheme

The cash accounting scheme enables businesses to account for VAT on the basis of cash paid and received. That is, the date of payment or receipt determines the return in which the transaction is dealt with. **The scheme can only be used by a trader whose annual taxable turnover (exclusive of VAT) does not exceed £1,350,000 (from 1 April 2007).** A trader can join the scheme only if all returns and VAT payments are up to date (or arrangements have been made to pay outstanding VAT by instalments).

If the value of taxable supplies exceeds £1,600,000 (from 1 April 2007) in the 12 months to the end of a VAT period a trader must leave the cash accounting scheme immediately.

Businesses which leave the scheme (either voluntarily or because they have breached the £1,600,000 limit) can account for any outstanding VAT due under the scheme on a cash basis for a further six months.

3.2 The annual accounting scheme

The annual accounting scheme is only available to traders who regularly pay VAT to HMRC, not to traders who normally receive repayments. It is available for traders **whose taxable turnover (exclusive of VAT) for the 12 months starting on their application to join the scheme is not expected to exceed £1,350,000**.

Under the annual accounting scheme traders file annual VAT returns but throughout the year they must make payments on account of their VAT liability by direct debit. The year for which each return is made may end at the end of any calendar month. Unless HMRC agree otherwise, the trader must pay 90% of the previous year's net VAT liability during the year by means of nine monthly payments commencing at the end of the fourth month of the year. The balance of the year's VAT is then paid with the annual return. There is an option for businesses to pay three larger interim instalments.

Late payment of instalments is not a default for the purposes of the default surcharge.

An annual VAT return must be submitted to HMRC along with any balancing payment due within two months of the end of the year.

It is not possible to use the annual accounting scheme if input tax exceeded output tax in the year prior to application. In addition, all returns must have been made up to date.

If the expected value of a trader's taxable supplies exceeds £1,600,000, notice must be given to HMRC within 30 days and he may then be required to leave the scheme. If the £1,600,000 limit is in fact exceeded, the trader must leave the scheme.

If a trader fails to make the regular payments required by the scheme or the final payment for a year, or has not paid all VAT shown on returns made before joining the scheme, he may be expelled from the scheme. HMRC can also prevent a trader using the scheme 'if they consider it necessary to do so for the protection of the revenue'.

Advantages of annual accounting:

- Only one VAT return each year so fewer occasions to trigger a default surcharge
- Ability to manage cash flow more accurately
- Avoids need for quarterly calculations for input tax recovery

Disadvantages of annual accounting:

- Need to monitor future taxable supplies to ensure turnover limit not exceeded
- Timing of payments have less correlation to turnover (and hence cash received) by business
- Payments based on previous year's turnover may not reflect current year turnover which may be a problem if the scale of activities has reduced

3.3 Flat rate scheme

The optional flat rate scheme enables businesses to calculate VAT due simply by applying a flat rate percentage to their turnover.

Under the scheme, businesses calculate VAT by applying a fixed percentage to their tax inclusive turnover, ie the total turnover, including all reduced rate, zero-rated and exempt income. The percentage depends upon the trade sector into which a business falls. It ranges from 2% for retailing food, confectionery or newspapers to 13.5% for construction services. For example, the percentage for accountancy and book-keeping is 13%, for financial services is 11.5%, for hotels 9.5% and for catering 12%. A 1% reduction off the flat rate % can be made by businesses in their first year of VAT registration.

Exam focus point

> The flat rate percentage will be given to you in your examination.

Businesses using the scheme must issue VAT invoices to their VAT registered customers but they do not have to record all the details of the invoices issued or purchase invoices received to calculate the VAT due. Invoices issued will show VAT at the normal rate rather than the flat rate.

To join the flat rate scheme businesses must have:

- **a tax exclusive annual taxable turnover of up to £150,000**; and
- **a tax exclusive annual total turnover, including the value of exempt and/or other non-taxable income, of up to £187,500.**

3.4 Example: flat rate scheme

An accountant undertakes work for individuals and for business clients. In a VAT year, the business client work amounts to £35,000 and the accountant will issue VAT invoices totalling £41,125 (£35,000 plus VAT at 17.5%). Turnover from work for individuals totals £18,000, including VAT. Total gross sales are therefore £59,125. The flat rate percentage for an accountancy businesses is 13%.

VAT due to HMRC will be 13% × £59,125 = £7,686.25

Under the normal VAT rules the output tax due would be:

	£
£35,000 × 17.5%	6,125.00
£18,000 × 7/47	2,680.85
	8,805.85

Whether the accountant is better off under the scheme depends on the amount of input tax incurred as this would be offset, under normal rules, from output tax due.

Chapter Roundup

- A taxable person making a taxable supply to another registered person must supply a VAT invoice within 30 days.
- Every VAT registered trader must keep records for six years.
- A default occurs when a trader either submits his VAT return late, or submits the return on time but pays the VAT late. A default surcharge is applied if there is a default during a default surcharge period.
- Special schemes include the cash accounting scheme, the annual accounting scheme and the optional flat rate scheme. These schemes make VAT accounting easier for certain types of trader.

Quick Quiz

1. Within what time limit must a VAT appeal be lodged?
2. What is a default?
3. What are the turnover limits for the annual accounting scheme?
4. What is the optional flat rate scheme?

Answers to Quick Quiz

1. Within 30 days of the date of the decision by HMRC.
2. A default occurs when a trader either submits his VAT return late or submits the return on time but pays the VAT late.
3. Turnover not exceeding £1.35 million to join the scheme. Once turnover exceeds £1.6 million must leave the scheme.
4. The optional flat rate scheme enables businesses to calculate VAT simply by applying a percentage to their tax-inclusive turnover. Under the scheme, businesses calculate VAT due by applying a flat rate percentage to their tax inclusive turnover, ie the total turnover generated, including all reduced-rate, zero-rated and exempt income. The percentage depends upon the trade sector in which a business falls.

Now try the questions below from the Exam Question Bank

Number	Level	Marks	Time
Q39	Examination	10	18 mins
Q40	Examination	10	18 mins

Exam question bank

1 Mary **13 mins**

Mary (aged 25) has partnership trading income of £14,000. She also receives building society interest of £6,400 net, dividends of £1,800 (net), and pays interest of £2,500 each year on a loan to purchase an interest in the partnership. How much cash will she have available to spend in 2007/08? Ignore national insurance. **(7 marks)**

2 Jane and Chris **13 mins**

Jane and Chris Bradbury, both in their 30s, had been married for only two years when Chris was killed in a car accident on 3 July 2007.

Jane and Chris had worked for the same company each earning £12,000 gross per annum. PAYE of £100 per month was deducted.

The couple's other income received in the year to 6 April 2008 was as follows:

	£
Jane	
Building society interest	800
Chris	
Building society interest	480

Required

Calculate the couple's tax payable or repayable for 2007/08. **(7 marks)**

3 Mr and Mrs Lowrie **27 mins**

John Lowrie and Helen Lowrie who are both in their thirties are a married couple. Mr and Mrs Lowrie received the following income in 2007/08.

	Mr Lowrie	*Mrs Lowrie*
	£	£
Salary (gross)	38,500	20,000
PAYE tax deducted	7,000	2,980
Dividends (amount received)	1,090	2,538
Bank deposit interest (amount received)	600	76
Building society interest (amount received)	592	420

Required

Compute the net tax payable by Mr Lowrie and by Mrs Lowrie for 2007/08. **(15 marks)**

4 Employment and self-employment **27 mins**

Discuss the factors to be taken into consideration when deciding whether a person is employed or self employed for the purposes of income tax. **(15 marks)**

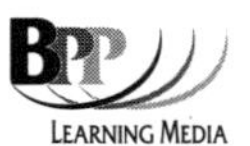

5 Cars and loans **27 mins**

The following items have been provided by a UK company to employees earning more than £8,500 a year.

(a) A loan of £16,000 at 1% a year to Mr Andrews on 6 October 2007 which has been used to improve his private residence.

(b) A £1,000 interest free loan to Mrs Preece on 6 April 2007 which was used to finance her daughter's wedding.

(c) The loan of a TV and video system to Mr Charles from 6 June 2007, the asset having cost the company £800 in 2005 and having had a market value of £500 in June 2007.

(d) A long service award in December 2007 to Mrs Davies, the company secretary, comprising a gold wrist watch costing £400. Mrs Davies has been employed by the company since December 1982.

(e) The loan of a petrol engined BMW motor car to Mr Edgar from 6 April 2007. The company had acquired the car new on 1 August 2004 at a cost of £23,000 and its market value in April 2007 was estimated to be £15,000. The car emits CO_2 of 139g/km. The company pays all running costs, including fuel.

(f) The exclusive private use of a company flat in central London, by Mr Ford, the managing director. The company acquired the flat in February 2005 for £100,000 and Mr Ford has used it since that date. The flat is fully furnished at a cost of £5,000 and the council tax paid by the company amounted to £500. The annual value is £900. The running costs of the flat amounting to £1,200 for 2007/08 were paid directly by Mr Ford.

Required

State in detail how each of the above items would be treated for 2007/08, computing the amount of any taxable benefit. Assume an official rate of interest of 6.25%. **(15 marks)**

6 Gary and George **13 mins**

(a) Gary had employment income of £50,000 for 2007/08. He paid £3,900 into his personal pension scheme.

Required

Calculate Gary's income tax payable. **(2 marks)**

(b) What would your answer in part (a) be if Gary paid £60,000 (gross) into his personal pension scheme?

(2 marks)

(c) George is due to inherit a substantial amount of wealth following the death of his aunt. He wishes to put £250,000 (gross) into his personal pension scheme in 2007/08.

Required

Outline the tax implications of this investment. Assume his employment income will be £300,000 in 2007/08. **(3 marks)**

(Total = 7 marks)

7 Mr Lee **27 mins**

You have received the following e-mail from a client, Mr Lee:

'I have just started a new job and thought that I ought to start making some pension provision now that I am in my mid-30s. My initial salary is £100,000 a year, but I am hoping that, with bonuses, it may increase in the next few years to around £500,000.

My employer operates a pension scheme and I have been given a booklet about it. The booklet says that the scheme is a 'money purchase' scheme. If I join the scheme, my employer will make contributions to the scheme in addition to the amount that I pay into it.

Could you answer the following questions:

(1) Do I have to join my employer's pension scheme or can I make other pension arrangements? What is a 'money purchase' scheme?

(2) If I join my employer's pension scheme, how much can I contribute to the scheme and how much can my employer contribute?

(3) I have heard that there is tax relief on my contributions to a pension scheme. How does that work if I join my employer's pension scheme?

Required

Draft an e-mail in response. **(15 marks)**

8 Hamburg **27 mins**

On 1 May 2007, Hamburg started to invest in rented properties. He bought three houses in the first three months, as follows.

House 1

Hamburg bought house 1 for £62,000 on 1 May 2007. It needed a new roof, and Hamburg paid £5,000 for the work to be done in May. He also spent £1,200 on loft insulation. He then let it unfurnished for £600 a month from 1 June to 30 November 2007. The first tenant then left, and the house was empty throughout December 2007. On 1 January 2008, a new tenant moved in. The house was again let unfurnished. The rent was £6,000 a year, payable annually in advance.

Hamburg paid water rates of £320 for the period from 1 May 2007 to 5 April 2008 and a buildings insurance premium of £480 for the period from 1 June 2007 to 31 May 2008.

House 2

Hamburg bought house 2 for £84,000 on 1 June 2007. He immediately bought furniture for £4,300, and let the house fully furnished for £5,000 a year from 1 August 2007. The rent was payable quarterly in arrears. Hamburg paid water rates of £240 for the period from 1 June 2007 to 5 April 2008. He claimed the 10% wear and tear allowance for furniture.

House 3

Hamburg bought house 3 for £45,000 on 1 July 2007. He spent £1,200 on routine redecoration and £2,300 on furniture in July, and let the house fully furnished from 1 August 2007 for £7,800 a year, payable annually in advance. Hamburg paid water rates of £360 for the period from 1 July 2007 to 5 April 2008, a buildings insurance premium of £440 for the period from 1 July 2007 to 30 June 2008 and a contents insurance premium of £180 for the period from 1 August 2007 to 31 July 2008. He claimed the 10% wear and tear allowance for furniture.

During 2007/08 Hamburg also rented out one furnished room of his main residence. He received £4,600 and incurred allowable expenses of £875.

Required

Compute Hamburg's property business income for 2007/08. **(15 marks)**

9 A Trader

27 mins

A Trader's profit and loss account for the year to 31 March 2008 was as follows.

	£		£
General expenses	73,611	Gross trading profit	246,250
Repairs and renewals	15,000	Impairment losses recovered	
Legal and accountancy charges	1,200	(previously written off)	373
Subscriptions and donations	7,000	Profit on sale of office	5,265
Impairment losses	500	Building society interest	1,900
Salaries and wages	30,000		
Travel	8,000		
Depreciation	15,000		
Rent and rates	1,500		
Net profit	101,977		
	253,788		253,788

Notes

(1) *General expenses include the following.*

	£
Entertaining staff	1,000
Entertaining suppliers	600

(2) *Repairs and renewals include the following.*

	£
Redecorating existing premises	300
Renovations to new premises to remedy wear and tear of previous owner (the premises were usable before these renovations)	500

(2) *Legal and accountancy charges are made up as follows.*

	£
Debt collection service	200
Staff service agreements	50
Tax consultant's fees for special advice	30
45 year lease on new premises	100
Audit and accountancy	820
	1,200

(4) *Subscriptions and donations include the following.*

	£
Donations under the gift aid scheme	5,200
Donation to a political party	500
Sports facilities for staff	500
Contribution to a local enterprise agency	200

(5) Travel expenses included A Trader's motoring expenses of £2,000. 25% of his use of his car was for private purposes.

(6) Capital allowances amounted to £2,200.

Required

Compute A Trader's taxable trading profits for the accounting period to 31 March 2008. **(15 marks)**

10 Tom Hardy **27 mins**

Tom Hardy makes accounts to 30 June. Despite substantial investment in new equipment, business has been indifferent and he will cease trading on 31 December 2010. His last accounts will be prepared for the six months to 31 December 2010.

The tax written down value of fixed assets at 1 July 2006 was as follows.

	£
General pool	32,000

Fixed asset additions and disposals have been as follows.

		£
20.9.06	Plant cost	1,917
25.9.06	Computer cost	4,400
15.7.07	Car for own use cost	13,400
14.7.09	Plant sold for	340
10.5.10	Computer sold for	2,200

An election to depool the computer was made when it was acquired in 2006. Private use of the car was agreed at 20% for all years.

At the end of 2010, the plant would be worth £24,000 and the car £10,600.

Tom has always been a medium sized enterprise for FYA purposes.

Required

Calculate the capital allowances for the periods from 1 July 2006 to 31 December 2010, assuming FY07 rates and allowances continue to apply in the future. **(15 marks)**

11 Saruman **27 mins**

Saruman is the sole proprietor of a small engineering business. He prepares accounts annually to 31 March and has been in business since 1 June 2001.

(a) General pool brought forward on 1 April 2007 £52,000

Tax written down value of motor car for Saruman's use on 1 April 2007 £600

Private use of this car has been agreed with HMRC at 25%.

The following events occurred during the year ended 31 March 2008:

Disposals:	20 April 2007	–	Plant £12,000 (original cost £10,000)
	21 May 2007	–	Motor car for Saruman's own use £920 (original cost £1,896)
	20 June 2007	–	Plant £800 (original cost £3,000)
Additions:	21 May 2007	–	New car for Saruman's use £19,000
	1 October 2007	–	Estate car for use by sales representative £4,800

(b) A new small factory was bought from a builder for a total cost of £40,000, including land £10,000 and office accommodation £3,000. The factory was purchased and brought into use on 10 August 2002.

Required

Calculate capital allowances for the purpose of the trading income assessment for the year ended 31 March 2008. **(15 marks)**

12 Mr Cobbler **27 mins**

Mr Cobbler starts a business as a sole trader on 1 January 2008.

His business plan shows that his monthly profits are likely to be as follows.

January 2008 to June 2008 (inclusive)	£800	a month
July 2008 to December 2008 (inclusive)	£1,200	a month
Thereafter	£2,000	a month

Mr Cobbler is considering two alternative accounting dates, 31 March and 30 April, in each case commencing with a period ending in 2008.

Required

Show the taxable trading profits which will arise for each of the first four tax years under each of the two alternative accounting dates, and recommend an accounting date. **(15 marks)**

13 Miss Farrington **27 mins**

Miss Farrington started to trade as a baker on 1 January 2007 and made up her first accounts to 30 April 2008. Adjusted profits before capital allowances are as follows.

	£
Period to 30 April 2008	20,710
Year to 30 April 2009	14,916

Miss Farrington incurred the following expenditure on plant and machinery.

Date	*Item*	£
4.1.07	General plant	2,280
1.3.07	Second-hand oven acquired from Miss Farrington's father	1,200
25.3.07	Delivery van	1,800
15.4.07	Typewriter	340
15.5.07	Car for Miss Farrington	6,600
30.1.09	General plant	1,000
30.4.09	Computer	1,945

In addition Miss Farrington brought into the business on 1 January 2007 a desk and other office furniture. The agreed value was £940.

The agreed private use of the car is 35%. Miss Farrington's business is a small enterprise for capital allowance purposes. Assume FYA for small enterprises from 6.4.08 is 40%.

Required

Calculate the taxable profits for the first four tax years and the overlap profits carried forward. **(15 marks)**

14 Langland **27 mins**

Langland started to trade on 1 February 2004 and decided to retire on 31 October 2009. His accounts show the following profits as adjusted for income tax purposes.

	£
P/e 30 April 2005	12,000
Y/e 30 April 2006	6,000
Y/e 30 April 2007	8,000
Y/e 30 April 2008	10,000
Y/e 30 April 2009	6,000
P/e 31 October 2009	4,000

Required

Calculate the trading assessments for all tax years in question. **(15 marks)**

15 Morgan **27 mins**

Morgan started to trade on 6 April 2004. His business has the following results.

Year ending 5 April		£
2005	Profit	12,000
2006	Profit	16,000
2007	Profit	18,000
2008 (projected)	Profit	15,000
2009 (projected)	Loss	(32,000)

It is expected that the business will show healthy profits thereafter. In addition to his business Morgan has gross investment income of £8,000 a year.

Required

(a) Outline the ways in which Morgan could obtain relief for his loss. **(5 marks)**

(b) Prepare a statement showing how the loss would be relieved assuming that relief were to be claimed as soon as possible. Comment on whether this is likely to be the best relief **(5 marks)**

(c) Describe briefly how the situation would alter if Morgan were to cease trading on 5 April 2009. **(5 marks)**

(Total = 15 marks)

16 Adam, Bert and Charlie **27 mins**

Adam, Bert and Charlie started in partnership as secondhand car dealers on 6 April 2004, sharing profits in the ratio 2:2:1, after charging annual salaries of £15,000, £12,000 and £10,000 respectively.

On 5 July 2005 Adam retired and Bert and Charlie continue, taking the same salaries as before, but dividing the balance of the profits in the ratio 3:2.

On 6 May 2007 Donald is admitted as a partner on the terms that he received a salary of £18,000 a year, that the salaries of Bert and Charlie should be increased to £18,000 a year each and that of the balance of the profits, Donald should take one tenth, Bert six tenths and Charlie three tenths.

The trade profits of the partnership as adjusted for tax purposes are as follows.

Year ending 5 April	*Profits*
	£
2005	102,000
2006	208,000
2007	126,000
2008	180,000

Required

Show the taxable trade profits for each partner for 2004/05 to 2007/08 inclusive. **(15 marks)**

17 Partnerships **27 mins**

(a) *Required*

Briefly explain the basis by which partners are assessed in respect of their share of a partnership's taxable trading profit. **(3 marks)**

(b) Anne and Betty have been in partnership since 1 January 2001 sharing profits equally. On 30 June 2007 Betty resigned as a partner, and was replaced on 1 July 2007 by Chloe. Profit continued to be shared equally. The partnership's taxable trading profits are as follows:

	£
Year ended 31 December 2007	60,000
Year ended 31 December 2008	72,000

As at 6 April 2007 Anne and Betty each have unrelieved overlap profits of £3,000.

Required

Calculate the taxable trading profits of Anne, Betty and Chloe for 2007/08. **(6 marks)**

(c) Daniel and Edward have been in partnership since 6 April 2000, making up accounts to 5 April. On 31 December 2007 Edward resigned as a partner, and was replaced on 1 January 2008 by Frank. For 2007/08 the partnership made a trading loss of £40,000, and this has been allocated between the partners as follows.

	£
Daniel	20,000
Edward	15,000
Frank	5,000

Each of the partners has investment income. None of them have any capital gains.

Required

State the possible ways in which Daniel, Edward and Frank can relieve their trading losses for 2007/08. **(6 marks)**

(Total = 15 marks)

18 Denise **18 mins**

Denise started business on 6 April 2007 as a designer dressmaker, having been a housewife for many years. Her trading profits in her first year of trading were £115,000.

Required

(a) Outline briefly what payments Denise could make into a personal pension scheme and the tax relief such payments would receive. **(7 marks)**

(b) Show the Class 2 and Class 4 contributions payable by Denise in 2007/08. **(3 marks)**

Assume 2007/08 tax rates and allowances apply throughout.

(Total = 10 marks)

19 Sasha Shah **27 mins**

Sasha Shah is a computer programmer. Until 5 April 2007 she was employed by Net Computers plc, but since then has worked independently from home. Sasha's income for the year ended 5 April 2008 is £60,000. All of this relates to work done for Net Computers plc. Her expenditure for the year ended 5 April 2008 is as follows:

(1) The business proportion of light, heat and telephone for Sasha's home is £600.

(2) Computer equipment was purchased on 6 April 2007 for £8,000.

(3) A motor car was purchased on 6 April 2007 for £10,000. Motor expenses for the year ended 5 April 2007 amount to £3,500, of which 40% relate to journeys between home and the premises of Net Computers plc. The other 60% relate to private mileage.

Required

(a) List eight factors that will indicate that a worker should be treated as an employee rather than as self-employed. **(4 marks)**

(b) (i) Calculate the amount of taxable trading profits if Sasha is treated as self-employed during 2007/08.

(ii) Calculate the amount of Sasha's taxable earnings if she is treated as an employee during 2007/08. **(7 marks)**

(c) (i) Calculate Sasha's liability to Class 2 and Class 4 NIC if she is treated as self-employed during 2007/08.

(ii) Calculate Sasha's liability to Class 1 NIC if she is treated as an employee during 2007/08. **(4 marks)**

(Total = 15 marks)

20 Andrea **20 mins**

Andrea made the following disposals in 2007/08:

	Gain £	*Loss* £
Non business asset (1)		
Acquired June 2004: disposal December 2007	16,000	
Non business asset (2)		
Acquired August 2005: disposal January 2008		6,000
Business asset		
Acquired July 1990: disposal March 2008	35,000	

Andrea had unrelieved losses of £5,000 to 5 April 2007. Her taxable income for 2007/08 was £32,500.

Required

Calculate Andrea's CGT liability for 2007/08. **(11 marks)**

21 Peter Robinson **18 mins**

Peter Robinson made the following disposals of non-business assets during the tax year 2007/08.

30 April 2007

Investment property for £150,000 less costs of disposal £1,280. Acquired December 1995 for £80,000. The indexation allowance available on the sale was £6,320.

27 June 2007

Part of a plot of land. The proceeds of sale were £35,000. The costs of disposal were £700. The original cost of the land on 15 April 2004 was £54,000. The remainder of the land is worth £70,000.

1 September 2007

A vase which was destroyed. It cost £12,000 on 30 June 2002. Compensation of £20,000 was received on 30 September 2007. John bought a new vase as a replacement for £17,000 on 21 December 2007.

Required

Calculate Peter's capital gains tax payable for the year 2007/08. Peter's taxable income (after personal allowances) for income tax purposes was £30,000. **(10 marks)**

22 John Harley **18 mins**

(a) John Harley purchased a property in England on 1 August 1986 for £40,000 and lived in it until 31 May 1987 when he moved overseas to take up an offer of employment. He returned to the UK on 1 August 1991 and took employment in Scotland until 31 October 1997. During these periods he lived in rented accommodation. On 1 November 1997 he moved back into his own house until he moved out permanently on 30 June 2000. The house was then put up for sale and was finally sold on 30 November 2007 for £120,000. At all times when John was not in the house it remained empty.

Required

Prepare a schedule of periods of exemption and non-exemption, together with the reasons where applicable. **(5 marks)**

(b) Elsie Phillips made the following disposals of non-business assets during the tax year 2007/08.

2 June 2007

An oil painting for £5,000 (net of £400 commission). She had purchased this in 1994 at a cost of £11,500.

1 February 2008

A crystal chandelier for £7,500. He had purchased this on 11 January 2006 for £4,000.

Required

Calculate Elsie's chargeable gains or allowable losses on these two transactions. **(5 marks)**

(Total = 10 marks)

23 The White family **27 mins**

(a) Mr White is a sole trader. He bought a factory for use in his trade on 10 July 2004 for £150,000.

On 1 December 2007, Mr White gave the factory to his son, Gary. The market value of the factory at that time was £260,000. Gary rented out the factory to a quoted company.

Required

Show the chargeable gains (if any) for Mr White for 2007/08 assuming that any claims to defer gains are made and taking account of taper relief. **(5 marks)**

(b) Gary sells the factory to a developer on 1 March 2009 for £320,000.

Required

Compute the gain on the sale for Gary and explain the taper relief situation. **(6 marks)**

(c) Mrs White is also a sole trader. She acquired a freehold shop for use in the business in May 2002 for £40,000 and sold it in August 2007 for £80,000.

Mrs White is considering buying a new shop. She has located two possible shops. One is a small freehold shop which would cost £72,000. The other is a larger leasehold shop with a lease of 55 years. The cost of the lease would be £90,000.

Required

Explain the tax consequences of acquiring each of the shops. **(9 marks)**

(Total = 20 marks)

24 Alice **9 mins**

Alice decided to incorporate her sole trader business on 9 January 2008. She started this business in 1992. All of the business assets were transferred to the new company. The consideration consisted of 200,000 £1 ordinary shares valued at £200,000 and £100,000 in cash. The transfer of the business assets resulted in total indexed gains of £120,000.

Required

Calculate the chargeable gain arising on the transfer and the base cost of the shares for the future.

(5 marks)

25 Mary and Robert Green **27 mins**

(a) Mary Green made the following purchases of ordinary shares in Read plc, a quoted company.

Date	*Number*	*Cost*
		£
15 May 2006	1,800	1,900
1 March 2007	1,000	1,260

On 12 July 2007 there was a 1 for 1 bonus issue.

On 30 September 2007 she sold 3,200 of the shares for £14,000.

(b) On 26 May 2007 Robert Green sold 1,450 quoted ordinary shares in Greengage Supermarkets plc for £10,150. His previous dealings in these shares had been as follows.

15 April 1985	Purchased 900 shares for £3,408. Indexed cost 5.4.98 £5,845
11 November 2006	Purchased 1,000 shares for £6,000

None of the shares are business assets for taper relief purposes.

Required

(a) Compute the chargeable gain or allowable loss on the sale of Mary's shares. **(8 marks)**
(b) Compute the chargeable gain on Robert's disposal of his shares. **(7 marks)**

(Total = 15 marks)

26 Tim **15 mins**

Tim is a medical consultant. His total tax liability for 2006/07 was £16,800. Of this £7,200 was paid under the PAYE system, £800 was withheld at source from bank interest and £200 was suffered on dividends received during the year.

Tim's total tax liability for 2007/08 was £22,000. £7,100 of this was paid under PAYE system, £900 was withheld at source from bank interest and there was a £250 tax credit on dividends.

Tim did not make any claim in respect of his payments on account for 2007/08. HM Revenue and Customs issued a 2007/08 tax return to Tim on 5 May 2008.

Required

State what payments Tim was required to make in respect of his 2007/08 tax liability and the due dates for the payment of these amounts. **(8 marks)**

27 Lai Chan **45 mins**

Until 31 December 2007 Lai Chan was employed by Put-it-Right plc as a management consultant. The following information relates to the period of employment from 6 April to 31 December 2007.

(1) Lai was paid a gross salary of £3,250 per month.

(2) She contributed 6% of her gross salary into Put-it-right plc's registered occupational pension scheme. The company contributed a further 6%.

(3) Put-it-Right plc provided Lai with a motor car with a list price of £26,400. The motor car's CO_2 emissions were 190g/km. Lai paid Put-it-Right plc £130 per month for the use of the motor car.

Put-it-Right plc paid for the petrol in respect of all the mileage done by Lai during 2007/08. She paid the company £30 per month towards the cost of her private petrol.

The motor car was returned to Put-it-Right plc on 31 December 2007.

(4) Put-it-Right plc provided Lai with an interest free loan of £30,000 on 1 January 2004. She repaid £20,000 of the loan on 30 June 2007 with the balance of £10,000 being repaid on 31 December 2007.

On 1 January 2008 Lai commenced in self-employment running a music recording studio. The following information relates to the period of self-employment from 1 January to 5 April 2008.

(1) The trading profit for the period 1 January to 5 April 2008 is £19,900. This figure is *before* taking account of capital allowances.

(2) Lai purchased the following assets:

1 January 2008	Recording equipment	£5,952
15 January 2008	Motor car	£14,800
20 February 2008	Motor car	£10,400
4 March 2008	Recording equipment	£1,664

The motor car purchased on 15 January 2008 for £14,800 is used by Lai, and 40% of the mileage is for private purposes. The motor car purchased on 20 February 2008 for £10,400 is used by an employee, and 10% of the mileage is for private purposes.

The recording equipment purchased on 4 March 2008 for £2,080 is to be treated as a short-life asset.

Lai's business meets the definition of small enterprise for FYA purposes.

(3) Since becoming self-employed Lai has paid £390 (net) per month into a personal pension scheme. Payments are made on the 20th of each month.

Required

(a) Calculate Lai's income tax liability for 2007/08. **(20 marks)**

(b) Briefly explain how Lai's income tax liability for 2007/08 will be paid to the HM Revenue and Customs. **(5 marks)**

(Total = 25 marks)

28 P Ltd **18 mins**

P Ltd starts to let out property on 1 July 2007. The company has the following transactions.

(a) On 1 July 2007, it lets an office block which it has owned for several years. The tenant is required to pay an initial premium of £20,000 for a 30 year lease, and then to pay annual rent of £4,000, quarterly in advance. The office is let unfurnished.

(b) On 1 October 2007 it buys a badly dilapidated office block for £37,000. During October, it spends £8,000 on making the office block useable. It lets it for £600 a month from 1 November 2007, but the tenant leaves on 31 January 2008. A new tenant moves in on 1 March 2008, paying £2,100 a quarter in arrears. Water rates are £390 a year, payable by P Ltd. P Ltd also pays buildings insurance of £440 for the period from 1 October 2007 to 31 August 2008. P Ltd financed the purchase (but not the repairs) with a bank loan at 7% interest. This office is also let unfurnished.

Required

Compute P Ltd's property business income for the year to 31 March 2008. **(10 marks)**

29 E Ltd **9 mins**

E Ltd disposed of assets as follows.

(a) On 1 January 2007 it sold a car which had been used by a company director at a loss of £10,700.
(b) On 28 February 2007 it sold some shares at a loss of £16,400.
(c) On 1 May 2007 it sold some shares and realised a gain of £17,700.
(d) On 1 October 2007 it sold some shares at a loss of £6,000.
(e) On 1 December 2007 it sold a picture to a collector for £50,000, making a gain of £3,000.

Required

What loss, if any, is available to be carried forward at the end of its year ended 31 March 2008? **(5 marks)**

30 Hardup Ltd **27 mins**

Hardup Ltd made the following disposals in the year ended 31 March 2008.

(a) On 31 May 2007 it sold an office block for £120,000. The company had bought the offices for £65,000 on 1 July 1992. The company had invested £100,000 in another office block on 1 May 2006.

(b) On 18 June 2007 it sold a plot of land for £69,000. It had bought it for £20,000 on 1 April 1985 and had spent £4,000 on defending its title to the land in July 1989.

(c) On 25 June 2007 the company exchanged contracts for the sale of a workshop for £173,000. Completion took place on 24 July 2007. It had bought the workshop for £65,000 on 16 October 1987.

Required

Compute Hardup Ltd's chargeable gains for the year end 31 March 2008. **(15 marks)**

Assume retail prices index

May 2007 = 205.2	July 1992 = 138.8
June 2007 = 205.9	July 1989 = 115.5
July 2007 = 206.6	October 1987 = 102.9
	April 1985 = 94.78

31 Tree Ltd **27 mins**

(a) Tree Ltd, a company with no associated companies, had the following results for the twelve months to 31 March 2008:

	£
Trading profits	180,000
Chargeable gain	105,000
Gift aid donation	27,000
Bank interest	36,000
Dividend received	29,700

The bank interest accrued evenly over the period.

Required

Compute the corporation tax liability in respect of the profits arising in the twelve months to 31 March 2008. **(7 marks)**

(b) Dealers plc had profits chargeable to corporation tax of £420,000 for its six month accounting period ended 31 March 2008. No dividends were received by the company during the year.

Required

Compute Dealers plc's corporation tax liability for the period. **(3 marks)**

(c) Springer Ltd had profits chargeable to corporation tax of £600,000 in the year to 31 December 2007. It received a dividend of £27,000 on 1 September 2007.

Required

Calculate Springer Ltd's corporation tax liability for the year. **(5 marks)**

(Total = 15 marks)

32 Righteous plc **18 mins**

Righteous plc used to make its accounts up to 31 December. A decision has been made to change its year end to 31 May. The following information relates to the period of account from 1 January 2006 to 31 May 2007.

	£
Trading profits	500,000
Bank interest receivable	
30.6.06	15,000
31.12.06	6,000
31.5.07	2,500
30.6.07	7,000
Capital gain on property sold on	
1 May 2007	5,000
Gift Aid donations paid	
28.2.06	15,000
31.8.06	15,000
28.2.07	40,000
31.8.07	40,000

No capital allowances are claimed.

Required

Calculate the corporation tax liability. **(10 marks)**

33 Ferraro Ltd

27 mins

Ferraro Ltd has the following results.

	y/e 31.12.04	*y/e 31.12.05*	*9m to 30.9.06*	*y/e 30.9.07*
	£	£	£	£
Trading profit (loss)	34,480	6,200	4,320	(100,000)
Bank deposit interest accrued	200	80	240	260
Rents receivable	1,200	1,420	1,440	1,600
Capital gain			12,680	
Allowable capital loss	5,000			9,423
Gift aid donation paid (gross)	1,000	0	1,000	1,500

Required

Compute all profits chargeable to corporation tax, claiming loss reliefs as early as possible. State any amounts carried forward as at 30 September 2007. **(15 marks)**

34 P Ltd

27 mins

P Ltd owns the following holdings in ordinary shares in other companies, which are all UK resident.

Q Ltd	83%
R Ltd	77%
S Ltd	67%
M Ltd	80%
T Ltd	70%

In each case, the conditions for claiming group relief, where appropriate, are satisfied.

The following are the results of the above companies for the year ended 31 March 2008.

	M Ltd	*P Ltd*	*Q Ltd*	*R Ltd*	*S Ltd*	*T Ltd*
	£	£	£	£	£	£
Income						
Trading profit	20,000	0	64,000	260,000	0	70,000
Trading loss	0	226,000	0	0	8,000	0
Property business income	0	6,000	4,000	0	0	0
Charges paid						
Gift aid donation	4,000	4,500	2,000	5,000	0	0

Required

(a) Compute the corporation tax payable for the above accounting period by each of the above companies, assuming group relief is claimed, where appropriate, in the most efficient manner.

(b) Advise the board of P Ltd of the advantages of increasing its holding in S Ltd, a company likely to sustain trading losses for the next two years before becoming profitable. P Ltd itself is likely only to break even in the next few years.

(15 marks)

35 Apple Ltd **27 mins**

Apple Ltd owns 100% of the ordinary share capital of Banana Ltd and Cherry Ltd. The results of each company for the year ended 31 March 2008 are as follows:

	Apple Ltd	*Banana Ltd*	*Cherry Ltd*
	£	£	£
Tax adjusted trading profit/(loss)	(125,000)	650,000	130,000
Capital gain/(loss)	188,000	(8,000)	–

Apple Ltd's capital gain arose from the sale of a freehold warehouse on 15 April 2007 for £418,000. Cherry Ltd purchased a freehold office building for £290,000 on 10 January 2008.

Required

(a) Explain the group relationship that must exist in order that group relief can be claimed. **(3 marks)**

(b) Explain how group relief should be allocated between the respective claimant companies in order to maximise the potential benefit obtained from the relief. **(4 marks)**

(c) Assuming that reliefs are claimed in the most favourable manner, calculate the corporation tax liabilities of Apple Ltd, Banana Ltd and Cherry Ltd for the year ended 31 March 2008. **(8 marks)**

(Total = 15 marks)

36 M Ltd **27 mins**

M Ltd is a UK resident company which owns controlling interests in two other UK resident companies and in two non-resident companies.

It also has the following interests in three non-resident companies:

Company	*Shareholding*	*Rate of Withholding tax*	*After tax Profits*	*Foreign tax paid*
	%	%	£	£
A Inc	6	15	400,000	80,000
B P G	8	25	900,000	300,000
C S A	12	20	800,000	200,000

M Ltd had experienced a prolonged period of poor trading and, as a result of losses brought forward from earlier years, its chargeable trading profits for the year ended 31 March 2008 are only £20,000.

During the year, a gift aid donation of £75,000 had been paid to charity and this had been added back in arriving at the adjusted taxable trading profits.

The only other income received by M Ltd during the year consisted of dividends from the above three companies, each of which had substantial undistributed profits. The figures (net of withholding tax) were:

	£	*Date received*
A Inc	170,000	1.6.07
B PG	150,000	10.9.07
C SA	120,000	31.12.07

Required

Compute the corporation tax payable by M Ltd in respect of the year ended 31 March 2008. Your answer should show clearly your treatment of the gift aid payment and of the foreign taxes suffered. You should explain why you are dealing with items in a particular way and you should use a columnar layout.

(15 marks)

37 Hogg Ltd **9 mins**

(a) Hogg Ltd prepares accounts for the year to 31 December 2007. Its profits chargeable to corporation tax for the year will be £1,750,000. The company has always paid corporation tax at the full rate.

Required

State the amounts and due dates for the payment of corporation tax by Hogg Ltd in respect of the year to 31 December 2007. **(3 marks)**

(b) State the due date for submission of Hogg Ltd's corporation tax return assuming a notice to file the return is issued on:

(i) 12 March 2008

(ii) 12 November 2008 **(2 marks)**

(Total = 5 marks)

38 Newcomer Ltd and Au Revoir Ltd **18 mins**

(a) Newcomer Ltd commenced trading on 1 October 2007. Its forecast sales are as follows.

		£
2007	October	11,500
	November	14,200
	December	21,400
2008	January	17,300
	February	14,700
	March	15,200

The company's sales are all standard rated, and the above figures are exclusive of VAT.

Required

Explain when Newcomer Ltd will be required to compulsorily register for VAT. **(6 marks)**

(b) Au Revoir Ltd has been registered for VAT since 1996, and its sales are all standard rated. The company has recently seen a downturn in its business activities, and sales for the years ended 31 October 2007 and 2008 are forecast to be £60,000 and £57,500 respectively. Both of these figures are exclusive of VAT.

Required

Explain why Au Revoir Ltd will be permitted to voluntarily deregister for VAT, and from what date deregistration will be effective. **(4 marks)**

(Total = 10 marks)

39 Justin — 18 mins

Justin has the following transactions in the quarter ended 30 September 2007. All amounts exclude any VAT unless otherwise stated.

	£
Purchases (all standard rated)	
Furniture for resale	275,000
Computer for use in the business	2,400
Restaurant bills: entertaining customers	1,900
Petrol for cars owned by Justin and used only by his employees	2,800
Sales	
Furniture (standard rated)	490,000
Books on interior design (zero rated)	2,400

Only one employee's car has petrol for private motoring provided by Justin (the appropriate fuel scale charge is £426 inclusive of VAT).

Required

Calculate the amount of VAT which Justin must pay to HM Revenue and Customs for the quarter.

(10 marks)

40 Ongoing Ltd — 18 mins

Ongoing Ltd is registered for VAT, and its sales and purchases are all standard rated. The following information relates to the company's VAT return for the quarter ended 30 September 2007:

(1) Standard rated sales amounted to £120,000. Ongoing Ltd offers its customers a 5% discount for prompt payment, and this discount is taken by half of the customers.

(2) Standard rated purchases and expenses amounted to £35,640. This figure includes £480 for entertaining customers.

(3) On 15 September 2007 the company wrote off impairment losses (bad debts) of £2,000 and £840 in respect of invoices due for payment on 10 February and 5 May 2007 respectively.

(4) On 30 September 2007 the company purchased a motor car at a cost of £16,450 for the use of a salesperson, and machinery at a cost of £21,150. Both these figures are inclusive of VAT. The motor car is used for both business and private mileage.

Unless stated otherwise, all of the above figures are exclusive of VAT. Ongoing Ltd does not operate the cash accounting scheme.

Required

Calculate the amount of VAT payable by Ongoing Ltd for the quarter ended 30 September 2007.

(10 marks)

41 Industrial Ltd

54 mins

Industrial Ltd is a UK resident company that manufactures furniture. The company's results for the year ended 31 March 2008 are summarised as follows:

	£
Trading profit (as adjusted for taxation but before taking account of capital allowances)	1,677,710
Income from property (note 1)	110,400
Bank interest received (note 2)	12,500
Loan interest received (note 3)	36,000
Profit on disposal of quoted shares (note 4)	90,622
Donation to charity (note 5)	(1,500)

Note 1 – Income from property

Since 1 January 2008 Industrial Ltd has leased an office building that is surplus to requirements. On that date the company received a premium of £80,000 for the grant of a ten-year lease, and the annual rent of £30,400 which is payable in advance.

Note 2 – Bank interest received

The bank interest was received on 31 March 2008. The bank deposits are held for non-trading purposes. There were no accruals of bank interest at the beginning or end of the year.

Note 3 – Loan interest received

The loan interest was received on 31 March 2008. The loan was made for non-trading purposes to another UK company. There were no accruals of loan interest at the beginning or end of the year.

Note 4 – Profit on disposal of quoted shares

The profit on disposal of quoted shares is in respect of a shareholding that was sold on 15 January 2008 for £230,906. The shareholding was purchased on 1 April 2003 for £135,800. The indexation allowance from April 2003 to January 2008 is £22,184.

At 1 April 2007 Industrial Ltd had unused capital losses brought forward of £10,800.

Note 5 – Donation to charity

The donation to charity was the amount paid under the gift aid scheme.

Note 6 – Industrial building

Industrial Ltd has a new factory constructed at a cost of £400,000 that was brought into use on 30 September 2007.

	£
Land	80,000
Levelling the land	9,200
Architects fees	24,300
Heating system	12,800
Fire alarm system	7,200
Strengthened concrete floor to support machinery	16,500
General offices	62,500
Factory	187,500
	400,000

Note 7 – Plant and machinery

On 1 April 2007 the tax written down values of plant and machinery were as follows:

	£
General pool	84,600
Expensive motor car	15,400

The expensive motor car was sold on 31 August 2007 for £19,600.

In addition to any items of plant and machinery included in the cost of the industrial building (see note 6), the following assets were purchased during the year ended 31 March 2008.

		£
15 June 2007	Computer	3,400
15 August 2007	Motor car	17,200
12 October 2007	Lorry	32,000

Industrial Ltd is a medium-sized company as defined by the Companies Acts.

Note 8 – Other information

Industrial Ltd has no associated companies. For the year ended 31 March 2007 Industrial Ltd had profits chargeable to corporation tax of £1,650,000.

Required

(a) Calculate the corporation tax payable by Industrial Ltd for the year ended 31 March 2008. **(25 marks)**

(b) (i) Explain why Industrial Ltd is required to make quarterly instalment payments in respect of its corporation tax liability for the year ended 31 March 2008. **(2 marks)**

(ii) State the relevant due dates for payment of the corporation tax liability. **(3 marks)**

(Total = 30 marks)

Approaching the answer

You should read through the requirement before working through and annotating the question as we have so that you know what you are looking for.

Industrial Ltd is a UK resident company that manufactures furniture. The company's results for the year ended 31 March 2008 are summarised as follows:

ALL in FY 07

	£
Trading profit (as adjusted for taxation but before taking account of capital allowances)	1,677,710
Income from property (note 1)	110,400
Bank interest received (note 2)	12,500
Loan interest received (note 3)	36,000
Profit on disposal of quoted shares (note 4)	90,622
Donation to charity (note 5)	(1,500)

Note 1 – Income from property

Since 1 January 2008 Industrial Ltd has leased an office building that is surplus to requirements. On that date the company received a premium of £80,000 for the grant of a ten-year lease, and the annual rent of £30,400 which is payable in advance.

Prorate × $^{3}/_{12}$

Property income charge on short leases

Note 2 – Bank interest received

The bank interest was received on 31 March 2008. The bank deposits are held for non-trading purposes.

There were no accruals of bank interest at the beginning or end of the year.

Investment income received

Note 3 – Loan interest received

The loan interest was received on 31 March 2008. The loan was made for non-trading purposes to another UK company. There were no accruals of loan interest at the beginning or end of the year.

Received gross

Also investment income

Note 4 – Profit on disposal of quoted shares

The profit on disposal of quoted shares is in respect of a 2% shareholding that was sold on 15 January 2008 for £230,906. The shareholding was purchased on 1 April 2003 for £135,800. The indexation allowance from April 2003 to January 2008 is £22,184.

Set off capital loss b/f against gain

At 1 April 2007 Industrial Ltd had unused capital losses brought forward of £10,800.

Note 5 – Donation to charity

The donation to charity was the amount paid under the gift aid scheme.

Deduction

Note 6 – Industrial building

Industrial Ltd has a new factory constructed at a cost of £400,000 that was brought into use on 30 September 2007.

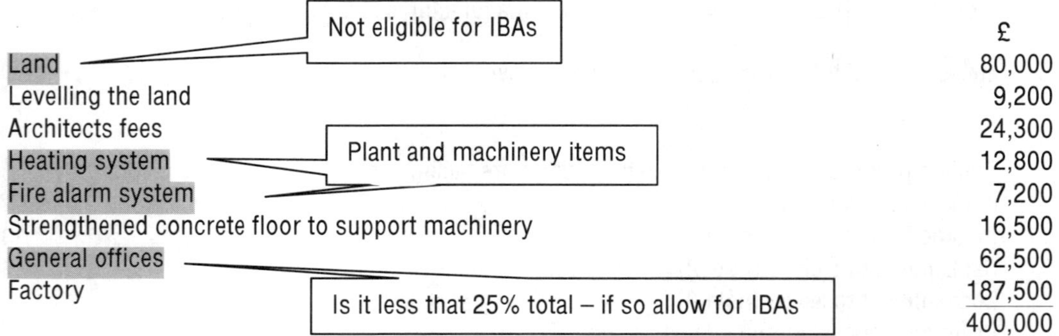

	£
Land	80,000
Levelling the land	9,200
Architects fees	24,300
Heating system	12,800
Fire alarm system	7,200
Strengthened concrete floor to support machinery	16,500
General offices	62,500
Factory	187,500
	400,000

Note 7 – Plant and machinery

On 1 April 2007 the tax written down values of plant and machinery were as follows:

	£
General pool	84,600
Expensive motor car	15,400

The expensive motor car was sold on 31 August 2007 for £19,600

Balancing charge

In addition to any items of plant and machinery included in the cost of the industrial building (see note 6), the following assets were purchased during the year ended 31 March 2008.

		£
15 June 2007	Computer	3,400
15 August 2007	Motor car	17,200
12 October 2007	Lorry	32,000

Industrial Ltd is a medium-sized company as defined by the Companies Acts.

40% FYA available

Note 8 – Other information

Industrial Ltd has no associated companies. For the year ended 31 March 2007 Industrial Ltd had profits chargeable to corporation tax of £1,650,000.

Paid CT at full rate

Required

(a) Calculate the corporation tax payable by Industrial Ltd for the year ended 31 March 2008. **(25 marks)**

(b) (i) Explain why Industrial Ltd is required to make quarterly instalment payments in respect of its corporation tax liability for the year ended 31 March 2008. **(2 marks)**

(ii) State the relevant due dates for payment of the corporation tax liability. **(3 marks)**

Instalment dates

(Total = 30 marks)

Answer plan

Then organise the things you have noticed and your points arising into a coherent answer plan. Work through the items in a logical order and tick them off once you have dealt with them.

(a) Set out proforma on first page with trading profit at top.
Deduct capital allowances to give the taxable trading profit.
Add other sources of income – Property business income, investment income.
Add gains (after losses).
Deduct gift aid payment to give PCTCT.
Calculate tax.

Workings

IBAs

Not on land, heating system, fire alarm system.
Check % on general offices – allowable if less than 25%.

P&M

Remember to add in heating system, fire alarm system – 40% FYAs.
Lorry qualifies for 40% FYAs also.
40% FYA on computer.

Property business income

Premium on short lease.
Add in rental.

Gains

Calculate gain after indexation allowance.
Deduct loss b/f.

(b) (i) Company is large this year and last.

(ii) Instalments required. Payable every 3 months starting in 7th month of accounting period on 14th day of the month.

42 Susan White **36 mins**

Susan White disposed of the following assets during 2007/08.

1 On 15 July 2007 Susan sold 20,000 £1 ordinary shares in Red Ltd for £55,000. Susan bought 25,000 shares in the company on 2 June 2006 for £37,500. She bought a further 5,000 shares on 18 July 2007 for £15,000.

2 On 25 August 2007 Susan sold 50,000 £1 ordinary shares in Blue Ltd to her son for £70,000. The market value of the shares on this date was £200,000. The shareholding was purchased on 15 April 1985 for £18,000. Take the indexation allowance from April 1985 to April 1998 to be £12,800. Susan and her son are to elect to hold over the gain as a gift of a business asset.

Red Ltd and Blue Ltd are unquoted trading companies. Susan's shareholding in each company qualifies as a business asset for the purposes of CGT taper relief.

3 On 12 October 2007 Susan sold a vintage Mercedes car for £27,000 that had been left to her by her grandfather on his death on 1 June 2003 when the car was worth £23,000.

4 On 23 February 2008 Susan sold the following antiques: (i) a table for £12,000 which she had purchased for £5,500 in May 2001, (ii) a war medal for £2,500 that she had bought for £8,735 on 5 August 2000, and (iii) a painting for £2,750 that she had purchased on 14 September 2003 for £1,500.

Required

(a) Describe the types of shareholding that qualify as a business asset for the purposes of CGT taper relief. **(4 marks)**

(b) Calculate the chargeable gains arising from Susan's disposals during 2007/08. You should ignore the annual exemption. **(16 marks)**

(Total = 20 marks)

Approaching the answer

You should read through the requirement before working through and annotating the question as we have so that you know what you are looking for.

Susan White disposed of the following assets during 2007/08.

[Matching rules for shares]

1 On 15 July 2007 Susan sold 20,000 £1 ordinary shares in Red Ltd for £55,000. Susan bought 25,000 shares in the company on 2 June 2006 for £37,500. She bought a further 5,000 shares on 18 July 2007 for £15,000.

[Post 5/4/98 acquisition]

[Next 30 days post sale acquisition]

Sale at undervalue

2 On 25 August 2007 Susan sold 50,000 £1 ordinary shares in Blue Ltd to her son for £70,000. The market value of the shares on this date was £200,000. The shareholding was purchased on 15 April 1985 for £18,000. Take the indexation allowance from April 1985 to April 1998 to be £12,800.

Susan and her son are to elect to hold over the gain as a gift of a business asset.

Gift relief – how does it work?

Red Ltd and Blue Ltd are unquoted trading companies. Susan's shareholding in each company qualifies as a business asset for the purposes of CGT taper relief.

Taper relief years?

All cars are exempt

3 On 12 October 2007 Susan sold a vintage Mercedes car for £27,000 that had been left to her by her grandfather on his death on 1 June 2003 when the car was worth £23,000.

4 On 23 February 2008 Susan sold the following antiques: (i) a table for £12,000 which she had purchased for £5,500 in May 2001, (ii) a war medal for £2,500 that she had bought for £8,735 on 5 August 2000, and (iii) a painting for £2,750 that she had purchased on 14 September 2003 for £1,500.

Watch for chattels costing or sold for < £6,000

Required

(a) Describe the types of shareholding that qualify as a business asset for the purposes of CGT taper relief. **(4 marks)**

Brief description only for 4 marks

(b) Calculate the capital gains arising from Susan's disposal during 2007/08. You should ignore the annual exemption. **(11 marks)**

Make sure you do!

(Total = 15 marks)

Answer plan

Then organise the things you have noticed and your points arising into a coherent answer plan. Not all the points you have noticed will go into your answer – you should spend a few minutes thinking them through and prioritising them.

(a) Trading co. shares:

(1) unquoted – all
(2) director/employee
(3) holds 5 % votes.

Non trading co. shares:

Only employees holding 10% or less of votes.

(b) **Red Ltd shares**

Matching rules for individuals:

(1) same day
(2) next 30 days
(3) post 5.4.98.

Apportion cost/proceeds as necessary.

Taper relief periods – none for next 30 days
– 1 year for post 5/4/98.

Blue Ltd shares

Gain based on MV not cash.

'Cash' gain (ie proceeds over cost (no IA)) remains in charge. Taper relief applies from 6.4.98 – maximum taper after two years ownership for business assets. Rest can be held over to son – no taper relief.

Mercedes

Cars are not chargeable assets ∴ exempt

Antiques

Chattels rules apply

War medals acquired by purchase – not exempt assets

Summary of gains.

Set losses off v. gains with least taper relief.

Exam answer bank

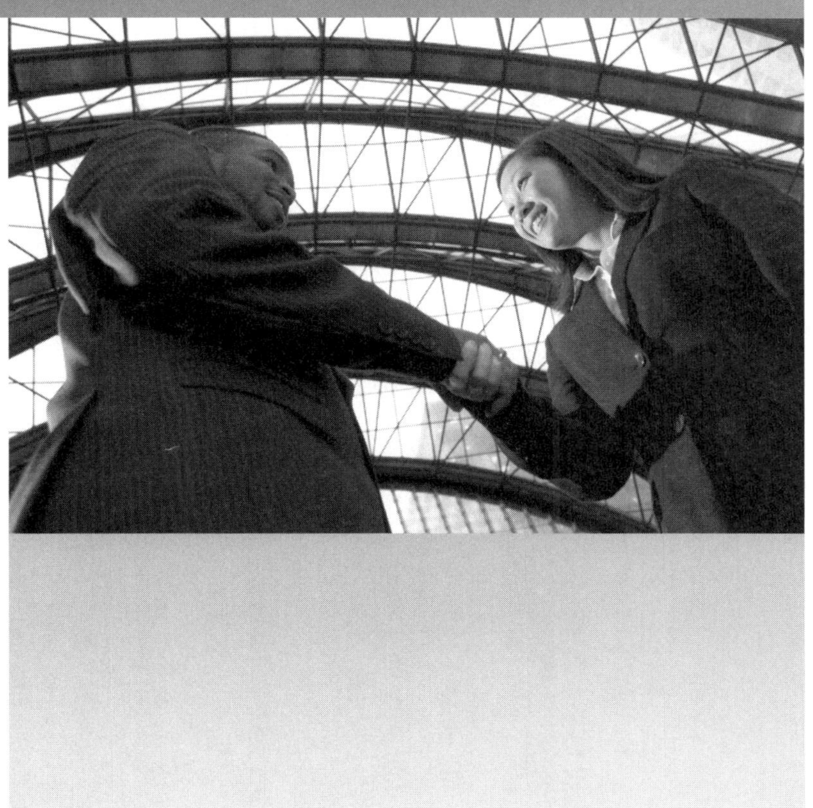

1 Mary

Tutorial note. If you get into the habit of setting up your income tax computations with three columns like this you should have a good chance of getting them right. Remember that savings income in the basic rate band is taxed at 20%, *not* 22%. Dividend income within the basic rate band is taxed at 10%.

	Non-savings income	*Savings income*	*Dividend income*	*Total*
	£	£	£	£
Trading income	14,000			
Building society interest × 100/80		8,000		
Dividends × 100/90			2,000	
Total income	14,000	8,000	2,000	
Less interest paid	(2,500)	0	0	
Net income	11,500	8,000	2,000	21,500
Less personal allowance	(5,225)	0	0	
Taxable income	6,275	8,000	2,000	16,275

	£
Non-savings income	
Starting rate band £2,230 × 10%	223
Basic rate band £4,045 × 22%	890
Savings income	
£8,000 × 20%	1,600
Dividend income	
£2,000 × 10%	200
	2,913
Less tax credit on dividend income	(200)
tax suffered on building society interest	(1,600)
Balance of tax still to pay	1,113

	£	£
Profits received		14,000
Building society interest received		6,400
Dividend received		1,800
		22,200
Less interest paid on loan	2,500	
income tax to pay	1,113	
		(3,613)
Available to spend		18,587

2 Jane and Chris

Tutorial note. Remember that building society interest is received net of 20% tax. This tax credit is repayable (unlike the tax credit attaching to dividends)

Jane 2007/08

	Non-savings income	*Savings income*	*Total*
	£	£	£
Employment income	12,000		
BSI × $^{100}/_{80}$		1,000	
Net income	12,000	1,000	13,000
Less personal allowance	(5,225)	–	
Taxable income	6,775	1,000	7,775

Non-savings income	
	£
£2,230 × 10%	223
£4,545 × 22%	1,000
Savings income	
£1,000 × 20%	200
Tax liability	1,423
Less: tax suffered at source £(100 × 12) + £200	(1,400)
Tax payable	23

Chris 2007/08

	Non-savings income	*Savings income*	*Total*
	£	£	£
Employment income × 3/12	3,000		
BSI × $^{100}/_{80}$		600	
Net income	3,000	600	3,600
Less personal allowance	(3,000)	(600)	
Taxable income	0	0	0

	£
Tax liability	0
Less: tax suffered at source £(100 × 3) + £120	(420)
Tax repayable	(420)

3 Mr and Mrs Lowrie

Tutorial note. Mr Lowrie's dividend income is above the higher rate threshold, so it is taxed at 32.5%. Mrs Lowrie's dividends, however, fall below this threshold and are consequently taxed at 10%.

	Non-savings income	*Savings income*	*Dividend income*	*Total*
Mr Lowrie	£	£	£	£
Employment income	38,500			
Dividends × 100/90			1,211	
Bank deposit interest × 100/80		750		
Building society interest × 100/80		740		
Net income	38,500	1,490	1,211	41,201
Less personal allowance	(5,225)			
Taxable income	33,275	1,490	1,211	35,976

	£	£
Non savings income		
£2,230 × 10%		223
£31,045 × 22%		6,830
Savings income		
£1,325 × 20%		265
£165 × 40%		66
Dividend income		
£1,211 × 32.5%		394
		7,778
Less: tax credit on dividend	121	
tax suffered on savings income	298	
PAYE	7,000	
		(7,419)
Tax payable		359

	Non-savings income	*Savings income*	*Dividend income*	*Total*
	£	£	£	£
Mrs Lowrie				
Employment income	20,000			
Dividends × 100/90			2,820	
Bank deposit interest × 100/80		95		
Building society interest × 100/80	–	525		
Net income	20,000	620	2,820	23,440
Less personal allowance	(5,225)			
Taxable income	14,775	620	2,820	18,215

	£	£
Non-savings income		
£2,230 × 10%		223
£12,545 × 22%		2,760
14,775		2,983
Savings income		
£620 × 20%		124
Dividend income		
£2,820 × 10%		282
Tax liability		3,389
Less: tax credit on dividends	282	
tax suffered on savings income	124	
PAYE	2,980	
		(3,386)
Tax payable		3

4 Employment and self-employment

Tutorial note. In general, individuals prefer self employment to employment because NICs are lower and the rules on the deductibility of expenses are less onerous. HM Revenue and Customs will decide any particular case of employment or self employment by looking at all the relevant facts.

You are unlikely to get a full question with no computation in the exam but do ensure that you are comfortable providing brief written answers.

The factors to consider in deciding whether someone is employed or self-employed for income tax purposes are as follows.

(a) How much control is exercised over the way work is done? The greater the control, the more likely it is that the worker is an employee.

(b) Does the worker provide his own equipment? If so, that would indicate self-employment.

(c) If the worker hires his own helpers, that indicates self-employment.

(d) If the worker can profit by his own sound management, or lose money through errors, that indicates self-employment.

(e) If there is a continuing obligation to provide work for the worker, and an obligation on the worker to do whatever job is offered next, that indicates employment.

(f) If the worker accepts work from any independent sources, that indicates self-employment.

(g) If the worker can work whenever he chooses, that indicates self-employment.

These tests are summed up in the general rule that there is employment when there is a contract **of** service, and self-employment when is a contract **for** services.

5 Cars and loans

Tutorial note. The calculation of car and loan benefits are particularly important for exam purposes. Ensure that you pro-rate the benefits if they are not available for the entire year.

(a) A taxable benefit must be computed for Mr Andrews. The benefit will equal the difference between the interest which would have arisen at the official rate and the actual interest paid. The benefit for 2007/08 is therefore £16,000 × (6.25 – 1)% × 6/12 months = £420.

(b) The loan to Mrs Preece is less than £5,000, so the taxable benefit is nil.

(c) Mr Charles will have a taxable benefit of the annual value of the TV and video system, which will be computed as 20% of the value of the asset when first provided as a benefit to any employee. If the system had been lent to an employee when it was bought, the benefit for 2007/08 would be £800 × 20% = £160 × 10/12 = £133. If the system was first provided as a benefit in June 2007, the benefit would be £500 × 20% = £100 × 10/12 = £83.

(d) Long service awards of tangible property to employees with at least 20 years service are not taxed provided the cost to the employer does not exceed £50 for each year of service and no similar award has been made to the same person within the previous ten years. In Mrs Davies's case the limit on value would be £50 × 25 = £1,250, so there will be no taxable benefit.

(e) The car benefit and fuel scale benefit will apply to the car provided for Mr Edgar. The car benefit is calculated as price of car × %. The % depends on the CO_2 emissions of the car.

  (i) Because CO_2 emissions are 139g/km the percentage is 15%. The emissions figure is rounded down to the nearest 5 below ie to 135g/km. This is below the 140g/km baseline so the percentage is 15%.

  (ii) The fuel scale benefit will be at £14,400 multiplied by the percentage used in calculating the car benefit, in this case 15%.

  (iii) The charges will not be reduced on a time basis because the car was provided for the whole of 2007/08.

  The taxable benefit will therefore be as follows.

	£
Car £23,000 × 15%	3,450
Fuel £14,400 × 15%	2,160
	5,610

(f) Mr Ford will be taxed on the annual value of the flat and of the furniture. The company's payment of his council tax will also be a taxable benefit.

The following rules will apply.

  (i) There will be a basic accommodation benefit equal to the annual (or rateable) value.

  (ii) There will be an additional accommodation benefit equal to the excess of the flat's cost over £75,000, multiplied by the official rate of interest at the start of the tax year.

  (iii) There will be a benefit in respect of the use of the furniture, equal to 20% of its value when first provided as a benefit to any employee.

The taxable benefit will therefore be as follows.

	£
Flat: annual value	900
additional charge £(100,000 – 75,000) × 6.25%	1,562
	2,462
Furniture £5,000 × 20%	1,000
Council tax	500
	3,962

6 Gary and George

Tutorial note. Tax relief is available on pension contributions up to the higher of relevant earnings and the basic amount (£3,600). However, tax relief on contributions in excess of the annual allowance are clawed back by the excess contributions charge.

(a) *2007/08*

	Non-savings income
	£
Employment income	50,000
Less personal allowance	(5,225)
Taxable income	44,775

Tax

	£
£2,230 × 10%	223
£32,370 × 22%	7,121
£5,000 (£3,900 × $^{100}/_{78}$) × 22%	1,100
£5,175 × 40%	2,070
44,775	10,514

(b) As Gary's earnings are only £50,000 for 2007/08 only £50,000 of his contribution of £60,000 would qualify for tax relief.

His income tax liability will be:

	£
£2,230 × 10%	223
£32,370 × 22%	7,121
£10,175 × 22%	2,238
44,775	9,582

(c) All of George's contribution of £250,000 will qualify for tax relief. He will therefore pay £250,000 × 78% = £195,000 to the scheme. As he is a higher rate taxpayer his basic rate band will be extended by £250,000. However there will be a 40% tax charge on the excess contribution above the annual allowance of £225,000. His income tax liability is as follows:

	Non-savings income
	£
Employment income	300,000
Less personal allowance	(5,225)
Taxable income	294,775
Tax	£
£2,230 × 10%	223
£32,370 × 22%	7,121
£250,000 × 22%	55,000
10,175 × 40%	4,070
294,775	66,414
Excess contribution charge £(250,000 – 225,000) × 40%	10,000
Tax liability	76,414

7 Mr Lee

Tutorial note. Although you are writing an e-mail it is to a client and you should aim to be clear but concise.

To: Mr Lee@red.co.uk
From: An Advisor@taxadvice.co.uk
Date: [ ]
Re: Pension advice

Thank you for your e-mail about pension advice. My answers to your questions are as follows:

(1) You do not have to join your new employer's pension scheme. Instead you could start a pension with a financial institution such as a bank or insurance company. However, your employer may not want to contribute to private pension arrangements so you need to bear this in mind when considering whether or not to join your employer's scheme.

A money purchase scheme is one where the value of your pension benefits depends on the value of the investments in the pension scheme at the date that you set aside ('vest') funds to produce those benefits. This is distinct from a defined benefits scheme where the benefits are defined from the outset. If you decide to use private pension arrangements, these are also likely to be money purchase arrangements.

(2) You can contribute an amount up to your earnings into the pension scheme and obtain tax-relief on those contributions. You can also make any amount of further contributions, for example out of capital, but these will not obtain initial tax relief. However, since there is no income tax or capital gains tax payable by a pension fund, it may still be beneficial for such extra contributions to be made into this tax-exempt fund.

In addition, your employer can make any amount of contributions provided that the tax authorities are happy that such contributions are not excessive and so not for the purposes of the employer's trade.

However, there are two limits that you need to be aware of. First, there is an annual allowance which limits the inputs that can be put into the pension fund. For 2007/08, this limit is £225,000. The amounts that you contribute **and** obtain tax relief on, plus any contributions made by your employer, will count towards the annual allowance. If those contributions exceed the annual allowance, there will be a tax charge at 40% on the excess which is payable by you. This might be relevant in later years when your earnings may be above the annual allowance limit.

The second limit is the lifetime allowance limit. This is the maximum value of the pension fund that you are allowed to build up to provide pension benefits without incurring adverse tax consequences. The lifetime allowance is £1,600,000 in 2007/08. This limit is tested against the value of your pension fund when you vest pension benefits. If your fund exceeds the lifetime allowance at that time, there will be a tax charge of 55% on funds vested to provide a lump sum and 25% on funds vested to provide a pension income. Although there are no adverse tax consequences if your pension fund exceeds the lifetime allowance other than at the time that pension benefits are vested, it would be wise to keep an eye on how your fund is growing so that you can adjust your contributions accordingly so as to keep within the lifetime allowance.

(3) Your employer will deduct your pension contributions gross from your pay before applying PAYE. This means that tax relief is given automatically at your highest rate of tax and no adjustment is needed in your tax return. As an example, if you contribute £1,000 to your pension and that amount of income would have been taxed at 40%, your pay will be reduced by £1,000 but the amount of tax that would be deducted from your pay would be reduced by £400, so that the net amount of the contribution payable by you would be £600.

The above is only an outline of the basics of pension provision as this is very complex area, so I suggest that we meet once you have decided how you wish to proceed.

AN Advisor

8 Hamburg

Tutorial note. Remember to accrue the rents receivable and expenses payable for the tax year. Where you disallow an expenses, such as the new roof, note this in your computation to show that you have considered it.

	£	£
Rent		
House 1: first letting £600 × 6		3,600
House 1: second letting £6,000 × 3/12		1,500
House 2: £5,000 × 8/12		3,333
House 3: £7,800 × 8/12		5,200
		13,633
Expenses		
House 1: new roof, disallowable because capital	0	
House 1: loft insulation	1,200	
House 1: water rates	320	
House 1: buildings insurance £480 × 10/12	400	
House 2: water rates	240	
House 2: wear and tear £(3,333 – 240) × 10%	309	
House 3: redecoration	1,200	
House 3: water rates	360	
House 3: buildings insurance £440 × 9/12	330	
House 3: contents insurance £180 × 8/12	120	
House 3: wear and tear £(5,200 – 360) × 10%	484	
		(4,963)
Income from houses		8,670
Rent a room (*Working*)		350
Total property business income		9,020

Working

Hamburg should claim rent a room relief in respect of the letting of the furnished room in his main residence, since this is more beneficial than the normal basis of assessment (£4,600 – £875 = £3,725). This means that Hamburg will be taxed on an additional £350 (£4,600 – £4,250) of property business income.

9 A Trader

Tutorial note. You are extremely likely to be required to adjust accounts profit in your exam to arrive at your taxable trading profits. The best way to familiarise yourself with the adjustments required is to practise plenty of questions like this.

	£	£
Net profit per accounts		101,977
Add: entertaining customers	600	
tax consultancy	30	
lease on new premises	100	
gift aid donation	5,200	
political donation	500	
private travel expenses 25% × £2,000	500	
depreciation	15,000	
		21,930
		123,907
Less: profit on sale of office	5,265	
capital allowances	2,200	
building society interest	1,900	
		(9,365)
Taxable trading profits		114,542

10 Tom Hardy

Tutorial note. The key to being able to deal with a capital allowances computation correctly is to get the layout right. Once you have done this, the figures should fall into place.

	FYA	*Pool*	*Expensive car (80%)*	*Short life asset*	*Allowances*
	£	£	£	£	£
1.7.06 – 30.6.07					
Brought forward		32,000			
WDA @ 25%		(8,000)			8,000
		24,000			
Additions	1,917			4,400	
FYA @ 40%	(767)			(1,760)	2,527
		1,150		2,640	10,527
		25,150			
1.7.07 – 30.6.08					
Additions			13,400		
WDA		(6,287)	(3,000)	(660)	9,347
		18,863	10,400	1,980	
1.7.08 – 30.6.09					
WDA		(4,716)	(2,600)	(495)	7,291
		14,147	7,800	1,485	
1.7.09 – 30.6.10					
Disposals		(340)		(2,200)	
		13,807		(715)	
Balancing charge				715	(715)
WDA		(3,452)	(1,950)		5,012
		10,355	5,850		4,297
1.7.10 – 31.12.10					
Disposals		(24,000)	(10,600)		
		(13,645)	(4,750)		
Balancing charges		13,645	4,750		(17,445)

Tutorial note. The capital allowances are restricted as a result of the private use of an asset by the proprietor.

11 Saruman

> **Tutorial note.** Balancing adjustments where there has been private use of the asset are restricted to the business use element.

Capital allowances computation for year ended 31 March 2008

Plant and machinery

	General Pool	*Saruman's car (75%)*		*Allowances/ (charges)*
	£	£		£
TWDV b/f	52,000	600		
Additions	4,800			
Disposals (10,000 + 800)	(10,800)	(920)		
	46,000			
Balancing charge		(320)	× 75%	(240)
Private use car		19,000		
WDA 25%	(11,500)	(3,000)	× 75%	13,750
TWDV c/f	34,500	16,000		13,510

Industrial building

Cost excluding land (office accommodation included as less than 25% of qualifying cost)	£30,000
WDA @ 4% =	£1,200

Total capital allowances are £13,510 + £1,200 = £14,710

12 Mr Cobbler

> **Tutorial note**. Significant cash flow advantages can be gained with a careful choice of accounting date.

THE TAXABLE PROFITS FOR THE FOUR YEARS 2007/08 TO 2010/11

The accounts profits will be as follows.

Period ending in	*Working*	*Accounting date* 31 March	30 April
		£	£
2008	3 × £800	2,400	
	4 × £800		3,200
2009	3 × £800 + 6 × £1,200 + 3 × £2,000	15,600	
	2 × £800 + 6 × £1,200 + 4 × £2,000		16,800
2010	12 × £2,000	24,000	24,000
2011	12 × £2,000	24,000	24,000

The taxable profits will be as follows.

		Accounting date	
		31 March	*30 April*
		£	£
2007/08	Actual basis	2,400	
	£3,200 × 3/4		2,400
2008/09	Year to 31.3.09	15,600	
	First 12 months		
	£3,200 + £16,800 × 8/12		14,400
2009/10	Year to 31.3.10	24,000	
	Year to 30.4.09		16,800
2010/11	Year to 31.3.11	24,000	
	Year to 30.4.10		24,000
		66,000	57,600

30 April is the better choice of accounting date as it will give a considerable cash flow advantage.

13 Miss Farrington

Tutorial note. In a question like this, work out the capital allowances for each period of account before you think about allocating profits to tax years.

Writing down allowances are time apportioned in a long period of account but first year allowances are not.

As Miss Farrington's business is a 'small enterprise' for capital allowance purposes, 50% FYAs are available for expenditure incurred in the two year period to 5.4.08.

We must first work out the capital allowances.

	FYA	*Pool*	*Car (65%)*	*Allowances*
	£	£	£	£
1.1.07 – 30.4.08				
Car			6,600	
WDA @ 25% × 16/12			(2,200) × 65%	1,430
Desk and office furniture (1.1.07)	940			
General plant (4.1.07)	2,280			
Secondhand oven (1.3.07)	1,200			
Delivery van (25.3.07)	1,800			
Typewriter (15.4.07)	340			
	6,560			
FYA @ 50%	(3,280)	3,280		3,280
		3,280	4,400	4,710
1.5.08 – 30.4.09				
WDA @ 25%		(820)		820
			(1,100) × 65%	715
		2,460		
General plant (30.1.09)	1,000			
Computer (30.4.09)	1,945			
	2,945			
FYA @ 40%	(1,178)	1,767		1,178
		4,227	3,300	2,713

Profits are as follows.

Period	*Profit*	*Capital allowances*	*Adjusted profit*
	£	£	£
1.1.07 – 30.4.08	20,710	4,710	16,000
1.5.08 – 30.4.09	14,916	2,713	12,203

The taxable profits are as follows.

Year	*Basis period*	*Working*	*Taxable profit*
			£
2006/07	1.1.07 – 5.4.07	£16,000 × 3/16	3,000
2007/08	6.4.07 – 5.4.08	£16,000 × 12/16	12,000
2008/09	1.5.07 – 30.4.08	£16,000 × 12/16	12,000
2009/10	1.5.08 – 30.4.09		12,203

The overlap profits are the profits from 1 May 2007 to 5 April 2008: £16,000 × 11/16 = £11,000.

14 Langland

Tutorial note. Work out the tax years which the trading covers, then allocate the profits to the relevant years. Don't forget overlap profits. A good check is to add up the profits throughout the life of the business: the result should be the same as the total of the profits assessed in each tax year.

		£
2003/04	1.2.04 – 5.4.04	1,600
	$(12{,}000 \times \frac{2}{15})$	
2004/05	6.4.04 – 5.4.05	9,600
	$(12{,}000 \times \frac{12}{15})$	
2005/06	12m to 30.4.05	9,600
	$12{,}000 \times \frac{12}{15})$	
2006/07	Y/e 30.4.06	6,000
2007/08	Y/e 30.4.07	8,000
2008/09	Y/e 30.4.08	10,000
2009/10	Y/e 30.4.09	6,000
	P/e 31.10.09	4,000
		10,000
	Less: Overlap profits	
	1.5.04 to 5.4.05	
	$(\frac{11}{15} \times 12{,}000)$	(8,800)
		1,200

15 Morgan

Tutorial note. In a losses question take care to consider all available reliefs. When deciding on the best relief you must consider both the rate of tax saved and the timing of the relief.

(a) Loss relief could be claimed:

(i) against general income of the year of loss (2008/09), the investment income of £8,000;

against general income of the preceding year (2007/08). This would be trading profits of £15,000 plus investment income of £8,000;

against the first available future profits of the same trade.

(b) *The quickest claim*

The quickest way to obtain relief would be for Morgan to use loss relief against general income in both years. The tax computations would then be as follows.

	2007/08	*2008/09*
	£	£
Trading profits	15,000	0
Investment income	8,000	8,000
Total income	23,000	8,000
Less loss relief against general income	(23,000)	(8,000)
Net income	0	0

The balance of the loss, £1,000, would be carried forward and relieved against future trading income.

Although this proposal produces loss relief quickly, it has the disadvantage of wasting Morgan's personal allowance in both years. Morgan could, if he chose, delay his relief by carrying the loss forward. The loss would then be set off only against trading income, with the investment income using his personal allowance.

(c) On a cessation, terminal loss relief would be available. The loss could be set against profits taxable in the tax year of cessation and the three preceding tax years, later years first. This would probably be the best claim for Morgan. The effect would be as follows.

Year	*Original*	*Loss relief*	*Revised*
	£	£	£
2008/09	0	0	0
2007/08	15,000	(15,000)	0
2006/07	18,000	(17,000)	1,000
2005/06	16,000	0	16,000

Tutorial note. Because of Morgan's choice of accounting date, no overlap profits arose on commencement.

16 Adam, Bert and Charlie

	Total	*A*	*B*	*C*	*D*
	£	£	£	£	£
Year ending 5 April 2005					
Salaries	37,000	15,000	12,000	10,000	
PSR (balance)	65,000	26,000	26,000	13,000	
Total	102,000	41,000	38,000	23,000	
Year ending 5 April 2006					
6 April to 5 July					
Salaries	9,250	3,750	3,000	2,500	
PSR (balance)	42,750	17,100	17,100	8,550	
Total	52,000	20,850	20,100	11,050	
6 July to 5 April					
Salaries	16,500		9,000	7,500	
PSR (balance)	139,500		83,700	55,800	
Total	156,000		92,700	63,300	
Totals for the year	208,000	20,850	112,800	74,350	
Year ending 5 April 2007					
Salaries	22,000		12,000	10,000	
PSR (balance)	104,000		62,400	41,600	
Total	126,000		74,400	51,600	
Year ending 5 April 2008					
6 April to 5 May					
Salaries	1,833		1,000	833	
Balance	13,167		7,900	5,267	
Total	15,000		8,900	6,100	
6 May to 5 April					
Salaries	49,500		16,500	16,500	16,500
Balance	115,500		69,300	34,650	11,550
Total	165,000		85,800	51,150	28,050
Totals for the year	180,000		94,700	57,250	28,050

Taxable trade profits are as follows.

	A	*B*	*C*	*D*
	£	£	£	£
Year				
2004/05	41,000	38,000	23,000	
2005/06	20,850	112,800	74,350	
2006/07		74,400	51,600	
2007/08		94,700	57,250	28,050

17 Partnerships

Tutorial note. This is a comprehensive question as it asks you to explain how partners are taxed, followed by a computation including joining and retiring partners, and finishes with a discussion of losses.

Overlap profits are relieved either on a change of accounting date or on a cessation. Each partner obtains relief for their own overlap profits and their own losses.

(a) Each partner is taxed like a sole trader who runs a business which starts when he joins the partnership, finishes when he leaves the partnership, has the same periods of account as the partnership, and makes profits or losses equal to the partner's share of the partnership profits or losses.

(b)

	Total	*Anne*	*Betty*	*Chloe*
	£	£	£	£
1.1.07 – 31.12.07				
January to June	30,000	15,000	15,000	
July to December	30,000	15,000	–	15,000
Totals	60,000	30,000	15,000	15,000
1.1.08 – 31.12.08	72,000	36,000	–	36,000

Trading profit assessments 2007/08

	Anne	*Betty*	*Chloe*
	£	£	£
Profits y/e 31.12.07	30,000		
Profits 1.1.07 – 30.6.07		15,000	
Profits 1.7.07 – 31.12.07			15,000
Profits 1.1.08 – 5.4.08			
3/12 × £36,000			9,000
	30,000	15,000	24,000
Less overlap relief for Betty on cessation		(3,000)	
Profits assessable 2007/08	30,000	12,000	24,000

(c) (i) *Daniel*

Daniel can use his £20,000 loss:

- against general income of 2007/08 and/or of 2006/07
- against future trading profits

(ii) *Edward*

Edward can use his £15,000 loss:

- against general income of 2007/08 and/or of 2006/07
- if there is a terminal loss in the last 12 months of trading, against trading profits of the tax year of cessation and the three preceding years, later years first

(iii) *Frank*

Frank can use his loss of £5,000:

- against general income of 2007/08 and/or 2006/07
- against general income of 2004/05, 2005/06 and 2006/07
- against future trading profits

18 Denise

> **Tutorial note**. It is important that you can calculate and distinguish NICs for the self employed and employed individuals. Here both Class 2 and Class 4 were required for a self employed individual.

(a) Denise can contribute an amount up to her earnings into a personal pension scheme and obtain tax relief on those contributions ie up to £115,000 for 2007/08. She can also make any amount of further contributions, for example out of capital, but these will not obtain initial tax relief. However, since there is no income tax or capital gains tax payable by a pension fund, it may still be beneficial for such extra contributions to be made into this tax exempt fund.

However, there are two limits that Denise needs to be aware of. First, there is an annual allowance which limits the inputs that can be put into the pension fund. For 2007/08, this limit is £225,000. The amounts that Denise contributes **and** obtains tax relief on, will count towards the annual allowance. If those contributions exceed the annual allowance, there will be a tax charge at 40% on the excess which is payable by Denise. This might be relevant in later years when Denise's earnings may be above the annual allowance limit.

The second limit is the lifetime allowance limit. This is the maximum value of the pension fund that Denise is allowed to build up to provide pension benefits without incurring adverse tax consequences. The lifetime allowance is £1,600,000 in 2007/08. This limit is tested against the value of her pension fund at the date she sets aside (vests) the fund to provide these benefits. If her fund exceeds the lifetime allowance at that time, there will be a tax charge of 55% on funds vested to provide a lump sum and 25% on funds vested to provide a pension income.

Personal pension contributions are entitled to tax relief at source. The pension payments made will be treated as being net of basic rate tax at 22%. As she is a higher rate tax payer, she will then need to claim higher rate tax relief of 18% through her tax return. Thus for a gross contribution of £1,000, Denise would pay £780 to the pension provider and then she would claim an additional £180 through her tax return.

(b)

	£
Class 2 NICs	
£2.20 × 52	114

	£
Class 4 NICs	
£(34,840 – 5,225) × 8%	2,369
£(115,000 – 34,840) × 1%	802
	3,171

19 Sasha Shah

Tutorial notes.

1. Strictly, expenses are only deductible in calculating net taxable earnings if they are incurred wholly, necessarily and exclusively in the performance of the duties. In practice, however, HM Revenue and Customs allow an apportionment between private and business use as here.
2. Capital allowances are available to an employee who provides plant and machinery necessarily for use in the performance of his duties, in the same way as a sole trader.
3. The use of the car for travel between home and work is ordinary commuting and not business use.
4. 'Earnings' for Class 4 NIC purposes are trading profits. However, earnings for Class 1 NIC purposes are gross earnings before the deductions of any expenses.

(a) Factors that will indicate that a worker should be treated as an employee rather than as self employed are:

(i) control by employer over employee's work;

(ii) employee must accept further work if offered (and employer must offer work);

(iii) employee does not provide own equipment;

(iv) employee does not hire own helpers;

(v) employee does not take substantial financial risk;

(vi) employee does not have responsibility for investment and management of business and cannot benefit from sound management;

(vii) employee cannot work when he chooses but when an employer tells him to work;

(viii) described as an employee in any agreement between parties.

(b) (i) *Income assessable as trading profits*

Note. It is assumed that Sasha's business meets the definition of 'small business' for FYA purposes.

	£	£
Gross income		60,000
Less: business expenses on heating etc	600	
FYA @ 50% on computer	4,000	
business expenses re car (£3,500 × 40%)	1,400	
WDA @ 25% on business car		
£10,000 × 25% × 40% (business proportion)	1,000	(7,000)
Assessable as trading profits		53,000

(ii) *Net taxable earnings*

	£	£
Gross income		60,000
Less: business expenses on heating etc (note 1 above)	600	
FYA @ 50% on computer (note 2 above)	4,000	(4,600)
Net taxable earnings		55,400

(c) (i) *Class 2 and Class 4 NIC*

		£
Class 2	£2.20 × 52	114.40
Class 4	£(34,840 – 5,225) × 8%	2,369.20
	£(53,000 – 34,840) × 1%	181.60
Total		2,665.20

(ii) *Class 1 NIC (Primary)*

	£
£(34,840 – 5,225) × 11%	3,257.65
£(60,000 – 34,840) × 1%	251.60
Total	3,509.25

20 Andrea

Tutorial note. The losses are set against the gain arising on the non business asset as this asset attracts the lowest amount of taper relief (ie the highest percentage of the gain remains taxable). The taxable gain is taxed as if it were savings income, ie at 20% on any gain falling within the unused portion of the basic rate band and at 40% on the excess.

	£	£
Non business asset (1)	16,000	
Less: loss on non business asset (2)	(6,000)	
	10,000	
Less: loss b/f	(5,000)	
Gain before taper relief	5,000	
Gain after taper relief		
Ownership June 2004 – December 2007 = 3 years		
95% × £5,000		4,750
Business asset	35,000	
Gain after taper relief		
Ownership April 1998 – March 2008 = 9 years		
25% × £35,000		8,750
		13,500
Less: annual exemption		(9,200)
Taxable gains 2007/08		4,300

CGT liability 2007/08	£
£34,600 – £32,500 = £2,100 × 20%	420
£4,300 – £2,100 = £2,200 × 40%	880
	1,300

21 Peter Robinson

> **Tutorial note**. The first disposal is a basic computation with indexation allowance and taper relief. The second disposal tests the A/(A+B) formula and the third part tests compensation for the destruction of an asset.

Peter Robinson CGT payable 2007/08

Summary of gains

	£
Investment property £62,400 × 60% (W1)	37,440
Land £16,300 × 95% (W2)	15,485
Destroyed asset £3,000 × 85% (W3)	2,550
	55,475
Less: annual exemption	(9,200)
Taxable gains	46,275
CGT payable	
£(34,600 – 30,000) = 4,600 × 20%	920
£(46,275 – 4,600) = 41,675 × 40%	16,670
CGT payable	17,590

Workings

1 *Investment property*

	£
Proceeds	150,000
Less cost of disposal	(1,280)
Net proceeds	148,720
Less cost	(80,000)
	68,720
Less indexation allowance	(6,320)
Indexed gain	62,400

Taper relief period – 6.4.98 – 30.4.07 = 9 years + bonus year = 10 years

2 *Land*

	£
Proceeds	35,000
Less cost of disposal	(700)
Net proceeds	34,300
Less cost	
$£54{,}000 \times \frac{35{,}000}{35{,}000 + 70{,}000}$	(18,000)
Gain	16,300

Taper relief period – 15.4.04 – 27.6.07 = 3 years

3 *Vase*

	£
Proceeds	20,000
Less cost	(12,000)
Gain	8,000
Gain immediately chargeable £(20,000 – 17,000)	3,000

Remainder rolled into base cost of new vase (£8,000 – £3,000 = £5,000)

Taper relief period – 30.6.02 – 1.9.07 = 5 years.

22 John Harley

Tutorial note. Part (a) is a typical question examining principal private residence relief. You are asked to present your answer as a schedule (ie table) showing periods of exemption and non-exemption with reasons (ie explanation of your application of the rules). To obtain good marks you must comply with these instructions.

(a) **John Harley – Gain on house**

	Chargeable months	*Exempt months*
1.8.86 – 31.5.87 – actual residence		10
1.6.87 – 31.7.91 – employed abroad any period		50
1.8.91 – 31.7.95 – up to 4 years work elsewhere		48
1.8.95 – 31.10.97 – up to 3 years any reason		27
1.11.97 – 30.6.00 – actual residence		32
1.7.00 – 30.11.04 – absent	53	
1.12.04 – 30.11.07 – last 3 years ownership for any reason		36
Totals	53	203

(b) **Elsie Phillips**

1 *Painting*

	£
Proceeds (deemed)	6,000
Less costs of disposal	(400)
Gain	5,600
Less: cost	(11,500)
Loss	(5,900)

Indexation cannot increase a loss.

2 *Chandelier*

	£
Proceeds	7,500
Less: cost	(4,000)
Gain	3,500
Cannot exceed £(7,500 – 6,000) × 5/3 =	2,500

Ownership period less than 3 years so no taper relief available.

23 The White family

Tutorial note. In an exam question you should watch out for the CGT reliefs. When dealing with rollover relief look out for depreciating assets.

(a) 2007/08

Gift relief can apply to the gift of the factory because it is an asset used in the trade of the donor. Full relief is available as no payment is made by Gary ie it is an outright gift.

	£
Market value at gift	260,000
Less cost	(150,000)
Gain heldover	110,000

Taper relief in respect of Mr White's period of ownership is lost.

(b) Gary's gain on sale is:

	£
Proceeds	320,000
Less cost £(260,000 – 110,000)	(150,000)
Gain before taper relief	170,000

The taper relief period for Gary begins on the date of the gift to him (1 December 2007). This is a non-business asset for Gary and so he has not accrued the minimum period for non-business asset taper relief to apply (3 years). Thus no taper relief is due.

(c) Mrs White has made a gain before taper relief of £40,000 (£80,000 – 40,000) on the sale of the shop. If she acquires a replacement shop within 3 years of the sale, she can claim rollover relief.

Freehold Shop

Less than the full proceeds have been reinvested. A gain before taper relief equal to the amount not reinvested (£80,000 – £72,000 = £8,000) will remain in charge. As the shop has been owned for more than two years full business asset taper relief is due.

The remainder of the gain before taper relief of £32,000 can be rolled over into the base cost of the freehold shop. The base cost will therefore be £72,000 – £32,000 = £40,000 for the purposes of computing a gain on its disposal. Taper relief will accrue from the date the new freehold shop is acquired.

Leasehold Shop

Full deferral of the gain before taper relief is available as the whole of the proceeds of sale are reinvested.

The leasehold shop is a depreciating asset as the lease has less than 60 years to run. The gain is not deducted from the base cost of the leasehold shop, but is deferred until the earliest of the disposal of the leasehold shop, ceasing to use it in the business or 10 years from its acquisition. The gain which will come into charge at that date will be £40,000 but it will be eligible for the maximum rate of business asset taper relief as that was available on the original sale.

If a non depreciating asset is acquired before the gain crystallises it can be rolled over into that new asset.

24 Alice

Tutorial note. Remember that incorporation relief only applies to the extent that shares are received in exchange for the assets transferred to the company.

	£
Indexed gains on incorporation	120,000
Less: incorporation relief $\frac{200,000}{200,000 + 100,000} \times$ £120,000	(80,000)
Gain before taper relief	40,000
Chargeable gain after taper relief (25%)	£10,000
Base cost of shares £(200,000 – 80,000)	£120,000

25 Mary and Robert Green

Tutorial note. Remember to allocate bonus shares to the original holdings. The key to part (b) is the matching rules.

(a) *Match post April 1998 acquisitions on a LIFO basis*

1 March 2007

Shares held after bonus issue 1,000 + 1,000 = 2,000

No change to base cost

	£
Disposal proceeds (£14,000 × $\frac{2,000}{3,200}$)	8,750
Less cost	(1,260)
Gain	7,490

No taper relief – owned less than one year

15 May 2006

Shares held after bonus issue 1,800 + 1,800 = 3,600

No change to base cost

	£
Disposal proceeds (£14,000 × $\frac{1,200}{3,200}$)	5,250
Less cost (£1,900 × $\frac{1,200}{3,600}$)	(633)
Gain	4,617

No taper relief – non business asset held less than 3 years.

The total chargeable gain on the sale of Mary's shares in Read plc is £12,107 (£7,490 + £4,617).

(b) *The disposal of Greengage Supermarkets plc shares*

(i) *Post 5 April 1998 acquisition*

	£
Proceeds $\frac{1,000}{1,450} \times$ £10,150	7,000
Less: cost	(6,000)
Gain	1,000

No taper relief – owned less than one year

(ii) *The FA 1985 pool*

	£
Proceeds $\frac{450}{1,450} \times$ £10,150	3,150
Less cost (W1)	(1,704)
	1,446
Less indexation allowance £(2,923 – 1,704) (W1)	(1,219)
Indexed gain	227

Gain after taper relief (10 complete years ownership after 6.4.98 including additional year) 60% × £227 = £136

The total chargeable gain on the disposal of Robert's shares in Greengage Supermarkets plc is £1,136 (£1,000 + £136)

Working

The FA 1985 pool

	No of shares	*Cost*	*Indexed cost*
	£	£	£
Value at 5 April 1998	900	3,408	5,845
Disposal (May 2007)	(450)	(1,704)	(2,923)
FA 1985 pool value remaining	450	1,704	2,922

26 Tim

Tutorial note. Three payments of income tax may need to be made in respect of a tax year. Two payments on account are normally made on 31 January in the tax year and on the following 31 July. These are based on the prior year tax payable under self assessment. A final balancing payment of the income tax due for a year is normally made on the 31 January following the year.

Tim's payments on account for 2007/08 were based on the excess of his 2006/07 tax liability over amounts deducted under the PAYE system, amounts deducted at source and tax credits on dividends:

	£
2006/07 tax liability	16,800
Less: PAYE	(7,200)
tax deducted at source	(800)
tax credit on dividends	(200)
Total payments on account for 2007/08	8,600

Two equal payments on account of £4,300 (£8,600/2) were required. The due dates for these payments were 31 January 2008 and 31 July 2008 respectively.

The final payment in respect of Tim's 2007/08 tax liability was due on 31 January 2008 and was calculated as follows:

	£
2007/08 tax liability	22,000
Less: PAYE	(7,100)
tax deducted at source	(900)
tax credit on dividends	(250)
	13,750
Less payments on account	(8,600)
Final payment due 31.1.09	5,150

27 Lai Chan

Tutorial notes. This is a good example of the type of question that you might find as question 1 of the exam.

1 For capital allowance purposes the WDA is restricted by the length of the basis period, but the FYA is not.

2 There is no capital allowance restriction in respect of the private use of an asset by an employee.

3 The basic rate band is extended by the gross amount of personal pension contributions made. Occupational pension contributions are, however, deducted in computing total income.

4 There is no taxable benefit in respect of the company's contribution to the occupational pension scheme.

(a) *Income tax liability*

	£	*Non-savings income* £
Gross salary 9 × £3,250	29,250	
Less pension contribution (6%)	(1,755)	
	27,495	
Car benefit (W1)	3,780	
Fuel benefit (W2)	2,700	
Taxable cheap loan (W3)	781	
Employment income		34,756
Trading profit	19,900	
Less Capital allowances (W4)	(4,908)	
Taxable trading profit		14,992
Net income		49,748
Less personal allowance		(5,225)
Taxable income		44,523

Tax

	£
£2,230 × 10%	223
£33,870 × 22% (W5)	7,451
£8,423 (44,523 – 36,100) × 40%	3,369
Tax liability	11,043

Workings

1 *Car benefit*

	£
25% × £26,400 × 9/12 (note)	4,950
Less contribution £130 × 9	(1,170)
	3,780

Note. The % depends on the CO_2 emissions of the car.

CO_2 emissions = 190 g/km

Amount above baseline figure 190 – 140 = 50 g/km

Divide by 5 = 10 g/km

Taxable percentage = 15% + 10% = 25%

The benefit is time apportioned as the car is available for only nine months of the year.

2 *Fuel benefit*

£14,400 × 25% × 9/12 = £2,700

No reduction for partial reimbursement of private fuel cost. The benefit is time apportioned as the car was available for only nine months of the year.

The taxable percentage used in calculating the fuel benefit is the same as the percentage used in calculating the car benefit.

3 *Taxable cheap loan*

Average method

$$6.25\% \times \frac{30{,}000 + 10{,}000}{2} \times 9/12 = £937$$

Alternative method (strict method)

	£
£30,000 × 3/12 × 6.25% =	469
£10,000 × 6/12 × 6.25% =	312
	781

Elect for strict method

4

	FYA	General pool	Private use car (60%)	Short life asset	Allowances
	£	£	£	£	£
Additions not qualifying for FYA					
– private car			14,800		
– employee car		10,400			
WDA @ 25% × 3/12		(650)			650
		9,750			
WDA @ £3,000 (restricted) × 3/12			(750) × 60%		450
			14,050		
Additions qualifying for FYA					
– recording equipment	5,952				
– recording equipment				1,664	
Less: FYA @ 50%	(2,976)			(832)	3,808
TWDV c/f		2,976			
Allowances		12,726	14,050	832	
					4,908

5 Basic rate band

£34,600 + (£390 × 100/78 × 3) = £36,100

(b) Up to 31.12.07, PAYE will have been deducted from Lai Chan's salary. It is likely that her PAYE code was adjusted to take account of her benefits. Further tax payable (or tax repayable) will be dealt with under the self-assessment system.

As Lai Chan was employed before starting in business on her own account, she is unlikely to have made any payments on account for 2007/08. Therefore, the tax on her trading profit will be collected in full on 31 January 2009 under the self assessment system.

28 P Ltd

Tutorial notes.

1 The interest on the loan is dealt with under the loan relationship rules. It is not a property business expense.

2 Income and expenses are dealt with on the accruals basis when calculating the property business profit.

P LTD: PROPERTY BUSINESS INCOME

	£	£	£
First Property			
Premium £20,000 less [2% × (30 – 1) × £20,000]			8,400
Rent £4,000 × 9/12			3,000
			11,400
Second Property			
Rent £600 × 3		1,800	
Rent £2,100 × 1/3		700	
		2,500	
Less: water rates £390 × 6/12	195		
insurance £440 × 6/11	240		
repairs: capital	0		
		(435)	
			2,065
Property business income			13,465

29 E Ltd

Tutorial note. Current year losses are dealt with before losses brought forward. Companies do not get taper relief or an annual exemption.

Motor cars are exempt assets, so the loss brought forward from the year ended 31 March 2007 is £16,400.

The position for the year ended 31 March 2008 is as follows.

	£
Gains	
Shares	17,700
Picture	3,000
	20,700
Less loss on shares	(6,000)
	14,700
Less loss brought forward	(14,700)
Chargeable gains	Nil

The loss carried forward at 31 March 2008 is £(16,400 – 14,700) = £1,700.

30 Hardup Ltd

Tutorial note. The date of disposal for chargeable gains purposes is the date that the disposal becomes unconditional. In this case the date of exchange, not the date of completion.

Rollover relief is not available to defer the gain arising on the sale of the office block, because the reinvestment was not made in the qualifying period, commencing one year before and ending three years after the disposal.

CAPITAL GAINS COMPUTATION

	£
Office block (W1)	23,930
Plot of land (W2)	18,428
Workshop (W3)	42,935
Chargeable gains	85,293

Workings

1 *The office block*

	£
Proceeds	120,000
Less cost	(65,000)
	55,000
Less indexation allowance $\frac{205.2 - 138.8}{138.8}$ (0.478) × £65,000	(31,070)
Chargeable gain	23,930

Rollover relief is not available as replacement asset acquired outside the qualifying period.

2 *The plot of land*

	£
Proceeds	69,000
Less cost	(20,000)
expenditure in July 1989	(4,000)
	45,000
Less indexation allowance	
$\frac{205.9 - 94.78}{94.78}$ (1.172) × £20,000	(23,440)
$\frac{205.9 - 115.5}{115.5}$ (0.783) × £4,000	(3,132)
	18,428

3 *The workshop*

	£
Proceeds	173,000
Less cost	(65,000)
	108,000
Less indexation allowance $\frac{205.9 - 102.9}{102.9}$ (1.001) × £65,000	(65,065)
	42,935

31 Tree Ltd

Tutorial note. You need to calculate both PCTCT and 'profits'. 'Profits' determine which tax rate applies.

(a) Tree Ltd

	Year to 31.3.08
	£
Trading profits	180,000
Chargeable gain	105,000
Investment income	36,000
Less: Gift aid donation	(27,000)
Profits chargeable to corporation tax	294,000
FII: £29,700 × 100/90	33,000
'Profits'	327,000

Marginal relief applies

Year to 31.3.08	£
Corporation tax (FY 07)	
£294,000 × 30%	88,200
Less 1/40 (1,500,000 – 327,000) × $\frac{294,000}{327,000}$	(26,366)
	61,834

(b) Dealers plc's profits for small companies' rate purposes are £420,000 so tax is payable at the small companies marginal rate.

	6 months to 31.3.08
	£
Profits chargeable to corporation tax	420,000
'Profits'	420,000
Upper limit £1,500,000 × 6/12	750,000
Lower limit £300,000 × 6/12	150,000

	£
Corporation tax (FY 07)	
£420,000 × 30%	126,000
Less small companies' marginal relief	
£(750,000 – 420,000) × 1/40	(8,250)
	117,750

(c) Springer Ltd's accounting period to 31 December 2007 falls partly in FY 06 and partly in FY 07. PCTCT and 'profits' are apportioned to each FY.

	£
PCTCT	600,000
FII: £27,000 × 100/90	30,000
'Profits'	630,000

	FY 06 3 months to 31.3.07 £	FY 07 9 months to 31.12.07 £
PCTCT (3:9)	150,000	450,000
'Profits' (3:9)	157,500	472,500
Lower limit:		
£300,000 × $^3/_{12}$ / $^9/_{12}$	75,000	225,000
Upper limit:		
£1,500,000 × $^3/_{12}$ / $^9/_{12}$	375,000	1,125,000
Marginal relief applying in both FYs		
FY 06		
£150,000 × 30%	45,000	
Less: marginal relief		
$£(375{,}000 - 157{,}500) \times \frac{150{,}000}{157{,}500} \times {}^{11}/_{400}$	(5,696)	
	39,304	
FY 07		
£450,000 × 30%		135,000
Less: marginal relief		
$£(1{,}125{,}000 - 472{,}500) \times \frac{450{,}000}{472{,}500} \times {}^{1}/_{40}$		(15,536)
		119,464
Total corporation tax £(39,304 + 119,464)		158,768

32 Righteous plc

Tutorial note. Where a company has a long period of account, it has two accounting periods: first 12 months and then the remainder.

	1.1.06- 31.12.06 (12m) £	1.1.07- 31.5.07 (5m) £
Trading income (12:5)	352,941	147,059
Investment income (15,000 + 6,000)	21,000	2,500
Chargeable gain	–	5,000
	373,941	154,559
Less: gift aid donations (15,000 + 15,000)	(30,000)	(40,000)
Profits chargeable to CT	343,941	114,559

12 m/e 31.12.06

PCTCT/'profits' £343,941

FY05 and FY06

Upper limit: £1,500,000
Lower limit: £300,000

Marginal relief applies for both FYs

Tax payable	£
£343,941 × 30%	103,182
Less £(1,500,000 – 343,941) × $^{11}/_{400}$	(31,792)
	71,390

5 m/e 31.5.07

'Profits'/PCTCT	£114,559

Lower limit:

FY06/FY07 £300,000 × $^5/_{12}$ = £125,000

Small companies' rate applies for both years

	£
FY 06 £114,559 × $^3/_5$ × 19%	13,060
FY 07 £114,559 × $^2/_5$ × 20%	9,165
	22,225

33 Ferraro Ltd

Tutorial note. The pro-forma for loss relief is important. If you learn the proforma you should find that the figures slot into place. Note that the result of a losses claim may be that, as here, gift aid donations become unrelieved.

	Accounting periods			
	12m to 31.12.04	*12m to 31.12.05*	*9m to 30.9.06*	*12m to 30.9.07*
	£	£	£	£
Trading profits	34,480	6,200	4,320	0
Investment income	200	80	240	260
Property business income	1,200	1,420	1,440	1,600
Chargeable gain (12,680 – 5,000)	0	0	7,680	0
	35,880	7,700	13,680	1,860
Less current period loss relief	0	0	0	(1,860)
	35,880	7,700	13,680	0
Less carry back loss relief	0	(1,925)	(13,680)	(0)
Less Gift Aid donations	(1,000)	(0)	(0)	(0)
PCTCT	34,880	5,775	0	0
Unrelieved charges			1,000	1,500

Loss memo	£
Loss of y/e 30.9.07	100,000
Less used y/e 30.9.07	(1,860)
	98,140
Less used 9m/e 30.9.06	(13,680)
	84,460
Less used 3m/12 × £7,700	(1,925)
c/f	82,535

The allowable capital loss of £9,423 during the year ended 30 September 2007 is carried forward against future chargeable gains.

The gift aid donation made in the 9 months to 30 September 2006 remains unrelieved. Similarly the gift aid donation in the year 30 September 2007 remains unrelieved. Unrelieved gift aid donations cannot be carried forward.

Tutorial note. The loss is carried back to set against profits arising in the previous 12 months. This means that the set off in the y/e 31.12.05 is restricted to 3/12 × £7,700 = £1,925.

34 P Ltd

Tutorial note. You are asked to use group relief in the most efficient manner. This means giving it first to companies in the small companies' marginal relief band, then to companies paying tax at the full rate.

Note that groups will be tested only as part of the longer question in the exam.

(a) There are six associated companies, so the lower and upper limits for small companies' rate purposes are £50,000 and £250,000 respectively.

S Ltd and T Ltd are outside the P Ltd group for group relief purposes. P Ltd's loss should be surrendered to Q Ltd, to bring its taxable profits down to £50,000, and to R Ltd to bring its taxable profits down to £50,000. The balance of £5,000 should be surrendered to either M Ltd, Q Ltd or R Ltd. In this case M Ltd has been selected. A claim by P Ltd against its own profits would have wasted gift aid, and carrying the loss forward would not obtain relief for several years.

	M Ltd	*P Ltd*	*Q Ltd*	*R Ltd*	*S Ltd*	*T Ltd*
	£	£	£	£	£	£
Trading profits	20,000	0	64,000	260,000	0	70,000
Property business income	0	6,000	4,000	0	0	0
	20,000	6,000	68,000	260,000	0	70,000
Less Gift aid donation	(4,000)	(4,500)	(2,000)	(5,000)	0	0
	16,000	1,500	66,000	255,000	0	70,000
Less group relief	(5,000)	0	(16,000)	(205,000)	0	0
PCTCT	11,000	1,500	50,000	50,000	0	70,000
Corporation tax:						
at 20%	2,200	300	10,000	10,000	0	
at 30%						21,000
Less small companies						
Marginal relief						
1/40 (£250,000 – 70,000)						(4,500)
MCT payable	2,200	300	10,000	10,000	0	16,500

(b) If P Ltd were to acquire another 8% of the share capital of S Ltd, bringing the total holding to 75%, S Ltd's losses could be surrendered to P Ltd, Q Ltd, R Ltd or M Ltd.

35 Apple Ltd

Tutorial note. The marginal rate of tax of 32.5% is an effective tax rate only. It is never actually used in working out corporation tax.

Again remember groups will form part of a longer question in the exam.

(a) Group relief is available within a 75% group. This is one where one company is a 75% subsidiary of another company or both are 75% subsidiaries of a third company. The holding company must have at least 75% of the ordinary share capital of the subsidiary, a right to at least 75% of the distributable income of the subsidiary, and the right to at least 75% of the net assets of the subsidiary were it to be wound up.

Two companies are in a group only if there is a 75% effective interest eg if Company A holds 90% of Company B which holds 90% of Company C, all three companies are in a group because 90% × 90% = 81%.

(b) Losses should be allocated to the company with the highest marginal rate of tax. This is Cherry Ltd and Apple Ltd to the extent that profits exceed £100,000 since the small companies rate lower limit is £300,000 ÷ 3 = £100,000. Such profits are taxed at the marginal rate of 32.5%. Then, the remainder of the loss should be set against the profits of Banana Ltd which bears tax at 30%. The capital loss cannot be group relieved.

(c) Rollover relief for part of Apple Ltd's gain can be claimed in respect of the investment by Cherry Ltd. The excess of amount of proceeds over the amount invested remains in charge ie £(418,000 – 290,000) = £128,000.

An election should be made so that the asset disposed of at a loss by Banana Ltd is treated as having been disposed of by Apple Ltd. Apple Ltd will then be able to offset the loss of £8,000 against the gain of £128,000, leaving £120,000 chargeable.

Apple Ltd should then make a current year loss relief claim to bring its profits down to £100,000.

	Apple Ltd	*Banana Ltd*	*Cherry Ltd*
	£	£	£
Trading profits	–	650,000	130,000
Net capital gain	120,000	–	–
	120,000	650,000	130,000
Less: loss relief against total profits	(20,000)		
group relief		(75,000)	(30,000)
PCTCT	100,000	575,000	100,000
Tax @ 20%	20,000		20,000
Tax @ 30%		172,500	

Note that the SCR upper limit is £1,500,000 ÷ 3 = £500,000.

36 M Ltd

Tutorial note. In order to maximise the set off of double tax relief, gift aid payments are allocated firstly to UK profits and then to overseas sources of income that have suffered the lowest rate of overseas tax.

There are five associated companies so the full rate of corporation tax applies.

Take care to identify when relief for underlying tax is available and when it is not. If relief for underlying tax is available you will need to gross the net dividend up for both withholding and underlying tax.

The overseas aspects of corporation tax will only be tested as part of a longer question in the exam.

Year ended 31 March 2008

	Total	*UK*	*A Inc*	*B PG*	*C SA*
	£	£	£	£	£
Trading profits	20,000	20,000			
Foreign income (W1 and W2)	587,500	–	200,000	200,000	187,500
	607,500	20,000	200,000	200,000	187,500
Less Gift aid donations	(75,000)	(20,000)	(55,000)	–	–
Profits chargeable to corporation tax	532,500	–	145,000	200,000	187,500
CT @ 30%	159,750	–	43,500	60,000	56,250
Less DTR (W2)	(136,250)	–	(30,000)	(50,000)	(56,250)
Corporation tax	23,500	–	13,500	10,000	–

Workings

1 *Dividend from C SA*

Since M Ltd's shareholding in C SA is at least 10%, relief for underlying tax is available:

	£
Dividend from C SA	120,000
Withholding tax (× 20/80)	30,000
	150,000
Underlying tax	
£150,000 × $\frac{200,000}{800,000}$	37,500
Gross dividend	187,500

2 *Overseas dividends*

			Net	*Tax credit*	*Gross*
			£	£	£
A	Inc	(15%)	170,000	30,000	200,000
B	PG	(25%)	150,000	50,000	200,000
C	SA	(20%) (see W1)	120,000	67,500	187,500

3 *Double tax relief*

		A Inc	*B Pg*	*C Sa*
		£	£	£
Lower of				
(i)	UK tax	43,500	60,000	56,250
(ii)	Overseas tax	30,000	50,000	*67,500
		£30,000	£50,000	£56,250

* Underlying tax + withholding tax.

37 Hogg Ltd

Tutorial note. 'Large' companies must pay their CT liabilities in quarterly instalments.

(a) Hogg Ltd's corporation tax liability for the year is £1,750,000 × 30% = £525,000. The due dates for the payment of corporation tax by Hogg Ltd in respect of the year to 31.12.07 are:

	£
14 July 2007 1/4 × £525,000	131,250
14 October 2007 1/4 × £525,000	131,250
14 January 2008 1/4 × £525,000	131,250
14 April 2008 1/4 × £525,000	131,250
Total	525,000

(b) (i) 31 December 2008 – 12 months after the end of the accounting period.

(ii) 12 February 2009 – 3 months after the notice to file the return.

38 Newcomer Ltd and Au Revoir Ltd

> **Tutorial note**. This question is a typical question on registration and deregistration. Note the importance of the dates.

(a) The registration threshold is £64,000 (from 1.4.07) during any consecutive 12 month period.

This is exceeded in January 2008:

		£
2007	October	11,500
	November	14,200
	December	21,400
2008	January	17,300
		64,400

Therefore, Newcomer Ltd must register within 30 days of the end of the period ie by 2 March 2008.

Newcomer Ltd will be registered from 1 March 2008 or an earlier date agreed between the company and HM Revenue and Customs.

(b) A person is eligible for voluntary deregistration if HM Revenue and Customs are satisfied that the rate of his taxable supplies (net of VAT) in the following one year period will not exceed £62,000 (from 1.4.07). However, voluntary deregistration will not be allowed if the reasons for the expected fall in value of taxable supplies is the cessation of taxable supplies or the suspension of taxable supplies for a period of 30 days or more in that following year. HM Revenue and Customs will cancel a person's registration from the date the request is made or an agreed later date.

39 Justin

> **Tutorial note**. This question is a very basic VAT computation. Note how the input and output VAT is accounted for in respect of petrol. Note also that the VAT incurred on the entertaining is blocked from recovery.

	£	£
Output VAT		
Furniture: £490,000 × 17.5%	85,750	
Books: £2,400 × 0%	0	
Petrol (VAT scale charge): £426 × 7/47	63	
		85,813
Input VAT		
Furniture: £275,000 × 17.5%	48,125	
Computer: £2,400 × 17.5%	420	
Entertaining: irrecoverable	0	
Petrol: £2,800 × 17.5%	490	
		(49,035)
VAT to account for		36,778

40 Ongoing Ltd

Tutorial notes.

1. Where a discount is offered for prompt payment, VAT is chargeable on the net amount, regardless of whether the discount is taken up.
2. VAT on business entertaining is not recoverable where the cost of the entertaining is not a deductible trading expense.
3. Impairment loss (bad debt) relief is only available for debts over six months old (measured from when the payment is due).
4. VAT incurred on the purchase of a car not used wholly for business purposes is not recoverable.

	£	£
Output tax		
£120,000 × 95% = 114,000 × 17.5% (note 1)		19,950
Input tax		
£(35,640 – 480) = 35,160 × 17.5% (note 2)	6,153	
£2,000 × 17.5% (note 3)	350	
£21,150 × 7/47 (note 4)	3,150	(9,653)
VAT payable		10,297

Notes

1. VAT is calculated after the deduction of the prompt payment discount.
2. Entertaining is not an expense on which input tax can be recovered.
3. The debt must be 6 months old to claim bad debt relief.
4. Input tax on motor cars is blocked.

41 Industrial Ltd

Tutorial note. This question is a typical example of the compulsory 30 mark question that you will be faced with in question 1 or 2. Do not allow the length of the question to overwhelm you – you should break the question down into parts as you work through it.

(a) *Corporation tax payable y/e 31.3.08*

	£	£
Trading profit	1,677,710	
Less: capital allowances		
– on Factory (W1)	(12,000)	
– on Plant and machinery (W2)	(42,110)	
Trading profit		1,623,600
Investment income	12,500	
Loan interest received	36,000	48,500
Property business income (W3)		73,200
Capital gains (W4)		62,122
Total profits		1,807,422
Less: Gift aid donation		(1,500)
PCTCT		1,805,922

Tax

£1,805,922 × 30% = £541,777

Workings

1 *IBA*

Expenditure eligible for IBAs

	£
Levelling the land	9,200
Architect's fees	24,300
Concrete floor	16,500
Factory	187,500
General offices (less than 25% of total)	62,500
	300,000
IBA @ 4% (building in use on 31.3.08)	£12,000

2 *Plant and machinery*

	FYAs	*General pool*	*Expensive car (1)*	*Expensive car (2)*	*Allowances given*
	£	£	£	£	£
TWDV b/f		84,600	15,400		
Addition not qualifying for FYAs				17,200	
Disposal			(19,600)		
Balancing charge			4,200		(4,200)
WDA @ 25% /max £3,000		(21,150)		(3,000)	24,150
		63,450		14,200	
Additions qualifying for FYA @ 40%					
Heating system	12,800				
Fire alarm system	7,200				
Computer	3,400				
Lorry	32,000				
	55,400				
Less: FYA @ 40%	(22,160)				22,160
		33,240			
TWDV c/f		96,690	–	14,200	
Allowances given					42,110

Note. The plant does not qualify for 50% FYA as Industrial Ltd is not a 'small' enterprise.

3 *Property business profit*

	£	£
Premium		
Amount received	80,000	
Less 2% × (10 – 1) × 80,000	(14,400)	
Assessable as property income		65,600
Rental (3/12 × £30,400)		7,600
Property business profit		73,200

4 *Capital gain on sale of shares*

	£
Proceeds	230,906
Less cost	(135,800)
Unindexed gain	95,106
Less indexation allowance	(22,184)
Indexed gain	72,922
Less loss b/f	(10,800)
Net gains	62,122

(b) (i) Industrial Ltd is a 'large' company as it pays corporation tax at the full rate and did so in the previous year. Therefore it is required to make quarterly payments on account of corporation tax.

(ii) Industrial Ltd must pay its liability in four equal instalments. These are due on: 14 October 2007; 14 January 2008; 14 April 2008 and 14 July 2008.

42 Susan White

Tutorial note. Losses are allocated to gains before taper relief is applied. They should be allocated to the gain which attracts the lowest amount of taper relief (ie where the highest percentage of the gain remains chargeable).

(a) The following shareholdings in trading companies qualify for CGT business asset taper relief.

(i) shares in unlisted companies;
(ii) shares in a company of which the shareholder is an officer or employee;
(iii) shares in a company in which the shareholder can exercise at least 5% of voting rights.

In addition, an employee of a non trading company qualifies for business asset taper relief on a disposal of his shareholding providing he (together with any connected persons) does not own more than 10 per cent of (generally) the voting rights in the company.

(b) *Capital gains*

Summary

	NBA *80%* £	*BA* *50%* £	*BA* *25%* £
Red Ltd (W1)		18,750	
Blue Ltd (W2)			52,000
Car (W3) – exempt			
Table (W4)	6,500		
Painting (W4) – exempt			
	6,500	18,750	52,000
Less loss on shares (W1)	(1,250)		
Less loss on medal (W4)	(2,735)		
Gains before taper relief	2,515	18,750	52,000
Gains after taper relief @ 80%/50%/25%	2,012	9,375	13,000
Total chargeable gains			24,387

1 *Red Ltd*

	£
5,000 shares (acquired within next 30 days)	
Proceeds $\frac{5,000}{20,000} \times £55,000$	13,750
Less cost	(15,000)
Loss	(1,250)
15,000 shares (post 6.4.98 acquisition)	
Proceeds $\frac{15,000}{20,000} \times £55,000$	41,250
Less cost $\frac{15,000}{25,000} \times £37,500$	(22,500)
Gain before taper relief	18,750

Taper relief period (2.6.06 – 1.6.07) = 1 year. 50% of any net gain will remain chargeable after taper relief.

2 *Blue Ltd*

	£
MV (sale between connected persons)	200,000
Less cost	(18,000)
Unindexed gain	182,000
Less indexation allowance to April 1998	(12,800)
Indexed gain	169,200
Gift relief (balancing figure)	(117,200)
Chargeable gain £(70,000 – 18,000)	52,000

Taper relief period (6.4.98 – 5.4.07) = 2+ years: 25%

3 *Vintage car – exempt*

4 *Antiques*

Where chattels cost or are sold for < £6,000 some restriction applies.

Table

	£
Proceeds	12,000
Less cost	(5,500)
Gain before taper	6,500

Restricted to 5/3 × £(12,000 – 6,000) = £10,000
ie £6,500

Taper relief period (5.01 – 2.08) = 6 years: 80%

Medal
Only medals awarded for bravery (and not purchased) are exempt.

	£
Proceeds (deemed – to restrict loss)	6,000
Less cost	(8,735)
Allowable loss	(2,735)

Painting
Both proceeds and cost < £6,000, therefore exempt.

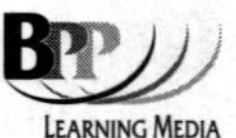

Pilot paper

Pilot paper

Paper F6 (UK)

Time allowed

Reading and planning: 15 minutes
Writing: 3 hours

ALL FIVE questions are compulsory and MUST be attempted.

Do NOT open this paper until instructed by the supervisor.

During reading and planning time only the question paper may be annotated. You must NOT write in your answer booklet until instructed by the supervisor.

This question paper must not be removed from the examination hall.

Warning

The pilot paper cannot cover all of the syllabus nor can it include examples of every type of question that will be included in the actual exam. You may see questions in the exam that you think are more difficult than any you see in the pilot paper.

Question 1

On 31 December 2007 Mark Kett ceased trading as a marketing consultant. He had been self-employed since 6 April 2002, and had always made his accounts up to 5 April. On 1 January 2008 Mark commenced employment as the marketing manager of Sleep-Easy plc. The company runs a hotel. The following information is available for the tax year 2007/08:

Self-employment

(1) Mark's tax adjusted trading profit for the nine-month period ended 31 December 2007 is £20,700. This figure is before taking account of capital allowances.

(2) The tax written down values for capital allowances purposes at 6 April 2007 were as follows:

	£
General pool	13,800
Expensive motor car	14,600

The expensive motor car was used by Mark, and 40% of the mileage was for private purposes.

(3) On 15 June 2007 Mark had purchased office furniture for £1,900. All of the items included in the general pool were sold for £18,800 on 31 December 2007. On the cessation of trading Mark personally retained the expensive motor car. Its value on 31 December 2007 was £11,800.

Employment

(1) Mark is paid a salary of £3,250 (gross) per month by Sleep-Easy plc, from which income tax of £620 per month has been deducted under PAYE.

(2) During the period from 1 January 2008 to 5 April 2008 Mark used his private motor car for business purposes. He drove 2,500 miles in the performance of his duties for Sleep-Easy plc, for which the company paid an allowance of 16 pence per mile. The relevant HM Revenue & Customs authorised mileage rate to be used as the basis of an expense claim is 40 pence per mile.

(3) On 1 January 2008 Sleep-Easy plc provided Mark with an interest free loan of £64,000 so that he could purchase a new main residence.

(4) During the period from 1 January 2008 to 5 April 2008 Mark was provided with free meals in Sleep-Easy plc's staff canteen. The total cost of these meals to the company was £400.

Property income

(1) Mark let out a furnished property throughout the tax year 2007/08. He received gross rents of £8,600, 5% of which was paid to a letting agency. During December 2007 Mark spent £540 on replacing dilapidated furniture and furnishings.

(2) From 6 April 2007 to 31 December 2007 Mark let out a spare room in his main residence, receiving rent of £350 per month.

Investment income

(1) During the tax year 2007/08 Mark received dividends of £2,880, interest from government stocks (gilts) of £1,900, and interest of £430 from an individual savings account (ISA). These were the actual cash amounts received.

(2) On 3 May 2007 Mark received a premium bond prize of £100.

Other information

(1) On 15 December 2007 Mark made a gift aid donation of £780 (net) to a national charity.

(2) Mark's payments on account of income tax in respect of the tax year 2007/08 totalled £11,381.

Required

(a) Compute the income tax payable by Mark for the tax year 2007/08, and the balancing payment or repayment that will be due for the year. **(22 marks)**

(b) Advise Mark as to how long he must retain the records used in preparing his tax return for the tax year 2007/08, and the potential consequences of not retaining the records for the required period. **(3 marks)**

(Total = 25 marks)

Question 1

There is likely to be a comprehensive question covering a wide range of income. You will be expected to complete detailed workings and you must always state why you have excluded any item from your computation rather than ignoring it. You do not have to use the three column approach to calculating taxable income, but it does make the income tax computation much simpler and less prone to error if you do. In a computational question you are likely also to see a written part where you are required to discuss some aspect of income tax, such as administrative requirements.

Question 2

(a) Scuba Ltd is a manufacturer of diving equipment. The following information is relevant for the year ended 31 December 2007:

Operating profit

The operating profit is £170,400. The expenses that have been deducted in calculating this figure include the following:

	£
Depreciation and amortisation of lease	45,200
Entertaining customers	7,050
Entertaining employees	2,470
Gifts to customers (diaries costing £25 each displaying Scuba Ltd's name)	1,350
Gifts to customers (food hampers costing £80 each)	1,600

Leasehold property

On 1 April 2007 Scuba Ltd acquired a leasehold office building that is used for business purposes. The company paid a premium of £80,000 for the grant of a twenty-year lease.

Purchase of industrial building

Scuba Ltd purchased a new factory from a builder on 1 July 2007 for £240,000, and this was immediately brought into use. The cost was made up as follows:

	£
Drawing office serving the factory	34,000
General offices	40,000
Factory	98,000
Land	68,000
	240,000

Plant and machinery

On 1 January 2007 the tax written down values of plant and machinery were as follows:

	£
General pool	47,200
Expensive motor car	22,400

The following transactions took place during the year ended 31 December 2007:

		Cost (Proceeds)
		£
3 January 2007	Purchased machinery	18,020
29 February 2007	Purchased a computer	1,100
4 May 2007	Purchased a motor car	10,400
18 August 2007	Purchased machinery	7,300
15 November 2007	Sold a lorry	(12,400)

The motor car purchased on 4 May 2007 for £10,400 is used by the factory manager, and 40% of the mileage is for private journeys. The lorry sold on 15 November 2007 for £12,400 originally cost £19,800.

Scuba Ltd is a small company as defined by the Companies Acts.

Property income

Scuba Ltd lets a retail shop that is surplus to requirements. The shop was let until 31 December 2006 but was then empty from 1 January 2007 to 30 April 2007. During this period Scuba Ltd spent £6,200 on decorating the shop, and £1,430 on advertising for new tenants. The shop was let from 1 May 2007 to 31 December 2007 at a quarterly rent of £7,200, payable in advance.

Interest received

Interest of £430 was received from HM Revenue & Customs on 31 October 2007 in respect of the overpayment of corporation tax for the year ended 31 December 2006.

Other information

Scuba Ltd has no associated companies, and the company has always had an accounting date of 31 December.

Required

(i) Compute Scuba Ltd's tax adjusted trading profit for the year ended 31 December 2007. You should ignore value added tax (VAT); **(15 marks)**

(ii) Compute Scuba Ltd's corporation tax liability for the year ended 31 December 2007. **(4 marks)**

(b) Scuba Ltd registered for value added tax (VAT) on 1 April 2005. The company's VAT returns have been submitted as follows:

Quarter ended	*VAT paid (refunded)*	*Submitted*
	£	
30 June 2005	18,600	One month late
30 September 2005	32,200	One month late
31 December 2005	8,800	On time
31 March 2006	3,400	Two months late
30 June 2006	(6,500)	One month late
30 September 2006	42,100	On time
31 December 2006	(2,900)	On time
31 March 2007	3,900	On time
30 June 2007	18,800	On time
30 September 2007	57,300	Two months late
31 December 2007	9,600	On time

Scuba Ltd always pays any VAT that is due at the same time that the related return is submitted.

During February 2008 Scuba Ltd discovered that a number of errors had been made when completing its VAT return for the quarter ended 31 December 2007. As a result of these errors the company will have to make an additional payment of VAT to HM Revenue & Customs.

Required

(i) State, giving appropriate reasons, the default surcharge consequences arising from Scuba Ltd's submission of its VAT returns for the quarter ended 30 June 2005 to the quarter ended 30 September 2007 inclusive. **(8 marks)**

(ii) Explain how Scuba Ltd can voluntarily disclose the errors relating to the VAT return for the quarter ended 31 December 2007, and state whether default interest will be due, if (1) the net errors in total are less than £2,000, and (2) the net errors in total are more than £2,000. **(3 marks)**

(Total = 30 marks)

Question 2

You are likely to get a detailed corporation tax question, requiring workings supporting each of the figures in the final computations of corporation tax payable. Part (b) of the question deals with VAT. Taking a methodical approach to part (b) is crucial. Ensure that adequate reasoning is given in your answer to obtain the maximum marks. In part (b)(ii) you are asked to give an explanation in two scenarios – be sure that you cover both.

Question 3

Paul Opus disposed of the following assets during the tax year 2007/08:

(1) On 10 April 2007 Paul sold 5,000 £1 ordinary shares in Symphony Ltd, an unquoted trading company, for £23,600. He had originally purchased 40,000 shares in the company on 23 June 2005 for £110,400.

(2) On 15 June 2007 Paul made a gift of his entire shareholding of 10,000 £1 ordinary shares in Concerto plc to his daughter. On that date the shares were quoted on the Stock Exchange at £5.10–£5.18, with recorded bargains of £5.00, £5.15 and £5.22. Paul's shareholding had been purchased on 29 April 1992 for £14,000. The shareholding is less than 1% of Concerto plc's issued share capital, and Paul has never been employed by Concerto plc. The indexation factor from April 1992 to April 1998 is 0.170, and from April 1992 to June 2007 it is 0.483.

(3) On 9 August 2007 Paul sold a motor car for £16,400. The motor car had been purchased on 21 January 2004 for £12,800.

(4) On 4 October 2007 Paul sold an antique vase for £8,400. The antique vase had been purchased on 19 January 2007 for £4,150.

(5) On 31 December 2007 Paul sold a house for £220,000. The house had been purchased on 1 April 2001 for £114,700. Paul occupied the house as his main residence from the date of purchase until 30 June 2004. The house was then unoccupied until it was sold on 31 December 2007.

(6) On 16 February 2008 Paul sold three acres of land for £285,000. He had originally purchased four acres of land on 17 July 2006 for £220,000. The market value of the unsold acre of land as at 16 February 2008 was £90,000. The land has never been used for business purposes.

(7) On 5 March 2008 Paul sold a freehold holiday cottage for £125,000. The cottage had originally been purchased on 28 July 2006 for £101,600 by Paul's wife. She transferred the cottage to Paul on 16 November 2007 when it was valued at £114,800. The cottage is not a business asset for taper relief purposes.

Paul's taxable income for the tax year 2007/08 is £15,800.

Required

Compute Paul's capital gains tax liability for the tax year 2007/08, and advise him by when this should be paid. **(20 marks)**

Question 3

This question included seven disposals of assets on which you had to calculate the gain. Although each computation was straight forward it tested a different aspect of CGT. Remember always to include your workings, and state why you exclude any disposal ('motor cars are exempt assets') to obtain maximum marks. Part (2) required you to calculate the indexation allowance on a disposal of shares from the FA 1985 pool. The study guide states that '*where shares and securities are concerned, a figure will be given for the value of the 1985 pool as at 5 April 1998*' so this was strictly outside the scope of your studies.

Question 4

Li Fung commenced in self-employment on 1 October 2003. She initially prepared accounts to 30 June, but changed her accounting date to 31 March by preparing accounts for the nine-month period to 31 March 2007. Li's trading profits since she commenced self-employment have been as follows:

	£
Nine-month period ended 30 June 2004	18,600
Year ended 30 June 2005	24,900
Year ended 30 June 2006	22,200
Nine-month period ended 31 March 2007	16,800
Year ended 31 March 2008	26,400

Required

(a) State the qualifying conditions that must be met for a change of accounting date to be valid. **(3 marks)**

(b) Compute Li's trading income assessments for each of the five tax years 2003/04, 2004/05, 2005/06, 2006/07 and 2007/08. **(9 marks)**

(c) Advise Li of the advantages and disadvantages for tax purposes of changing her accounting date from 30 June to 31 March. **(3 marks)**

(Total = 15 marks)

Question 4

This was a question on basis periods in opening years and on a change of accounting date. As well as calculating assessable profits you were required to state conditions (facts) and also advantages and disadvantages (conclusions). This combination of facts, calculations and conclusions is likely to be typical of the sort of question that you will meet.

Question 5

Loser Ltd's results for the year ended 30 June 2005, the nine month period ended 31 March 2006, the year ended 31 March 2007 and the year ended 31 March 2008 are as follows:

	Year ended 30 June 2005	*Period ended 31 March 2006*	*Year ended 31 March 2007*	*Year ended 31 March 2008*
	£	£	£	£
Trading profit/(loss)	86,600	(25,700)	27,300	(78,300)
Property business profit	–	4,500	8,100	5,600
Gift aid donations	(1,400)	(800)	(1,200)	(1,100)

Loser Ltd does not have any associated companies.

Required

(a) State the factors that will influence a company's choice of loss relief claims. You are not expected to consider group relief. **(3 marks)**

(b) Assuming that Loser Ltd claims relief for its losses as early as possible, compute the company's profits chargeable to corporation tax for the year ended 30 June 2005, the nine month period ended 31 March 2006, the year ended 31 March 2007 and the year ended 31 March 2008. Your answer should clearly identify the amount of any losses that are unrelieved. **(5 marks)**

(c) Explain how your answer to (b) above would have differed if Loser Ltd had ceased trading on 31 March 2008. **(2 marks)**

(Total = 10 marks)

Question 5

This was a question on corporation tax losses. First it required a written explanation, then a calculation and it ended with a comment on the effect of slightly changing the scenario, thereby encompassing a range of issues. Always read the question carefully, part (b) told you to assume that loss relief was claimed as early as possible, and to state clearly any unrelieved losses. If you did not, you would lose easy marks.

1 Mark Kett

Text references. Chapters 2, 6 to 9 and 18 are required reading for this question.

Top tips. Set out your proformas in the correct layout to assist the marker to award you maximum marks.

You cannot avoid administration questions in the exam so make sure you learn the rules.

Marking scheme

			Marks
(a)	Trading profit	½	
	Capital allowances – Pool	2	
	– Motor car	2	
	Salary	1	
	Beneficial loan	1	
	Staff canteen	½	
	Expense claim	1½	
	Property business profit	2	
	Furniture and furnishings	½	
	Rent-a-room scheme	1	
	Interest from government stocks	1	
	Dividends	1	
	Individual savings account	½	
	Premium bond prize	½	
	Personal allowance	½	
	Extension of basic rate band	1	
	Income tax	2½	
	Tax suffered at source – PAYE	1	
	– Dividends	1	
	Balancing repayment	1	
			22
(b)	Business records	1	
	Other records	1	
	Penalty	1	
			3
			25

(a) Mark Kett income tax computation 2007/08

	Non-savings income	*Savings income*	*Dividend income*	*Total*
	£	£	£	£
Trading income (W1)	22,120			
Employment income (W3)	10,150			
Property income (W6)	7,310			
Gilt interest (received gross)		1,900		
Dividends × 100/90			3,200	
Net income	39,580	1,900	3,200	44,680
Less PA	(5,225)			(5,225)
Taxable income	34,355	1,900	3,200	39,455

Tax

	£
£2,230 @ 10%	223
£32,125 @ 22%	7,067
£245 @ 20%	49
£1,000 @ 20% (W8)	200
£655 @ 40%	262
£3,200 @ 32.5%	1,040
	8,841
Less tax credits	
PAYE (3 × £620)	(1,860)
Dividends	(320)
Tax payable	6,661
Less POAs	(11,381)
Repayment due from HMRC	(4,720)

Note. Both the ISA interest and premium bond winnings are exempt from tax.

Workings

1 *Trading income*

	£
Trading profit	20,700
Balancing charge (W2)	1,420
	22,120

2 *Capital allowances*

	General Pool	*Exp car (60%)*		*CAs*
	£	£		£
TWDV b/f	13,800	14,600		
Additions	1,900			
	15,700	14,600		
Disposal	(18,800)	(11,800)		
Balancing charge	(3,100)			(3,100)
Balancing allowance		2,800	@ 60%	1,680
No WDA in year of cessation				
Balancing charge				(1,420)

3 *Employment income*

	£
Salary (1.1.08 – 5.4.08)	9,750
Loan (W5)	1,000
Canteen meals – not taxable	nil
Less mileage deduction (W4)	(600)
Employment income	10,150

4 *Mileage allowance*

	£
Company pays: 2,500 @ 16p	400
Less: mileage allowance 2,500 @ 40p	(1,000)
Deduction (expense claim)	600

5 *Loan*

£64,000 × 6.25% × 3/12 = £1,000

6 *Property income*

	£
Income	
Rent	8,600
Less expenses	
letting agent fees	(430)
wear & tear (£8,600 @ 10%)	(860)
	7,310

Note. There is no relief for expenditure on furniture as wear and tear allowance is given.

7 *Rent-a-room relief*

Received: £350 × 9 = £3,150

This is below the limit of £4,250 and therefore this income will be exempt.

8 *Basic rate band*

Extended by gift aid: £780 × 100/78 = £1,000

(b) **Retaining records**

(i) As Mark has self employment and property income he must retain his records for five years and ten months from the end of the tax year ie until 31 January 2014.

(ii) He must also retain the records for his other income until this date (even though the usual period would be one year ten months).

(iii) If he does not retain his records for this period of time HMRC can fine him up to £3,000 (although this is usually only collected in serious cases).

2 Scuba Ltd

Text references. Calculation of taxable profits, PCTCT and CT in Chapters 19 and 20. Chapter 8 for IBAs and capital allowances. Administration in Chapter 24. VAT in Chapter 26.

Top tips. When dealing with an adjustment to profits, make a brief note to the examiner about why you have treated an item in a particular way. Ensure that you comment on every item in the question to obtain maximum marks.

Most of the calculations are fairly straightforward with perhaps the lease premium being the most challenging and only possible if you have studied this topic.

The most likely trap is not reading the question carefully and missing some information. It is good to mark the question in some way when you have dealt with each item (eg tick off or highlight each item dealt with).

With plant and machinery be careful with dates of purchase and which rate of FYA applies.

Easy marks. The adjustment to profit was straightforward, as was the calculation of corporation tax.

Once again using a proforma for

- adjustments of profit
- capital allowances
- calculation of PCTCT

would have helped gain marks. You can slot the appropriate item into the proformas as you read through the question in many cases.

Marking scheme

			Marks
(a)	Trading profit		
	Operating profit	½	
	Depreciation	½	
	Entertaining	1	
	Gifts to customers	1	
	Lease premium – Assessable amount	1½	
	– Deduction	1½	
	IBA – Land	½	
	– General offices	1	
	– Eligible expenditure	1	
	– Allowance	1	
	P & M – Pool	2	
	– Motor car	1	
	– 50% FYA	2½	
			15
	Corporation tax computation		
	Trading profit	½	
	Property business profit – Rent receivable	1	
	– Expenses	1	
	Interest	½	
	Corporation tax	1	
			4
(b)	Default surcharge		
	Quarter ended 30 June 2005	1	
	Quarter ended 30 September 2005	1	
	Quarter ended 31 March 2006	2	
	Quarter ended 30 June 2006	1	
	Extension of surcharge period	1	
	Four consecutive VAT returns on time	1	
	Quarter ended 30 September 2007	1	
			8
	Errors on VAT return		
	Net errors of less than £2,000	1	
	Net errors of more than £2,000	1	
	Default interest	1	
			3
			30

(a) (i) **Scuba Ltd – tax adjusted trading profit year ended 31 December 2007**

	£	£
Profit before tax		170,400
Add depreciation	45,200	
customer entertaining (N1)	7,050	
gifts to customers (N2)	1,600	
		53,850
Less lease premium (W1)		(1,860)
Adjusted profits		222,390
Less IBAs (W2)		(6,880)
Capital allowances (W3)		(27,510)
Taxable trading profit		188,000

Notes

(1) Customer entertaining is never an allowable expense. Staff entertaining is allowable.

(2) Expenditure on gifts to customers is only allowable if the gift (i) costs less than £50 per item, (ii) is not food, tobacco, alcohol or vouchers, and (iii) clearly advertises the business's name.

(ii) **CT liability year ended 31 December 2007**

	£
Taxable trading profit (above)	188,000
Property income (W4)	11,570
Interest (W5)	430
PCTCT	200,000

Small company (profits < £300,000)

		£
FY 2006	3/12 × £200,000 × 19%	9,500
FY 2007	9/12 × £200,000 × 20%	30,000
Total CT liability		39,500

Workings

1 *Lease premium*

	£
Premium (P)	80,000
Less 2% × (n – 1) × P	
2% × (20 – 1) × 80,000	(30,400)
Taxable as Landlord's income	49,600

This amount is deductible for the company over the life of the lease:

$$\frac{£49,600}{20} = £2,480$$

Allowable on an accruals basis ie 1 April 2007 to 31 December 2007 = 9/12 × £2,480 = £1,860

2 *IBAs*

	£
Allowable cost	
Expenditure	240,000
Less land	(68,000)
Total cost	172,000

Expenditure on offices only allowable if represents < 25% × total cost:

$$\frac{40,000}{172,000} = 23\% \text{ therefore allowable}$$

IBA: 4% × £172,000 = £6,880

3 *Capital Allowances*

	FYA	*Pool*	*Exp. car*	*Allowances*
	£	£	£	£
TWDVs b/f		47,200	22,400	
Additions not qualifying for FYAs				
4 May 2007		10,400		
		57,600		
Disposal				
15 November 2007		(12,400)		
		45,200		
WDA @ 25%		(11,300)		11,300
		33,900		
WDA (restricted)			(3,000)	3,000
Additions qualifying For FYAs				
3 January 2007	18,020			
29 February 2007	1,100			
18 August 2007	7,300			
	26,420			
FYA @ 50%	(13,210)	13,210		13,210
TWDVs c/f		47,110	19,400	
Allowances				27,510

4 *Property income*

1 May 2007 to 31 December 2007 = 8m

	£
£7,200 × 4 = £28,800 × 8/12 =	19,200
Less expenses:	
decorating	(6,200)
advertising	(1,430)
Property income	11,570

5 *Interest*

Non-trading loan relationship therefore £430 is taxable as non-trading interest receivable.

(b) (i) **Default surcharge**

	Quarter ended	Circumstance	Default surcharge consequence
1	30 June 2005	Late return and payment	Surcharge liability notice (SLN) issued, ending 30 June 2006. As this is the first default there is no surcharge.
2	30 September 2005	Late return and payment	SLN extended to 30 September 2006 Surcharge @ 2% = £644
3	31 December 2005	On time	SLN remains in place until 30 September 2006
4	31 March 2006	Late return and payment	SLN extended to 31 March 2007 Surcharge @ 5% = £170 Not collected as < £400
5	30 June 2006	Late return but no VAT due	SLN extended to 30 June 2007 No surcharge as no VAT due
6	30 September 2006 to 30 June 2007	On time	As returns and payments have been on time until the end of the SLN period, the SLN record is wiped clean
7	30 September 2007	Late return and payment	New SLN issued to 30 September 2008 As this is the first default there is no surcharge.
8	31 December 2007	On time	SLN remains in place until 30 September 2008

(ii) **Voluntary disclosure of errors**

- Voluntary disclosure can be made of errors whether they are more or less than £2,000.
- If the error is <£2,000 it can be reported on the next VAT return ie for the quarter ended 31 March 2008 and no interest will be collected.
- If the error is >£2,000 it must be disclosed separately to HMRC and default interest may be charged.

3 Paul Opus

Text references. Chapters 13 to 17 for CGT.

Top tips. There is no reason why you cannot do the workings first and then feed the results into a summary table. Make sure that when you put your answer together that the summary is on top – followed by the workings.

Marking scheme

	Marks
Symphony Ltd – Proceeds	½
– Cost	1
– Taper relief	1½
Concerto plc – Proceeds	2
– Cost	½
– Indexation	1
– Taper relief	1½
Motor car	½
Antique vase	2
House – Proceeds	½
– Cost	½
– Exemption	2
– Taper relief	1
Land – Proceeds	½
– Cost	2
Holiday cottage	1
Annual exemption	½
Capital gains tax	1
Due date	½
	20

Paul Opus – 2007/08 CGT Liability

Summary

	NBA 100%	*NBA 80%*	*NBA 60%*	*BA 50%*
	£	£	£	£
Symphony Ltd shares (W1)				9,800
Concerto Plc shares (W2)			34,720	
Car – exempt				
Vase (W4)	4,000			
House (W5)		7,800		
Land (W6)	117,800			
Cottage (W7)	23,400			
Gains before taper relief	145,200	7,800	34,720	9,800
Gains after taper relief	145,200	6,240	20,832	4,900
Total gains before taper relief	177,172			
Less AE	(9,200)			
Taxable gains	167,972			

	£
£(34,600 – 15,800) = 18,800 @ 20%	3,760
£(167,972 – 18,800) = 149,172 @ 40%	59,669
CGT due 31.1.09	63,429

Workings

1 *Symphony Ltd shares*

	£
Proceeds	23,600
Less cost £110,400 × 5,000/40,000	(13,800)
Gain before taper relief	9,800

Business asset with 1 complete year of ownership: 50%

2 *Concerto Plc shares*

	£
Proceeds (W3) £5.11 × 10,000	51,100
Less: cost	(14,000)
Less: IA 0.170 × 14,000	(2,380)
Gain before taper relief	34,720

Non business asset with 9 complete years of ownership plus the bonus year: 60%

Note. Although strictly the shares are in the FA 1985 pool, as there was only one acquisition you can treat this as a single asset.

3 *Market value of Concerto Plc shares*

As this is a gift, the market value is used as the proceeds.

For quoted shares this is the lower of the:

(i) Quarter up:

[¼ × £(5.18 – 5.10)] + 5.10 = 5.12

(ii) Average:

£(5.00 + 5.22) / 2 = 5.11, ie £5.11 per share

4 *Vase*

This is a non wasting chattel and a restriction therefore applies:

	£
Proceeds	8,400
Less cost	(4,150)
Gain before taper relief	4,250

Restricted to:

5/3 × £(8,400 – 6,000) = 4,000, ie £4,000

Non business asset with < 3 complete years of ownership therefore no taper relief available

5 *House*

Total ownership period: 1.4.01 – 31.12.07 = 81 months

PPR period:

Actual occupation 1 April 2001 to 30 June 2004	= 39 months
Last 36 months	= 36 months
	= 75 months

	£
Proceeds	220,000
Less cost	(114,700)
	105,300
Less PPR relief	
75/81 × £105,300	(97,500)
Gain before taper relief	7,800

Non business asset with 6 complete years of ownership: 80%

6 *Part disposal of land*

	£
Proceeds	285,000
Less cost £220,000 × $\frac{285,000}{285,000 + 90,000}$	(167,200)
Gain before taper relief	117,800

Non business asset with < 3 complete years of ownership therefore no taper relief available

7 *Cottage*

Spouse transfer takes place at no gain, no loss therefore Paul takes on his wife's original base cost.

	£
Proceeds	125,000
Less cost	(101,600)
Gain before taper relief	23,400

Non business asset with < 3 complete years of ownership therefore no taper relief available

4 Li Fung

Text references. Self-employment is covered in Chapters 7 to 9.

Top tips. There are 3 marks for part (a); you should aim to state 3 conditions.

Marking scheme

				Marks
(a)	Notification date		1	
	18 month limit		1	
	Change within five years		1	
				3
(b)	Assessments	– 2003/04	1	
		– 2004/05	1½	
		– 2005/06	1	
		– 2006/07	1½	
		– 2007/08	1	
	Overlap profits	– 1.10.03-5.4.04	1	
		– 1.7.04-30.9.04	1	
		– Relieved in 2006/07	1	
				9
(c)	Basis periods correspond		1	
	Overlap profits		1	
	Disadvantages		1	
				3
				15

(a) **Change of accounting date conditions**

(i) Must notify HMRC by 31 January following the tax year of the change of accounting date.

(ii) The new accounts must not exceed 18 months in length.

(iii) There must not have been a change of accounting date in the previous 5 years unless there is a commercial reason for this later change.

(b) **Trading income assessments**

	£	£
2003/04		
Actual basis: 1.10.03 – 5.4.04		
6/9 × £18,600		12,400
2004/05		
<12 months therefore tax first 12 months		
9m to 30.6.04	18,600	
1.7.04 – 30.9.04: 3/12 × £24,900	6,225	
		24,825
2005/06		
CYB: y/e 30.6.05		24,900

	£	£
2006/07		
Year of change (two periods ending in same tax year)		
Tax both periods and relieve overlap profits		
Y/e 30.6.06	22,200	
9m to 31.3.07	16,800	
	39,000	
Less overlap relief (W1)	(18,625)	
		20,375
2007/08		
CYB: y/e 31.3.08		26,400

Working

Overlap profits are any profits that are taxed twice when a business starts (or on a change of accounting date):

		£
1.10.03 – 5.4.04	= 6m	12,400
1.7.04 – 30.9.04	= 3m	6,225
Total	= 9m	18,625

(c) **Advantages and disadvantages of changing accounting date**

Advantages	Disadvantages
All of the overlap profits will be relieved	Tax on the profits of a tax year will be due sooner
The year end will now correspond with the tax year so will make basis periods easier	The profits taxable for a tax year will not be known until after the end of the tax year.
On cessation, only the profits earned in the tax year of cessation will be taxed.	

5 Loser Ltd

Text references. Chapter 21 deals with loss relief for companies.

Top tips. In a loss relief question, set out your proforma then copy in the numbers from the question – remember the trading profits figure is 'nil' when there is a loss in a period. You can then apply the loss relief rules.

Remember that a company **must** make a current year claim if it wishes to then carry back losses to an earlier period (individuals may choose which claim, if any, to make first.)

Marking scheme

			Marks
(a)	Rate of corporation tax	1	
	Timing of relief	1	
	Gift aid donations	1	
			3
(b)	Trading profit	½	
	Property business profit	½	
	Loss relief against total profits	2	
	Gift aid	1	
	Unrelieved trading loss	1	
			5
(c)	Extension of relief	1	
	Year ended 30 June 2005	1	
			2
			10

(a) **Choice of loss relief factors**

(i) The marginal rate of tax – losses will be better used in years where the tax rate is higher.

(ii) Timing – it will be preferable to obtain relief in earlier years as this will result in a repayment of tax already paid.

(iii) Gift aid – loss relief may lead to gift aid donations becoming wasted (as they cannot be carried forward – only group relieved in the current period) in which case it may be better to use the loss in a year where they will not be wasted.

(b) **Losses**

	y/e 30.6.05	*9m to 31.3.06*	*y/e 31.3.07*	*y/e 31.3.08*
	£	£	£	£
Trading profit	86,600	Nil	27,300	Nil
Property income		4,500	8,100	5,600
Total profits	86,600	4,500	35,400	5,600
Less CY loss		(4,500)(i)		(5,600)(iii)
Less loss carried back	(21,200)(ii)		(35,400)(iv)	
Revised profits	65,400	Nil	Nil	Nil
Less Gift aid donations	(1,400)	–	–	–
PCTCT	64,000	–	–	–

Loss memo

		£
Loss of 9m to 31.3.06		25,700
(i)	CY	(4,500)
(ii)	CB	(21,200)
c/f		Nil
Loss of y/e 31.3.08		78,300
(iii)	CY	(5,600)
(iv)	CB	(35,400)
c/f		37,300

(c) **Difference if company ceased trading 31 March 2008**

(i) If the year to 31 March 2008 had been the company's final period it would have been able to carry back the losses of the year to 31 March 2008 against the profits of the previous 36 months, compared to the normal 12 month carry back period.

(ii) It would be therefore be able to reach back to the trading profits of the year ended 30 June 2005.

(iii) It would have been able to set off the lower of the profits and the unrelieved loss ie £37,300.

Tax tables

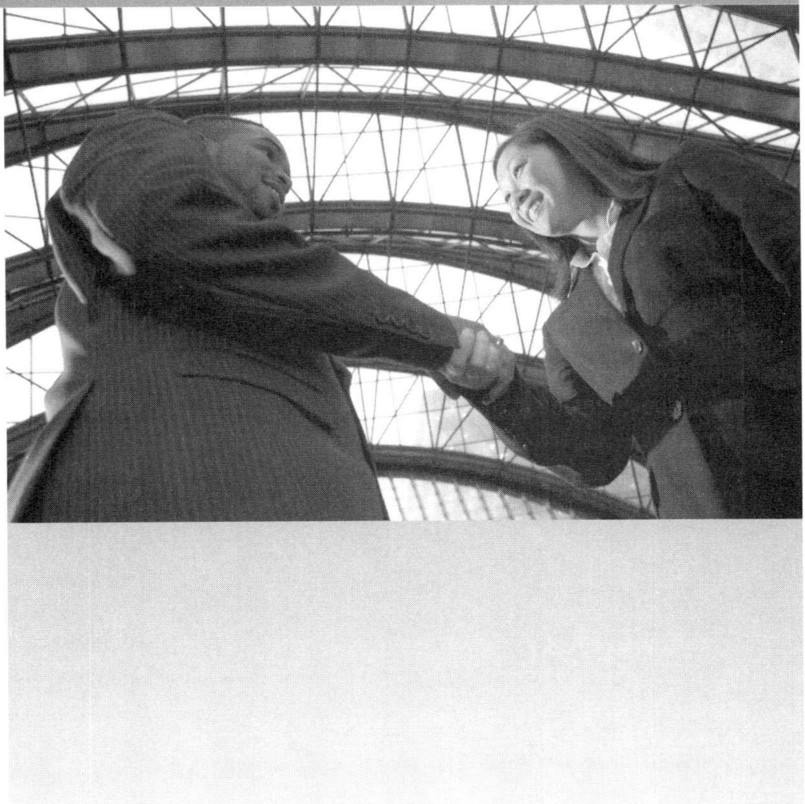

The following tax rates and allowances are to be used in answering the questions

Income tax

Starting rate	£1 – £2,230	10%
Basic rate	£2,231 – £34,600	22%
Higher rate	£34,601 and above	40%

Personal allowances

	£
Personal allowance	5,225
Personal allowance aged 65 to 74	7,550
Personal allowance aged 75 and over	7,690
Income limit for age-related allowances	20,900

Car benefit percentage

The base level of CO_2 emissions is 140 grams per kilometre.

Car fuel benefit

The base figure for calculating the car fuel benefit is £14,400.

Pension scheme limits

Annual allowance	£225,000

The maximum contribution that can qualify for tax relief without any earnings is £3,600.

Capital allowances

	%
Plant and machinery	
Writing down allowance	25
First year allowance – plant and machinery	40
– low emission motor cars (CO_2 emissions less than 120 g/km)	100

For small businesses only: the rate of plant and machinery first-year allowance is 50% for the period from 1 April 2006 to 31 March 2008 (6 April 2006 and 5 April 2008 for unincorporated businesses).

Long-life assets

Writing-down allowance	6

Industrial buildings

Writing-down allowance	4

Corporation tax

Financial year	*2005*	*2006*	*2007*
Small companies (SC) rate	19%	19%	20%
Full rate	30%	30%	30%
Lower limit	£30,000	£300,000	£300,000
Upper limit	£1,500,000	£1,500,000	£1,500,000
Marginal relief fraction:	11/400	11/400	1/40

Marginal relief

$(M - P) \times I/P \times$ marginal relief fraction

Value Added Tax

Registration limit	£64,000
Deregistration limit	£62,000

Capital gains tax: annual exemption

Individuals	£9,200

Capital gains tax: taper relief

The percentage of the gain chargeable is as follows:

Complete years after 5 April 1998 for which asset held	*Gains on business assets (%)*	*Gains on non-business assets (%)*
0	100	100
1	50	100
2	25	100
3	25	95
4	25	90
5	25	85
6	25	80
7	25	75
8	25	70
9	25	65
10	25	60

National insurance (not contracted-out rates)

		%
Class 1 employee	£1 – £5,225 per year	Nil
	£5,226 – £34,840 per year	11.0
	£34,841 and above per year	1.0
Class 1 employer	£1 – £5,225 per year	Nil
	£5,226 and above per year	12.8
Class 1A		12.8
Class 2	£2.20 per week	
Class 4	£1 – £5,225 per year	Nil
	£5,226 – £34,840 per year	8.0
	£34,841 and above per year	1.0

Rates of Interest

Official rate of interest	6.25%
Rate of interest on underpaid tax	7.5% (assumed)
Rate of interest on overpaid tax	3.0% (assumed)

Calculations and workings need only be made to the nearest £.

All apportionments may be made to the nearest month.

All workings should be shown.

Index

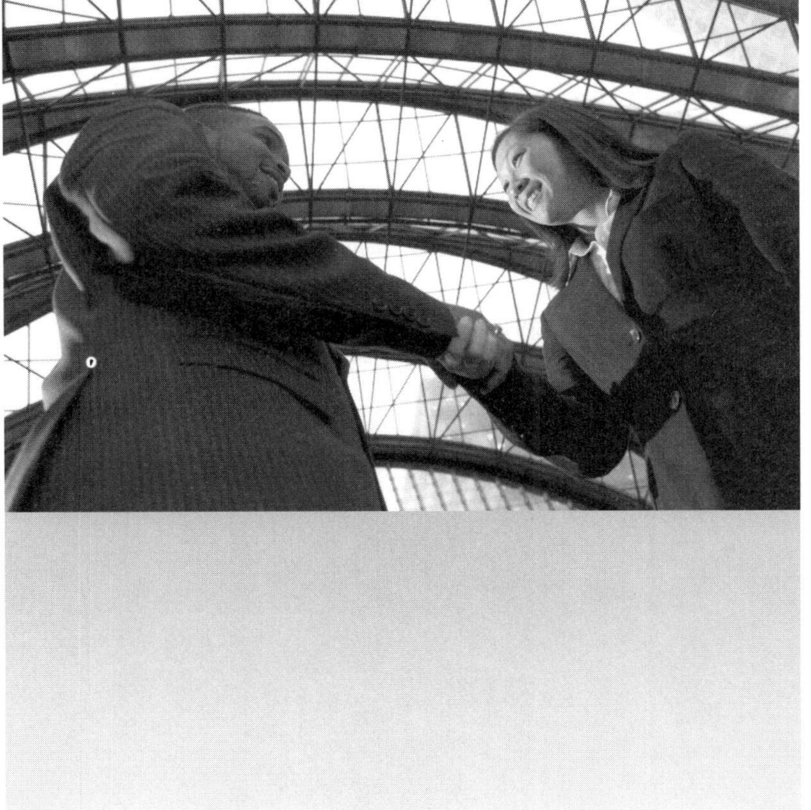

Note. **Key Terms** and their page references are given in **bold.**

75% subsidiary, 305

Accounting period, 269
Adjustment of profits, 121
Age allowance, 63
Allowable deductions, 74
Annual allowance, 108
Annual exemption, 202
Appeals, 342
Appropriations, 125
Associated companies, 288

Badges of trade, 120
Balancing adjustments on sale, 146
Balancing charges and allowances, 139
Basis periods, 152
Beneficial loans, 90
Bonus issues, 244
Branch or subsidiary abroad, 314

Capital allowances, 113, 132, 272
Capital expenditure, 122
Capital gains group, 309
Capital gains tax (CGT)
  Annual exemption, 202
  Capital losses, 202
  Chargeable asset, 201, 202
  Chargeable disposal, 201
  Chargeable person, 200
  Chattels, 220
  Computation, 210
  Damage, loss or destruction of an asset, 215
  Enhancement expenditure, 211
  Exempt asset, 201
  FA 1985 pool, 242
  Gifts, 210
  Holdover relief for gifts, 234
  Incorporation relief, 236
  Letting relief, 225
  Matching rules for individuals, 241
  Overseas aspects of CGT, 201
  Principal private residence, 223
  Rollover relief, 230
  Taper relief, 203
  Tax payable, 206
  Valuing quoted shares, 240
  Wasting assets, 222
Capital losses (corporation tax), 301
Capital receipts, 128
Car fuel, 89
Carry forward trade loss relief (corporation tax), 292
Carry forward trade loss relief (income tax), 167
Cars, 86, 346
Cessation, 157
Cessation of a trade, 140
Change of accounting date, 160
Chargeable gain, 204, 273
Charitable donations, 79, 126
Chattels, 220
Childcare, 95
Choice of an accounting date, 156
Claims, 256, 326
Commencement, 153
Company, 268
Computer software, 134
Corporation tax, 268
Corresponding accounting period, 307

Deductible expenditure not charged in the accounts, 128
Depreciating asset, 233
Determinations, 262, 327
Discovery assessments, 262, 327
Dispensation, 96
Dividend income, 61
Donations, 126
Double taxation relief (DTR), 315

Early trade losses relief, 172
Earnings, 73
Employer pension contributions, 107
Employment, 72
Enquiries, 326
Enquiries into returns, 261
Entertaining, 124, 346
European Union, 54
Excluded employees, 82
Exempt benefits, 94
Exempt income, 61
Expenses, 86
Extra-statutory concessions, 54

FA 1985 pool, 275
Filing date for a personal tax return, 253
Financial year, 269
First year allowances, 136
Franked investment income (FII), 282
Furnished holiday lettings, 114

General Commissioners, 53
Gift aid donations, 277
Gift aid donations (individuals), 67
Gift relief, 234
Gifts, 124
Gilts, 247
Goods for own use, 127
Group relief, 304

Her Majesty's Revenue and Customs, 53
Hotels, 144

Impairment debts, 124
Income taxed at source, 61
Incorporation relief, 236
Indexation allowance, 212, 274
Individual savings accounts, 62
Industrial buildings, 143
Instalments, 328
Interest on late paid tax, 259, 328
Interest on overdue tax, 127
Intra-group transfers, 310

Jointly held property, 68

Land and buildings in the UK, 112
Legal and professional charges, 126
Lifetime allowance, 109
Limited liability partnerships, 186
Living accommodation, 84, 86
Loan relationships, 272
Long life assets, 142

Medium sized enterprise, 136
Miscellaneous income, 273
Mobile phone, 95
Motor cars, 139

National insurance, 190
Net income, 60
Net pay arrangements, 106
Non-savings income, 60, 65
Notification of chargeability, 325
Notification of liability to income tax and CGT, 253

Occupational pension scheme, 104
Other expenses, 76

Overlap profits, 158

P11D employees, 82
Part disposals, 214
Partnership loss reliefs, 185
Partnerships, 180
PAYE settlement agreements, 100
PAYE system, 96
Payment of corporation tax, 327
Payment of income tax and capital gains tax, 257
Payments on account, 257
Payroll deduction scheme, 79
Penalties, 100, 263, 329
Pension scheme, 104
Pension tax relief, 106
Period of account, 269
Personal allowance, 63
Personal pensions, 105
Personal tax computation, 59
Plant and machinery, 133
Postponement of payment of tax, 262
Premiums on leases, 116
Pre-trading expenditure, 129, 272
Principal private residence, 223
Private incidental expenses, 86
Private use assets, 139
Private use of other assets, 92
Profits, 282
Profits chargeable to corporation tax (PCTCT), 270
Property business, 112
Property business income, 272
Property business losses, 117
Property business losses (corporation tax), 301

Qualifying corporate bond (QCB), 248
Qualifying loans, 92

Records, 254, 325
Removal expenses, 95
Rent a room scheme, 115
Reorganisations, 246
Repayment supplement, 260
Replacement of business assets, 230
Residence, 59
Residence of companies, 269
Residual charge, 94
Returns, 325
Rights issues, 244
Rollover relief, 230
Rollover relief (groups), 311

Savings income, 61
Scholarships, 93
Self assessment, 252, 324, 255
Self employment, 72
Share matching rules for companies, 275
Shares, 241
Short life asset, **141**
Small companies marginal relief, 283
Small companies rate (SCR), 283
Small enterprise, **136**
Special Commissioners, 53
Staff parties, 96
Statements of practice, 54
Statute, 52
Statutory Instruments, 54
Statutory mileage allowances, 78
Subscriptions, 126
Surcharges, **259**

Takeovers, 247
Taper relief, 203
Tax avoidance, 55
Tax Bulletin, 54
Tax evasion, 55
Tax law, 52
Tax liability, **60**
Tax payable, **60**, 64
Tax returns, 253
Taxable benefits, 83
Taxable earnings, 73
Taxable gain, **204**
Taxable income, 59
Taxable supply, **335**
Taxation in a modern economy, 50
Taxes, 52
Temporary workplace, 75
Terminal trade loss relief (income tax), 174
Total income, 60
Trade loss relief against general income, 168
Trade loss relief against total profits, 293
Trading losses relieved against capital gains, 169
Transfer pricing, 320
Transfers between spouses/civil partners, 213
Travelling expenses, 74

UK resident company, 314

Value added tax (VAT)
- Administration, 342
- Annual accounting scheme, 356
- Car fuel, 347
- Cash accounting scheme, 356
- Deregistration, 340
- Exempt supplies, 337
- Flat Rate Scheme, 357
- Impairment losses, 348
- Input tax, 345
- Non-deductible input tax, 346
- Penalties, 353
- Pre-registration input tax, 341
- Records, 353
- Registration, 338
- Substantial traders, 343
- Supplies of goods, 336
- Supplies of services, 336
- Tax point, 343
- Taxable persons, 336
- VAT fraction, 345
- VAT invoices, 352
- VAT periods, 342
- Zero rated supplies, 337

Valuing quoted shares, 240
Vans, 90
Vouchers, 83

Warehouses, 143
Wasting assets, **220**
Wear and tear allowance, 113
Wholly and exclusively for the purposes of the trade, 123
Writing down allowance (WDA), **135**, 145

Review Form & Free Prize Draw – Paper F6 Taxation (UK) FA 2007 (8/07)

All original review forms from the entire BPP range, completed with genuine comments, will be entered into one of two draws on 31 July 2008 and 31 January 2009. The names on the first four forms picked out on each occasion will be sent a cheque for £50.

Name: ______________________ **Address:** ______________________

____

____

How have you used this Text?
(Tick one box only)

☐ Home study (book only)

☐ On a course: college ______________

☐ With 'correspondence' package

☐ Other ______________

Why did you decide to purchase this Text? *(Tick one box only)*

☐ Have used BPP Texts in the past

☐ Recommendation by friend/colleague

☐ Recommendation by a lecturer at college

☐ Saw advertising

☐ Saw information on BPP website

☐ Other ______________

During the past six months do you recall seeing/receiving any of the following?
(Tick as many boxes as are relevant)

☐ Our advertisement in *ACCA Student Accountant*

☐ Our advertisement in *Pass*

☐ Our advertisement in *PQ*

☐ Our brochure with a letter through the post

☐ Our website www.bpp.com

Which (if any) aspects of our advertising do you find useful?
(Tick as many boxes as are relevant)

☐ Prices and publication dates of new editions

☐ Information on Text content

☐ Facility to order books off-the-page

☐ None of the above

Which BPP products have you used?

Text	☑	*Success CD*	☐	*Learn Online*	☐
Kit	☐	*i-Learn*	☐	*Home Study Package*	☐
Passcard	☐	*i-Pass*	☐	*Home Study PLUS*	☐

Your ratings, comments and suggestions would be appreciated on the following areas.

	Very useful	*Useful*	*Not useful*
Introductory section (Key study steps, personal study)	☐	☐	☐
Chapter introductions	☐	☐	☐
Key terms	☐	☐	☐
Quality of explanations	☐	☐	☐
Exam focus points	☐	☐	☐
Questions and answers in each chapter	☐	☐	☐
Fast forwards and chapter roundups	☐	☐	☐
Quick quizzes	☐	☐	☐
Question Bank	☐	☐	☐
Answer Bank	☐	☐	☐
Index	☐	☐	☐

Overall opinion of this Study Text *Excellent* ☐ *Good* ☐ *Adequate* ☐ *Poor* ☐

Do you intend to continue using BPP products? *Yes* ☐ *No* ☐

On the reverse of this page are noted particular areas of the text about which we would welcome your feedback.
The BPP author of this edition can be e-mailed at: suedexter@bpp.com

Please return this form to: Nick Weller, ACCA Publishing Manager, BPP Learning Media Ltd, FREEPOST, London, W12 8BR

Review Form & Free Prize Draw (continued)

TELL US WHAT YOU THINK

Please note any further comments and suggestions/errors below

Free Prize Draw Rules

1. Closing date for 31 July 2008 draw is 30 June 2008. Closing date for 31 January 2009 draw is 31 December 2008.
2. Restricted to entries with UK and Eire addresses only. BPP employees, their families and business associates are excluded.
3. No purchase necessary. Entry forms are available upon request from BPP Learning Media. No more than one entry per title, per person. Draw restricted to persons aged 16 and over.
4. Winners will be notified by post and receive their cheques not later than 6 weeks after the relevant draw date.
5. The decision of the promoter in all matters is final and binding. No correspondence will be entered into.